The former Swedish Bishop Bo Giertz was a man of clarity and simplicity. At the same time, he was a thinker of profound knowledge and understanding. Every time he picked up his pen, his writings started to live their own life. They have inspired the reader ever since, even after the death of the author. Now, *The New Testament Devotional Commentary* can be read in English. The exceptional character of the whole series proves that Bo Giertz was a man with a mission. He was sent by God to speak to you.

Reverend Timo Laato
Dr. Theol. and Master of Arts

The legacy of Bo Giertz is multifaceted. He was a gifted pastor, theologian, and novelist. As a bishop of the church, he wanted the pastors and people under his care to love the Holy Scriptures and to delight in reading them. His devotional commentaries are devoid of extended arguments regarding authorship and background of the individual New Testament books. Rather, Giertz provides a concise and coherent exposition of the biblical text always centered in the Gospel of Jesus Christ. Like the first two volumes this final volume reflects Giertz's commitment to the Scriptures as the Word of God and it radiates the warmth of evangelical faith. This volume like the previous two lends itself well for use in personal and group Bible study.

John T. Pless
Concordia Theological Seminary
Fort Wayne, IN

The volume completes Bror Erickson's splendid offering of access to the witness of Swedish bishop Bo Giertz. While Giertz was a contemporary of the great theologians of the Swedish Luther Renaissance like Wingren, Aulén, and Nygen, he understood that the theology they explained had to serve a higher purpose: proclamation of the gospel. Volume 3 of the *New Testament Devotional Commentary* is the culmination of a short course for pastors in how to preach and for lay people in what to look for in a sermon. For Giertz, Christ *is* the same yesterday, today, and forever, that is, he remains crucified and risen Lord "for you," the center of all things. This is preaching we need today.

Ken Sundet Jones
Professor of Theology and Philosophy
Grand View University

THE NEW TESTAMENT DEVOTIONAL COMMENTARY

VOLUME 3:
GALATIANS THROUGH REVELATION

The New Testament Devotional Commentary, Volume 3: Galatians through Revelation
© 2023 New Reformation Publications

All rights reserved. No part of this publication may be reproduced, distributed, or transmitted in any form or by any means, including photocopying, recording, or other electronic or mechanical methods, without the prior written permission of the publisher, except in the case of brief quotations embodied in critical reviews and certain other noncommercial uses permitted by copyright law. For permission requests, write to the publisher at the address below.

Unless otherwise indicated, all Scripture quotations are from The ESV® Bible (The Holy Bible, English Standard Version®), copyright © 2001 by Crossway, a publishing ministry of Good News Publishers. Used by permission. All rights reserved.

Published by:
1517 Publishing
PO Box 54032
Irvine, CA 92619-4032

Printed in the United States of America

Cover art by Zachariah James Stuef.

Names: Giertz, Bo, 1905-1998, author. | Erickson, Bror, translator.
Title: The New Testament devotional commentary. Volume 3,
  Galatians through Revelation / by Bo Giertz ; translated by Bror Erickson.
Other titles: Förklaringar till Nya testamentet. D. 3, Galaterbrevet, Efesierbrevet,
  Filipperbrevet, Kolosserbrevet, Tessalonikerbreven, Breven till Timoteus,
  Brevet till Titus, Brevet till Filemon, Hebre´erbrevet, Jakobs brev,
  Petrusbreven, Johannesbreven, Judas brev, Uppenbarelseboken. English |
  Galatians through Revelation
Description: Irvine, CA : 1517 Publishing, [2023] | Series: The New Testament
  devotional commentary series ; volume 3 | Translation of Förklaringar till Nya
  testamentet. D. 3, Galaterbrevet, Efesierbrevet, Filipperbrevet, Kolosserbrevet,
  Tessalonikerbreven, Breven till Timoteus, Brevet till Titus, Brevet till Filemon,
  Hebre´erbrevet, Jakobs brev, Petrusbreven, Johannesbreven, Judas brev,
  Uppenbarelseboken. | Includes bibliographical references.
Identifiers: ISBN: 978-1-956658-60-6 (hardcover) |
  978-1-956658-61-3 (paperback) | 978-1-956658-62-0 (ebook)
Subjects: LCSH: Bible. New Testament—Commentaries. | Bible. New Testament—
  Devotional literature. | LCGFT: Devotional literature. | BISAC: RELIGION /
  Biblical Commentary / General. | RELIGION / Biblical Commentary /
  New Testament / General. | RELIGION / Christian Living / Devotional.
Classification: LCC: BS2555.3 .G5413 2023 | DDC: 226/.07—dc23

THE NEW TESTAMENT DEVOTIONAL COMMENTARY

VOLUME 3:
GALATIANS THROUGH REVELATION

BY BO GIERTZ

TRANSLATED BY BROR ERICKSON

Contents

Preface xi

Galatians:
Introduction 1
   Galatians 1 3
   Galatians 2 5
   Galatians 3 8
   Galatians 4 12
   Galatians 5 15
   Galatians 6 18

Ephesians:
Introduction 21
   Ephesians 1 25
   Ephesians 2 29
   Ephesians 3 33
   Ephesians 4 36
   Ephesians 5 41
   Ephesians 6 46

Philippians:
Introduction 51
   Philippians 1 53
   Philippians 2 56
   Philippians 3 59
   Philippians 4 63

Colossians:
Introduction 67
   Colossians 1 69
   Colossians 2 74
   Colossians 3 79
   Colossians 4 83

First Thessalonians:
Introduction 87
   1 Thessalonians 1 89
   I Thessalonians 2 91
   1 Thessalonians 3 94
   1 Thessalonians 4 96
   1 Thessalonians 5 99

Second Thessalonians:
Introduction 103
   2 Thessalonians 1 105
   2 Thessalonians 2 107
   2 Thessalonians 3 110

First Timothy:
Introduction 113
   1 Timothy 1 119
   1 Timothy 2 122
   1 Timothy 3 127
   1 Timothy 4 130
   1 Timothy 5 133
   1 Timothy 6 137

CONTENTS

Second Timothy:
Introduction 141
- 2 Timothy 1 143
- 2 Timothy 2 146
- 2 Timothy 3 149
- 2 Timothy 4 151

Titus:
Introduction 155
- Titus 1 157
- Titus 2 159
- Titus 3 161

The Letter to Philemon:
Introduction 165

Hebrews:
Introduction 171
- Hebrews 1 177
- Hebrews 2 179
- Hebrews 3 182
- Hebrews 4 184
- Hebrews 5 186
- Hebrews 6 189
- Hebrews 7 191
- Hebrews 8 194
- Hebrews 9 196
- Hebrews 10 200
- Hebrews 11 204
- Hebrews 12 208
- Hebrews 13 212

Introduction to James 217
- James 1 221
- James 2 225
- James 3 229
- James 4 231
- James 5 233

First Peter:
Introduction 237
- 1 Peter 1 241
- 1 Peter 2 245
- 1 Peter 3 249
- 1 Peter 4 252
- 1 Peter 5 254

Second Peter:
Introduction 257
- 2 Peter 1 263
- 2 Peter 2 267
- 2 Peter 3 270

First John:
Introduction 273
- 1 John 1 277
- 1 John 2 280
- 1 John 3 284
- 1 John 4 287
- 1 John 5 290

Second And Third John:
Introduction 293
- 2 John 295

CONTENTS

3 John 298

Jude:
Introduction 301

Revelation:
Introduction 309
   Revelation 1 323
   Revelation 2 328
   Revelation 3 333
   Revelation 4 336
   Revelation 5 339
   Revelation 6 342
   Revelation 7 345
   Revelation 8 348
   Revelation 9 350
   Revelation 10 353
   Revelation 11 356
   Revelation 12 360
   Revelation 13 363
   Revelation 14 367
   Revelation 15 371
   Revelation 16 372
   Revelation 17 375
   Revelation 18 379
   Revelation 19 383
   Revelation 20 386
   Revelation 21 390
   Revelation 22 394

Appendix:
The Bible's View of Itself. 399

PREFACE

Bo Giertz loved the Scriptures and made the New Testament the subject of a life-long in-depth study to which the commentaries he wrote testify. This study began under the mentorship of Anton Fridrichsen while Giertz was studying for a bachelor's degree in theology in Uppsala as a young man. It continued until late in life when he recorded the Greek New Testament onto cassette tapes so he could continue to listen to it when his eyesight failed. Fridrichsen is not well known in the English-speaking world, but he had an incredible influence on biblical studies through his students such as Bo Reicke and Krister Stendahl, who later taught at Harvard Divinity School.

Fridrichsen was a form critic who earned his PhD. at the University of Strasbourg. His thesis was entitled "The Problem of Miracle in Primitive Christianity." In it, Fridrichsen began to highlight the problems of higher criticism and its operative assumptions. Later he would advocate for a "Biblical Realism" in an essay titled "Realistic Interpretation of the Bible" (which can be found in Anton Fridrichsen, "Exegetical Writings: A Selection" [Eugene, OR: Wipf and Stock Publishers, 1994]). Fridrichsen argued against liberal exegesis in this essay and maintained that the "foundation of all theological interpretation must be the early Christian kerygma, the message and confession: Jesus is Lord, Kyrios Jesus!" (pg. 28) and that any interpretation of the Scriptures which starts with presuppositions other than the New Testament's own is nothing but a "re-interpretation in modern style. Even such an interpretation has its rightful place, but not in theological scholarship, where strict realism and an unconditional sense of reality must be demanded" (pg. 29).

As late as 1991, Bo Giertz was quoted in his biography *Atiesten som blev biskop* (*The Atheist that Became Bishop*) saying that he was still a student of Fridrichsen and that much of what he wrote was an attempt to pass on to another generation what he had learned from him (pg. 68). Bo Giertz was also an independent thinker who developed his own style and approach to Biblical studies even if he remained indebted to his college mentor and travel companion to Palestine. It was typical of Bo Giertz's "all in" approach to topics of interest to him that he should travel to Palestine and spend six months surveying the terrain and visiting archeological digs. This trip first bore literary fruit in *With My Own Eyes*, a particularly striking and impactful novelization of the life of Jesus. However, his memories and experiences of Palestine in 1931 would serve to color and add texture to his sermons (see *A Year of Grace*, volumes 1 and 2), devotions (*To Live with Christ*), and perhaps most stunningly in these commentaries.

In all these literary endeavors, Bo Giertz sought to build up the church and edify the laity. This was his primary concern. He especially wanted to make the Scriptures accessible to the laymen of the church. Thus, he wrote in a style that avoided theological jargon as much as possible. Where it was necessary, it is thoroughly explained. Still, these commentaries show—despite their simplicity—intimate knowledge of scholarly research. He can, like Fridrichsen, be critical of both liberal and conservative positions from time to time. However, he was not interested in controversies and tried to avoid them. He would occasionally pass over a controversy by lightly touching upon it only to highlight the meaning of the text that he wanted to expound. In this way he forced the reader, scholar and layman alike, to be confronted with the word of God—both in law and gospel—rather than avoiding it all by getting caught up in minutia, which can often spill ink for pages in more scholarly commentaries that never get around to expounding the word of God.

I suppose a person could go on for some time explaining the approach Bo Giertz wanted to take with these commentaries. Perhaps the best way is to let him explain. I've thus included his essay "The Bible's View and the View of the Bible" in the back of this book, which was translated and previously published in *Then Fell the Lord's Fire*, a collection of ordination sermons and essays in pastoral theology by Bo Giertz.

I have owned these commentaries for almost a decade and have often referenced them in sermon preparation. They have deeply enriched my own life and understanding of Scripture. Perhaps, from time to time, I'm given to pause and contemplate a disagreement I have with Bo Giertz on a point or two, but even then I find I have been blessed for the conversation.

I want to thank 1517 for encouraging me to translate and publish these volumes. My editor Steve Byrnes was incredibly supportive during this endeavor, as have been the rest of the team members at 1517 who have become great friends, brothers and sisters in the work of gospel proclamation. I also want to give thanks to Birgitta Giertz and the Giertz estate who have graciously given permission for these translations. Many of you have enjoyed Bo Giertz's devotional commentary on Romans, which was published separately (and will be included in volume 2). I thank you all for sharing your reviews and appreciation of that work. They too have been an inspiration to me and an encouragement to complete the project. I know you will find the rest of Bo Giertz's New Testament commentaries a rich treasure trove of blessing and enlightenment.

Pastor Bror Erickson
Exaudi Sunday,
May 16th 2021

GALATIANS
Introduction

The Galatians were what the Greeks called the Celts (the same group of people that the Romans called Gauls). Celtic tribes had been wandering down toward the Mediterranean since the fifth century before Christ. In the year 387 BC, they burned Rome, and a hundred years later they swept through Greece and plundered Delphi. They moved on and crossed the Bosporus and pushed into Asia Minor where they eventually settled in the heart of the land, in the tracts surrounding modern Ankara. This area was then named Galatia after them.

When the Romans subjugated the area, it became a Roman province. To this region they also incorporated tracts to the south where a completely different people lived, the Lycaonians.

Even in Paul's day, a person could mean two different things by "Galatians." Just as when we say Norrbotten we can mean the old region by the Gulf of Bothnia or the county (that is now a bit bigger), so Galatia could mean either the old region or the new and rather larger province. This means that we cannot be sure who Paul means when he writes to the "congregations of Galatia." He had travelled through the southern part of the province on his first missionary trip. There he had established congregations in Iconium, Lystra, and Derbe. Then it is said, on his second trip, that he visited these places again and then continued through the "areas of Phrygia and Galatia" (Acts 16:6). This could refer to the old Galatian heartland in the north or a "Phrygian Galatia" further to the west where there were also Galatian people. On the third mission trip Paul came back to the same areas (Acts 18:23). It is certain that he calls his recipients Galatians. He could have hardly done this with Lycaonians who spoke a completely different language and did not have any kinship with the Galatians though they happened to end up in the same Roman province.

If we ask when this letter was written, then we have a clue in that which Paul says about the trip he made to Jerusalem, "after fourteen years," probably figured from his conversion. Unfortunately, we then have two trips to choose from, both known to us from Acts, and the meanings differ greatly about what it is Paul has in mind. It can be the one in which he took Barnabas to bring a gift to the congregation in Antioch (Acts 11:29f, 12:25). However, it can also mean the trip to the great "Apostolic Council" that Luke describes in chapter 15. At that meeting, Paul gained a great victory when it was established that gentiles did not need to be circumcised to be Christian. It is also precisely this controversial question that plays a dominant role in Galatians though Paul never invokes this decision. There are authorities who think that the reason for this is that Galatians was written before the council in Jerusalem (that is usually dated to the year 49/50). The congregations to whom it is directed to then must have been established on the first missionary trip. If this theory holds, then Galatians is the oldest among the letters of Paul that were preserved and ought to have been written at latest in the year 49.

Against this theory stands another theory that says that the letter is directed to the Galatians among whom Paul worked during the second and third mission trip. There is strong support for this when Paul says that it was because he was sick that he first preached the gospel to the Galatians (Galatians 4:13). He seems to also have already been with them a couple of times when he writes this. A person is reminded that Luke says (Acts 16:6) the Holy Spirit hindered them from proclaiming the Word where they wanted, and so they took the road through the Galatian countryside. The hindrance could have been due to illness that Paul took as a sign and a guide.

Consequently, according to this theory, Galatians was written sometime after Paul had visited the Galatians on his third mission trip. On this trip he then came to Ephesus where he stayed for more than two years. It is possible that during this time he received the disturbing news from his Galatian congregations that were not that far away. There must have been Jewish Christians who, despite what was said at the Apostolic Council in Jerusalem, held fast to the idea that circumcision was necessary and now attempted to undermine the work that Paul had carried out. If Paul wrote the letter from Ephesus, then it came into existence sometime around the years 54-56, just two decades after the death of Jesus.

A choice between the two theories has hardly any bearing on the meaning of the letter. Though the letter formally deals with something so outdated as circumcision, it is an invaluable Christian document. Paul saw with sharp eyes how the demand for circumcision springs from a false view of salvation, a doctrine of works that perpetually pops up anew and threatens to disempower the gospel. So, the letter has been one of Christendom's most important writings about Law and Gospel.

Galatians is one of the most engaging letters Paul wrote. It is passionate, personal, and pulsating with enthusiasm that only vital questions can bring to life. This question here is decisive for all true Christendom. Here today is the watershed between the true gospel and the false that is no longer any gospel. However, Paul himself can speak about this matter now.

Galatians 1

1-5 Letterhead and Greeting

Paul begins with his own name. This is not egocentricity. It belongs to the letter writing style of antiquity. The name of the sender comes first, sometimes as it is here, with a presentation. The reason Paul emphasizes that he is an apostle, i.e., one sent out as a fully authorized envoy, not from men but from God will be understood later. It is also why, even here, he emphasizes that which is the chief summary of Christ's work of salvation: that He has made us free by His death.

6-10 The Reason for the Letter: The Galatians are About to Fall from the Gospel

Paul explodes. Otherwise, he usually begins by giving thanks where he does not neglect to mention what joy he receives from them to whom he now writes. Yet here he has nothing to rejoice for. He is shaken and upset. He writes, or rather, he dictates, with a passionate engagement that reverberates through his whole letter. Something dangerous has happened. He must warn and shout as a person does when someone goes straight for a precipice in the dark. His Galatians have fallen from the gospel!

They have not returned to heathendom. Neither have they made themselves guilty of any grave moralistic misstep. They believe that they are good Christians, even better Christians, stricter and with greater demands on themselves. Yet, all is lost if Paul cannot bring them to their senses.

This is remarkable about Galatians. This deals with a problem that is just as real in all ages. What happened in the congregations of Galatia is constantly happening.

What was it that had happened?

Strict teachers had come, certainly Jewish Christians, who wanted to improve upon the gospel. It was certainly true that we must believe in Jesus Christ, but we must also . . . and then they came with new conditions for salvation, conditions that all added up to something we must do. So, they preached a way of salvation different from the gospel. They laid another foundation for salvation and for the right to be called Christian and to be God's child rather than this belief in Jesus.

Paul begins by noting that there is only one gospel. He does it with implacable sharpness, as uncompromisingly and emphatically as he can. In God's kingdom there is no pluralism. When it comes to our salvation, there is only one great truth.

If anyone adds something to it or takes something from it, then the gospel is no longer the saving gospel. Then a person draws people into perdition and comes under judgment themselves.

The opponents have apparently tried to undermine the allegiance the Galatians had for Paul by saying that Paul was not a real apostle. He did not belong to the twelve. At most, he was a disciple of Peter and the others. Moreover, they said that he tried to curry favor with gentiles. He wants to be popular, and therefore he preached a more convenient way of salvation than the strict law of obedience.

First Paul takes up the later accusation. Here you can see, he says, that I really am not afraid to offend men. He knows that he has a truth to stand for, and it must be brought forth whatever the cost.

11-24 Paul is Christ's Apostle, Entrusted with Christ's Gospel

Next Paul shows that he really is an apostle called by Christ Himself, and that he received his gospel directly from Christ. By this he means the foundational truth around which there is now conflict: that salvation depends on faith. All that Paul knew about the life of Jesus, about His deeds and His word, this he, like other Christians, had obviously learned from those who were "eyewitnesses and servants of the word from the beginning" (Luke 1:1). Already at the beginning there were some who "were notified" and "received" when the message of Jesus Christ was carried out into the world. Paul refers to this solidly conceived tradition, for example, when he says: "I have received from the Lord what I also have handed over to you" (1 Corinthians 11:23). But here it is the very core: that Christ died on the cross means that every sinner, even the greatest one (such as Paul, the persecutor), could be forgiven of everything.

Paul also describes how it goes when a person is converted. He emphasizes that he is not just the disciple of an apostle. Christ has really shown Himself to him and given him insight into a truth that he is now obligated to spread. He is "set apart from the womb" (like Jeremiah) and "called" (like the prophet Jeremiah). God has revealed His Son in Paul and taken possession of him. He is now a servant of Christ, His serf, His slave (the Greek uses the same word for all three). He has not been taught and sent by the other apostles. So, he tells in detail how little he had to do with the congregation in Jerusalem. Luke has described the same events from a different viewpoint in Acts, chapter 9. As so often in the Bible, there are two stories that don't quite match each other, so without further information, we cannot really harmonize them into a united story. In his commentary on Galatians, Luther jokes about the church father Hieronymus, who toils hard with such problems. He says: "Hieronymus sweats here and says that Luke does not write anything about Paul traveling to Arabia, as if it was necessary to write a chronicle over what he did day by day! This is completely impossible. It may suffice that we have a few moves and a summary of the events from which we can find examples and instruction."

Galatians 2

1-10 Paul's Gospel was Confirmed by the Other Apostles

Paul tells about his trip to Jerusalem where he received solemn confirmation that his gospel was the true gospel. He emphasizes that Titus, who was along on the trip, was accepted even though he was not circumcised. Those who had demanded that the gentile Christians should be circumcised were wrong. Paul does not hesitate to call them "false brothers." He disavows their Christianity. They step up as representatives of the doctrine of works have done in every era. They spied to find out what their free brothers now had in order to report it to James, in hope that he would intervene and see to it that everyone followed the example that the doctrine of works prescribed. Paul emphasizes that he will not give them an inch. He was otherwise willing to meet anyone where they were and could be a Jew for Jews and a Greek for Greeks. He gave an uncompromising no in this case. Here it was the truth of the gospel. This applied to the foundation upon which the church stands or falls (*articulus stantis et cadantis ecclesiae*). Then one cannot give in. There are things which a man can very well do in and of themselves, and which can be useful (for example, to fast, observe particular feast days, let all pastors be ordained by a bishop, and abstain from alcoholic drinks). However, if someone makes such a thing a condition for true Christianity and demands that it shall be observed before someone can have Christian communion, then a person must say no. Then a person has come to a point where the truth of the gospel applies. Then he stands "*in statu confessionis,*" which is where a person must give a witness to the gospel by saying no.

There was only one thing that Paul was able to promise: that he should "remember the poor." Thereby is meant the congregation in Jerusalem. Those who became Christians often lost their jobs and were ostracized from their family, which in antiquity meant losing all that we call social benefits. The outcasts shared what they had freely, and their fellow Christians sold their assets. Now they lived in great affliction. This was the reason behind the resolution to organize a collection in the other congregations. Paul has much to say about this in his letter.

11-14 The Conflict with Peter in Antioch

However, Paul has more to say. Apparently, there were Jewish Christians that did not accept the settlement in Jerusalem. They did not keep quiet, rather they travelled around and agitated. Now they had also come to the congregation in Galatia. Paul speaks of how he encountered them in Antioch. He speaks about what he said on that occasion. He allows us to imagine the secret fears those lawgivers could instill. They appeared as if they decided and wholeheartedly. They demanded that a person should go the way of obedience to the end, whatever the cost. They were understood to imply that they had James, even the brother of Jesus, behind them. So, it went as it so often does. Peter did not want to risk being portrayed as less reliable. He even broke communion with the gentiles whom he had eaten with before, something that was unthinkable for a pious Jew.

We notice that "Jews" and "heathen" (gentiles) are used here as names for peoples, not for religions. "Heathen" was the name for anyone that was not a Jew. Even the gentile Christians could be called heathen (because they did not belong to the Jewish people), just as the Jewish Christians could still be called Jews when a person wanted to distinguish them from the Greeks in the same congregation.

15-21 One is Justified by Faith, not by Works

The conflict in Antioch now gives Paul occasion to speak about the most important thing he has to say concerning the question of salvation. We cannot determine where the story about what happened in Antioch ends. Imperceptibly, he glides over to speaking directly to the Galatians. It is just that which is the chief thing for him: to be able to say the same thing as he had already said.

So, Paul declares what he thinks. Certainly, he was born a Jew and would be able to claim all that which a pious Jew expects to benefit. He is not some "heathen sinner." It was just that which his compatriots saw concerning other people. However, Paul knows that both Jews and heathen alike are far from God, and that there is only one path that leads home to Him, as for them all. Certainly, the Jews have the law, but it does not help them. "No man is justified by works of the law." Here Paul uses an expression from the Old Testament that is not easy to translate into English. By works of the law or deeds of the law he means such works as the law demands. So, it is not only a question concerning external commands such as fasting, sacrifices, the Sabbath, and purity regulations, but above all the demands for uprightness, love, truth, and godliness. The word "flesh" can mean the body or men. "All flesh" then means "all living," "all creatures." However, and especially in the New Testament, it also means our depraved nature. In this place it means "no living man," and "no created creature," but there lies in the expression a hint of why we are never finished with the law's good deeds: we are "of the flesh by nature." We have something within us that strives against God and is never submissive to Him. What "righteous" finally means can perhaps be most simply translated with the word "finished with doing right." Righteousness is that which fulfills all that God demands of us.

Paul thus concludes that it is just this that we are never finished with. Therefore, God has opened another path for us. He has allowed His Son to die as atonement for our sin. If we believe in Him, then all is forgiven.

But then, does not Christ become a servant of sin? Paul has certainly heard this accusation many times. Christ becomes just a help for incorrigible sinners, an excuse for nothing being as it should. No, says Paul. Certainly, Peter and Paul are both sinners, just as all who believe in Christ. But there is a difference between sinners. They who believe and live in forgiveness, they are also affected by it (Paul takes up this matter later on). It is not a question of consciously being shameless trespassers. I would be that, Paul says, if I took it upon myself to build a fake bridge to salvation that I have now destroyed at Christ's command! (The words, "The false faith," are not in the original text; Paul only speaks of building up that which has been destroyed, but one can figure from context that it is the false faith in works that he has in mind.)

So, Paul says, that through the law I have died to the law. By really trying to be righteous through the law I have learned the bitter lesson that it is impossible for me. The conclusion is that the law condemns me to death. Thus, I have said farewell to the law as a way to God. Now the real life has begun for me, life in Christ. Believe not that I am free from the law in the manner that I can do what I want. No, I am crucified with Christ. I have left my life with Him. It is He who answers for me. It is He who lives in me. He has made me a member of His body, a part of Himself. So, I live in faith in Him, though I remain here "in the flesh." This means that a created creature, like other men, subject to the same temptations and the same corruption and with the same old Adam is still within me, though crucified, not free to do what he wants! This life I now live in faith in the Lord, who has sacrificed Himself for me and given me the right and possibility to be God's child. It is this great offer, the inconceivable and fantastic grace of God that I may not toss aside. I should do it, if I now began to come with my works and offer them to God as payment for salvation. If this payment could suffice, then Christ would never have needed to suffer death.

Galatians 3

1-5 Experience shows that Righteousness comes through Faith

Paul reminds us again of how it was when the Galatians heard the gospel. Christ was painted for them so that they saw the crucified One. (Paul uses an expression that could also be used for public notice, visible to all.) And the Holy Spirit comes with faith in the Crucified. The experience must have been stark and palpable, possibly through speaking in tongues, and certainly through some sort of miraculous work, because immediately afterward Paul refers to them. This is evidence enough, Paul means. Here you can see for yourself that it depends on faith and not in the works of the law.

The Galatians had thus "begun in the Spirit." That which happened in their midst was God's own work, that which only the Spirit could carry out. Should now everything "end in the flesh"? Thus, as a work of man? Should the old man receive back his dominion with his self-righteousness and his desire to make himself valid? It is just as bad, Paul means, as if it should all end in hedonistic immorality and depravity. Both mean that one "finishes in the flesh," apart from God.

6-14 The Scriptures teach that Righteousness comes from Faith

Paul transitions from experience to the evidence of Scripture. Already, Abraham was made righteous through faith. Paul has seen what is written in Scriptures (Genesis 15:6). The old, childless Abraham had received the promise that he would be the father of a people as innumerable as the stars of heaven. It was unreasonable. But "he believed in the Lord," and it was counted to him as righteousness. In the Old Testament, Abraham stands as the key figure in the history of salvation. He left everything in order to be someone who would prove to be a blessing for all peoples. This calling out from God and this promise has a foundational meaning. In a different context (Romans 4) Paul mentions that the promise was given before Abraham had even received circumcision. So, it had nothing to do with the law. It was pure grace. And Abraham believed, even where it could seem completely impossible, just as impossible as that God would be able to raise Jesus (Romans 4:20-25) or that God would be able to make the ungodly righteous (Romans 4:5). Yet that is precisely how God operates! He has shown this from the very beginning, precisely when He dealt with Abraham and intervened in the history of the world in a decisive manner.

There is also a promise from God, a promise that already spoke from the beginning about how salvation would be given to the world. Paul means that there is a particular meaning in the promise given to Abraham's "seed," a word that has a plural in Greek in contrast to Swedish, [and English]. Here it is written in the singular, and there is an allusion to Christ in it, Paul says. (A person could use a word like "descendant" or "offspring" to reproduce Paul's course of thought in English.) In other contexts, he shows that he is very well conscious that the word can hint at a whole people, to all of Israel. However, he apparently means that here there is a particular meaning for the choice of words. The biblical word often has a depth that is not plumbed with the first perusal. The Jews knew this, and Jesus shows us this. So, Paul means that here the word choice witnesses to God's deepest plan of salvation. God began the work of salvation by calling one man, the father of faith, Abraham. In the fullness of time, the whole work of salvation was encompassed in another single man, Abraham's descendant, his "seed," Jesus. Just as Abraham was made into a great people, so Christ would also be the head for an innumerable generation, that all would be "of Abraham's faith."

Now, the important thing for Paul is that this promise of God becomes the basis for His work of salvation in all times. Even at the very beginning, God had promised to save each and every one who believed. So, a man can draw a line straight through all people. There are those who "hold to faith" and those who "hold to works." So, the usual division between evil and good, moral and immoral, good people and bad people, does not apply before God. Those who believe that they have the right place before God because they live an honorable life and behave—whatever a man means by that—in actuality, they live under a curse. If the law is to apply, then it shall apply completely. Then a man shall fulfill all of it. Then we are all lost.

However, Christ has now redeemed us from the curse of the law. He took the curse upon Himself. The law cannot be repealed; it is an expression of God's will. So, Jesus was also placed under the law. He fulfilled it. He alone has done all that the law demands. However, He took upon Himself what we others had broken. When He was condemned to death and crucified, the opponents thought that God had shown that He was a deceiver, condemned by God. This was precisely why they wanted Him crucified. It was written in the law that He who was crucified (hung on a tree): He is cursed, condemned by God himself (Deuteronomy 21:23). However, when God let this happen, it was to show that His judgment over sin stood firm, at the same time He wanted to redeem us who pulled this judgment over us. The word "redeemed" is taken from the slave trade. A person could lose his freedom, for example a prisoner of war or a debtor, and end up in the slave market. Yet in this distraught situation a person could also be saved, if someone wanted to pay what it cost.

15-18 Here the Law does not Apply but the Promise

Then Paul makes a comparison with that which is applicable for a testament. What he wants to say becomes even more clear if a person knows that "testament" and "covenant" are the same word in Greek. (This is why we speak of the Old and New

Testament when we mean the Scriptures that deal with the old and new covenant.) Paul posits that the covenant of grace with Abraham that still applies to us is older than the covenant of Law on Mt. Sinai. And just as an applicable testament cannot be repealed, so neither can the law nullify God's immutable promise and His plan of salvation.

19-29 The Law is a Schoolmaster to Christ

So why did we receive the law? Well, says Paul, God wants sin to be revealed. It should reveal the breaking of the law as something that is contrary to the will of God. We men should know when we oppose God. And we should learn that we need grace and forgiveness.

Neither does the law lead us to God. On the contrary: It locks us in prison where we sit as convicted criminals. Before Jesus came, the law held God's people under this strict castigation. The law was a "guardian." The Greek uses the word "pedagogue," and by it is meant a slave who would follow and monitor a child equipped with a cane and instructed not to let his fingers get in between if there was any reason whatsoever for the use of corporal punishment and beating. However, Paul adds a pedagogue to Christ. God's intention was to lead Israel's people and all of humanity to Christ. Even today He uses the law to show us why we need Christ.

So, the law is something secondary, an aid to faith. Paul highlights that there were 430 years after the promise to Abraham. Exodus says that Israel was in Egypt for 430 years. Of course, there ought to have been a lot more time than that between Abraham and Moses. Paul only mentions an approximate figure. It is not his purpose to give an exact chronological account (as one would have done in a reference book or an historical essay) but only to show that the law was given long after the promise. The actual number of years has no significance. So, it often is with the notices about external conditions that we have in the Bible. A person should not read them the same way as data in a reference book but remember Luther's words that we have already cited: "It may suffice that we have a few moves and a summary of the course, whereby we can find examples and instruction."

Now Paul also mentions that the law was given by angels and a mediator. The mediator is Moses. The angels on Sinai are not mentioned in our Old Testament, but we know that among others who cited the Septuagint, the Greek translation of the Old Testament, Jews presupposed that the angels appeared. Even Steven says this (Acts 7:53). Even in this, Paul sees a difference with the promise. The promise was given by God Himself. This time it was only He who operated, by pure grace, without the help of any man. The covenant of the law on Sinai was a different matter. It was cut between two parties, between God and His people (who were represented by the mediator Moses). Israel received the law and promised to live according to it. They would be God's people upon this condition. Israel broke this covenant too many times to count. It is nothing to build upon as a basis for salvation. However, the promise that God gave to Abraham, that stands fast.

So, salvation does not come through the law. On the contrary, the Scriptures have "included everyone under sin." It shows us that, as it says in the Psalm, "here on earth sin is with everyone." Nothing that we are or do is perfect. It does not correspond to the law's demand for a perfect love that causes a person to love God above all and his neighbor like himself. Yet when Scripture convicts us of this matter, it causes us to understand what it really wants to say: "That which God has promised should be given to those who believe through faith in Jesus Christ."

When Christ has come, a completely new era has begun in the history of the world. Paul says: faith has come. He means: The Savior has come. Him, we may believe in and Him we can believe upon, because the Spirit has also come with the gospel, with the Word that creates faith in our hearts. Through this faith, we are all God's children. We are that "in Christ Jesus." This "in" is meant literally. We are incorporated in Christ. This happened to us in baptism. All who have been baptized have clothed themselves with Christ. They are sealed in Him. They are His members. They are enveloped in a mercy that is completely drenched with forgiveness. They are clothed in the true wedding clothes, Christ's righteousness. It conceals and obliterates all guilt. It makes it so that we can be, and we may be God's beloved children, when we believe in Christ.

So, faith in Christ is the crucial condition. If a person has this, then he is God's child, and as God's children, we are all the same: beloved by God, worth the same in His eyes, embraced the same by His love. Here, when it comes to our right to be children of God, all lines of division, that otherwise apply to people, cease. Here, it is no longer a matter of Jew or Greek. Christians of all people and all races stand just as close to God. Here, there is no question of slave or free. Christians of all types, regardless of relationships and societal class, are just as precious in the eyes of God. Here there is neither question of man nor woman. Here Paul says man and woman because it touches upon the first chapter of the Bible. Essentially it says, "no male or female." When it comes to salvation, the right to be children of God is for men and women (and children!) perfectly equal. This does not mean that the difference that God created when He "created them male and female" should be done away with. So long as we live here on earth shall "a man cleave to his wife and the two shall be one flesh." They have partially different functions as Paul develops in more detail in other places (Ephesians 5). Paul specifically rejects homosexual acts. Yet the differences between the sexes are abolished in this manner, that all are one in Christ. We are not all the same. The differences that God has created still remain, but we are all just as worthy because we belong to Christ. This means, and Paul here summarizes, that we belong as "descendants" to that which was promised. We are His siblings. So, we too are descendants of Abraham and heirs to the promise.

Galatians 4

1-11 We who were Slaves to the Powers of the World are now Children of God

A person can differentiate between two epochs in the spiritual history of humanity. They can be compared with the time in which a ward is under tutors and the time he may take over his heritage. There enters a fundamental change the day he comes of age. The change enters for us people on the day when Christ redeemed us. Before then we were held "in slavery to the authorities of this world." Here Paul uses an expression that means element, basic rules, constituents such as those who have a fundamental and controlling interest. For the Jews this was the law; for the gentiles the authorities of nature and society behind which a person perceived divine spiritual beings: justice, fate, the planets, guardian spirits, demons, and many other things. Paul knows that all this is connected. God's law is not only the Law of Moses; it is also written in the hearts of the gentiles. We encounter this everywhere in existence. It is God who has established "powers," i.e., governments. God has given nature a law, "and it shall not pass" (Psalms 148:6). If a person is not a child of God, then he experiences all this as a constraint. He is trapped by demands and claims on all sides. To give it modern expression, he feels pressure from his surroundings. He can't fool himself. He has to do the work. He knows what people expect of him. Yet at the same time, he feels the threat from the forces of nature, the threat of cancer, from car accidents. Or perhaps from a downturn in the market with the risk for lay off. A person can be tempted to glance at horoscopes in the newspaper when he is supposed to do something important. Or to try semi superstitious treatments to keep himself young and healthy. This is "slavery to the powers of this world."

Christ has freed us from this slavery. He has made us children of God. When we believe, we can say, "Abba, Father." It is really something incredible. Contemporaries of Jesus were shocked that He called God, "Abba,"—Dad. God was the most holy and exalted, demanding, and jealous. That Jesus could call Him "Dad" shows the uniqueness of His position. He was God's Son. However, the fantastic thing now is that He made it possible for us to be sons and daughters of God, who may say "Dad" in the same manner.

So it is when a person learns to know God, such as He is revealed by Christ. We really ought not say that we have learned to know God, but that we have been "known by God." This means God has acknowledged His children, however disfigured they are. He has made it possible for them to be embraced in His arms without being devoured by His purity and holiness.

And now Paul comes to the core point. If we have now received this glorious freedom, the right to be God's children, how then can someone be so foolish that he can consider turning back to slavery under the world's completely dark powers and under the terrible and impossible task of earning God's grace by fulfilling all that which the law demands? It is just this that the Galatians want to do. They are already snug in the noose. They have begun to believe in particular days and seasons. Perhaps Paul hints that they began to observe Jewish holy days and the Sabbath day. Perhaps they have also begun to comply with astrologers and their horoscopes, something that was very common at the time, even among religious and cultured people.

12-20 Remember How it Was and Make it Clear for Yourself What is Happening

Now Paul entreats them: Be as I am, free in Christ. Though I could live as a Jew, I have for your sake shown that it is not important. Paul reminds them of how good the relationship between him and the Galatians had always been. We learn that the first time he came to stand before them he was sick, apparently with some disfiguring disease, perhaps an eye disease that had been able to make them think that he looked obnoxious and dissuasive. But they listened and received him, and it became a jubilant joy. What then has taken the joy away? There they go, sour and suspicious, strict with themselves and critical of others.

Yet they are still zealous; no one objects to these lawgivers. They still want your best. Foolish zeal! Paul says. They want to shut you out, isolate you, only so that they can keep you for themselves. Here, with a few short sentences, Paul shows the picture of the typical formation of a sect, a tragedy that is often repeated—a zeal and eagerness that seems genuine but only leads to splintering and separation.

A person notices how engaged Paul is. It is important to take notice that it is not moral mistakes and debauchery that he wants to correct. Instead, it is a misguided piety, a doctrine of works, moralism, the belief that good deeds are the right and important way to God. Such can also be just as dangerous and devastating as immorality.

4:21-5:1 The Covenant of the Law and that of the Promise

So, Paul comes with yet another argument. Perhaps it was during his three years in Arabia that he had been able to hear that Mount Sinai had the same name as Hagar, Abraham's slave and concubine. Now he makes an allegorical explanation of the story about Hagar and Sarah. Such allegories are often used in Biblical commentaries by Jews, as in the early church and during the Middle Ages. Luther was skeptical of them, and Paul makes sparse use of them. The method means that one uses an historical story as if it were a parable where the different details can illustrate something completely different than what the story is concerned with. Thus, Paul allows Sarah and Hagar to illustrate the two covenants and the great differences between them. We could say: he uses both women and their sons as symbols. Hagar's children are born "according to the flesh." This means in the normal, natural course, like other children. Isaac was born according to the particular promise of God, contrary to everything that could be expected. By him, God's Word continued the work that He had begun with Abraham, that which would give rise to God's people Israel and finally to the salvation of the whole world. Isaac was thus the bearer of God's plan of salvation and the tool for His work of salvation, just as Christ's church that is the new Israel and the heavenly Jerusalem.

In the 21st chapter of Genesis, it is said that Ishmael, Hagar's son, who was many years older than Isaac, displeased Sarah. She asked Abraham to drive Hagar and her son away, so that he would not inherit anything with her own. This displeased Abraham greatly, but God promised to provide for them and make Ishmael the father of a people. Then Abraham sent them away. It was important to Paul that Isaac, the son of the free woman was the heir of God's promise of righteousness through faith. So he stands as the symbol of the New Testament (covenant). We are not born to slavery. We are children of the promise.

Paul also finds another parallel. Ishmael persecuted Isaac. It can point to the events that awakened Sarah's dissatisfaction. It is written in our translation that Ishmael "played and joked." It can also mean that he "mocked and teased." However, Paul can also have in mind that Ishmael's descendants, the Ishmaelites, were desert tribes; the Mideanites also belonged to them, and during the long time were a plague for the Israelites by their raids on the coastal country. Paul is reminded that it is still this way. The old Israel persecutes the new. We are reminded that Judaism at that time was the more powerful party, something of a worldwide church, with synagogues and missionaries all over the Roman world, while the Christians were a small, persecuted minority. Yet Paul says that it is this minority that now has the promise of God. They are those who shall be a great people. He cites the passage from the prophet Isaiah that speaks about God's people, who seem to be just as hopeless without a future as a childless and hated mother, but who had God's promise and therefore would bloom again. He sees that such is the promise to God's people, which now applies to them, who have received God's Messiah and become citizens of the true Israel. They shall be a great people, however despised they may be just now. For just this reason they should stand firm and not receive the yoke of slavery again.

Galatians 5

2-6 To Trust in Your Deeds is to Reject Christ

Now Paul will summarize everything he has wanted to say up to this point. He does it with extreme sharpness. When it comes to the basis for our right to be children of God, then it is implacably either/or. Either we receive forgiveness on account of Christ alone, or we receive it because we live righteously, and this means only the law and the whole law. A person cannot build partially on Christ and partially on his own good will and his moralistic way of life. To come clinging to something of your own means to displace Christ and no longer give Him the glory of being our Savior. Naturally, Paul does not reject good works. On the contrary, they follow from faith. If faith in Christ is genuine then it is active in love. Yet works will not do as the basis for salvation. They may not be that which we trust in when we ask ourselves if we are true Christians. Not even if it means such good things as devotional prayers, great missionary offerings, overcoming alcohol abuse, or a self-sacrificing work in the congregation and at home.

7-12 Warning and Plea

As so often, Paul uses a picture from sports. Galatians had "pressed on to the goal" (Philippians 3:14), but now they have left the course. It is so serious with the doctrine of works. It can look as if it is concerned with some minor detail, like circumcision; however, if a person makes the detail the basis of salvation, then every little thing is devastatingly dangerous. Paul reminds us of how little yeast is needed for the whole dough to rise (he seems to cite a proverb). Then he strikes a new tone and asks if it can really be so bad with the Galatians. "In the Lord"—i.e., because they are all incorporated into Christ—he dares to hope that the Galatians still know what they build their faith on. They have only been delivered. Paul reminds them how serious it is to lead people astray when it comes to the actual ground of salvation. He coarsely says that those who lay such importance on circumcision would just gladly go "circumcise themselves till it is cut all the way off" (as it says in some translations). There were heathen priests—not the least in Galatia—who did this. But in Israel no such person could be a priest. There is a subtext in Paul's words that these erring men could so happily give such external evidence of how useless they were as spiritual leaders. At the same time, he reminds us that he really didn't preach evangelical freedom to be popular. He would have it much easier if he stuck to preaching the law. Now he suffers persecution, and it shows in its way that he stands for the gospel.

13-18 The Struggle Between Spirit and Flesh

Paul devotes the rest of the letter to the other side of the same thing. He has made that which is the basis of our salvation clear: Christ and not our own works. Now he goes on to show that works still have their obvious place in a Christian life. If a person has received life through faith in Christ, then good works follow as an important consequence. Both faith and works are a work of the Spirit.

This means that we are free from the slavery of the law and compulsion to earn our salvation. Yet we are not free from service. Our new life in forgiveness means that we have Christ as our Lord, and we will gladly serve Him. The problem is that we still have within ourselves a power that struggles against this. It is our natural, innate selfishness. Here Paul uses the word "flesh." Among other things it can mean the body that God created (so something good), but it often means something that God has not created: the evil will within us. It is our nature that is adversarial toward God, something that God's enemy Satan has sown there. This, our innate egotism, remains even in a Christian that has become God's child through faith in Christ. So, it can be called "the old man." Sometimes we call it original sin, the inherited corruption in our nature, or merely depravity. A person can attempt to express it in English with such words as "selfishness" or "egotism" or "self-interest," but this only partially expresses what the issue is. So, we say "the flesh" when the original text uses the word in this particular meaning.

The truth is, there are two powers at work within a Christian: the Spirit and the flesh. They are in constant strife with one another. So, there is always something that attempts to hinder us from carrying out our determination. If we want to think of Christ, then the flesh attempts to check us. Should we follow the suggestion of the flesh, then the Spirit says no. Within this strife, we have now taken the Spirit's side. The flesh is crucified, nailed fast so that it does not have freedom of movement, which does not hinder it from attempting to come with his proposals and try to see them through. Here it is the matter of two contrasting programs for life. The one is the Spirit's: to serve each other and love one another. The second is that of the flesh: to assert oneself, which leads to biting at each other. So, it is important to walk in the Spirit and be driven by the Spirit. It is that which happens when we love Christ, hold fast to Him, listen to Him, speak with Him, and live before His face. Then we don't carry out what the flesh proposes. And then we no longer stand under the law. We live under grace, in perpetual forgiveness, even for the enmity with God that remains within us and that perpetually tempts us to cheating and misconduct.

To "walk in spirit" can also be translated "to walk in the Spirit." It is a question of living a life that is ruled by the Holy Spirit. (The translation "let your spirit lead you" does not correspond with the original text.) "Driven by spirit" can all be expressed with "being driven by the Spirit." The former is the common translation; the latter expresses the meaning. In the former case, "spirit" is normally with a small letter. In the latter the "Spirit" is with a capital, because in the latter it is a question of a proper name; in the former it was more the work of the Spirit. However, where it is a question about the name of the Holy Spirit, a person ought to always use the capital letter, because it touches upon a personal being that bears His name. Yet even in such expressions as "walk in spirit," it is a question of something that happens only where the Spirit is and works. Jesus says: "That which is born of the Spirit, it is Spirit" (John 3:6).

19-24 Works of the Flesh and the Fruits of the Spirit

When Paul lists works of "the flesh," a person quickly notices how deficient the normal conception is, according to which "flesh" means our body with its needs, perhaps above all the sexual drive. The "flesh" is not the body but the will's hostility toward God and selfishness. This can certainly reveal itself in immorality, vice, drunkenness, and orgies (Paul also mentions those), but such things only account for a third of the examples that Paul lists. To a high degree, the rest have to do with the life of the soul, the intellect, or even religion. To the deeds of the flesh also belong false worship and all sorts of magic. To this belong all the everyday outbreaks of egocentricities and aggressiveness, just as in the social world we desire to form cliques and into collectives that push for group interests at the expense of others.

Paul calls that which the Spirit works "fruit." We are branches in the vine of Christ. So, a new power is at work in our life. It is not a question of human ambition and our own performance. It is something that grows forth because we are "in Christ" and live in relationship with Him. First Paul mentions love, and then joy and peace. It is no accident. Love is that which supports and characterizes all the others. Joy and peace are also fundamental. They are not just feelings, and they do not depend on everything going as we desire. They can also be found when we suffer injury and in the midst of persecution. We are still God's children. All the other fruits (naturally, they are only examples and not a systematic accounting) could be a description of Jesus Himself. The life from Him creates a similarity with Him. Here, it is not a question of "virtues" or "properties" that we possess, but gifts that come from Christ. They are all typical for the Kingdom of God where a person has everything forgiven and no longer needs to assert oneself.

"Against such there is no law," Paul says, and by this he means that it is not the law that brings about all these good things. The law can forbid evil and set boundaries for it, but to set forth something really good, this it is not able to do. Only the Spirit can do that.

Galatians 6

5:25-6:10 Admonitions

Paul now turns to admonitions. As usual, he does it only when the basis has been made clear, that the whole of the Christian life must grow forth from communion with Christ. Otherwise, the admonitions only lead to moralism. The admonitions he now gives are not a complete explanation of what a person should do in different situations (that which is called "casuistry") but scattered, ostensibly unconnected advice and rules, certainly in many cases a result of the knowledge Paul had concerning conditions in the Galatian church.

First, he makes the basic rule, but from that which he just said: We have life through the Spirit; we are born again in baptism. So, then we should let ourselves be driven by the Spirit and "walk in Spirit." To "walk" is the Biblical word for "to carry oneself," to behave, to make one's way through life. To walk in the Spirit means to bear the fruit of the Spirit, that which Paul has now exemplified. Here what he exemplifies is repeated to not "thinks he is something" neither "be self-absorbed, conceited, or hungry for prestige." Such only leads to us challenging each other, to criticism and to trying to "one up" each other, and that we are jealous. Now Paul knows very well that such things happen. However, he says, even if you catch someone doing something that is obviously wrong, then you should help him correct himself "in a spirit of gentleness" as it is usually said with a difficult translation; and this we ought to be able because we have "the Spirit." However, because we also have an old man within us, we may suit ourselves even when we admonish. It is in precisely this context, when it comes to restoring a fallen brother, that Paul says the famous words: "bear each other's burdens." It is to fulfill Christ's law, the law of love. Yet precisely when a person may help others it is so easy to believe that he is himself something. It is to deceive himself. We should quit comparing ourselves with each other. It is one's own deeds one should test. The result is most often confession of sin, but also thanksgiving, the "boasting" that Paul speaks of and which we have a right to, the joyful pride concerning Christ, and what He has done even in our lives. However, a person may not compare this with that which others have received or done. This possible "boast" may be used in prayer and thanks to Christ. Finally, a person stands alone before Him, even with his burdens. We shall bear each other's burdens, worries, and weaknesses; but the burden of guilt is my own. A person cannot share this. Only Christ can lift that. Paul rounds out the whole thing with a serious admonition to "walk in the spirit" and to adhere to the Spirit against the flesh.

GALATIANS 6:11-18

11-18 Letter Closing in Paul's Own Hand

Up till now Paul dictated. Now he grabs the pen himself and writes in big letters (perhaps as we do for emphasis). He summarizes yet again that chief thought of the letter. The demand of circumcision means the denial of that which happened on the cross. It is a false spirituality that in itself means that a person lets his old man raise its head and assert itself. For Paul, the cross is decisive. It condemned all of that which the world and the old man lust for, even the lust to be someone through his religion and to achieve something on one's own before the eyes of God. Here neither circumcision nor uncircumcision matter. All depend upon us participating in Christ and His life and also being a new creation. Faith in Christ, not self-redemption, is the foundation. And so, Paul finishes with a blessing over those who follow the foundation, over "God's Israel," the true Israel, God's own people who are Christ's Church.

When Paul finishes, he adds a little postscript, a thing he was not going to say but just now came to memory. He appeals to the Galatians to not cause him more troubles. He now "bears the marks of Jesus" in his body. He thinks about all of his scars, those which remind him that five times he received the harshest punishment that the Jews could measure out, "forty stripes save one." In Lystra he had been stoned and left for dead on the ground. And three times he had been whipped, probably by Romans during torturous interrogation. He must have been covered over with scars. And this is his legitimacy, the consequences of his true faithfulness to his Lord, and so he is worth listening to.

EPHESIANS
Introduction

Among the letters of antiquity that have been preserved for us, there are two main categories that can be distinguished. The first are real letters that were once sent to a particular addressee for a particular reason. Some of them—written on papyrus or pottery shards—have been dug up by archeologists. So, they are real original letters. Others have been written and preserved as literature because they were considered too valuable to be forgotten. It is in this way, for example, that a great portion of Cicero's letters have been preserved for today.

The other group of letters (that one sometimes calls "epistles") have from the beginning been intended for a larger audience. Even if they were sometimes sent to certain addressees they have simultaneously gone out in copies and kept accessible for whoever wants to read them. They can be compared with tracts or pamphlets.

In the New Testament we have examples of both types. Hebrews, for example, belongs to the latter group. Paul's letters belong to the former. For the most part they show that they came about because of particular situations; they deal with conditions and spiritual problems in a certain congregation. Sometimes it is hard to understand what it is that Paul is referencing. For the addressees it was obvious. So it is with real letters that were originally meant to be read by a particular audience.

Ephesians takes a special place among the letters that Paul sent to his congregations. It contains no greetings to individually named people and no information concerning Paul himself. We learn that Paul sends it with a coworker named Tychicus and that he can tell more about how Paul's imprisonment is going. The first part of the letter is closer to a meditation over God's ineffably great gift in Christ, and the second half contains admonitions that Paul could direct to any Christian congregation. It lacks any references to local conditions or to current misunderstandings or false doctrines such as occupy a great place in Galatians and the letters to the Corinthians.

In actual fact, there is a strong reason to believe that here we have a circular letter written to many congregations at the same time or perhaps from congregation to congregation. The actual words "in Ephesus" at the beginning of the letter is actually lacking in the oldest Bibles we have preserved (they are from the beginning respectively from the fourth century). It seems from the beginning that there was an empty space here where a person could insert the name of the congregation where the letter was to be read. A person may also notice that Paul says he heard of the faith in Christ that the people receiving the letter had (1:15). Otherwise, he normally only says this when he writes to congregations to which he himself has not been (such as Romans and Colossians). However, he had worked in Ephesus for more than two years. Such an expression is conceivable in a circular, but hardly in a letter written only for the congregation in Ephesus that Paul knew inside and out.

In large part Ephesians is reminiscent of Colossians. All this speaks to the idea that they were both written in connection with each other during the time that Paul sat in prison. Both had been sent with Tychicus who likely had them with him on the same trip. The conclusion to Colossians speaks about a letter to the neighboring city of Laodicea. Paul apparently thinks that it should have arrived at approximately the same time as the letter to Colossians. Already in the early church there were those who assumed that this letter was our Ephesians. If this was a circular it ought to have gone to Laodicea also and arrived at the same time as Colossians because both the letters were carried by the same traveler.

In questions of word choice and style, Ephesians has a tone that separates itself, for example, from Romans and Corinthians. There are scholars who because of this have questioned whether it really was written by Paul. Yet in conceptual content it is truly Pauline, and in this it is closely related to Colossians, which in its turn has a connection to the undisputed true letter to Philemon. The letter is so completely on the same wavelength with Paul that a person has to ask what unknown genius in the early church could have written it if Paul was not the author. A person might also remember that we all can change style and vocabulary when we change themes. In this letter we do not encounter Paul as the apologist, defender of justification by faith, taskmaster over apostate Christians—as in different areas—but as meditational practitioner of prayer. The long passages in the first chapters can be changed into prayer without difficulty. If a person wants to get an idea of what prophecy might have sounded like in the early church, they should read verses three through fourteen of the first chapter. It is completely natural that this language receives a different character in such praise and prayer than it has in instruction and polemics. As a popular speaker, Paul is abrupt and drastic. Here we encounter him as a man of prayer, lost in the vision of God's mystery with constantly new words for the ineffable wealth in God's mysterious council.

Finally, a person may remember that as a rule Paul writes using a secretary. He often wrote his letters together with some of his coworkers who then were also mentioned as authors. Now as Paul sits in prison, he may have delegated more of the work to his coworkers. Usually, he dictated word for word that then included a greeting written by his own hand, which at the same time served as legitimation. But during his imprisonment there may have been periods when he could not work in this manner without giving instruction to some coworker to write down a letter which they would then both review for content. This must have actually left its tracks in the linguistic formulation.

Ephesians was likely written in Rome during the early years of the sixties when Paul sat in prison there. It is possible that it was written during his incarceration in Caesarea, and in such a case. it would have been written a couple of years earlier.

That this came to be called the letter to the Ephesians might be because it was also sent to them. If this copy was written, then the actual word Ephesus followed in the preamble.

Ephesians 1

1-2 As always, the letter begins with the author's name, to which he has added his title

Paul is an apostle, which means a fully authorized envoy of Christ. Here as so often, Christ comes before Jesus because it is not a surname but a title. It means "the anointed" and is a translation of the Hebrew Messiah, the name for the future King. As we saw in the introduction, the words in Ephesus are lacking in the two oldest manuscripts. Here there seems to have been a space where a person could insert the name of the congregation that would receive the circular letter.

The letter is written "to the Christians." Paul uses the word "the saints," which in the New Testament was the most common self-designation among Christians. Paul essentially calls them "believers in Christ Jesus" because faith in Jesus means that a person has been incorporated into Him as a branch in the vine or as a member of the body. With that, a person becomes holy, which means set aside for God, given over to his possessions and service. This word which we translate with "one who believes" or "a believer" means both one who has confidence and one who is worth believing and shows himself faithful. Those who believe in Christ are simultaneously His faithful.

3-14 The Blessing in Christ

Paul begins, as usual, with a thanksgiving. It is not easy to translate. Modern English hardly has any counterparts to any of these pregnant and content laden words that Paul uses. It is difficult for us to think that a person "blesses God," but for the Jews this was as natural as praying for His blessing. To say, "Blessed be (or rather are) you God" (as Jews did with every table prayer and often at other times) means to confess that God is the source of all blessings and to praise Him for it. The blessing begins with God's being, His creating goodness. The blessing is a power. He who receives it is also able to bless others. In his joy, he blesses God who gives such blessing. It is this praise that Paul now begins with. Here he gives thanks for that which is the most extreme, greatest, and deepest of all God's blessings: His plan of salvation and the whole of His work of salvation in Christ. The words shall be read with emphasis. It stands as a superscription over all that follows.

What is it that happens with us in Christ?

1. We have been chosen (4-6). This happened before the creation of the world, in "the heavenly world." Outside of our universe there is another world. It

too is created, but it is "spiritual," "heavenly," not made of the same stuff as ours but still completely real, filled with living, individual beings to whom God has given life and their own existence, so that they should receive joy with Him for being. Now God has blessed us with "all the heavenly world's spiritual blessing." He has chosen us, and us particularly, that we should be His children; He chose us "for adoption" as the Greek word says. This He has done before the world began. He knew what it would cost. Christ must become man and die for us. Only in this way could God actualize His determination that we should be "holy and without spot in his eyes." This we are when we partake in the Savior's righteousness and become members of Christ. Then we stand before God "in Christ." God sees His Son and not our sins when He sees us. Then God has "pardoned us in the beloved" (=in Christ). This He has done so that "the glory in his grace should be praised." The glory (in Greek, *doxa*) is God's own being, unfathomable, overpowering, fortune creating, the light who blends us and at the same time lets us meet the innermost existence of power, the Father of mercy. He now speaks of the glory in God's grace. The grace is God's salvific, active goodness that takes form in Christ and His work. In this work the glory breaks through. God's transcendent and inaccessible clarity, the "light that no man has seen or can see" presses into our world, envelops us and unites us with God—in Christ. And there it happens, there jubilee breaks loose—"to the praise of his glory."

2. In Christ, we have received forgiveness for all and have learned to know God's mysterious plan of salvation (7-10). Grace has spilled over all the banks, Paul says. He has given us opportunities that are beyond all that man is capable of: we have seen God's eternal plans and been given to know what He thought and determined before our world even existed. We now know God's ultimate intentions and know that which is the meaning for the whole course of the world. It is that everything in heaven and on earth ("the whole universe" we would say) shall be "united in Christ," so that Christ holds together the whole, rules over the whole and is the final answer and the ultimate declaration. We can wonder why God started the course of the world, and why He created independent individuals with their own will, though He must have known that it gave them opportunity to be evil. The answer lays in Christ. He would unite all and open an opportunity for forgiveness and salvation for all. He would restore that which had been destroyed. This was "the plan which would be fulfilled in the fullness of time." Concerning this plan, the original text uses the word "economy," also a type of household plan. God had made up His budget and figured the risks and rewards before He created the world. The whole comes to be in the surplus, thanks be to Christ.

3. In Christ we have our hope already before we know of it. (v. 11-12)
In Christ we have received our "inheritance." One does not receive an inheritance through his own merits. Here everything depends on that which God

has determined and carried through. All Christians shall know that they are Christians because God has willed it. They have "already in advance possessed a hope." This hope is not really just a feeling. In reality it is something that exists there, an access that a person can put their hope in. So, Christ is our hope, and He was that long before we became conscious of it.

4. In him we come to faith. (v. 13-14)

The inheritance will come to be before the day when Christ comes and establishes His kingdom. Yet even now we receive a "seal," a confirmatory deposit, and it is the Spirit. The Spirit is the "seal" in that here there is power on the move that is not of this world. The Spirit has "sealed" us, set a seal upon us, God's own seal that confirms what God promised.

Naturally, a man can ask how it is with all of them who have not come to faith. Does God not want them to be saved? The answer lies in the known word that "God desires all men to be saved" (1 Timothy 2:4). However, we know from Jesus's own Word that there are those who "loathe the council of God about themselves." There are men of whom Jesus says: "you have not desired." To be chosen to blessedness means to belong to them of whom God beforehand has known, that they would not despise His love. Yet God also loves the others, and He seriously means it when He calls them. God has not chosen any to damnation.

15-23 Through the Spirit we learn to know God in Christ and His Church

As in many other letters, Paul mentions here that he prays for those he is writing to. He knows that the prayer binds him together with them. He and they are members in the same body. The same life streams from Christ out into all the limbs, and from the limbs, thanks and intercessions return and meet in Christ—similar hands folded in each other.

Here we also hear what it is Paul prays for. It is that which we all need badly and which only God can give through His Spirit. A man can receive knowledge in God's word with the help of his understanding and memory. However, there is something that we usually call insight, an experience of one's own, something experienced by an individual that makes the knowledge come alive, applicable to oneself and their circumstances, and so addition constantly deepened.

Paul mentions some of the points where insight usually grows, and perspective widens for a Christian man. The first is the hope that we are called to. This hope is not that which we expect or anticipate or hope for. It is a reality before us, a reality that lies before us. We have become citizens of a new world and a coming kingdom. It is a fantastic future that opens before us through communion with Christ. We have received an inheritance—so something that falls out in the future—that is "rich in glory," God's own glory, His inconceivably beautiful essence. This inheritance falls out "among his saints," so in the church among us Christians. It works—or ought and could work—God's own, overwhelming power, the same power with which He awakened Christ. Paul means this literally. In Christ we have stepped into connection with a new life, the same victorious, immortal life that He brought with Him from the grave. All this belongs to the experience of life that becomes all the more certain and convincing when a person lives in communion with Christ.

Finally, Paul paints a picture of the Church—the common body of Christ, the church which we speak about in the creed and used to write with a capital C in order to mark that this is not a question of a church building or a particular society. It has its origin and its anchoring in heaven. God has placed Christ on His right side, over all the spiritual powers and angelic beings that are in the heavenly world. Paul mentions, just as in many other places, different groups or classes among them without giving us any opportunity to say what separates them or why they are given different names. The names are there only as reminders that the heavenly world is not empty. It is not an abstract world of ideas, but a concrete and noticeable existence filled with "a great multitude of the heavenly host," a world where Gabriel "stands before God" and where the small children's angels "always see my heavenly father's face," as Jesus says.

From this heaven Christ guides and governs His church. He is its head. This means that He is its Lord and leader, but also something more. The body, the limbs—we—are united with Him in an organic communion and partake in His own life. A Christian does not live according to directives and instructions that come from without. He lives as a member who has within him a web of nerves and therefore functions through impulses from the head, impulses that work from within as a part of the member's own life.

With Christ there is "the fulness" of all the conceivable good, all that we and the world could ever need. In Him we have received a share of this fulness. The Church is fulfilled by it—not so that here there are all parts in all the individual limbs, but so that Christ with His life fills them all—with so much as they are more than needed. He is "all in all." In each and every one of the limbs, it is He who works all of that which can be called Christian faith and Christian life.

Ephesians 2

1-5 With Christ from Death to Life

Paul reminds us of what it was like before we came to believe. We lived as a person would without God. Perhaps we thought it was completely natural: "Everyone does this." In actual fact, we followed the enemy of God, Satan. Between God and Satan there is no neutrality; there is no "no man's land." What Paul says is literally translated "of the prince of the power of the air," and apparently it means the same as what he later calls (6:12) "the spiritual forces of evil in the heavenly places." There are evil spiritual forces. They were created by God at one time but fallen from Him. So, the Bible speaks about Satan and his angels and about Satan's kingdom. We are surrounded by them in the same manner as the air. If we do not belong to Christ, we are left to their influence. They press in upon us and are a power that works within us, "in the sons of disobedience." Paul says this with a Semitic expression. It means all the sons of man created by God who do not listen to Him but have received another father and come under another's influence.

When a person lives in such a manner, he follows his "flesh," that is, his old man. As a matter of course, the old man will assert himself so as to get as much as possible for their own share of this life, with everything that means in business, sexual life, careers, food and drink, or what one incidentally likes. So we all lived, Paul says. It does not mean a vicious life, but it was a life where God's will was replaced by our own—and behind that, the powers of opposition. In and of ourselves, our nature, our innate "sinful depravity," we were children of wrath. God's wrath is His unreconciled opposition to all evil, the zeal that is like a burning fire when it encounters that which is evil, impure, cruel, petty, and cowardly.

So we were all dead, i.e., separated from the real life, the life with God. And still! Paul cannot emphasize strongly enough the inconceivable and overwhelming aspects in this fact, that God did not quit loving those who were so unthankful but was willing to sacrifice His only Son to save us and waken us to new life.

6-10 With Christ in Heaven and on Earth

This salvation consists in being united with Christ through baptism and faith. It is in baptism that a person is buried with Christ and raised up with Him to new life. (Paul speaks closer to this matter in Romans 6.) A person is incorporated into Christ, joined as a member in His body. We can see just how literally Paul means this by the expression that God "has placed us with him in the heavenly world." Previously, Paul had described how God with His overwhelming power awakened Christ and sat Him at His right side in heaven. With the same power He has now done the same with us, "in Christ Jesus." This means in the invisible but real union that has happened between us and Christ when we were taken up in Him. Through this, we are already now placed in His kingdom. There we have our heart, our source of life, the Lord who we are incorporated into. In the future, in "the coming ages" when God has created a new heaven and a new earth, we come to experience the overwhelming wealth of this communion with Christ. When Paul says that such a salvation does not depend on what we have accomplished, he means it lays in the open daylight. It is a pure gift. No one has anything to be proud of. What we are as Christians, we are this completely through His work. Just as once the whole world was created in Christ, so now a new creation has happened in Christ. Even the good that we now can do, is His work. He has in advance prepared good deeds for us. These lie in wait for us down the road. They too are a gift we receive by grace.

11-18 Included in God's People, United with God and with One Another

Paul now highlights from another point of view the immense change that happens when a person becomes a Christian: a person is in-grafted into his own people, those who belong to God. God had made a covenant with Israel. They had received the promise that no one else could plead. Israel was God's people, and the heathen were not. Yet it was precisely through Israel that salvation would come to all people. The Jews were wrong when they prided themselves for their peculiarity, their law, and their circumcision so that they looked down on other people. Paul reminds the gentile Christians of how it felt. They were called the uncircumcised by those who in actual fact only possessed a circumcision that was "of the flesh, made by hands." Paul describes the counterpoint in Romans (2:29). It is the circumcision of the heart by the Spirit. At that time, there was a wall of enmity between the people of God and those who stood outside. Now this has been torn down, and Christ has declared peace. He has done this on the cross where He bore all sins, the sins of both Jews and heathen, and died for them. He attained atonement with God for all of us. He abolished the law; it no longer applies as the way of salvation. There is forgiveness for everything when a person comes to Christ and is united with Him through faith in Him. Just as He once united us all in His suffering body when He bore all our sins, so He unites us now when we believe in Him, and He makes us all members of His body. They who belonged to Israel before are united with them who once stood outside, "in a single new man." The wall between us is broken down, and the enmity is put aside. Yet at the same time as the wall that separated us from God has been broken down, so now we all have "entrée to the Father." Even the enmity between us and God is repealed. We are God's children, united with God.

In Christ there is also an atonement between people and races. This atonement can find expression in new laws that promote equality and justice. Yet it cannot be brought about by legislation. It will only become a reality through men being one with one another because they have been united with Christ. It is He who is our peace. This means two things: peace with God and peace with one another. Here peace does not mean a mood nor a feeling of calm and harmony, but an actual relationship: a peace that has stepped between two fighting parties. Peace with God rests on the fact that Christ has died for me and answers that I may be God's own child, though God had every reason to be angry with me. It is Christ who is our peace.

19-22 Built up in Christ into a Temple of God

So we are members of Christ. The same thing can be expressed with another picture. We are the house people of God. Or, we are a temple, a building built for God and consecrated for His service.

Paul begins with the picture of house people (household of God). We are no longer strangers and "guests" as it used to be translated. Paul uses an expression here that signifies immigrants that do not have the rights of citizens. Through Christ we have received citizenship in God's people. The Church is the true Israel, His own people. We have become "The household of God." We belong to God's "house" and by "house" is meant, as in earlier times, the whole family and all the slaves that were subject to a housefather. It was in "the house" that an individual found security and protection. There he was cared for and received the equivalent of what we call social benefits and what we expect of a welfare society. If a person stood outside, he had no rights, left out and abandoned. Yet now God has also taken us in to be among His household, in His family, and we remain under His protection.

The same thing can now be expressed with the picture of a building. It is under construction. The foundation is laid. It is made of the Apostles and Prophets. The prophets are the inspired worshipers and proclaimers of the early congregations. We hear a lot of talk about them, but we do not know much about what they said. All the more, we know about what the Apostles said. It is worth remembering what is written here: this is the foundation for all Christendom. The cornerstone is Christ. Without Him, everything is razed. (It possibly means "keystone," the downward tapered stone that a man would place at the top of an arch and made it so that the other stones in the arc could remain in place. The meaning is the same; without this stone the whole thing collapses.) The foundation rests on this cornerstone, that which proceeds from the apostles and prophets. On this foundation we are all built up. This means that all true Christians rest upon this basis that is laid once and for all in the apostolic era. It was Christ who with His Spirit worked in the Apostles. So, the church came to be what it is. This Christian faith is the apostolic faith, and we confess together that the church is one, holy, catholic, and apostolic.

On this foundation, the church now grows into "a holy temple in the Lord." "In the Lord" here means as elsewhere "in Christ," in communion with Christ. A house of stone cannot really have any communion of life, but the whole time Paul has had the living church in mind, that which is the body of Christ. This temple is perforated with life from Christ. In the same manner, Peter says that we are living stones that are built up into a spiritual house (1 Peter 2:5).

Paul repeats this crucial statement one more time: in Him (for the twelfth time since he placed it as a rubric in the beginning of his letter). In Him you are also built up, he says, together with all the others. You are inserted into this living building, where God Himself works through the Spirit. This building is Christ.

Here we can also see what man in the early church meant by "being built up." It does not mean to be touched or seized or pleasantly comforted, but it literally means to be inserted into the Church's building, to be a living stone in Christ and so grow in faith, love, and holiness.

Ephesians 3

1-13 The Great Mystery that has been Revealed

Paul returns to the prayer that he never finished. He calls himself a prisoner of Christ. This could mean "a prisoner for the sake of Christ," but here he certainly means something more: a man who is imprisoned by Christ, bound to Christ, inextricably and forever. Before he even had time to say what he is praying about he breaks off again. He has something more to say about the great mystery, God's eternal plan that is now being fulfilled. Paul himself has been able to see it revealed. He has received a chief role assigned to this great drama. He knows that it is a complete gift, something that was given to him even though he did not deserve it. Of course, he is the least among all the Christians ("all the saints" as one said in the early church); he persecuted God's church. So consequently, he speaks here about something that was given to him: gifted, revealed. Through the millennia God had this plan ready. Yet only now has it been revealed and set-in motion—through Christ, through the Spirit, in the Church. First and foremost, Paul is thinking about how the mystery was revealed to him in the Damascus revelation where Christ made him the apostle to the gentiles. However, the spirit has also revealed this mystery even for "his holy apostles and prophets." We are accustomed to using the word 'holy' as a designation for a saint. In the New Testament this word originally meant something that belongs to God and is set apart for God, for His service. So, a person said, 'the holy' when they meant 'the Christians.' For this reason, it was obvious that the apostles and prophets were holy. They were God's chosen instruments—but without the halo. So, this mystery—that the gentiles just like the Jews would be God's people in Christ—was revealed to them. It happened through the interventions of the Holy Spirit such as the baptism of the Spirit at the house of Cornelius (Acts 10) or the resolution that was approved by the church council in Jerusalem (Acts 15), where a person could say: "The Holy Spirit and we have determined . . ." This happened completely by the Spirit-inspired understanding of Christ's death and resurrection that carried the proclamation of the apostles and prophets.

This great mystery that Paul speaks about here has become almost a banal truth for us. It seems so obvious to us that all people should have a right to salvation. The Epistle to the Ephesians can give us a useful reminder that salvation in Christ is least of all an obvious right, but instead a fantastic, unlikely, and completely undeserved favor. We need to rediscover the overwhelming joy in this happy news that even we have received the right of inheritance in Christ's kingdom, that we have been grafted on to Christ's body, that we have a share in the promise that applied to Israel.

This hidden plan of God's has thus been revealed—even for "the princes and powers in the heavenly realms." And it has been "through the church." The church has, as we have already heard, Christ as her head. From His place in heaven, He guides His church on earth, sends His Holy Spirit and His Word, and stands in a living, organic relationship with the members on earth. The church is something that is found in the heavenly realms too. Through that which happens in the church, God's plan is revealed even to the heavenly powers.

Now we can see what God always had in mind, and now realizes. When we believe in Jesus we can all boldly step before God and be taken up into a covenant where everything rests on forgiveness and redemption. So, we need not allow ourselves to be beaten down by opposition and persecution. That Paul sits in prison is just a consequence of the commission he received, part of God's great plan. It is not meaningless. On the contrary, it is "for the honor" of all congregations. A person could even translate this: "for the glory." God's own glory enters into our world when through faith in Jesus we receive a share in the new life of the resurrection, even in suffering. What happens here is a little piece of the Word, by which God unites us with Himself and returns to us the glory we had lost.

14-21 The Apostle's Intercession

The prayer that then follows gives us a living picture of Paul as intercessor and of that which every Christian and every congregation needs to pray for more than anything. Paul bends his knees. He prays to the Father. He says something very thoughtful about the word "Father." We usually imagine that such words about God are defective images that we borrow from our earthly conditions. It is on the contrary; He gives to all true fatherhood on earth, such as He wants it to be, something of His own being. There is something of our heavenly Father's being that is reflected in every father on earth if he is a father after God's mind.

Now Paul asks the Father above all fathers for something to be done "according to the riches of his glory," that is with a lavish wealth and the boundless joy that wells up from out of His fatherly heart. The first thing Paul prays about, and also something of the most important, is that we shall be "strengthened in power to your inner being." Through faith in Christ, a new life has been born within us. A new man has been created, "have put on the new self, which is being renewed in knowledge after the image of its creator" (Colossians 3:10 [ESV]). This new man needs to be perpetually renewed, perpetually strengthened and constantly nourished from Christ, just as the branch cannot live apart from the tree. This happens through the Spirit, He who works in the means of grace. That this new man is with us, this means that God allows "Christ to live in our hearts through faith." We also see that which for Paul is the primary thing—not one's own resolutions and propositions, not one's own sacrifices or promises, but this: that we believe in Christ and through this faith are renewed with Him. This is also what used to be called something "purely religious," not at first a question of ethics and morals. But this "purely religious" has an important consequence that follows, that which is the other chief theme in this prayer: that we shall be "rooted and grounded in love." The picture is easy to understand. The plant sinks its roots down into the earth and finds nourishment. We sink our roots down into Christ's love and take it to us. A house needs a firm ground. Our life as Christians must also have a firm foundation, something which holds in all weather. That foundation is Christ's love. Growth here is not a question of our love, but of Christ. In actual fact, this leads to absorbing all the nutrients and building their entire lives on the love of Christ, even so that one bears the fruit of love. Yet here (typically enough), Paul does not mention the fruit, but another consequence of being rooted in Christ's love, all that "purely religious" something. Essentially, that one can, together with all the saints—in the church's communion—understand that which is "the breadth, the length and the depth and height," of this boundless love and so learn to know it, though it surpasses all knowledge. Here Paul gives a classic expression for a true aspect of the Christian experience. There is something that surpasses all knowledge, something that never can be expressed exactly and correctly in definite terms, but which is still real and which through personal experience through meeting it in life and being engaged by it, a person can learn to know that which is most real of all. In this way God wants for us all to be fulfilled by His gift, "filled to the fullness of God," which naturally does not mean that God's fullness can be accommodated by any of us, but well to this limitless wealth stays open for us and that God would set any limit. He has perpetually new wealth to give.

So, Paul finishes, as a pious Jew, just as Jesus Himself had to have done countless times, with a doxology, a song of praise to God. This praise shall be heard, he says "in the church and in Christ Jesus." Perhaps he thinks that the praise now ascends from all congregations on earth and shall make it "throughout all generations" until Christ comes again, and the earthly churches' time is past. Then the praise shall continue to sound "in Christ Jesus," before the Lamb's throne, "for all eternity." But it is also possible that both of these expressions, as so often, shall be taken as a unity. The praise in the church is a blessing of thanks "in Christ Jesus" in the indissoluble communion with Him. From His heart, life and forgiveness pulsate out into all limbs and returns in the flow of life as praise and jubilee.

Ephesians 4

1-6 Christian Unity

The admonitions, of which there are so many in Paul's letters, always come after the message of salvation. Paul first makes what we have received clear, by grace and for nothing, and then he points to the consequences of that for our living. So also, here. This admonition for unity that he gives builds point for point on the fact that he has just laid out. We shall lead a life that is worthy of the calling we have received, he says. Through baptism we are incorporated into Christ, so we should function as members of Christ's body. This means that we should begin to live in a way that goes stick to stave against our selfishness. Paul mentions—only as an example—humility, gentleness, patience, and naturally, also love. It is needed if a person should have forbearance with each other's weaknesses. Paul is a realist and knows that even believing Christians have their problems to deal with and that this can mean both tolerance and mutual forgiveness in the daily being together. It is just here that unity is put to the test. It means to preserve "through the bond of peace." Paul has just spoken of this peace. It is the peace with God and with each other that Christ attained for us when He died for our sake. So, it is not a question of a feeling but a fact, something that already exists and which we have received as a gift, and which we should now care for.

So, Paul considers all the other factors that make all Christians one. They are members in Christ's body, they have received the same Spirit, they have all been called to the same hope (namely, that Christ comes again and receives us into His kingdom), they have the same Lord (Christ), the same faith, the same baptism, and the same Father. The situation we modern Christians have found ourselves in—with different doctrines and baptisms—is an absurdity for Paul. There is only one church, and a man is received into it through baptism—the only one that exists—and there the same faith is confessed. If anyone would not do this, but preach "a different gospel," then he no longer belongs to Christ's church. Paul says this with all emphasis at the beginning of Galatians. The admonition to preserve the Spirit's unity through the bonds of peace does not apply to other teachings and paths of salvation. There is only one faith, and the Spirit's unity exists only between them who share this faith. It is their unity that shall be preserved during daily stressors. It is this the admonition deals with here. It is concluded with a reference that God is everyone's Father—namely the Father of all believers, He who is above them all, works through them all, and lives in them all. (The context is different here than in Romans 11:36; there Paul speaks about the Creator who sovereignly rules over His creation, even over those who do not believe.)

7-12 Servants of the Word are Gifts from God

We are one in Christ. However, we are not the same. Equality is not the same as similarity. We are all God's children, but we are different from each other, and we have different functions. Christ has given each and every one of us some particular tasks and gifts that are adapted to the tasks. That Christ gives us gifts is illustrated by Paul with a citation from Psalm 68 (though Paul's formulation departs from the Hebrew text). What this psalm says about God, the Victor, who ascends to heaven, Paul reads as an expression concerning Christ, the Victor who first descended in order to then return to heaven. So, Paul says the same as Jesus in the conversation with Nicodemus (in the third chapter of the Gospel of John, which at the time Paul writes this was nonexistent): No one has ascended to heaven except for Him who has descended from heaven, the Son of Man, who was in heaven. Paul adds: "to fill all things." Christ is not gone. He has not abandoned us. On the contrary, He ascended into heaven to be the Lord, who is with us and by us everywhere and at all times.

The importuning thing that Paul wants to say is that now this Victor has given His church gifts. These gifts consist of servants of the Word, who in their different offices and ministries are to build up the congregation. First, he mentions apostles, Christ's fully authorized envoys, the obvious leaders of the church. Then come the prophets, men and women with the "gift of prophecy," through whom the Spirit could speak with comfort and admonition in the hour that the Spirit gave them something to say. (They were not regular preachers, as the others who are mentioned here.) Concerning the third group, the evangelists, we do not know much. They seem to have been coworkers in mission work. Finally, Paul mentions "shepherds and teachers," apparently two names for the same ministry. They were the leaders and seelsorgers[1] of the local congregations responsible for the regular proclamation and instruction, what we would normally call pastors.

These ministries and offices are then a gift from Christ. He has given them to "the saints," meaning we Christians would be in position to complete the task we have: to build up the body of Christ. Paul has already spoken about the matter: we are built upon the foundation of the apostles and prophets, and the cornerstone is Christ Himself. There we are included as living stones in a spiritual temple; this can only happen through the preached word. For precisely this reason, Christ has provided that there shall be proclaimers. They are sent by Him as His gifts to the church.

---

[1] Seelsorger means one who cares or even worries for souls, it is a term Lutheran's use as a term of endearment for particularly loved and faithful pastors.

13-16 Proper Proclamation Creates Unity

Now Paul receives occasion to clarify what it means that the congregation is built up through a proper exercise of office and proclamation. The result should be that "we," the whole congregation, approach the true unity (that which Paul has just spoken about), a unity in faith and in knowledge of God's Son. The faith's most important and most critical point is called the truth, that Christ is God's Son. It is here that the false conceptions easily enter, those that disintegrate unity and break up the congregation. A true faith makes it so that we all together are "one fully formed man" (the expression that the original text uses means a man, who is perfected, whole, and completely matured). Paul has spoken before (Ephesians 2:15) about how Christ has made us "a single new man," when He made us all members in His body. This new organism—the church—needs to be nourished, grow up and mature. So, this happens when the gospel is rightly preached and received. Then the congregation grows up and matures so that it can receive the fulness of Christ—not in each individual, but so that the church, Christ's body, within itself contains all the wealth that Christ wants to give us. Then it has become a "perfected man" in possession of all the gifts and abilities that God wants to give through Christ.

And what happens now if the congregation is not built up in this way? Paul describes it with a series of graphic pictures. Then we remain children—small children, infants, immature. We are tossed to and fro upon the waves, like bits of bark in the fire. We are driven by the wind and wave for every new doctrinal fad. Every new fashionable theology drives the church in a new direction. The pastors and laymen strain to keep up with the turns and changes, of course, all because new winds blow.

Paul—along with the whole of the New Testament—takes all false teachings very seriously. Delusions are a work of evil powers. Just as the truth does not only mean a theoretical truth but God's true purpose for the real true life, so are lies, delusions, and false beliefs a work of a will that is opposed to God's will. What false teachings do is promote this evil will, Paul says. They "cheat." (Paul uses an expression that could be used concerning playing with false dice.) He says that it is craftiness and deceitful schemes that they practice.

The opposite, the true, is to "hold to the truth" such as can be revealed for us in the gospel. The expression can also be rendered with "to live in truth," "act according to truth, "do the truth" (as Jesus says in John 3:21). So, in this way we live in the truth so that we, i.e., the congregation, come to grow together and be all the more formed and ruled by our head, Christ. Here Paul still receives an occasion to remind us that we are Christ's body, and that it is He who holds us all together in His church. We are joints in the body, each in his place and according to the measure of his ability. We need true posture. Yet we are only part of the whole, ingrafted by Him.

17-24 The Old and the New Man

The unity is also created by Christ. It is only found where we take Him seriously. It is this that Paul now admonishes us emphatically to do. He talks to people who live in a hedonistic environment, and his word has found a new reality for those of us who live in a pluralistic society. He gives us a picture of the ancient heathenism as he encountered it in practice. (If one reads only the most noble philosophers, the picture is more beautiful.) He gives the following characteristics: the thoughts are filled by things that have no real, lasting meaning. One lives to get by. One lives in darkness because he has fallen so far from God and does not see the meaning of existence. The heart has been hardened. The Greek word means hard like a stone or a calcification in a gouty joint, something living that has hardened and died. The healthy reaction to right and wrong is no longer functioning. One has become jaded. God is absent, and everything can go on by itself. A person no longer reacts to shamelessness but can give themselves to it with a fury. And a person can do it with an appetite that is never satiated. Paul is not only thinking about sexual things. When he speaks about "insatiable desires," he uses a word that means "greed," covetousness, perpetual lust for more. Today we only need to stand in front of the weekly headlines at a newspaper kiosk to see how similar people can be across the ages when they fall away from God.

In such a world, a man must live differently and break with a lot that seems to be a given in the environment. All Christendom means a new life in Christ. In the letter to the Galatians, Paul expressly speaks about the old man, the flesh that should be put off, crucified, and set aside. It is not done once and for all. The flesh also remains among true Christians. Here, a daily repentance must happen; this means to shed the old Adam and put on the new. The new man lives as a limb of Christ. He is created, as man was originally created before the fall, in God's image. The right communion with God is reestablished. We are God's children again. But we are not free of sin.

25-32 As New Men We shall lay aside all Evil

We are not called new men because sin has once and for all been eradicated from our lives. This puts everything on you. Yet with Christ a new life begins, and this means a declaration of war on the old man. When we read how Paul admonishes his fellow Christians, we understand all the more without further ado that he does not demand an advanced stage of sanctification. The Christians that he speaks to have been usual sinners and are tempted all the same to be this. They have lied and stolen. They have sworn, raved, and barked at one another. Now he admonishes them not to lie any longer. Now they are one. The body's limbs have to hold together and not try to deceive one another. A person can be angry, Paul says, but a person can also constrain his wrath and see to it that it does not become entrenched. When the sun goes down, everything should be forgiven. Otherwise, the devil gets his chance, and then he comes to take advantage of it. The thief ought to work, not only to feed himself, but for something better: to be able to help others instead of living at their expense. We all have to fit our words. There are poor words. Paul uses an expression that means rotten, decayed, odorous—such as one would never put in his mouth. If one does that, one grieves the good Spirit of God that has taken up residency in us and who is Himself the sign and seal that we are really God's children and shall experience the great day of emancipation when all becomes new. It is He who shall steer us. This means a new manner of socializing, soft and considerate, thoughtful, and heartfelt. This means mutual forgiveness, or at least that I forgive those who sin against me. I live under Christ's forgiveness, that which I need every day, and so I cannot deny forgiveness.

Ephesians 5

1-2 Those who Follow God

To try and imitate God and be His "imitators," as the expression literally means, can appear to us to be an almost irreverent thing. Yet it is clearly New Testamental. Jesus admonishes us to be merciful, as our heavenly Father is merciful, forgive like Him and be perfect like Him. He is serious about this, that we are His beloved children and shall be like our Father. Christ and His love is the great demonstration, when it comes to finding the forms of a new way of life in this world. Christ does not live for Himself. He gave His life as a sacrifice and as a "pleasing aroma before God." Here Paul uses an expression that often appears in the Old Testament and is picked up from the sacrificial worship that was a foreshadowing of the atoning sacrifice that Jesus made once and for all.

3-7 Two Chief Sins: Fornication and Greed

All sin stems from an improper relationship to God, and all unforgiven sin separates us from God. So, a person cannot grade sins as small and great. Yet if a person looks at sin's ability to dominate a man and keep him from God, then there are sins that are particularly disastrous, and Paul – like the entire New Testament—points out two of these in particular. They are fornication, a sexuality that has freed itself from responsibility before God and does not concern itself with His will, and the other is greed, the craving after money. Paul uses a word that means to want to have more, to have a craving that seems insatiable. Such ought not even be named, Paul says. "You are Christians!" Paul actually writes "so as becomes saints," but the translation we use here can perhaps help us to see that these were things that could not even be mentioned if a person wanted to be a Christian. If a person looks at the history of Christianity in the western lands, a remarkable fact can be noted: fornication has as a rule stood out as a serious sin, but the greed for money has not always received the same stamp. There is good reason to listen to the New Testament on both points. Such things cannot be united with life in God. It shuts us out from God's kingdom. If anyone excuses it, they are empty words that we should not listen to.

8-14 Darkness and Light

Paul does not say: you once lived in darkness. Now the light shines on you. But he says: you were darkness. You are now light. Just as Jesus says: "you are the light of the world." The light and darkness are really two kingdoms, God's and Satan's. We do not stand before them independently and autonomously, without belonging to either of them, and then we are dominated and filled by their power. We are either light or darkness. Or, as it can be said in the Semitic expression: we are children of light or children of darkness. Paul also says: "you are light in the Lord." The light is not some gift or property of ours. It is Christ who is the light of the world. We are the limbs of His body, so we are also light. And then we shall walk as children of light. Again, Paul proceeds from the gift, from that which Christ has given us, not from some moral housecleaning that we have already implemented and that makes us deserving of being called Christians. The order is the opposite: because Christ made us light, we shall also carry ourselves as children of light. We shall bear "fruit of light." And children of the light can assess and see what it is that their Lord expects of them. It is the love of Christ that is the new motivation, both when it comes to understanding that which is right and carrying it out.

This also means to no longer have any dealings with darkness and their deeds. Paul intentionally does not speak of the fruit of darkness. Fruit is something good, something positive, but the darkness achieves nothing of the sort. So a person should not let himself be impressed by it, but instead disclose it and show what it is worth. This exposure is something positive, not only a judgment but also a possibility for salvation. This is probably what Paul means when he says, as it is literally translated, that "all that is exposed is light." If Christ's light illuminates something then the light's power works upon it; it is penetrated by light and can be taken possession of by the light. The poet that Paul cites here also speaks about this. It is not some direct citation out of Scripture, but possibly a free paraphrase of a couple of passages from Isaiah. Most probable is that we have a verse from some early Christian hymn that was sung during the divine service and was thus well known to the readers. To be away from Christ, where one is heathen or nominally Christian, means that one sleeps the sleep of death. When the gospel is heard, a person has the possibility of waking up. And the awakening means that one may see Christ, in "the true light, that which shines upon all men" (John 1:9).

15-21 The New Life in the Spirit

Therefore, a person must carefully ensure the establishment of this life. A person cannot just do what everyone else is doing. It is unreasonable because a non-Christian environment obviously establishes itself in a way that is contrary to God's will in many aspects. Here you have to have understanding and seize opportunities. There are moments and situations that are given by God; perhaps there are not many if a person lives in an evil time. Thus, it is all the more important for you not to be blind and foolish without understanding what it is God wants at just this occasion.

Next follows a warning against getting drunk with wine, something that most drank daily. Instead, a person should let himself be filled by the Spirit. The connection can seem to be a bit loose, but here there is an interconnecting thought. If one drinks too much wine, one becomes drunk, and it usually leads to brawling and scenes. However, now there is a completely different way to be lifted out of everyday boredom, a Spirit-induced enthusiasm that can sometimes lead to ecstasy (for example, the speaking in tongues). To outsiders, it can look like madness or drunkenness. At Pentecost, the people believed the Apostles were drunk. But here, it is a question of something else altogether, Paul says. To be filled with the Spirit, as it happens now, certainly means to possess something that gives color, joy, and excitement to everyday life. It is something that would provide an outlet, just like intoxication. However, here it is thanksgiving, songs of praise and worship.

Life in the Spirit also consists in that we begin "to speak with each other in psalms, hymns, and spiritual songs." By Psalms means the psalter. Hymns are what they called newly penned songs that were sung in the divine service. We don't know much about "spiritual songs." The Greek word "ode" (we have it as a loan word) means neither something particularly folkish nor an easy-going song; it assumes a certain solemnity. Perhaps it stands here only as a synonym without any clearly defined meaning.

But what does Paul mean with this admonition? How does it go? For contemporaries, it was quite clear. They had learned to celebrate the divine service from the Jews. The body of the Jewish devotional life was the Psalter. It was used for devotions, both morning and evening, at table prayers and naturally in the synagogue. A person would recite them, read them in a half singing voice in particular tones. It often happened alternately. This could be what Paul means by "speak with one another." Our Canonical Hours (services such as Matins, Vespers, and Compline, which can still be found in our hymnals) can give us an approximate idea of how the Psalter was used. They are the direct continuation of this way of praying.

This can be done only by external habit. But if the Spirit can fill us this way, then it becomes something more, Paul says. A person begins to sing and play in the heart (also after or during the day's work), and thanks to God breaks forth. Again, Paul has a particular meaning with every word he says: there is always thanks, even during sorrows and persecutions. We can be thankful for everything that we encounter when we receive it from God's hand. We thank God, who contrary to everything we deserve, is Our Father. The thanks are offered up in the name of Jesus, because He is the guarantee that we can speak to God as to a father.

Finally, Paul names one thing that belongs with all the new life in the Spirit: that we submit to one another. This expression stands parallel with the foregoing as further explanation of what it means to "be filled by the Spirit."

To "submit" in the New Testament is one of the characteristic signs of life in Christ. It is often misunderstood. For he who lives in the manner of the world there lies something degrading, or, in any case, unpleasant in having to submit to someone else. It is seen as obvious that power is a benefit because it is that which gives the powerful the ability to use another's services. In the New Testament, it is to the contrary. To "submit" means just what the word literally means (both in Greek and Swedish): to enter an order. And here it is God's order, something God wills, that we shall function properly and serve one another. And this applies to all: we shall enter into this order where we are all servants. He who in the world's eyes is "superior" is in actual fact merely a servant of God who has His "power" to serve others and benefit them (as Paul also says of the political powers, Romans 13:4).

This distinctiveness for the new life in Christ is now that of his own freewill, a person enters into God's order with joy, without in anyway being downgraded or slighted when one submits to one another. The whole time a man knows the Lord he serves, and he serves Him gladly. Then the service also receives a new meaning; it is carried out in a new manner and in a different spirit.

22-33 As Christ Relates to the Church, so Relate Husband and Wife to Each Other

Paul proceeds to the application of this "submitting" so immediately that it does not even begin a new subject in the Greek text. It applies to three important areas of life: the relationship between a man and wife, between children and parents, and between masters and servants. Such sections (there are similar ones in Colossians and First Peter) were once called house tables and read as a type of bourgeois instruction for everyday life. This is to misunderstand Paul. As we have seen, here we receive an example of new life in the Spirit. A person lives in this way as a born again Christian, as a member of Christ's body. If a person makes this into a middle-class ethic, then it shall apply to all people, including those who do not stand in a living and transformative relationship with Christ; if not, the whole thing is skewed. Essentially then, a person turns this submission that happens of one's own free will for Christ's sake into an obligation that others have a right to demand, and that they can then misuse in order to obtain benefits at the expense of their fellow men. And this is not the purpose in the least. That which is said here is said as guidance for individual people who want to serve their Lord Christ and set up their life according to His will.

It is important to keep this in mind when reading what Paul has to say about marriage. It is a question of what Christian spouses do out of love for their Lord Jesus Christ when they want to submit to His order. Communion within marriage has a parallel with the communion between Christ and His church. Just as Christ is the head in this communion so shall the man according to God's will be a head for his wife. Naturally the difference is that the man never, as Christ, can be a savior for the one with whom he is united. This similarity is in this: that he is the head. For a non-Christian, this is highly objectionable because a person immediately thinks of a "headship" that can be exploited for egotistical purposes. However, Paul explains what the issue is. He paints a picture of Christ's sacrifice, how He gave Himself and did everything for His bride, the Church. (The word "bride" is not in the original text, but it is this that is referred to with talk about "presenting" the church pointing to the wedding ceremony.) And in this manner a husband shall love his wife. In the wedding ceremony, God has given just this woman to him. It is his life's task to make her life meaningful and happy, to take care of her with tenderness and caution, and be one with her, also when it comes to sharing her concern and responsibility for her failures.

Paul points to something here that ought to be completely clear for a Christian. Man and wife are one. It is abnormal to hate one's own body. Instead, a person devotes a particular care for it. Here Paul is only referring to that which, in fact, normally happens . . . in the same manner as Jesus when He says that we shall love our neighbor as we love ourselves. In this there lies no demand to love yourself, only an admonition to love others just as spontaneously and obviously as we, in fact, do love ourselves.

The wife on her side, naturally and of her own free will, enters into God's order that has ordered a head for the family, a head that has ultimate responsibility for it. Here it is the question of a working order, and no one is degraded because she operates according to the order that God has willed. On the contrary, greatest are those that serve. Every member finds their worth and greatness by finding their right place.

Is there any deeper cause for this parallel between marriage and the church? Paul implies this when he cites a word about marriage from Genesis as also Jesus did with the extension: "so they are no longer two but one flesh," so one organism, a single being before God, given to one another and joined by God. This is a great mystery, Paul says, a "mystery," something inscrutable. We see two people, and still God has established an invisible communion here. And this I will not apply to Christ and the Church, Paul says. God has united them in the same way. Where we see a mass of individuals, there God has established an invisible communion. We are one body with Christ. In both cases then it is a question of a spiritual organism, established by God, and in both cases, there apply some similar rules for life in this communion, and separation of functions between man and woman that are ordered by God and which a person submits to with joy.

Ephesians 6

1-4 Children and Parents

Respect for mother and father belonged to a Jew's most elementary religious duties. Paul stresses that it is the first of the Ten Commandments that comes with a promise. He means that a person can understand how important this is in God's eyes, and it is by no means less important since Christ has come. On the contrary, Paul emphasizes that it is "in the Lord," for the sake of Christ that a person should keep it. A person does not obey his parents because they are particularly remarkable or admirable, but because a person loves Jesus Christ and will gladly enter into an order that He has established.

In the Roman Empire an unlimited patriarchalism ruled. A father had absolute power over his family, literally for life and death. However, there is no question of patriarchalism here, and just as little in marriage, but a divine order where power means service. Even the parents are incorporated into this order. They have God's commission to serve their children for their best. So, they too receive an admonition. They may not "provoke their children to anger." A child is not a toy that a person can have fun with, for example, to belittle them. Neither are they cheap labor to do menial tasks that one uses for his own gain. The child is the Lord's and shall be fostered and raised so that he will receive both the education, theoretical and practical, and the corrections that Christ wants to give. So, then there is no talk about disposing of a child according to one's own discretion, but neither to let the child have full freedom to do whatever he himself wants.

5-9 Employees and Employers

Greek has the same word for servants and for slaves. On the one hand, it is without a doubt that Paul is speaking to slaves here because he speaks mostly of physical labor, and almost all servants were slaves in the Roman empire. So, "The Lord" is the one who owns them. In antiquity, a slave owner had unlimited authority over his slave. The slave was considered only as one thing: a work tool, not a person.

Now a person can ask if what Paul says here has any application for our day. The institution of slavery vanished from our land 700 years ago through the influence of Christianity. In our day, the wage earner and employees have the opportunity to influence their employment conditions and are not so helplessly dependent as before on their employers (and supervisors, which we must add to get a correct picture of those whom Paul calls "lords").

Still there is something here that is God's continuing order, the same in all times, an order that one willingly enters into for the sake of Christ. The external form of the relationship between employee and employer can change and improve. But even when slavery has been replaced by free agreement between equal parties, then this remains, that we—in all work, where we are still part of society—have instructions, regulations, or agreements that guide us. Most of us have some sort of supervisor over us. These correspond to the "earthly lords" that Paul speaks about here. And here his instructions also apply to us. We know the Lord we serve. God's purpose with the whole society with production and management is "to hold creation together with power"—to produce goods, food, housing, care for the sick, and everything else that is needed for this life. Here we are now placed as God's servants, for the benefit of our neighbor. The Savior wants us here. If we ask Him what we can do to show our thankfulness, He shows our fellowman to us. Thus, for a Christian there is nothing degrading about submitting to such an order that must be obeyed. It does not mean submitting to a man but to Christ. So here we can apply everything that Paul says to our day. We do not only give eye service: we do not work just for the sake of the career, but honestly, from the heart, willingly and gladly. We can apply the words 'with fear and trembling' the hardest. Yet here we may remember that Paul uses an expression that is used for a right relationship with God. It is a matter of deep respect that knows here, I also am dealing with God and fulfill a service as duty to Him.

What then Paul says to "the lords" was completely revolutionary at the time. Now it has more or less been generally accepted—at least in western Christendom—that he who has some sort of legal authority over other men shall always keep in mind that he has to deal with people who are just as worthy as he himself. Yet there still remains this useful reminder that we all are of equal value because we all have a Lord over us in heaven who has given us all this same value when He created us in His image. There is no remaining worth in man if a person maintains that we men are only some sort of intelligent animal that in the course of fighting for existence has developed into the best equipped, according to nature's order, to beat the system and win the awful lottery. If a person applies this "natural order" to society the consequences can be terrifying.

Again, we must now emphasize that here Paul is speaking to Christian men, who ask how they can best serve their Lord Christ. A person cannot make a civil law out of it. It is not a requirement that an unconverted supervisor or an impersonal company has the right to put on their employees. If a person abuses the gospel and makes it a law for the world, then a person can place the weapon, or at least the argument, in the hands of men who will only usurp private benefits. Yet here it is a question of how a Christian views his work. He knows whom he serves, both when he receives orders and when he gives them. Just as he is only a servant of his Lord, even when he is the one who rules.

10-20 "The Fight we all have to Fight"

After this long section that deals with entering into God's order there now follows the last admonition: to join the unavoidable fight. For this a person needs strength from Christ Himself, something of this "strength of his might" that Paul spoke about at the beginning of this letter, that with which God resurrected Christ and with which He also works in us when we believe in Jesus Christ. This means taking upon ourselves "the armor of God." When Paul describes this, a person can see that he had the prophetic word of Isaiah in his thoughts. There it speaks of how God clads Himself in armor. (Isaiah 59:17)

Neither is it here a question of any good properties of our own that we should develop, but it really means to be armored with something that comes from God. Essentially, it is not a matter of a fight against "flesh and blood," or against men who are opponents of Christendom and want us to live as they do. It is a question of a fight against spiritual powers that we are helpless to overcome if Christ does not fight for us. These spiritual powers are found "within the heavenly places," which were created before our universe and where the rebellion happened, that which led to Satan establishing his kingdom. Paul has spoken before (in the beginning of chapter 2) about the power that rules over the places of evil powers, and which is active in all those who oppose God. It is he we must encounter. Paul speaks of his "sneaky ambush." It is the same expression that we rendered "deceitful schemes" before. In the beginning, his proposals seldom appear evil. There are many reasons that speak for them, if a person sees the matter from the world's point of view. You have to see through them and resist.

Here it really is a fight between life and death. Paul uses thoroughly military terms to describe it. The armor is the heavy armament of the legions, with a heavy sword belt, a steel breast plate, a large square shield, and a helmet on the head. This is now all used to give a picture of the armament that is needed if a person is going to take a stand and win victory on the "evil day," when it really means eternal life or eternal death. That belt, which makes it so that a man can gird up his long clothes and always have his sword at hand, this is the truth, the great truth that there is a God, and He has intervened in our world through Christ, in a way that determines the whole of my existence. The breast plate that protects the breast is the righteousness, not my own, which has so many holes, but Christ's which is perfect and hides all my shortcomings.

The shoes that make it possible to walk unhindered over rubble and thorns is the readiness that comes from the peace of the gospel. It is not a question of continuing to be willing to serve, nor of any personal character. It is something that is born within me, when I receive the gospel of the forgiveness of sins and receive peace with God. Here Paul is thinking of Isaiah 52:7 that speaks about the feet of him who brings good news that bears him over the mountains, eager to "publish peace and bring good news." In this readiness, that Paul speaks about here, there also lies the will to be one who brings good news to others, one who conveys the great news of Jesus.

Again, the shield that shields me is faith in Christ. It also protects against the flaming darts (one of the most feared weapons of the time). It protects both against temptation and against the conscience's accusations that say, "I am never such a Christian as I ought to be." Christ has extinguished the fire with His blood when He died for me. The helmet is salvation. This word also means "rescuing." Again, it is something Christ has done. His redemption is my protection against the accuser's most murderous blows. And the sword, the weapon that gives those who are attacked the ability to fight back, is the Word of God. Just as the Savior in the desert used God's Word to fight back the evil one's cleverly thought-out proposal, so the best weapon in the fight is a firm anchoring in God's Word. Here Paul touches on that which we ourselves can do to arm ourselves. We can educate ourselves in Christian knowledge, live in the Scriptures, receive the Word with both head and heart. And Paul immediately adds to what we can do: we can pray constantly, without ceasing, persistently in the Spirit, which means our spirit both prays and cries, even when we are not praying with words, and that the Spirit prays within us and for us, when we do not know for what we shall pray. Finally, Paul also reminds us of intercession and prayer for our own share of this. He knows what we need most: the right words to interpret the mystery of the gospel, that which he speaks about so much in this letter. We anticipate how the apostles fought to be able to lay forth the incredible, which they had been present for and received the task of proclaiming. They had the promise of the Spirit's help for this, and they received it, but the Spirit's help is often something that forces its way into us through pain and struggle.

21-24 Personal Messages and Final Greetings

Paul usually finishes his letter with a series of personal greetings to named friends. Here these are completely lacking, which is a further sign that the letter had not been meant for one particular congregation, even less so Ephesus, where Paul must have had a great number of acquaintances and coworkers who were close to him. Neither does this letter contain any personal information about how Paul is doing. Paul only gives such details if he has particular reason to do so. As a rule, they are not needed. The letter is sent with some personal carrier, usually a coworker who made the long trip in service to the ministry, as a custom in mission work. So, it is the case also here. Paul mentions the coworker's name: Tychicus. We hear of him in both in the "Acts of the Apostles" and letters and so know that he also carried the letter to the Colossians, in all likelihood on the same trip.

If a person wants to characterize Ephesians with a modern description, a man could then call it a shepherd's letter. Here a leader of the church writes to his congregations, a word of comfort and admonition and, above all, an instruction concerning Christ. It is a word from a true father in God, both firm and tender. Above all, it is a powerful hymn of praise to the immeasurable wealth and power in God's deeds through Christ; this also reflects itself in the content laden words that the apostle hopes in his final wishes: peace, love, faith, grace, all gifts from God and Christ, gifts that make us love the Lord Jesus Christ "incorruptible" with a love that never perishes.

PHILIPPIANS
Introduction

The city of Philippi was named after the Macedonian King Philipp, the father of Alexander the Great. He established the city sometime around the year 360 BC after he had conquered the area. The place was strategic. You had to pass through here if you were taking the coastal road from Greece to Asia Minor, and there was an easily defended pass in the vicinity. So it was that a battle with decisive importance for the history of the world and the fate of the Roman empire for centuries played out here. It was the year 42 BC when Caesar was murdered, and the fight for world domination continued. Among the leaders of the victorious side was a man who would later be known as Caesar Augustus. He came to intervene in a decisive way in the history of Philippi. He converted the city into a Roman colony, which means that it was populated with old legionnaires who received Roman citizenship, Roman management, and Roman language. The Roman colonies there held tight to their privileges and were well aware of their special position.

Paul came here on his second missionary journey (probably in the year 50) and experienced a few dramatic events that Luke has described in Acts 16. Apparently, the city had no Jewish colony of importance, and there was no synagogue. We do not hear of any Jewish opposition, but there was a harsh reaction from some slave owners that lost a source of income through the actions of Paul. Their accusation was that Paul and Silas were Jews who attempted to establish new customs and laws, completely unacceptable for true Romans, and this was in Philippi!

In any case, a congregation was established here. It was the first in Europe, but nothing was thought of that at the time when all the lands surrounding the Mediterranean constituted a closed cultural circle. For Paul the congregation in Philippi was always a source of joy. Some ten years after the congregation was established, Paul wrote this letter. At that time, he was sitting in prison, possibly in Caesarea (in such a case between the year 57 and the summer of 59) but probably in Rome, where he was kept in prison from the summer of 60 until his case was finally heard two years later. He had a particular cause: He wanted to give thanks for the support he received. This became the external reason for this very personal letter with its particular charm and warmth, which has always caused it to be read and loved. It is not without reason that it is called "The Letter of Joy."

Philippians 1

1-2 Letter head

That Paul and Timothy stand side by side in the letterhead shows that the letter from the beginning was thought of as a greeting from them both. However, that it is Paul who carried the pen, or rather dictated the letter, is obvious. The whole time he says "I" and later he speaks of Timothy in the third person.

Among those who received the letter are named only particular Philippian "bishops and deacons." Here, Paul uses words that are still in use in the church today. The word "deacon" (i.e., servant, namely of the congregation) was already then used for a servant of the congregation in almost the same way it is today. However, this isn't the case with the word "bishop." From the beginning it meant "director" or "overseer" and is used in the New Testament of the men, apparently several in number, who had a hand in the leadership of the congregation, both spiritually and materially.

They were called bishops (*episkopoi*) and presbyter (same word we have for "priest") interchangeably. They functioned as the church's leaders in the first generation, the apostles, and then under such disciples were apostles such as Titus and Timothy. In the beginning of the second century, we find that the name bishop has begun to be used in the manner that has become common, for he who was leader of the congregations within a certain district (usually a city with surrounding villages).

3-11 Thanksgiving and Intercession

Paul begins, as so often, with a thanksgiving that here receives a particular warmth. A reader notices that he is happy for his Philippians. He had come to them for the first time approximately ten years earlier. He was not able to stay but for a short time in the city. After having been illegally abused, thrown in prison, and then set free again by the completely upset and embarrassed Roman authorities in the place—as it is told in Acts 16—he continued on to Thessalonica. But the consequences of the short visit had been a lively and faithful congregation in whom he apparently had pure delight. Paul is well aware that there still remains much to do, when men so suddenly have come to faith. (For example, the prison guard who was baptized with the whole of his house that night that an earthquake shook the city and the prison was opened.) Yet, Paul trusts in God. He has called a person who has answered yes, so he also carries out his work to completion. Paul implies what is needed: a Christian education that gives knowledge obviously in the Christian doctrine, and to that 'a mature discernment' (this could also be translated as: a balanced insight, a broadened experience, a sanctified understanding) that makes it possible to see clearly in new situations and shed real discernment in all the tangled issues that have meaning in a Christian life.

12-20 God Can Even Use a Tragedy

Now Paul changes topic to give some information about himself which the Philippians were certainly anxious to receive. He already hinted in the introduction that he thought about his friends both during the long hours in prison and when he was occupied by defense before the judge's seat (where, typically enough for Paul, it is not really about him, but rather to "defend and confirm the gospel"). Paul now finds himself in "the Praetorium." This can mean two things: either the residency in some provincial capital, which would mean Caesarea, where Paul sat in prison for two years, or the barracks of the imperial guard on the north edge of Rome, where Paul might have been held during the proceedings of his trial. The latter is the more likely, as we don't know if the purpose was for him to have a real court hearing in Caesarea. In any case, it is obvious that Paul expects a decision in the case that could carry the death penalty. He does not enjoy the relative freedom that he had during the first two years in Rome (Acts 28:30). He is detained and wears chains, but he is still free enough that he can receive visitors and speak with those around him. And now he shows precisely this: that being held in the Praetorium has meant opportunity for the gospel. Like everywhere else, Paul has found people to listen to him. He seems to have acquired a certain respect, just as he did in the stormy trip to Malta, where finally it was to him and in him that they all looked and trusted. In such a manner, the Christians in the city had become bolder. Apparently, it is a question of a great congregation, which also points to Rome rather than Caesarea. There were many who were missionaries, some of whom Paul views skeptically. They had to have prestige. They probably felt a little jealous that a newcomer should receive such great esteem. Now as he sits detained they find the time fitting to outmaneuver him. Yet Paul takes it calmly. Christ is still preached. It is not a question of different teaching. If that were the case, Paul would have reacted as sharp as he did with the Galatians. Here it is a question of personal shortcomings with those who preached a pure gospel. So what Paul says here cannot, as sometimes happens, be used as defense for there being different denominations with their own teachings.

21-26 Die or Remain Alive?

Paul has become acquainted with the thought that he may die in the near future. It fills him with joy rather than fear. Here we can see what creates the Christian hope before death. It is the communion of life with Christ that has already begun. Paul knows that he belongs to Christ. For him, to live means Christ, that is to constantly work with Christ and to always be in His hand. Should he die then he still gets to be with Christ. And it is far better at home with Him in His kingdom than here. However, now he has a task in this world, something that his Lord wants to use him for. Here Paul formulates a sentence that applies to all of us: so long as we are needed, we remain. It is just as incorrect to want to go to heaven in order to escape difficult duties here on earth, as it is to get so caught up in one's duties that one can't think of leaving them to someone else. Thus, Paul is certain that he will be acquitted and come to Philippi yet once more. That he was right about that is shown some years later by the letters he wrote to Titus and Timothy. Paul speaks about the "cause to glory in Christ Jesus" that a Christian can feel. He uses a word that is hard to translate, that meant that one triumphs and rejoices in a joy and bold certainty of having received something that one really can be proud of, in all humility because it is a gift from Christ.

27-30 Stand Fast in the Persecution

Persecution has broken out against the congregation in Philippi. Paul admonishes his friends to carry themselves in a manner that is worthy of the gospel even when they are treated badly. They shall stand together steadfast and firm, even when a person tries to scream at them with the worst threats. Such a steadfastness is a sign from God, he says. The persecutors cannot help but ask themselves if the Christians are still right and if they themselves are not on the way to destruction. The persecution is in a certain way a privilege, Paul says. We may hear together with Christ also in this way that we may share his suffering and reproach. It also applies to completely normal Christians. The Philippians can see themselves that they may now experience the same that they both saw and heard that Paul encountered.

Philippians 2

1-11 Be United and Humble, and Look to Christ

During the persecution, they must hold together in an unbreakable unity. Paul admonishes concerning the matter as earnestly as he can. He reminds the Philippians of all that they have experienced: The comfort they received from Christ, the encouragement that love (the love of God) gives them, their experience of the Spirit's communion (both in that they have the Spirit and that they are one in the Spirit), and all the mercy that they received from God and from each other. He means: if you now know what this means—and this you know!—then make my joy complete by holding together unwaveringly, united in the same faith and same love, not thinking of prestige or class. When Paul admonishes, he always proceeds from faith in Christ. He does not give good advice that anyone can follow with a little good will. It is only in communion with Christ that they receive any real meaning. Unfeigned modesty, so that a person regards others more than himself, is something only an exposed sinner gets, someone who knows that he lives in the grace of Christ. To see to the best of others and not his own is contrary to our nature. Yet it is natural and right to serve each other when we have become members of Christ.

Paul consistently points to Christ here as an example. Christ lived with God; He was equal with God. However, He regarded it not as "spoil," as "booty," something that one is excited to have found and wants to hold on to at any price (that is the meaning of the Greek word), but He was willing to empty Himself and become like one of us and come as a servant for our sake. He humbled Himself and became obedient even to death on the cross. Therefore, God has raised Him, He who we degraded and who let Himself be dishonored. God has raised Him as high as He can be raised. He has given Him the name that is above all names. This name is God's own name, the Lord (in the Greek "Lord," the word that in the Greek translation of the Old Testament is used for JHVH, the name that was too holy to be spoken by the lips of men). To this name, every knee shall bow. All come to see and recognize that it was so: this Jesus Christ was God. This does not lessen the glory of God. On the contrary, it happens "to the glory of God the Father." A person cannot glorify God more than by confessing that He gave His Son for our sake and made Him the Savior of all.

That which Paul says about Christ here has a linguistic structure, a rhythm and reverberation that causes a person to suppose that it comes from a hymn used in the divine service. In any case, here we have a summary of the early Christian message and the early congregation's confession of Jesus Christ. It is a confession of His "pre-existence," for His entry into the world where He lived with the Father and shared in the divinity of His Father. However, He put aside the full use of His divine character and took on the form of man. He was "born of a woman and put under the law" (Galatians 4:4). The difference from all other men is that He lived in perfect obedience, even to His atoning death on the cross. Therefore, God has raised Him and given Him victory, so that the whole world would be able to see the truth and worship Him as God and Savior.

12-18 Be Obedient Like Christ

Now Paul draws to a conclusion with the thought of the persecuted Philippians. If Christ was obedient to death, so should we be obedient to death. And the Philippians have always been obedient, he adds. The obedience to Christ shows itself in that a person works out his salvation in fear and trembling. A person knows that he can be lost. A person knows that there is something we must do: hold fast to the Word, receive it and take it seriously. But at the same time, we know that it is God who is at work here. Paul says it with such pointedness that it sounds like a paradox: work on your salvation, for God works here. But this paradox corresponds to the actual reality. God gives us the right will and leads our desires in the right direction. It is He who gives us both the desire and the power to do what is right. But when it happens within us, we experience it like a fight. We have the old man within us who would hinder us and needs to be constantly crucified. When God's good intentions for us are realized, the struggle within us continues. This cannot be carried out without "fear and trembling." We know that we can be lost. We can do all this that Paul admonishes us not to do here. We can grumble. We can hesitate. And this is just what our old man constantly does. Yet if we let ourselves "be driven by the Spirit" (Galatians 5:18), then we are "blameless and innocent children of God without blemish," who live under a constant forgiveness and are pure before God, though our sinful corruption remains.

The point is that we are to be points of light in this dark world and shine like stars in the night sky. We can do this if we hold fast to the Word, the Word that alone can give life. As always, Paul looks forward to the goal: the day when Christ comes. Then he hopes that his Philippians will step forth as the living proof that all his toil was not in vain. We notice that even Paul does his work in fear and trembling. He knows the risk. That which he fears for is not that he can now be executed, but it is that he himself or his spiritual children can be lost. He takes martyrdom with serenity. He compares it with the drink offering in the temple. Just as one poured out wine over the altar as an offering to God, he is prepared to let his blood be shed. He stands there as one of the priests in the temple and offers a sacrifice of thanksgiving to God, the offering of faith that he has woken to life among the heathen through apostolic service he has received to carry out. It is this gift that he lays down on the altar of God. Now if only this gift is received, if their faith is firmly anchored in God so will his blood gladly be poured over it as a drink offering over the gift. Paul only rejoices and asks the Philippians to share his joy. The next message from Rome that reaches the congregation in Philippi may be the message of his martyrdom. Should it go in such a manner, they shall not grieve but rejoice with him. This is the message he sends them.

19-30 Travel Plans and Instructions for Timothy and Epaphroditus

In the beginning of the letter Timothy is named as the sender. While Paul dictated, which could have taken some considerable time and probably had a few interruptions because a prisoner did not control his time, the letter became a very personal letter from Paul himself, and when Timothy now comes into the picture, he is no longer treated as a letter writer. Paul says things about Timothy that Timothy never would have said about himself. Paul hopes to be able to send him soon, apparently on a short visit so that he himself can receive news from Philippi. (Just as he once sent Timothy from Athens to Thessalonica, 1 Thessalonians 3: 1-8.) However, he first wants to see if the case is perhaps coming to a decisive decision. In such a case, he obviously wants to wait for the outcome before he sends Timothy. We notice how great a worth he sets on him. He loves him like a son. He speaks with clear disappointment about "all" the others. What he has in mind, we don't know. It must indicate a group of coworkers. That some preached Christ for impure motives, he has already said that. Yet he also mentioned that some had good intentions. Thus, here he must point to some other group of coworkers. Among them Timothy is the one he trusts. As a son serves his father, so Timothy served, not Paul, but together with Paul, in service to the gospel.

If Timothy is going to be delayed in travel, then in any case, Paul plans on sending Epaphroditus as soon as possible. He had come from Philippi at the behest of the congregation with a gift that they had gathered to make it easier for Paul while he was in prison. Apparently, Epaphroditus has stayed in Rome according to the congregation's desires in order to be a help for Paul. During his stay he became sick with something, perhaps one of the infections it was so easy to catch in the big city. He had been close to death. Now he longs for home and wants to return. Paul understands and clears the road for him so that no one will think that he shirked his duties. The apostle would love to keep him as a coworker, but he honestly means it when he says that he will be less anxious when Epaphroditus makes it home successfully.

We hear Paul use the expression "in the Lord" many times when he speaks about his plans and hopes. It shows how he planned: during prayer under the leadership of Jesus in order to serve His cause, in reliance on His help and willing to even let Him change that which Paul would rather have done.

Philippians 3

1-7 Warning Against False Righteousness

Paul the prisoner has spoken about the joy he has in the midst of uncertainty. Now he takes up the theme again and admonishes the Philippians to rejoice—during persecution. They shall rejoice in the Lord. Again, we encounter the word not as a pious expression, worn by old habit, but as a reminder of the actual chief matter. It causes him to rejoice in the midst of difficulties when a person lives in communion with Christ, has his forgiveness, has his presence and knows that no matter what happens the enemies cannot separate us from him.

Yet in the same breath Paul reminds them that it is possible to be separated from Christ. He knows that he repeats himself. He has said this before, perhaps personally in Philippi, perhaps in some letter that has now been lost. But he has not tired. He knows that it is safest that he says it one more time.

This is true of the Jewish lawgivers, those who want the Christians to submit themselves to the law of Moses. To understand this matter better a person ought to read Galatians. The same danger must have threatened Philippi—as so many other places in the early Church.

These "Judaizers" seem to have come with certain slogans and arguments that Paul now uses against them. They have said that everyone has to be circumcised. Otherwise, they are gentiles and gentiles were like dogs to the Jews—the ignoble scabby dogs of the orient. Furthermore, they have emphasized their nonsense for the church. They have presented themselves in the congregations as volunteer workers concerned for the church's best. Now Paul says: watch out for them. It is they who are the dogs. They are malicious workers that destroy everything in their path. It is we who are the circumcision, God's Israel. They are the mutilated, they who believe that the true faith has to do with an operation they have gone through. We know instead that it depends on the circumcision of the heart that one worships God in spirit and truth and counts Jesus Christ as the only one that a man can "glory in" and build his faith upon.

Paul is quick to explain that he is not speaking about foxes and rowanberries[1]. If there is anyone that can then it is he who can trust "in the flesh"—thus in such virtues that hang together with burdens and human achievements. He lists all that which were enviable precedents from a Jewish point of view. He was circumcised as a child, not only does he belong to the people of Israel but purely from the celebrated tribe of Benjamin. He is not one of the Jews who must read the Scriptures

---

[1] This references a Swedish saying "Sour, says the fox about rowanberries'" the idea is that a person decides not to like something because he cannot attain it.

in Greek, but he belongs to those who learned the language of the fathers already in childhood. He has kept the law and fought for it fanatically. It could really be a long list of merits. Yet all that which was accounted as spiritual assets, had turned into loss, to sin and vanity when he came to know Christ.

8-11 The Better Righteousness

All that which Paul was proud of before and trusted in, stands before him now like garbage, refuse, worthless crap, like nothing that matters before God. If God wants to examine, then the stitching of sin will be found everywhere. However, now Christ, he who emptied himself and became obedient to death, has given us a completely new opportunity to be children of God. So there is only one thing that is really meaningful. Paul wants to gain Christ, be incorporated into him through faith, receive his righteousness. He wants to learn to know the power of his resurrection. To be incorporated into Christ means to be permeated by the new life of the resurrection. He wants to fill every measure of "Christ's suffering" and die as Christ (he has martyrdom in mind) to finally also be able to rise and share in his victory. In another place (Romans 8:17) Paul expresses the matter so; we suffer with him in order to also be glorified with him. Paul knows that he has not deserved it. So, it comes in a tone of humiliating wonder: "If I should be able…" Paul does not doubt for a moment that the resurrection is there. But he knows that it is a miracle of grace if he is present.

12-14 Not There but on the Way

Paul has also found a completely different way to attain righteousness and be able to stand before God: to trust in Christ and to hold himself to Christ. This gives assurance but not self-assurance. The opponents seem to have made the claim that a person must be a "perfect" Christian and could be saved by obedience to the law. Paul now says that salvation is never finished here in time. It is a goal that we are on the way to. It is like a track in a sports stadium. The matter is not settled until the finish line. However, in the course one "forgets that which lies behind," both of his sin and misfortune that are sunk in the sea of oblivion, and his virtues that mean nothing. The only thing that matters is keeping the goal clearly before your eyes and not giving up.

15-19 Good and Poor Examples

So one also ought to consider this "perfect." Paul thinks that one or another among the Philippians think differently. He takes it easy. He trusts in God's ability to lead the upright forth to the truth. Just as he can be sharp towards the aggressive deceivers who falsify the gospel, so can he be just as patient and tender before doubt and those who find it hard to believe.

The whole time he stands before the truth and attempts to clarify it both with word and deed. The deeds were not the least important. The gentile Christians came directly for heathendom, most of them from the poorest neighborhoods of the city. The everyday life of the heathen could be unbelievably brutal and hard. It was obvious that a person stole, lied and cheated to get by. It was a world where bickering and growling filled the day. In sexual matters, promiscuity was the norm. For many, to be Christian meant to begin a new life that a person never saw anyone live before. It was one of the greatest tasks for the congregational leaders to give examples for how the new life should take shape practically. Not in the least did this mean Christian freedom, those who were not bound by the law of Moses but bound by love for Christ. For this reason, Paul says an obvious thing, without any arrogance: look at me and to those who live as I do. You have examples in us.

At the same time, he mentions that there are poor examples, perhaps within the congregation. A person wonders what these could have been. Perhaps it was a matter of Judaizers. Of them it is true that Paul had already warned about them often and that they are enemies of the cross of Christ. That they go to their destruction, is something Paul had already said in Galatians: He who will be righteous through deeds, he has fallen away from Christ. It is harder to determine what Paul means when he says that they have their bellies as their god. It can mean that they let "food determine our standing before God," (1 Corinthians 8:8) and judge men who eat anything "unclean." Perhaps it can simply mean that in the midst of their formal circumstantiality are gourmands who live to eat. That they seek their glory in that which is their shame can mean that they praise themselves for their good deeds when in actual fact they should be ashamed of their self-infatuation and self-obsession that stains them. For us it probably lays closer to hand to apply these words to those who are manifest enemies of Christ's cross and who have made the pleasures of life their highest good and even brag about that which they should be ashamed of. It is not out of the question that these were the types whom Paul is thinking about here, crass materialists, "with their minds set on earthly things." However, we cannot do away with the other interpretation. A person can be an enemy of the cross essentially by figuring that in the end at least some of his own merits should count for something before God, or by willingly receiving forgiveness from the cross but not taking the cross upon himself. To have the stomach for his god and to have all his thoughts directed toward earthly things, this belongs to the old Adam's obvious lifestyle, which comes to remain a temptation even for Christian men so long as the church lives in this world.

20-21 The New Citizenship

Philippi was a Roman colony, and the citizens had the enviable privilege of being Roman citizens. So, they knew what citizenship could mean. Paul certainly has this in mind when he says that we Christians have our citizenship in heaven, and that it is from there that we await "a savior." Paul does not say the Savior, but uses an indefinite form, perhaps because Caesar in Rome could also be called savior, *sotier*, a title that is found preserved in many inscriptions and expresses the contemporary thankfulness for the Roman peace that really had created order and tranquility around the Mediterranean. Paul's words hint at what he means: we have a different, better citizenship, and we have a better Savior, one who shall come and change everything so that finally there is real peace and tranquility in existence. He can make all things new, even our "lowly body," that which is marred by sin and drags along "the law of sin that is in my members" (Romans 7:23). It shall be like "his glorious body," that which He bears after the resurrection. It is the same thought that John in a later epistle expresses with the words: "What we shall be that is still not revealed. But this we know, that when he is revealed we shall be like him" (1 John 3:2).

Philippians 4

1-9 Advice, Encouragement, and Admonitions

The letter nears the end and Paul concludes. Again, love breaks forth for these Philippians for whom he longs. He calls them his "crown." It is the crown of victory that Christ once gives and which for Paul consists in that he may bring others to Christ.

Then follows a very personal admonition. A conflict has arisen between two women in the congregation. We do not know what it was all about. We see that Paul is careful to be impartial: he normally directs the same admonition to each and every one of them. Then he turns his attention to an unknown person that he calls Syntyche. This means, "one who bears the same yoke" and is sometimes used for a good friend or "sidekick." Perhaps it is not a nickname, but only a characteristic of a good friend. In such a case it ought to be translated: "also you, who have really been a faithful coworker." Here we receive an example of church discipline in the early church. Disagreements and discord were something that had to be. The apostle does not use the language of force, but he speaks with a spiritual authority that it could not have been easy to ignore. At the same time, he is appreciative of those he rebukes. He takes the opportunity to emphasize what these two women have done. And he takes occasion to also thank his other coworkers. We notice that these must have been many. All are born up volunteers: one drew others to the divine service, one stood for his new faith among old friends, one helped each other mutually, one opened his home, one prayed together. To "fight" meant first and foremost to pray (as we also see at the beginning of Colossians 2). It is worth taking notice of which roles women played as coworkers in the early church and how they are emphasized and glorified by Paul, at the same time as he makes clear that it is not the Lord's will that they should be shepherds and teachers of the congregation.

Then follows one more invitation to joy, the joy that is always found there, joy in the Lord over what He has done and does. He who died for us; He is with us every day and shall come again. He is near, Paul emphasizes. And precisely because we possess Him, we can be spiritually big and generous to others. Paul uses a word that is difficult to translate, that means that one is not petty, and neither selfish nor conceited, but is decent, helpful, willing to overlook, and outgoing—so just that which follows from the joy of Christ. Certainly, there are worries, but those a man may take to God. Paul emphasizes that this applies to all. It is just every day, awkward realities that we may speak to God about. Then they come to be put in the proper light, and we always have something to be thankful for. This is the way to peace. Peace is not a fragile mood that we must try to keep. On the contrary, it is

God's peace that keeps our hearts and thoughts because that is a true relationship to God, a happy childship[1] with Him.

Finally, Paul makes a great sweep over all the good and true that he can find words for and says: you should let your hearts and thoughts be filled with these. It is a very important council in a world where one who is with us is surrounded by a manner of thought that shapes us and distorts our conceptions if we do not consciously correct them. In every point it means to make clear for us how one lives in faith in Christ. And again, Paul says: Remember what you have learned from me.

10-20 Paul Gives Thanks for the Gift He Received

Paul has a particular reason for writing this letter. He wants to give thanks for a gift and acknowledge reception. He saved this for last. There were important things in the relationship between the apostle and his congregation, which had to precede. And when the thanks come now, the letter takes shape in such a way that gives the money a subordinate place. Many have thought that this thanks is fairly sparse. But this is because Paul and the Philippians had a sense for the proper proportions. What Paul rejoices over is first that the Philippians themselves got it a little better, even more that they remembered their imprisoned apostle and desired to ease his burden. Now what he wishes most of all is that this gift—which in actual fact is an offering to God from the love of Christ and for the sake of the gospel—should bear such fruit that the Philippians themselves benefit from it. Perhaps Paul means that the successes of the gospel in Rome must also profit the Christians out in the provinces. Or he thinks that such an unselfish gift usually means that God has prepared some sort of gift to give in return.

While Paul gives thanks, he finds opportunity to say a few essential things about the freedom of the Christian and independence from external relations. He has learned to be content with what he has. "To be content" could also be translated to "be independent," to be able to cope. Paul uses a word (the same as our "autarchy") which in the stoic philosophy described the elevation of indifference before all sorrows. With the stoics it was a cool unconcern, something that one put upon himself to escape worry and pain. Even while watching their loved ones suffer, the wise would be able to say: "this does not move me." For Paul, it was something that came from Christ and made him prepared to serve other men. When Paul says that he "was consecrated" in the art of living in all circumstances, he uses another expression that has the connotation of being consecrated in some secret rite of a mystery religion. Paul means that there is a better consecration here, that which God gives when we remain standing in the midst of the strains of everyday life to serve Him.

---

[1] The word here is sometimes translated awkwardly with sonship, however the Swedish uses a more inclusive term referring to children as sons and daughters rather than just the son.

PHILIPPIANS 4:10-20

Paul reminds the Philippians that they are the only congregation from which he received such a gift. He sees it as the external confirmation that they are particularly close to him. And then he gives it formal recognition, acknowledgment of the full amount. (In this section he uses the contemporary accounting terms and repeats them numerously.)

As usual, at the end come a few personal greetings. He sends them to all who are Christians in Philippi. (As usual, it says "Saints" in the original manuscript.) And then he greets first from those who are now with him, probably when he finishes the letter, and from all the Christians in the city. Last come the greetings from "those in Caesar's house." This expression does not mean the Caesar's relatives, but it is used of all his servants and officials (often slaves or freedmen), who had a hand in the imperial chief administration and economy. They were both in Rome and dispersed in the empire. Why Paul sends such a particular greeting we do not know. Perhaps the Philippians had acquaintances among them, and perhaps Paul did not want to name them in case the letter fell into the wrong hands. There was persecution in Philippi and he himself could be condemned as an enemy of the state at any time. It can also be thought that Paul sends this greeting as an encouragement. It was a reminder that Christianity permeated everywhere and now had followers even among the house of Caesar.

As usual, Paul does not end with the "Live Well!" which was otherwise common in antiquity but sends one of these final wishes that so easily become empty words for us, but which for the addressees were filled with living, self-perceived content. "The grace of the Lord Jesus Christ" was revolutionary and new: He who changed everything for the Philippians, the source of their joy, security during the persecutions, and the driving force that pushed them to pursue the goal.

COLOSSIANS
Introduction

As one can see looking at a map of Paul's travels in our Bibles, the city of Colossae is in Asia Minor, in the western region and a good bit inland. A little river, called Lykos at that time, runs between high mountains and peculiar limestone formations here. The area excelled at sheep grazing and the hard water contained an element that made it particularly suitable for the dying of yarn, and so the area became a center for production of woolen fabrics. There were three cities here within view of each other: Colossae, Laodicea and Hierapolis. All three are mentioned in this letter. The largest was Laodicea and the smallest was Colossae, which also lay high up in the valley. In all of these cities there were large Jewish colonies with tight relations to each other. If a person travelled to the east, he would come to Galatia. If he took the road west through the valley, he would come to the environs of Ephesus and Miletus by the sea. So, it was not remarkable that Christianity gained firm footing here early on. Of course, Paul had stayed in Ephesus for two years (around 54-56), and then the gospel had been preached in "almost the whole province of Asia," to which this province belonged (Acts 19:26). In Colossae, a man by the name of Epaphras had worked as a mission planter. Paul had never personally visited the cities of the Lykos valley.

The area was often plagued by earthquakes. We know that a severe one destroyed the cities there in the 60s. Laodicea and Hierapolis were rebuilt, but we hear nothing of Colossae after that. It is not found among the cities of this area mentioned in Revelation. The ruins of Laodicea and Hierapolis still remain, but of Colossae there is not a trace. Thus, a person has good grounds for positing that it was never restored after the earthquake. The city must have been destroyed rather quickly after Colossians was written. This letter is remarkably similar to the Epistle to the Ephesians and ought to have been written at the same time during Paul's imprisonment, probably in Rome during the first years of the sixth decade (or perhaps in Caesarea a couple of years earlier).

Upon what do the similarities between these two letters depend?

Exegetes from the school of Biblical Criticism had posited that the one is an imitation of the other. Someone attempted to produce a letter in Paul's name and had an already existing letter as an example. Yet the attempts to find out which of the two letters would be the original have turned out very differently and given rise to outlandish theories. The problem is the unrealistic assumption that some author was sitting with the one letter before him and writing from it, changing it, deleting and making additions in order to produce a new letter in Paul's name adapted to particular current conditions. In actual fact, we have here a typical example of how an author or preacher works when they have to speak on the same theme often. He has certain expressions he likes to use. Whole sentences can come together in approximately the same form. This is noticed if at approximately the same time he writes two speeches, or two pastoral letters on the same subject. Small sections can be almost identical. In other places the same thoughts and expressions are known without the need to say that the one is dependent on the other. The author has not used the one version as a model, but wrote them both independently, though with the help of common material that he has on his mind.

Everything speaks to Colossians and Ephesians being written at approximately the same time. It is not hard to find probable explanations for the differences between them. Yet a person has to remember that such explanations are always guesses that cannot be confirmed before we find more material to build upon, material we may never find. One such explanation could be that from his imprisonment Paul had wanted to send a sort of pastoral letter to the congregations of Asia Minor. He may have been expecting to be given the death sentence, and this could be his last letter. This circular, our letter to the Ephesians, would have also gone to Colossae. If Epaphras, who knew Colossae inside and out, had not given Paul some important information about the situation there, Paul would not have come to know that a new type of false doctrine had emerged there with a certain amount of success. He has immediately perceived that this teaching attacked the very foundation upon which the gospel stands or falls. So, he had to intervene. He decided to send a separate letter, partially with the same admonition as that of the circular but with particular focus upon the false teaching that has appeared there.

There is a third letter that has an apparent connection to Ephesians and Colossians. It is the little letter to Philemon, who apparently lived in Colossae. This letter gives us further insight into the early Christendom here in Asia Minor. The contents could have followed directly after Colossians, but in the New Testament it has its oldest place as last among Paul's letters.

Colossians 1

1-2 Opening

The heading to this letter is well known. Paul does not write alone, but as so often, he writes with a coworker. In this case, it is Timothy, the most faithful of them all. He also co-wrote five other letters with Paul. Perhaps, Paul had a particular reason to remind them that he is an apostle according to God's will. He writes to a congregation in which he himself never set foot. As an apostle, he still has something to say about God's assignment.

3-8 Prelude

There are three things that characterize the Epistle to Colossians. First, Paul writes to a congregation that he has never visited. Second, he writes for the particular purpose of opposing a counterfeit Christianity that began to have inroads in the congregation. Third, he wants to say some important things about Christian faith and Christian life that he knows always need to be said and so constantly come up again in his letters.

As so often, Paul first mentions how glad he is for the Christians that he is writing to, and how he prays for them. He attempts to say this in a manner that creates confidence and a feeling of fellowship between him and the Colossians. He reminds them of what they have in common though they have never seen each other. What is now happening in Colossae is happening all over the world: the Christian faith bears fruit and grows. He reminds them of Epaphras, the spiritual leader of the Colossians, who came to Rome and reported all of this and was possibly imprisoned there (in the letter to Philemon he calls him his prison mate). He praises his work, calls him a fellow slave (literally translated), and says that "he is a faithful Christian deacon in our place." The Greek has the same word for slave and servant. We usually translate the word with "servant." Yet "servant" can also be called *diakonos*, the same word as our deacon. When Epaphras is called "Christ's Deacon" here, it is possible that it means he had an office. In Philippians, which was written at about the same time, Paul already speaks about deacons in the congregation. Yet at the same time, the word keeps its original meaning of "servant." Paul calls himself a deacon at the end of this chapter. It is most probable that in our time Epaphras would have been considered part of one of the groups that Ephesians labels "evangelists" or "pastors" or "teachers."

As so often, here Paul also mentions what he prays about, and as always, it is not some common phrases but well-chosen essentials. He touches upon faith, love, and hope. Paul always posits faith in Christ as the foundation and love as a necessary function of faith. To this he usually adds a third chief point that can often be lacking in contemporary Christianity: hope. This hope is something very concrete. It is something that "remains in heaven." It is the fact that Christ comes again as victor and establishes His kingdom. This fact characterizes all genuine Christian life. Here Paul says that it is this hope that is the driving force behind the love of the Colossians for all their fellow Christians. Concerning this hope, they have received knowledge through the gospel "that is now heard among you." Here Paul brings up another fundamental truth: "faith in Christ is shaped by the word." The pervasive happenings in Colossae were happening because the gospel had now reached there.

Already in these introductory lines, Paul positions the great themes: Christ is the foundation, the one foundation, and the sufficient foundation for salvation. We immediately see that he says this in view of the perversion of Christianity that he deals with in this letter, and that is what makes his words so very relevant even for us.

9-12 What We Christians Need

As so often, when Paul speaks about what it is he prays for concerning his brothers in the faith it naturally becomes an admonition and a reminder concerning all the things he mentions. He wants to point out those things that we ourselves need and desire, the things we should pray for. As usual, he first points to the need for better knowledge concerning God's will. In a Christian land with Christian schools, it can seem quite obvious that people have reasonable knowledge concerning the will of God. Of course, even as a child a person has had to learn God's commandments. However, in Paul's day the situation was completely different, especially in these small mission congregations. A person had to start learning right from wrong at the very beginning, and it is becoming the same way in the secularized west. Society accepts a manner of living that is obviously against God's will on important points, in questions of sexuality, marriage, abortion, and family for example. In this situation, it becomes an elementary and vital question: What really is God's will? First a person needs knowledge, then "understanding" to apply the knowledge, and finally "insight"—thus, the Christian experience and maturity that make it so a person does the right thing even in new and unforeseen situations. It is not merely a question of rules and moral principles but about a right relationship with Christ who causes a person to "walk" (to live even in everyday life) in a manner that is worthy of Him, so as the disciple lives in the eyes of his master. Then a person can begin "to bear fruit" (like branches on a tree) in the form of all sorts of right and good dealings, and he can come to grow in knowledge not only concerning God's will but concerning God Himself, about the whole of the reality that one did not know before. It is this communion with God that gives a world-conquering power, and here Paul points to the result that was an obvious reality for the early Church, but that we would gladly escape accounting for: the persecution and badgering that a living faith can endure and that one bears with patience. Yes, Paul says it with complete joy and thankfulness because they show that we will inherit God's own kingdom.

13-20 Christ in All and Over All

Here Paul now finds occasion to develop the completely overwhelming significance of Christ. He does it with a clarity and power that has made the following passage into a chief passage for all Christian faith. And he has a particular reason for it. It is his desire to go directly to the crux of the issue of the false Christianity that threatens to destroy the faith of the Colossians, but in a manner that is free of polemics, and completely positive. We don't know the details of what the opponents had said and neither does it matter. In any case, the chief thing is clear and actually constant. It means faith in Christ is the only way to God. It is this faith that is being questioned, partially from a Jewish piety for the law, of a more folksy type than that which Paul fights against in Galatians. This Jewish folk piety was blended with elements of heathendom and primitive superstition. It was partially influenced by arguments from a new movement that we encounter here for the first time, and which grows to be a strong and real danger for the early church a couple of generations later. This movement is usually called Gnosticism. It is a syncretistic movement, thus an attempt to blend different religions together, gather together valuable thoughts and commonalities, and thereby achieve the true world religion. It also made claim to be scientific and to represent the true philosophy, humanity's deepest wisdom, in precisely the same ways that we see in similar movements today. In order to achieve such a blend, a person must (then as now) tone down the meaning of Jesus. So, they were willing to give Him approximately the same place as even Muslims and Hindus are willing to give Him: a place as one of the many revelations of god and god-sent guides that are in this world.

What Paul now says is this: Christ has an absolutely incomparable place. This is true both in the work of creation and in salvation, both in the universe and the church.

He was present before creation. He was present at creation. The world would never have come to be if Christ had not been there. And the world would not remain today if it were not for Christ's sake. This means the whole of our visible universe and the whole of the invisible world with all its spiritual powers that God has also created. There would not be any of this if it were not for the Savior's sake. With the creation of the heaven's spiritual powers and of us men came the possibility for sin and the fall. But the Savior was present in precisely this creation. The possibility of forgiveness was interwoven into God's plan already from the beginning.

So now the other part of Christ's all-encompassing work follows. He is the head of the church. Even here He is the first of them who bear all. He is the first who rose from the dead. First in Him the mortal has clothed itself in immortality. Already in His earthly body the fullness of God dwelt. This body was that which suffered on the cross to atone for the sin of the world. This atonement applies to all creation. All that was crooked and crazy can also be forgiven and re-established. However, it can only happen in Christ, only by being incorporated into Him and taken up into His kingdom.

A person can ask how Paul can know all this. He had of course never been a personal disciple of Jesus. We find the answer in the gospel of John. There a personal disciple speaks. He says the same as Paul, though in somewhat different terms. Even there we know that Christ is always there in the beginning, that He was present at the creation, and that all came to be through Him. Even there we may know that He gave His life so that the world shall live, and that we can all partake of His fullness if we come to Him. Again and again, John invokes the very words of Jesus. In Jesus Himself the truth returns as Paul so emphatically argues here against all those who say: "Certainly, Jesus gladly, also Jesus . . . but there is so much more that we must also have."

So, Paul says it as powerfully as it can be said: nothing can be put next to Christ. He is "the image of the invisible God." In Him dwells the "fullness" of divinity. The word "fullness" seems to have been widely used by the opponents in Colossae. They meant that God is so rich and so inexpressibly great that a person must have all religions and all great thoughts in order to get a true picture. Paul answers: It is true that God is inexpressibly and unfathomably rich. Yet the whole fullness of this is found in Christ. If we want to know who God, the invisible and unfathomable is, then we shall look to Jesus Christ. It is through Him that we learn to know God and, what is more, can come to God.

21-23 This is What shall be Held Firm

We are also involved in this powerful deed of Christ. Paul reminds the Colossians about this. They have experienced this themselves. They know how they once lived in all the evil deeds that were once natural to them, far away from God and with a hidden hostility towards Him in their hearts. While they still lived this way, God prepared their redemption. It happened, as it literally says, "in his body of flesh through death." Christ becomes man. The Word had become flesh, as John expresses it. In this earthly body Jesus took all of our sins upon Himself and bore them "in his body on the tree" as Peter says. For their sake He must die, and His death means the opportunity of forgiveness for us. We are sinners, but we are reconciled with God. Now the miracle of God setting us before His face can happen. We who still bear sin within us may still stand there holy and guiltless because

Christ has taken us into Him and made us members of His body. It is He who answers for our sins.

All this applies to us Christians, if really . . . and here Paul reminds us of the sine qua non: that we are really united with Christ, this Christ who alone can make a sinner righteous before God. Here Paul surrounds this mortal danger of believing in those who teach differently with a circle of arguments and points, yet without polemic. Of course, they are the ones who try to get us away from the only foundation, Christ. They are the ones who want to get us to budge at least a little from the gospel. The gospel says that Jesus and no one else is the way upon which a sinner can come home to God. It is this gospel that is now preached in the whole world and that Paul received Christ's own commission to bring forward.

Paul says this last bit here, as in Galatians, so that no one shall be able to say: "naturally, I believe in Jesus, but Paul, he is a different matter." Paul knows that he speaks by Christ's commission and stands for the true gospel. He knows that this gospel shall go out over the whole world. He can even say that it has been proclaimed in all creation. It goes like a trumpet blast throughout all creation and resonates all the way into the heavenly world, as Paul says in Ephesians (3:10). At last, the mystery of God is revealed, and His plan with the whole course of the world enters into day. Here Paul makes a digression to say something about this plan and about his own place in it, the whole time thinking about the situation in Colossae, so that all the reluctant shall understand what it is they are doing if they turn to another gospel.

24-29 God's Eternal Plan is fulfilled

Paul gives a reminder concerning the decisive time he and the Colossians live in. What had been God's plan for millennia, though hidden, has now been fulfilled, and God's holy people, the Christians, have been blessed to see it. Paul himself had received his particular task in a particular point in this great course of events. He shall spread knowledge of that which happened and get people to see it. It is a particular and limited commission (he uses the word "economy," which among the Greeks meant a plan for the household, even here a plan for God's "household of grace," in which Paul receives his particular post to manage). Paul is the apostle of the gentiles. As an apostle, he has received his particular and assigned measure of suffering. This, his particular measure, he now means to complete and fulfill. It happens to benefit those he shall serve, and the Christians in Colossae also belong to them. So, he rejoices because of his suffering. He toils and struggles, but he does it while a powerful force that is not his own (and he who can speak this without it being self-praise) carries him. Finally, it all depends on that great mystery of the gospel: That Christ can live in us and that this is the guarantee that we shall have a place in His glory, the unfathomable joy in communion with God.

Colossians 2

1-5 Paul Fights for the True Christian Faith

Now Paul says that even gentile Christians he had never seen belonged to the field of activity that he had received from God. He makes it clear that he really feels responsible for them. He "fights" for them, first of all in his prayers, but also by following their development and intervening where it is needed. He lets us hear what he sees like a picture for mission work: that the new congregations shall be strengthened, bound together in love and be firm in their conviction, through real insight into the great mystery of God, Christ. For in Christ there are all the treasures or wisdom (*sophia*) and knowledge (*gnosis*). Here Paul intentionally uses two terms that the false teachers used. They pretended to come up with a deeper wisdom and knowledge that would complete the gospel. No, Paul answers, here there is no completion necessary. All wisdom and knowledge are there already in Christ. And so he goes on the offense for the first time in this letter. He lets it be understood that he says all this about Christ because he knows that there are some in Colossae that say otherwise and come with specious arguments in order to find people to fall for their false claims. Now Paul has a personal word to say to the Colossians. Just as he has been there countless times in his prayers, he is now there again invisibly, "in spirit," to speak to them. However, first of all, as a wise debater he wants to prevent any misunderstandings. He does not want the Colossians to believe that he has heard some horror stories about the state of the congregation. So, he testifies to the good order among them and the firmness in their faith.

6-12 Baptism is our Christian Circumcision

Now Paul draws out the consequences of everything he has said before. If a person has received the true gospel, then he must not botch it. Faith in Christ cannot be improved or mixed with anything else. Paul says that the Colossians "received" Christ. He uses an expression that refers to the right knowledge that would be "transmitted" by the apostle or other teachers and "be received" by those who were Christian. It was a solidly formed instruction of what Jesus said and did. Because all Christians would know it, Paul never quotes it in his letter, unless he has special cause for it. However, the more eager he is to inculcate this shall you believe and nothing else, he says so even now. You have received Jesus as Lord, as God's Son. Now you shall hold fast to this, "walk in him" as it says in the Greek, so to live day to day in this communion, rooted in Him (like branches in a vine), and build upon this foundation, the only one that can be laid, firmly anchored in this faith, just as you have now been taught. The risk is really that a person is abducted—carried off as a slave—by those who come with some false teaching. Paul uses the word "philosophy" but means a blending of philosophy and religion, an outlook on life that is half built upon philosophical reasoning and rational arguments and half from articles of faith plucked together from different places; in this case, it is certain that it is mostly from Judaism and from the Christian proclamation. Paul says that it builds upon what men have learned, literally: on a tradition that comes from men, but not on the real gospel that comes from Jesus (and which one could also call a "tradition," something that is "handed down," i.e., "submitted"). Later, he says that this teaching has been formed by "the powers of this world." What he means we shall see immediately. The chief point is that this new wisdom will add something to the gospel. This puts authorities and powers next to Christ so that a person must also have regard for them. This is dangerous because if a person does this they are abducted and carried off into slavery.

In Christ there is actually all "fullness." Again, we encounter this word that was apparently a buzzword for the opponents. They used it to show that there was something more with God than that which Christ came with. Paul answers that the distinguishing thing about Christ, that which made the man Jesus to be Christ Jesus, is precisely this, that He bears within Him "the complete fullness of God." Again, it seems Paul uses the terms of the opponents. He hardly speaks of "divinity" at all. It is one of those empty clichés that men begin to use when God fades away and becomes a philosophical concept rather than a living Father. However, now Paul says, with emphasis, that the complete fullness of divinity dwells "corporally" in Jesus Christ. It is not a matter of an idea or principle. It is a matter of Jesus's body—He who was born in Bethlehem and with which He rose from the grave. There dwells the complete fullness of God. And there we have access to Him. We don't need anything more in order to find God. And it is this Christ that we are united with. This happened in Baptism. The opponents had apparently required that everyone be circumcised. Paul says: you are already circumcised. Not with hands, but with the real circumcision, that which Christ completed. This happened when you were baptized. There we were all united with Christ. First with His death. Your old man was condemned to death. You died to the old life. Then you were awakened and received life with Christ. Purely literal, so that His life now lives in you, you who believe in the Resurrected One.

So, baptism is the Christian parallel to circumcision. This is one reason why infant baptism was so obviously accepted in the early church. An Israelite would be circumcised already on the eighth day. Otherwise, he did not belong to God's people. So, it was natural for Christian parents to also have their children baptized, so that they too would be received into the people of God.

13-15 We Participate in Christ's Victory on the Cross

That God can do all this with us sinners, this is because of what He did on Golgotha. There He wiped out all that was written on the promissory note. Paul takes the picture of a contemporary IOU, a personally written (or at least signed) obligation of debt that laid out line for line what was required of the debtor. Paul says that every point on our ledger was against us. However, God wiped out all that was written there. It happened when He nailed our unredeemed and inconvertible promissory note on the cross. Then something happened that reverberated throughout the whole universe, even in the heavenly world. God disarmed the "rulers and authorities," all "the powers of the world" that Paul speaks about now. They were all the spiritual powers that rose in rebellion against God and took humanity with it and now make claim on all those who have fallen from God. They came to shame. Their claim lost its basis and its validity when Christ died for our sins.

16-19 By the Victory of Christ We are Liberated from all the Powers of the World

What is it that Paul is actually thinking of when he speaks of "the powers of this world"? He uses a word that means element, source, or basic principles, and basically indicates all spiritual powers that one thinks are behind them; above all these would be planets but also all sorts of guardian angels or evil spirits. Astrology played an immense role at the time, even in the highest strata of society. In Jewish folk piety, it was particularly angels (but also demons) that came to determine innumerable traditions and customs with which a person tried to protect themselves from misfortune and gain health and wealth. It is apparent that the half philosophical religious blending that began to gain ground in Colossae had strong strains of such Jewish folk piety. It concerned itself with a common religiosity that lost living communion with God. It went as it always does in such cases. There were two things that interested men in this. The one was speculations and explanations and "evidence" that could provide interesting insights into the invisible world. Some believed in secret [apocryphal] writings that revealed what Jesus really said, or in oracles and predictions that the ancient sages left, and that came to us today in secret ways. Some were interested in revelations and visions and phenomena of the occult. Alongside of this went the second chief line: the fear of powers. When the personal trust in God dies off, there can still remain a religious color, and somewhat rightly so, the feeling that we are left to the mercy of unknown powers that we can't control. These are what drive men to seek rules and advice that can guarantee that a person has evil powers under control and can exploit good powers. It may be a question of pure superstition like the fear of the number thirteen or the custom of "knocking on wood," but it can also be a half-religious reaction, a need for a refuge and sincere prayer (though in many cases the border between prayer and incantation can be hard to draw). In a Jewish context, it was obvious to all that the many rules concerning permitted foods and unclean foods or concerning good days and forbidden days would play a great role. Even the gentiles could anxiously begin to wonder if it was not best to correct themselves according to such rules and not get in trouble.

We might mention yet another feature. In such shallow but popular religiosities there are often ascetic traits. The thought that we put ourselves in the good graces of divine powers by abstaining from something and by being strict with ourselves is universal. The dark powers prefer sacrifice. A person acquires powers for themselves by afflicting their bodies, fasting, living like a Spartan, and denying themselves that which he actually desires.

A person could find all of these features in Colossae, just as in our day. If we want to have external examples from our own environment of that which Paul calls slavery to the powers of this world then we can think of the almost superstitious fear of fooling themselves, that is so normal, or in the unmerciful control that common opinion or the fad of the day or the demand to be skinny can exert over people.

Christ has made us free of all this. Paul emphasizes this constantly as a chief point in the gospel. So, he also says it to the Colossians. Do not belong to them who want to judge the genuineness of your Christianity according to what you eat or drink! They only show that they themselves do not know what the gospel is. It does not belong to those who make it into a matter of salvation to have a certain calendar of feasts or to hold the Sabbath in a Jewish manner! Certainly, such things are mandated in the Law of Moses, but they only applied until Christ. It is as a shadow of His figure that is there for Him. Yet when He Himself steps forward, the shadow no longer has meaning. You may not let yourselves be disqualified by such men! As so often, Paul uses a picture from the world of sport. Then as now, referees had the power to rule against the party that won if he broke the rules. Now the opponents step forward as such judges, and according to their own false rules want to declare forfeit for us Christians that victory we have through Christ. And what do they have to give us instead? They come with their "humility." This probably points to that which they wanted to claim they were taking seriously, the self-denial and the bearing the cross by ascetic exercises. Or perhaps humility consisted in that they bowed themselves to and also worshiped the angels that did not stand as high in rank as Christ. In any case, they made up a great number of angels and heavenly powers. They knew their names, and they could count up all the different classes in the heavenly hierarchy of both the evil and the good. Paul also mentions such powers. He knows that they are there. But he is completely uninterested with their rank and their characteristics. By his letter we cannot figure the matter out. There is only One. He says this over and over again: everything that is exists in Christ and He is the One who has the power.

Further, Paul mentions that these deceivers are inflated by their visions. They believe they have a covenant with the spiritual world, perhaps also with the dead, and not only with God. It is as if well is not enough for them. They are puffed up by their super-spirituality, and in actuality it is only a form of "carnal sensuality"—something that comes by flesh. These must have been hard words for the opponents to hear. They differentiated between reason, which they placed so highly and would help them get to a higher and more cultured Christendom, and the "flesh," the material body that was something inferior. Paul now draws up a new delineation instead. It does not go between spirit and material, neither between the soul and the body, but right through both these realities. It is the line between Christ's kingdom and the world. We only live in faith and forgiveness, and then both body and soul belong to Christ. Or we also live in unbelief and then there is evil in both body and soul. This is precisely the case with these puffed-up, clean-living people who in actual fact have only found a religious manner of making themselves noticeable.

20-23 Freedom in Christ may not be Bartered Against Slavery

To have been united with Christ means to have died to the world. All the bonds that held us prisoner for as long as we lived apart from Christ, whether they be the Law of Moses or normal consequences, superstitious fear, or human ambition, Christ has redeemed us from them. We have died to all these powers and found refuge in a different kingdom under a different Lord. Paul uses this fact as an inevitable argument when he wants to show how unreasonable it is that we, who have been freed from the world, should now carry ourselves as if we still lived in the kingdom of the world, and must then obey these rules and regulations. It ought to be observed that the whole time Paul speaks about that which makes us Christians, about the conditions for faith in the forgiveness of sins. A Christian can willingly take on rules and duties out of love for his neighbor and for the good of other men, but this is another matter. Here he is concerned with people who say: Don't touch that! And mean: in such a case, you can no longer be a Christian. Then a person has to stand in opposition to them for the sake of Christ. A person must not let himself be lured away by all that seems to be sincere, self-denying, and decisive piety. It is only an imaginary worship, and it only serves the good of the old man.

Colossians 3

1-4 Resurrected to New Life in Christ

We have died and risen with Christ. That is the meaning of baptism. In modern Christendom, it is often forgotten. In the New Testament it is the foundation upon which the whole Christian life is built. Now we hear Paul emphasize this yet again: you have now been raised up from the dead to live with Christ. Then it is obvious that you shall seek that which is found up there with Him in heaven. It is this you shall have as a landmark and checkpoint. You shall strive after and think about this. There you have your true life, that which we receive when we are baptized. You receive a share in Christ. You were incorporated into Him. This new life is certainly here on earth. Christ lives in us. Yet this life is invisible. It is a mystery that is inconceivable to the world and even to ourselves. In its visible reality it is only with Christ in heaven. For us, it is not visible before Christ returns, when He is revealed in His glory. Yet then it will not only be Him who steps forth in glory. We too shall do it. We shall be like Him.

5-11 The Old are Passed

In baptism, not only did we receive a share in Christ's resurrection, but also in His death. Just as Christ was condemned to death and was executed on Golgotha, so there was something within us that died in baptism. It was our old man, the flesh, the selfish ego, that is quite obviously the center within us if God doesn't become that. The ego has now been condemned to death, and this death shall be executed daily. "Put to death therefore the earthly members within you." By "members" Paul does not mean here certain parts of our body. He thinks the same as when he says we are members in Christ. Before, we were "members" in unrighteous service, who served as arms for sin (Romans 6:14). It is these members that shall be killed—or rather the functions, the deeds. So, Paul does not speak of body parts but about deeds when he now gives examples of these "members." He begins with such as we also hear mentioned in Ephesians as particularly dire sins: fornication and greed. Again, he says that such draw God's wrath upon us. There is something in God's own being that is inexorable against such things. Paul says why. Here it is a question of idolatry, of having chosen another god for oneself, he who is God's implacable enemy, Satan. He attracts first and foremost with these things: sex and money. Both things can be used rightly, but Satan changes these uses into fornication and acquisitiveness. However, it is not only things like this that shall be put away. Paul goes to the daily affairs of the sinner. Again, we receive a living picture of this world where the early Church recruited and the gospel meant a revolution, human and social. It was a world where men used all means to assert themselves and cope. Some scolded people, some quarreled and injured, some were indescribably coarse in speech and lied without hesitation. It is the whole of this lifestyle that shall now die away. It can be compared to soiled clothing that has been taken off and will not be put on again. Instead, a person dresses up in the new man, the new costume. Here it is not a question of a onetime thing. Paul says that this new man is renewed, perpetually anew, and that it happens because we receive more and more real knowledge of God. It is so "it is an image of whom who created them." Here Paul thinks of Christ. He has said before that Christ who was present at the first creation, is also He who creates the new creation when He gives life to the new man. So it is Christ who we come to resemble more and more if we are renewed in this manner.

Thereby a new relationship between us and men has also come into play. Before, there were hostile camps and inherited oppositions between races, social classes, and people. Now all these divided people are one, limbs in one and the same body; here Paul says the same as in Galatians. All baptized have clothed themselves in Christ. They are all God's children as long as they live in their baptism, and they are of the same value in God's eyes. Paul never says that we are all the same. On the contrary, we are different—sometimes very different, and therefore have very different functions just like members in the body. But we are all one in Christ. Christ lives in us all, and it is He, and nothing in us, that makes it so that we may be God's children. When it comes to salvation and the forgiveness of sins, it means that we are not . . . and so Paul enumerates a series of religious, national, and social limits that otherwise held up. All people who do not speak Greek or Latin are called "Barbarians." "Scythians" were the uncivilized tribes north of the Black Sea, and they are named here as examples of "independence."

12-17 Something New Has Come

Paul comes to that which is new, that which a person should put on like new clothes. Again, we notice that it is not a question of a single treatment. We have put on this new man in baptism, but it means that we shall put him on us every day, just as we put clothes on every day. Here too, Paul gives a series of examples. Yet a translator is given a perplexing problem here. He finds time after time that the words Paul uses, those that describe the Christian life, have no true correspondent in modern Swedish (or English). In the past they had words such as: humility, gentleness, meekness. However, these words have taken on the ring of old speech. They are not key words, and a person does not like to use them as a modern man when a person wants to say something appreciative. There are few expressions like generosity, decency, and helpfulness that come close to the Biblical expression, but to a great extent we must (to our shame!) recognize that we in our modern language hardly have any words that describe what the new life in Christ means. The words we use easily become tainted with blandness and weakness. This is partly because the life in Christ has always been something foolish, somewhat ridiculous, or unworldly in the eyes of outsiders. Yet there remains the impression of a poverty of speech that a Christian must keep in mind. He is called to live in a new way, so new that there are hardly words for it, at least not everyday words. This applies to most of the conduct that Paul lists here. "Heartfelt compassion" can also be translated "merciful heart." The Greek expression partially means something that engages us in our spirit, partially partaking in the suffering and worries of others. "Kindness" can also mean goodness, decency, and helpfulness. Here "modesty" is used to translate a word that is often translated "humility." The Greek word means that nothing is seen as remarkable, with the obvious meaning of being unnoticed and ignoring all prestige. "Gentleness" is not the same as indulgent, but a calm and firm kindness that can receive a scolding and suffer wrongs without getting angry. "Patience" is designated in the Greek with a word that normally means to be "longsuffering," to take a long time to flare up, to be strong enough to control yourself.

As always in such contexts, Paul reminds us of forgiveness. Christ's kingdom is a kingdom of forgiveness. As always, he points us to love. It is not a characteristic of oneself; it is the power and gift from Christ that holds together the whole and allows it to function properly. Of "peace" he says – here as in Philippians—that it shall rule and lord over our hearts. It is not a fragile and fleeting atmosphere that we shall attempt to keep, but an effective power. It shall teach us to keep the peace. We are members of the same body. So, we should work together, help out, and not be at war with one another.

This newness implies a perpetual new flood of life, power, and love from Christ. This flood comes through the Word. Even the Word shall receive a large space in the day's program and in the plan of the week. We receive a glimpse of the divine service (just like in Ephesians). There were psalms, newly composed hymns, and other songs there. There was also instruction and admonition. A person learns the Word of God, may hear and learn what Jesus said and did, and listen to admonition in the sermon. The conclusion is, to do everything in the name of Jesus, under His eyes, like the disciple to his Master, as faithful servants to Him who looks down on us from the right hand of the Father.

3:18-4:1 Home and Work Life "In the Lord"

What follows now has been encountered before in a more developed form in Ephesians. We have already seen that is not a "set of house rules" for all men. Here where Paul speaks as summarily as he can, there is still one thing that continually comes forth: this means "in the Lord," when a person lives as Paul now has described, as a member of Christ, as a man who "seeks that which is in heaven." This is no civil law code. It is a description of the life that follows when a man loves his Lord Christ.

We recognize all the instructions from Ephesians. What is meant by subordinate is explained in that commentary. It is to enter into God's order and function according to His will, something that makes a man free when he obeys. We also notice, here as in Ephesians, God's order encompasses everything. Everything stands under a demand of God, in its own way. Here Paul says some things that further highlight that which is written in Ephesians. When he says that the husbands should love their wives, he adds—literally translated—"do not be bitter against them." "Bitter," here it means that which tastes bitter. So at first hand, it does not mean to "be bitter to someone" or to "be embittered," but rather to be pith and vinegar, to be unfriendly, irritable, smug or ironic. Even that admonition to the parents is more detailed than in Ephesians on an important point. The admonition applies in Ephesians "to not provoke to anger." Here Paul uses a different word that can be translated "tease," but which has a wider meaning and could be rendered with "to mock" or "harm someone's self-esteem." It means all types of critique that—even if it is meant well—that only makes a person depressed and hurt. We can think of all pretentions and expectations on a child that makes it so that a person always finds something to remark upon, always something to nag and criticize, perhaps even taunts and humiliations. Such things cause children to lose heart. It cracks self-confidence and joy. With a modern expression we could translate: it can as giving an inferiority complex.

When it comes to admonishing workers and employers—something that is in complete agreement with what is said in Ephesians—a person should keep in mind that the Greek has the same word for servant and slave. When Paul says, "you stand in service to Christ," so can it also be rendered with the words: you are slaves to Christ. Paul normally calls himself "Christ's slave." We could say "live again under Christ," that is to have Him as Lord and belong to Him. It is great now that Christ's slave is simultaneously His sibling and co-heir. So here Paul says that the reward Christ gives is "your inheritance." The slave has become son and co-heir.

Colossians 4

2-6 Prayer and Mission

Paul calls for perseverance in prayer. As usual, he follows his Master's instructions. Yet he consistently uses other words. What Jesus says: all Christians should know that. Such things belonged to that which was handed down to them and which they received, "accepted." They are reminded of such things again and again in the instruction they receive from their "shepherds and teachers." Paul gives his own formulations and applications. He calls for perseverance in prayer and says—literally translated—"wakeful in it with thanksgiving." "Wakeful in it" can point to the custom of using the night hours for prayer (as Jesus normally did), but it can also mean with "spiritual vigilance" so that a person prays from the heart and watches for the temptations that also come during prayer. By "with thankfulness," he means the usual reminder to thank again and again and not just pray for help.

Paul cannot mention prayer without immediately entering upon the great subject of prayer: the spread of the gospel. He counts prayer as one of the most effective powers in his work. Finally, it is only God who can cause people to listen to the gospel and for it to be properly presented.

However, our daily conduct also belongs to mission work. This means to conduct ourselves rightly and wisely among those who are outside the faith, not to challenge and tease but to seize the opportunity when the door to a person's heart is ajar. At the very least, this means to speak and answer correctly, always friendly, but not meaningless. We shall be the salt of the earth. (Again, Paul alludes to the words of Jesus, without citing them directly.)

7-18 Personal Messages and Greetings

The following section is almost literally the same as in Ephesians. Paul does not say how it is going for him or about the legal case and future prospects. Though, in actual fact, this was something the addressees were eager to hear about. Tychicus, who brings this letter, can of course tell them this with far more in depth than it is possible to write in the expensive papyrus rolls.

Paul makes a little addition here. He says that he also sends Onesimus, "who is at home with you." He calls him a faithful (or believing—it is the same word) and beloved brother, thus a fellow Christian. There lies a long history behind these words that we will learn more of in the letter to Philemon. Onesimus was a runaway slave, who was converted and now wanted to return to his lord. Paul would commend him for a good reception. Because he belonged at home in Colossae, there was no reason to mention him in the letter—Ephesians—that would accompany it and go to the other congregations.

Then the greetings follow. These are easy for a Bible reader to pass over, but with examination and afterthought they have a lot to say about communion in the church. Many otherwise unknown people in the early church, the many coworkers and the common congregational members appear here. The first to be greeted are two of the more well known. The one is Aristarchus who had been with Paul in Ephesus and was dragged into the theater by the furious crowd, who then followed him to Jerusalem and eventually came to Rome by prison transport where he seems to have been imprisoned together with Paul. Then comes the greeting from Mark, usually called John Mark, who with his cousin Barnabas had followed Paul on the first missionary journey to Cyprus but didn't want to go any further when the trip went to purely gentile areas in the middle of Asia Minor. That was something that made Paul not want to take him along any further and thereby caused a rift between him and Barnabas. The conflict is obviously out in the open when Paul writes this letter, and Mark again belongs to the circle of faithful coworkers. According to what we know from the ancient church, it is this Mark who wrote our Gospel of Mark. Here we hear that he planned some trip to Asia Minor and that Paul sent letters of recommendation in advance. Perhaps they were needed if a person in the early church heard that Paul had been dissatisfied with his conduct earlier. Here Mark now gets the certificate that he had been one of the few among the Jews who faithfully stood by the Apostle's side during his imprisonment in Rome.

Then there is another, otherwise unknown, Jew named Jesus. This name was very common at the time. This Jesus also had—as many Jews—a Roman surname, Justus.

Then Epaphras, who apparently established the congregation in Colossae and was its leader, gives a greeting. We do not know why he was in Rome. In any case, Paul is keen to emphasize that Epaphras has not forgotten his old congregation but in his prayers, he fights for both it and for the Christians of the neighboring towns. Again, we see what a role prayer played and how conscious a person was of what a work it really was.

Next to last, Luke, the physician, also sends greetings. According to tradition, he is the author of the Gospel of Luke and Acts. We thus encounter in these short series, if we figure in Paul, the authors to a great majority of our New Testament.

Finally, there comes a greeting from Demas. He is also mentioned in the letter to Philemon, recognized among the coworkers of Paul. Here he does not receive any particular description. Perhaps Paul anticipated the tragedy that is spoken about in Second Timothy (4:10) where Paul mentions that Demas, in love with this world, has abandoned him.

Then Paul sends his own greetings, particularly to Laodicea and to one of the Christians who had leased his home for mission work (there were no churches) and gathered a "house congregation" there. According to the most faithful readings, it was a woman with the name Nympha, though a few old manuscripts propose that it was a man named Nymphos; in any case, it was one of the many unknown women and men who took an obvious share in the mission work with all that they possessed and had.

Finally, Paul gives an interesting admonition. This letter should be read in the surrounding congregations, and a letter that will arrive there shall be read in Colossae. Here we have a first hint about a development that would find meaning for the whole future. A person read the apostolic letters in the divine service, even those they had as copies from other congregations. When later the question came up as to what one should consider holy Scripture, then this became the defining criteria, that which since the oldest days had been read in the divine service.

We do not know what the greeting to Archipus means. It is the characteristic of a real, true letter that there can be something that is only comprehensible to the addressee. We do not know exactly what task or office it is that Archipus received. We come again to this matter because he is also mentioned in Philemon. The meaning with such a greeting, performed by the whole congregation, can be to nudge and spur him to boldness. It can also be to give him support if he must do something that falls on everyone's lap.

Finally, there comes what we would call the emphasis of his own hand. Here Paul follows a custom in antiquity. Even if a person, which was very common, made use of a scribe, a person finally wrote a greeting with his own hand. Sometimes it was only one word, "erros" ("live well"). A person could leave off his name when the addressee knew his handwriting. Here Paul puts his own name. He writes to strangers. And he writes down a little prayer together with the greeting. He asks them to think about his chains. That he mentions just this matter lets us understand how much he suffered being in fetters. Finally follows his personally written wish for freedom.

We only possess transcripts of Paul's letters. The original papyrus has long since deteriorated. If we had them remaining, we would be able to see how the handwriting changed where Paul himself grabbed hold of the pen. Yet even behind such verses we understand the everyday, tangible reality from which these letters sprang forth. And it also helps to understand that they also deal with the same reality that we live in.

FIRST THESSALONIANS
Introduction

It was during his "Second Missionary Journey" that Paul first came to Thessalonica, most likely in the summer of the year 50 A.D. Luke gives us a detailed account of this in The Acts of the Apostles (17:1f). Paul travelled together with Silas. A week before they had both been terribly abused in Philippi. Yet they immediately began to preach in the synagogue. Thessalonica (modern Saloniki or Salonica) was an important city. It had been the capital city of the Roman province of Macedonia for 200 years, and there was a strong Jewish colony there. Paul preached here for three weeks and as so often had great success among the Greeks who "feared God." Paul speaks about this in his letter, and we will return to it in the commentary. The result was that his adversaries among the Jews caused a malicious tumult and forced the authorities to intervene. Paul and Silas were forced to leave in a hurry. They came to Berea, but there too Paul was chased out after a short period of time, whereupon he made his way to Athens.

Paul himself says that in Athens he carried an almost unbearable anxiety for the newly founded congregation in Thessalonica. This is easy to understand. We do not exactly know how long he worked there, but it must have been a very short time, perhaps barely a month. He says that he had wanted to return but that some obstacles had presented themselves. When the anxiousness now overwhelmed him, he sent Timothy in order to ascertain what had happened. Apparently, Timothy had connected with Paul in Athens (something that Luke does not mention in Acts). He travelled to Thessalonica and then apparently returned in the company of Silas. They sought Paul who had continued to Corinth in the meantime and started new work (Acts 18:5). Timothy had good news with him from Thessalonica. Rejoicing in this, Paul now writes to the congregation.

We can also draw the conclusion that this letter ought to have been written sometime in the late autumn of 50 A.D. or the following winter. We know that Paul spent a minimum of a year and a half in Corinth. Towards the end of his sojourn there Paul was tried before the Proconsul Gallio. We can date the public service of Gallio in Corinth with the help of inscriptions discovered in Delphi to the time between midsummer 51 and 52 (or perhaps 52 and 53, which is less likely). This is the best anchor point we have when it comes to dating the events of Paul's life.

This letter would then be the oldest of all the letters of Paul that have been preserved for our day, barring the possibility that Galatians was written a year earlier, just before the great "apostolic counsel" that was held in Jerusalem. First Thessalonians would then be the oldest preserved Christian writing. We have reason to believe that the apostolic message of Jesus already had found its form in all of its essentials, that which we find in the first three gospels. But none of our gospels had yet been written.

So here before us we have a document that lets us encounter the very earliest church, not as it appeared when one looked back and shared their memory, but as one experienced it when one stood in the middle of the events. We encounter an outbreak of spontaneous joy against the background of tension and anxiety, which a great missionary feels for his spiritual children. We experience what a gamble it was to be a Christian. We notice that the whole of the Christian mission could appear as an unreasonable and impossible undertaking that a person would never have committed to if he had not known that God commanded it. A person experienced success as a miracle of God, an inescapable proof that the Resurrected One Himself still worked here through His Spirit.

There is no essential instruction that appears in this letter. Paul gives expression to his overwhelming joy and thankfulness for the good news that he has recently received through Timothy. Then he answers a couple of questions Timothy apparently carried with him. They deal with the return of Christ and how it should be with those who die before He comes. And finally, he gives admonitions that seem to assume a spiritual maturity in the congregation that one only rarely finds in congregations today. A person can marvel that Paul could assume so much faith and Christian maturity among men who just half a year earlier had never heard talk of the gospel. A person perceives the depth and power in his preaching. He knew how to lay the foundation. So, it also held.

1 Thessalonians 1

1 Letter Head

Paul names two of his most faithful coworkers at his side as fellow letter writers. These two had been his travel buddies during the last year and find themselves with him in Corinth when he writes, or rather dictates, this letter, sometime during the winter months of 50-51.

He met Silas in Jerusalem the year before at the great council of apostles where Silas received the commission to travel to Antioch as a representative of the original congregation and convey the decision that had been reached. So he accompanied Paul and Barnabas when they returned to Antioch. Silas was a prophet and proclaimer and worked for a season with the gentile Christians in Antioch before he returned to Jerusalem. His friendship with Paul made him a natural choice to accompany Paul when he began his second mission trip in the year 50.

He met Timothy in Lystra. He was the son of a Greek but had a Jewish mother. Apparently, he became a Christian when Paul and Barnabas preached in the city a few years earlier. Timothy became a coworker with Paul and seems to have remained so as long as Paul lived.

It was Silas who sat by Paul's side in the stocks in the innermost prison cell in Philippi and sang songs to God's glory in the middle of the night when they were both dragged before the judges in the square and abused. He then travelled with Paul to Thessalonica. Timothy probably followed soon after that. In any case the three were reunited a few months later in Berea. There they were separated for a time, and Paul travelled to Athens alone and then on to Corinth. Now they were together again and fully occupied with promising mission work.

The letter is addressed to "the congregation in Thessalonica," their church, which was established some months earlier. Paul says what separates them from every other congregation. (The word could be used for other "congregations," especially those who were held by voters in a free city like Thessalonica.) This church is a congregation "in God the Father and the Lord Jesus Christ." A person can clarify the words with additions, for example (to cite some modern translations): "who live in communion with," or "who have their life in," or "who belong" to God the Father and the Lord Jesus Christ.

2-10 What Thessalonica Meant

With noticeable joy, Paul speaks about his still fresh memory from Thessalonica. He seems to have stayed there for barely a month. He left the city after a violent tumult where the agitated masses tried to get hold of him but were only able to take hold of a few congregation members who were dragged before the magistrates and were only released after they provided bail, perhaps as assurance that Paul would vanish from the city.

Apparently, this is the first time that Paul wrote since he, as we will hear immediately, received good news. Now Paul lets them understand how joyful he is because of the Thessalonians. When he prays for them, which he does incessantly, the memories come to the fore. Their Christianity was true, both in questions of faith, hope, and love. Faith showed itself in deeds, love in all the effort they made, and hope in their endurance under persecution. Paul dares to assure them that they are God's beloved. For us it sounds like a banality. For the Jews it was something tremendous that could only be said of Moses and Elijah and other great men. He assures the Thessalonians that they belong to the chosen. So, it went as it went when he came to them. The gospel that he preached was filled with the overwhelming power of the Spirit. It was received with joy amidst persecutions. The rumor of what had happened went throughout all of Macedonia and Achaia—the two Roman provinces that correspond to the present Greece. The rumor was a powerful proclamation of Christ. Paul seems to have encountered it when he came to places that he had never before visited. He counts it as a part of the joyous message: Christ works even now, and the work testifies to Him.

In three lines Paul gives us the chief summary of the Christian mission: A person turned from false gods and idols to serve the one true God (with all that means a new way of life). It was a chief point even in the Jewish mission. However, here he added something decisive: Faith in Christ. He was the Resurrected One, He who could save from death and judgment. And so, a Christian waited for His arrival every day.

1 Thessalonians 2

1-4 "As False Teachers Though We Speak the Truth"

Now we may be aware that faith and the events in Thessalonica consist of a single victory for Paul and the gospel. Had Paul been the average modern man, we would have been prepared to draw this conclusion from his word. However, Paul knew that the successes of God's kingdom do not exactly resemble what the world calls success. They can be united with suffering and persecution and all sorts of harassments from the surrounding world. There is a paradox to them. Thus, Paul could say, "When I am weak, then I am strong" (2 Corinthians 12:10). So it was in Thessalonica too.

Luke described what happened there in Acts. Because it appears that Luke had stayed in Philippi of Macedonia at that time, he ought to have had a good opportunity to ascertain what had happened. His description posits that Paul and Silas went straightway to Thessalonica after they had been terribly abused before the court in Philippi and spent the night in jail. The trip ought to have taken six days if they went on foot, and half that time if they could afford to hire a wagon. In any case, hardly more than a week could have passed after the abuse.

These are the facts behind Paul's words here in this letter about boldness that he knew that he received from God when despite all his bruises and wounds that could have not yet been healed, he immediately began to preach in Thessalonica too. Luke says how it went and lets us know what lies behind Paul's word about "hard opposition." There was a synagogue in Thessalonica. Paul went there and preached as usual that Jesus was the Messiah and that the Scriptures taught that the Messiah must suffer and rise from the dead. Some of the Jews attached themselves to him and so did a great many of those who "feared God"—Greeks who believed in God but hesitated to take the final step and become proselytes. Among them were several leading ladies in the city. Paul maintained this for three weeks, but then the Jews caused a tumult to expel Paul. They took "some wicked men of the rabble and formed a mob" and attacked the house where Paul was staying. He happened to be out at the time, but they took his host and brought him and some other Christians before the court. There they yelled and shouted that these men "have turned the world upside down" acting against the decrees of Caesar and making Jesus king. The result was that the accused were released on bail after they apparently promised to have Paul leave the city. This happened the very same night. The mood was apparently so heated that a person did not dare let him show his face on the street in daylight.

When Paul writes this letter, now some months have passed since all this happened—perhaps even half a year. We have a living picture of how the Jews took to the streets to stir up the Greek population against Paul. It is their accusations that Paul takes up and refutes. They apparently used the opportunity to paint Paul as a wandering charlatan, who tried to gain influence and money by coming out with some fictional wisdom. In antiquity there were plenty of such hucksters and quacks, private philosophers and magicians who tried to cash in on the credulity of people. Paul first establishes that he has not come with anything he himself had discovered or has private benefits from. It is God who entrusted him with the gospel. This is why he speaks as he does.

5-12 To Be Able to Give Both the Gospel and Himself

Paul only needs to remind them of simple facts to show how unreasonable the adversaries' accusations are. At the same time, he, unconsciously, gives us a classic description of a true priest and his attitude towards both his proclamation and his congregation.

He has not come with flattery, nor tried to ingratiate and be popular, neither has he made himself remarkable in the power of his office. Just as slight has the attention his own finances been given in his thoughts. Paul—who is very conscious of the principle given by Jesus, that "those who proclaim the gospel shall live by the gospel" (1 Corinthians 9:14)—abstained for his own part from the right to pay and made his living as a tent maker. It was only from his friends in Philippi that he had at any time received a subsidy. They had helped him already in Thessalonica (Philippians 4:16), though he did not remind them of that here, perhaps so that it did not sound as if he expected anything of the like from other congregations.

This great love of the gospel, that makes him willing to make the greatest of sacrifices, is now paired with a similar righteous love for the congregation and individuals. It was not only his task to give them the gospel. Some attempt to fulfill this task without having any real interest for individuals. Paul cared for them. He can speak about how dearly he held these Thessalonians, and they must have known that he spoke the truth. He says that he and his coworkers were not only willing to give them the gospel, but even themselves. They gave them their time and their love, without reservation. They took care of each one especially when they admonished and encouraged. It is just what Luke says that Paul could say concerning his work in Ephesus a few years later (Acts 20:31). What he did in Thessalonica was no exception.

From other letters of Paul, we can see that the arguments of the adversaries remained the same in large part. They consisted of a personal attack that questioned Paul's integrity. Paul's counterargument, just as his performance under persecution, followed in large part along the same lines. What he says in this early letter comes up again almost point for point in other contexts (for example, 1 Corinthians 9 and 2 Corinthians 6 and 12).

1 THESSALONIANS 2:13-16

13-16 The Word Works Both Faith and Violent Opposition

This is something for which Paul must constantly thank God for when he remembers what happened in Thessalonica. It is that the people there rightly "accepted" the Word that they "heard from him" (that he mediated). Paul uses an expression that means that he mediated a given message that he himself had received from Christ and would spread unchanged as he had received it. This message was received as a Word from God, which it really is. And thereby, it also showed its power by being active in those who believed it.

But the Word also shows its power in those who do not believe it. It awakens violent opposition. He who rejects it does not remain untouched. He must harden himself. The Word unsettles him, and therefore he wants to silence it. This is what happened in Thessalonica. Here we know, from that which is told in Acts, that the Christians there were exposed to persecution from their Greek compatriots. We receive confirmation that the congregations in Palestine had received suffering from the Jews. The Jews appear as a warning example to Paul for how dangerous it is to hear God's Word without wanting to bow before it. He says that they have persecuted the prophets and killed their Messiah, and now they attempt to hinder the good message concerning salvation that now reaches the gentiles. They attempt to stir up unrest everywhere and have even successfully chased Paul away, most recently from Thessalonica and Berea.

What Paul says here about the Jews is not antisemitism. Paul loved his Jewish people. He has given captivating expression to this matter particularly in the ninth and tenth chapters of Romans. His conviction was that finally the whole of Israel will be saved (Romans 11:26). A person ought to take notice that when Paul here calls the Jews the "enemies of all people" (those who "oppose all mankind"), this is the conclusion of the reason that they try to hinder other people from being saved through faith in the Messiah that they themselves have rejected. In the measure to which they do this, they act as enemies to the humanity that God wants to reach with His gospel. Paul knew what he spoke about. He had experienced the bitterness of seeing his compatriots try to hinder precisely this that was their greatest task, that which gave them a particular place among all the people of the world: to come with the message of God's salvation to the gentiles.

1 Thessalonians 3

2:17-3:5 The Apostle's Concern and Longing

So long as Paul remained in Berea, which was in Macedonia, he was able to receive news from Thessalonica. Yet when he was forced to flee from Berea and travel to Athens, this became more difficult; he then lets us know that he lives in great anxiety. More than once he had resolved to travel back to Thessalonica—"but Satan hindered us." If we had written it we might have written something like "but unfortunately it did not happen." Or, "but we had bad luck and we met obstacles." However, Paul sees everything that happens during the mission work as part of the great struggle between God and Satan. If we would ask him and if he really means that Satan can thwart God's plans, he would presumably answer at present, "yes," but in the long run he pulls the shortest straw.

When Paul hurriedly left Berea, his friends helped him make it to Athens (Acts 17:14f). Then he was alone, but he sent word to Timothy and Silas to follow him as soon as possible. Apparently, at least Timothy came down to Athens, because here Paul says that it was from there that he sent him back to Macedonia in order to hear what was happening in Thessalonica. He says that he could "bear it no longer" when it came to his anxiety. His longing for news overwhelmed him. When he says that "we determined to remain alone in Athens," he apparently means himself because an author or letter writer of that time normally said "we" when they meant "I."

Paul had probably heard about persecution of the Christians in Thessalonica. Certainly, this was not a matter of an organized persecution from the Roman state. That would come later. In Acts, Luke speaks about "wicked men of the rabble" that the Jews had stirred up. We can guess that this concerned harassment, vandalism, and abuse. Paul notes soberly that a Christian has to deal with such things. From the very beginning he had told the Thessalonians that they would be persecuted. And so they were. In the New Testament, persecution is not anything incredible, that a person would be shocked by. Rather it is a sign that a person really belongs to Christ.

Paul knew that not everyone would receive the gospel. This was a matter that he received with equity. However, this did not prevent him from being anxious and worrying deeply over every single person who was in danger of being lost. This anxiety could be so stark that he "could no longer bear it" as he says here. He would continue to feel anxious. Six years later he writes to the Corinthians: "And, apart from other things, there is the daily pressure on me of my anxiety for all the churches. Who is weak, and I am not weak? Who is made to fall, and I am not indignant?" (2 Corinthians 11:28f)

1 THESSALONIANS 3:6-13

6-13 The Good News

Paul now gives a detail that makes it possible for us to date this letter rather exactly. He lets us know that Timothy has just come back from Macedonia. Luke tells the same story in Acts (18:5). Paul came to Corinth from Athens, apparently alone. He met a Jew who was also a tent maker and worked together with him, as he preached in the synagogue. "When then Silas and Timothy came down from Macedonia, Paul was occupied with the word" (could completely donate himself to the service of the Word) (Acts 18: 5). It ought to have happened in the fall in the year 50 or during the following winter.

Timothy had good news with him that meant much for Paul. Some years later he says (1 Corinthians 2:3) that he was in weakness and with fear and very anxious. He says that news came to him in "the midst of our distress and affliction (oppression)" and that they meant everything was different. He livened up again. He speaks of unmistakable joy and relief from the whole letter, and we then realize how intensively Paul was touched by all that happened in his congregations. Now without reason he called them his children. We can understand his uneasiness. It had not been many months before when these Thessalonians had been heathens and knew nothing about Jesus Christ; many of them did not know anything of one true God either. Paul had to leave them hastily. Now he hears that they "stand fast in the Lord."

His thankfulness is exuberant. He knows not how he shall be able to praise God rightly. He has one single great wish: to soon see them again to "supply what is lacking in your faith." Paul is real. He knows how much is still deficient with his spiritual children. They are of course "newborn children" (as he says in Corinth, 1 Corinthians 3:1). He knows his responsibility, and he prays for them and would wholly come to them. Yet for the moment it may stay with good wishes. Or rather a prayer first that the way to Thessalonica shall be open for him, then of that which the Thessalonians need most—the love that only God can give. That which prepares them to meet the Lord when He comes. That "Our Lord Jesus comes again" has obviously been a chief point in the gospel that Paul preached to them.

Thereby Paul has finished the first part of his letter, the spontaneous rejoicing. Now follows admonitions in series.

1 Thessalonians 4

1-8 The Christian Life is a Life in Purity

It is educational to see what Paul puts forth as essential here. It deals with people who were heathens just a year before and now begin to live a new life on a completely new foundation.

First Paul reminds them that it means "the life that you have learned from us" in accordance with "instructions that we gave you through Jesus Christ." The apostle admonishes "in the ways of the Lord Jesus." What he comes with is not a few private judgments. It is what a person in the early church called "parodosis," the solid, formed apostolic tradition of Jesus's Word and from words concerning Jesus that were taught throughout all mission work.

What Paul gives here is a "paranesis," i.e., ethical admonition. He is not speaking of the most important aspects of the Christian proclamation: Jesus's life, death, and resurrection. There are consequences for our way of life that apply.

The first consequence that Paul mentions is a life in purity. The Christian, just like the Jew, knows that they stand for a morality that radically separates itself from the world's morality. For the people of antiquity, it was almost self-evident that sexuality was the highest natural value. The great church historian Eusebius (died about 340) points out how all cultures that preceded the Christian saw the meaning of life in enjoyment, most of all sexual enjoyment. It was the Jews and the Christians that knew that sexuality like all other values must be subjected to God's will and His purposes. They knew through daily experience that fornication and heathendom belong together. Here went one of the obvious limits between a hedonistic and a Christian way of life. There is a limit that Paul now emphasizes again. Sexuality is not some obvious privilege. God has set a particular limit to it; each should have his own wife. However, the wife is not a sexual object, but the matrimonial relationship should be marked by "holiness," that is love, responsibility, compassion, and respect, and of modesty, that is respect for the other's intrinsic value and integrity. Therefore, faithfulness is essential. None may offend or deceive his neighbor "in this matter." The words probably point to the sexual life. However, since similar expressions can be used for litigation and sometimes business, the interpretation is unclear. In any case, the context talks about the right use of sexuality and emphasizes that one rejects God Himself if one sets himself over that which the apostles have taught in the commission of Christ.

On this point the early church had to fight a hard fight, also from directions that purported to be Christian (like Gnostics) but who wanted to adapt to the general pattern of life and accepted an emancipated sexuality. This has through

1 Thessalonians 5

1-11 Wait, Watch, and be Sober

The disciples had asked Jesus when He would come back. Briefly summarized, His answer was that no one could know the day but that they should always be watching and prepared. Paul reminds us of this now. As usual, he does not cite Jesus directly, but what he says is permeated by the words of Jesus. This is a distinguishing mark for Paul when he writes his letters. He assumes that the Christians have learned these words in about the same way that a person used to learn it in catechesis in an old church[1] congregation. Such things did not need to be repeated in the limited space of a letter. However, Paul alludes to it and reminds them of it with his own pictures and new expressions. The picture of the thief who comes unexpectedly at night is taken directly from the instruction of Jesus. However, even the talk of humanity's security, of the catastrophe that comes so suddenly and that cannot be escaped, as well as the urging of vigilance and the warning against sleep or intoxication have their counterparts in the words of Jesus, though Jesus uses different pictures (the flood, the destruction of Sodom, the servants who wait for their Lord, etc.).

Paul, like Jesus, lays all the weight on vigilance. It serves nothing to attempt figuring out when the Lord will come. We are to be prepared instead. Paul has a colorful picture concerning the matter. For a Christian, it is day. "The others" live in darkness. For them, it is night. They cannot see the way and do not know where they are going. Many sleep the spiritual sleep, far away from God, from the light and reality. Others get drunk; they live for the night and misuse God's good gifts. Yet for those who know Christ, the sun has ascended. He sees both the goal and the way. Therefore, he keeps himself sober both in the literal and metaphorical sense. The spiritual soberness, as it is called a dozen or so places in the New Testament, means a balance and reflection, a clear discernment and a sound realism that does not allow itself to be impressed by empty talk even if it sounds pious. Unbelief normally looks upon the Christian faith as unrealistic dreams and delusions. He who knows Christ knows that it is unbelief that does not look soberly upon reality because it will not see the truth of itself. It comforts itself with the illusion that

---

[1] GammalKyrklig, a reference to a movement within the Church of Sweden that has its roots in the revivals of the 17th and 18th centuries and led by Henric Schartau. This movement was very similar to the confessional revivals of Loehe and Walther with its emphasis on the confessions of the Lutheran faith, and somewhat in contrast to the experiential emphasis found in pietistic circles influenced by the Moravians and Halle Pietism.

men are basically good or that finally a better world will develop. The Christian knows what it means to fight and put on his armor that only Christ can give. Paul speaks about it expressly in Ephesians (6:11f). Here he only mentions the breastplate and helmet that gave the legionnaire the most important protection in battle. A Christian receives this protection through faith, hope, and charity. All three are insolubly bound in Christ. Faith is faith in Him, charity is His charity that we participate in, hope is the certainty that He returns, and the victory is His. He who is united with Christ in this way, he works to see the world soberly and realistically. However powerfully evil can still persecute, in the end it is Christ who has the victory.

Finally, Paul returns to the point of departure: the Thessalonians' uneasiness in the face of death. Paul has now made it clear that he who belongs to Christ, he belongs to Him in life and death. There is no difference if we are "awake or asleep." (Here Paul uses the words again in a metaphorical sense, but with a different content than just now.)

12-15 The Relationship of the Leaders and the Brothers in the Congregation

Paul adds—as so often—some short admonitions. They could have been difficulties that he knew existed in the congregation. They allow us to imagine what sort of inner problems a newly established congregation could have had to struggle with. At the same time, it shows that there was not only good will here, but a deep Christian conviction that could motivate people to be unselfish and forgiving far beyond the limits that are normally regarded as reasonable.

The first thing Paul takes up is the relationship to the congregational leadership. Obviously there existed such offices. Luke tells us that already in his first missionary journey Paul appointed "elders" in every congregation (Acts 14:23). He seems to have done this in Thessalonica also. The name of these congregational leaders could change. Sometimes, (like here), they were called "directors," sometimes they are called "elders," and sometimes "shepherds and teachers." Paul emphasizes that they are leaders "in the Lord," thus, by his commission and directing. Therefore, they have full authority and commission to "admonish." The word that Paul uses has a biblical meaning of giving a reprimand or a warning. It can (as further on in this piece) be translated with "rebuke." Perhaps one or another in the congregation has become upset. Therefore, Paul lets it be understood that this is precisely the purpose for having such leaders in the congregation, and that a person should appreciate them for their zeal and show them both respect and love. Then he adds "be at peace among yourselves"; it is in response to criticism given to the congregational leaders.

Later, Paul talks about the mutual responsibility within the congregation. He gives some practical applications of this view of the church that he has developed in other contexts. We are members in one and the same body. The strong members are to take care of the weaker. In the concrete it can mean to rebuke the "disorderly"—perhaps those who create conflict or neglect their work—or to have a heart for the wounded and unhappy and weak and take care of them. The obvious desire to let evil men be paid with the same coin must be kept in check. Evil should be repaid with good. A person should do good for everyone, not only for his friends and not merely once in a while.

16-22 A Living Christianity

A few loaded imperatives then follow. They masterfully capture some of the seemingly exorbitant consequences of having received God's great gift: Jesus Christ. To always be happy is an unreasonable thing, so long as we only have our own resources and those of this world to rely on. It is just as unreasonable to pray without ceasing. Yet in communion with Christ a person begins to comprehend what it is all about. They have something to be happy about whatever happens. Christians live in a communion that does not end when their thoughts must deal with something else. They always have Christ's presence and are conscious of this. And they can be thankful in all of life's relationships, perhaps not for everything but yet in the midst of everything that may happen.

What follows is even more special. A person should not despise "prophetic speech." Essentially Paul says, "the prophecies," and is certainly thinking of the prophetic, directly inspired elements in the divine service. Perhaps some had the inclination to disparage them. This has always been a temptation for those who stand for the organization of the church and the good order. However, the Spirit's fire may not be extinguished. The external order with its authority, which Paul has just argued for, is not at odds with the charismatic elements of the true Christendom. Both have their place. But a person should not uncritically accept all that is passed off as inspired by the Spirit. On the one hand, Paul thinks about the prophets when he says that he shall be tested and examined. He gives the same rule to the Corinthians (1 Corinthians 14:29), but the rule can also have a wider application. A person ought to take notice of the word that is here translated as "examined," which means to critically test and examine something to see if it fits with the goal. It says, "test everything," and some have taken it as an admonition to participate in everything to gain their own experiences. The word's real meaning is rather that a person should be careful and look before one gives himself to something new.

23-28 Final request

In his final request Paul reconnects to the chief theme: joy that the Thessalonians have received the gospel and now wait for the Lord Christ. He cannot wish them any better than that Christ shall complete this work. And he knows that Christ has the power for this.

Then comes the often-recurring admonition: pray for us.

With that Paul bids farewell in the oriental manner of a kiss that he prays the receivers will share with the whole circle of believers. Finally, he gives the command that his letter should be read before the whole congregation. It is the only time we hear him do this. Perhaps it was still something so unusual with a letter from an apostle that it must be emphasized that it is not a private letter. Later it became a self-evident thing. An apostolic letter is saved and read in the divine service. Of course, a person knows that the apostles spoke in Christ's stead and would receive their words as a word from the Lord Himself.

SECOND THESSALONIANS
Introduction

The letter to Thessalonica, which we call the second, is not as easy to date as the first. There are even some who believe the "second" was written before the "first," but they have seldom had any support. The information in the second letter suggests that it must have been written some time, probably a short time, after the first, so from Corinth during the first half of the year 51. The reason for the letter is obvious. Paul has received news from Thessalonica reporting that uneasiness has arisen in the congregation because some had imagined that Christ's return was immediately at hand and had stopped working. They had cited Paul as a sage. Now Paul wants to put everything right.

While the authenticity of the first letter to the Thessalonians has never been seriously questioned, the opinions have been divided on the second. Fifty years ago, it was not uncommon for it to be considered "Pseudo-Pauline," thus inauthentic. According to the most common theory, it had been added at that time when the hope of Jesus's quick return had begun to pale. Someone would then have attempted to replace the first, true letter to the Thessalonians that witness to a strong expectation of Parousia, with a new letter, in which long paragraphs used the former letter, but came with a new teaching concerning the return of Christ. The weakness with this theory is that Second Thessalonians does not speak to people who wonder why Christ is delayed, but on the contrary to such as those who have ended up with a false conviction concerning that He comes in the nearest future and who have therefore neglected their daily duties. The situation is thus typical for the first period mission. It is a strong argument for the authenticity. The newer research is dominated by the conviction that it is an authentic letter from Paul. The stylistic differences that undeniably exist between both the letter and the alleged contradiction between thoughts concerning Christ's return will be dealt with in the commentary.

Second Thessalonians belongs to those letters that received recognition as Holy Scripture. Bishop Polycarp in Smyrna cites him already in a letter to the congregation in Philippi from the time around the year 110. So, it must have already been known and read, obviously because it was apostolic. Polycarp also invokes the expression "the blessed Paul" when he cites. We can with good conscience follow his example.

2 Thessalonians 1

1-2 The Heading

The superscription is almost the exact same as in 1 Thessalonians. The greeting of peace is however something fuller and has the form that is the common one for Paul.

3-12 Thanksgiving and Intercession

As usual, Paul begins by saying how he prays for those who he now writes to and how he thanks God for them. If a person compares this part with the correspondence in First Thessalonians, he notices differences. The first time, in the thanksgiving with memories from Thessalonica, Paul could be thankful for what he himself had experienced. Now he talks about what he has been given to say. He speaks about how faith and love have grown in the congregation and how they have stood fast under persecution, so that Paul could proudly name the Thessalonians as an example for other congregations. However, the concretion is gone. In the place of memories there is a meditation concerning God's righteousness, and Christ is finally victorious. The language has a ring of prophecy. It is full of Biblical twists. The word streams forth in a single long sentence (the Greek sentence finally finishes in verse 10), where the one thought feeds the other. It is not a question of a doctrinal lesson that is thought through and planned beforehand. Later, it is a prayer of a type that is prayed by New Testament prophets at the Lord's Supper. A person can compare this chapter with the first in Ephesians, where we meet a long thanksgiving by the same type. All that is said here belongs to thanksgiving. It is thus the question of prayer, and not primarily about instruction.

However, the prayer is still an instruction. A person thinks how Paul has wrestled with a painful problem. Why should the decent and honorable people of Thessalonica need to suffer so much? Why should they be persecuted just when they finally quit repaying evil with evil and instead try to do good for all? How can God allow this evil? In the prayer these questions have been turned into thanksgiving. A Christian must suffer. Persecution is evidence that a man is on the right way. It is something to be thankful for. It is an omen and a sign. The evil powers are on the move. They know what it means. Christ comes. The great day approaches when God holds court and commands justice. The answer to all the questions concerning why the good must suffer and the faith seems to be trampled is found for Paul in the conviction that in the end God preserves the righteous with power and evil comes to be crushed. Where a man belongs at home is revealed before Christ. The light comes into the world, and they who are children of the light are drawn to the light. Others experience the light as a danger, something hostile that threatens their opportunity to live as they want. They are not obedient to the gospel of our Lord Jesus. The gospel comes with the greatest of all conceivable gifts: to be God's child. However, this gift can only be received in obedience. Some years later Paul writes (Romans 1:5) that his task is to "establish the obedience of faith among all nations." He knew that this was a great offense for many. They are happy enough to have a gracious God and an eternal life, but not a Father to obey and a Lord to follow in everything. It is this no to God Himself and to the communion with Him on His terms that finally becomes the reason that some are separated "away from the presence of the Lord and from the glory of his might." Here as elsewhere, the Lord means Christ. It is in Him that God has made Himself known in a final and decisive manner. Here we are placed before the choice. And Paul notes with deep thankfulness that the Thessalonians chose rightly when the gospel came to them.

Then follows a short prayer. It can sound incredible that Paul prays "that God make you worthy of his calling." The Thessalonians had already answered yes to the call. However, for Paul the call is not just a one-time thing. Seen most deeply it is God's whole work with a person, His will to save her[1] and all He does to draw her to Himself and hold her in His hand. So, Paul can use "the elect" as a name for Christians. And now he prays that God should continue His work and complete it.

---

[1] In Swedish, her is used as him is, or at least used to be, used to indicate a person of either gender. It is probable that a more correct translation would change the pronoun to account for this difference in language. However, the translator likes how it reads with her.

2 Thessalonians 2

1-12 The Lawless One and the Return of Jesus

Now Paul turns to the theme that is apparently the reason for his writing a new letter to the Thessalonians. He wants to correct a misconception in the matter of Christ's return. Some have imagined that the Lord's Day has already come, and the world will perish in the near future. Some had quit working. They referenced something that Paul had said when he spoke as a prophet in his instruction or in his first letter. However, it is not—as some think—a question of a forged letter from Paul. That conception follows from the word "purporting to be from us," which only refers to the letter (in the Greek it reads closer to "a letter"). However, it can just as well refer also to the preceding, and then the text receives the meaning that has been given here.

Paul wants to correct this now. He begins with the admonition: Let no one deceive you! It is probably a deliberate reminder of the admonition that Jesus once gave the disciples, just when it came to the time for his return (Mark 13:5). Jesus had said that many deceivers would come and that many would be confused but also that many things would happen before the end came. Now Paul reminds them of what must first happen. There will come a great apostasy (then the love of most will cool, Jesus had said, Matthew 24:12). "The Lawless one" shall step forth. It is apparently the same figure that John calls the "anti-Christ" and "the beast" in Revelation. It is an incarnation of evil. He is called "the Son of destruction" because he is thoroughly destroyed; he spreads destruction and he himself goes to destruction. He embodies the great rebellion against God. Yet he has not come, but the power he embodies is already now at work. Paul calls it "the mystery of lawlessness." In this expression there lies both that this power works in a hidden manner, even where one least expects it, and that it is a mystery (Paul uses precisely that word), something unfathomable that we can never fully fathom.

We meet the same perspective of the future as that of Jesus in Revelation. The world will not encounter a light and harmonious development. There is an ongoing fight for life and death between God and Satan. Satan leads the great rebellion against God; he musters up all his power and it looks like he will be victorious. But when it is time for the final showdown, then Christ will return.

All this is also spoken about in other places in the New Testament, even the thought that everything happens according to a plan that God has laid firm. This is why the man of lawlessness cannot step forth before his hour has come. However here we encounter a new thought that is only found in Paul: there is a hindrance. It can at the same time be said: "he who hinders" or "he who holds back." The path is not free for the man of lawlessness before this hindrance is removed, whether they are removed by the enemy or revoked by God (the word can mean both). Yet what is it that hinders? What does Paul think of? Some have proposed the Roman Empire and Caesar, or the gospel and its apostle, Paul, or some protective heavenly power that keeps other powers bound as it is hinted at in Revelation (9:14). The best is probably in agreement with Augustine: I must say it bluntly, that I do not know what he is speaking about.

Some have tried to find a completely different conception of the end times and Christ's return in Second Thessalonians than in First Thessalonians. According to the one conception Christ should come completely unforeseen, as a thief in the night, but according to the other His return should be preceded by signs that a person can observe. However, both of these manners of seeing are already found in the words of Jesus, so nearly interwoven in the tradition that it does not do to say that one of them should be the original. At the same time as Jesus stresses how surprisingly the day will come, "in a hour when you do not expect it," He speaks about how it is preceded by signs that allow a person to understand He is near. Both features are needed for the picture to be complete.

We shall know that the world is reaching a final crisis. We shall not lose our faith when it comes. At the same time, we should know that Christ's day comes as a surprise. We cannot foresee it; neither can we say that "it is far off" or so that we take it for granted that it is imminent, and we can shirk our earthly duties.

So, we live amidst the great settlement between God and Satan, between the truth and the lie. No one escapes the choice and how one chooses depends on what man basically thrives on and loves. The truth is not only a theoretical insight concerning facts. It is God's plan and meaning for existence. As a contrast to truth, He mentions evil twice. If a person wants to believe the truth and hold it to be right, a person is left out to evil with its eerie power to convince and blind. It can be a punishment that strikes a man already here. He can no longer see the truth. However, in such a case it is because he said no to it while he could still see.

13-17 You are Chosen so Stand Fast!

Paul is quick to reassure the Christians in Thessalonica that this evil shall not touch them. That they received the gospel shows that they belong to God's beloved, to those who are chosen for salvation from the beginning. This does not mean they can make themselves assured. On the contrary, this itself requires them to stand fast. Salvation does not happen automatically. This is the great paradox that we constantly re-encounter in the New Testament: God has loved me, He has received me as His child through Jesus, nothing shall be able to take me out of His hands. And for just this reason I must be vigilant and pray, prepared to fight and suffer in order to overcome that which wants to drag me away from God. Paul reminds them of what would be needed in the fight above all: to "hold fast to the apostolic instruction" (Acts 2:42). Here Paul uses the word paradosis, which indicates the holy tradition that the apostles received from their Master and through the Spirit whom He had promised to them. So, there was at this time already something of a written gospel that had arisen, a firm and defined Christian knowledge that a person could not be changed.

Then there follows a blessing that sounds as if Paul meant to finish the letter here. However, he has something more to say.

2 Thessalonians 3

1-5 Intercession and Obedience

Here, as so often, Paul also asks for prayer concerning his work, first and foremost for the success of the gospel and next for salvation from evil men. Paul constantly risked his life. He knew that the gospel must arouse violent opposition. "For not all have faith," he says literally. He does not just mean that there are some who still have not come to faith, but that there are those who through their whole being and way of life experience faith as a threat and an enemy that must be beaten down. When Paul says this, his thoughts immediately transition to the Thessalonians and the persecutions they are exposed to. So, he says, comforting, that God is faithful and will help them. Christ Himself shall lead them forth to that which they best need during the persecutions: God's own love that encompasses both friend and persecutor, and Christ's own perseverance that which He showed in His death. As an extreme ground for his conviction that it shall go well for them Paul mentions their obedience to the command, he and the apostles give them. He does it in the manner of Christ. The apostolic instruction is not one thought among many others that a person can discuss or negotiate. It comes from Christ and is applicable to all.

6-15 How A Person Comes to Correct the Disobedient

Now Paul gives one such apostolic command that he makes applicable in Christ's name. It concerns those who live a disorderly life in conflict with the apostolic paradosis (Paul uses precisely this word) that the congregation received. We may also know what exactly this "disorderly life" is that Paul points to. There are some who neglect their daily duties and occupy themselves in any other way possible. Most likely it was a consequence of believing they knew that world would immediately pass away. However, Paul lets it be understood that it could also be plain laziness and reluctance to work. Paul can now point to the example that he and his coworkers intentionally gave during their stay in Thessalonica. They had every right to let themselves be maintained, but they preferred to earn their upkeep in order to show that a person should not let others carry the load. Paul turns directly to those who do not ordinarily work and admonishes, in the name of Christ, thus with the greatest possible seriousness, that they must carry themselves better. He reminds them of a rule that he had included in his instruction (and which two thousand years later would come to be included in one of the world's first communist constitutions): he who will not work shall not eat. We may remember who this is directed to: men who will leave the demanding daily work to others and occupy themselves with "finer" things or be lazy, and simultaneously expect that they should be kept by those who still work.

Paul realizes the possibility that some will still not comply and continue loitering. In such a case the congregational discipline must be applied. Paul shows how it should go. The sinner should not be excluded but treated like a brother, thus as a member of the congregation. He may still come to divine service and communion. However, a person should not socialize with him, nor show him the fellowship in everyday life that was otherwise obvious between Christians. He should understand that a person should not just turn a blind eye to his carelessness and disobedience.

16-18 Final Greeting

Paul finishes with a wish for peace, perhaps with thoughts to all the unrest that the congregation may have experienced through persecution from without and problem children from within. "The Lord's Peace" is naturally Christ, He who prepared peace for us by dying for us and who can give a peace that the world does not know.

So far Paul has in his normal way dictated this letter and let someone else handle the pen. Now, he writes with his own hand a little greeting at the end. He was not alone in this custom. In many preserved papyri a man can see that the sender used a scribe but added some words with his own hand. That Paul usually did this we see openly in many of his letters (1 Corinthians 6:21, Galatians 6:11, Colossians 4:18). He now points out that his greeting is a guarantee that the letter really comes from him. This does not need to mean that there were also false letters of Paul circulating, neither, as has been maintained, that we have before us a false letter that someone tried to make trustworthy by falsifying a "certificate of authenticity." Paul knew that men invoked him when they spread false messages. He could now assume that one or another who had been convinced that Paul, in fact, said all this would question if the letter really did come from Paul. So, it was best to once and for all clarify that it was he and no one else who spoke here.

Paul references his name and his handwriting when with his own hand he now repeats the final greeting that the scribe had just set to paper. He changes "The Lord" to "The grace of our Lord Jesus Christ" and thereby gives us a reminder of what was the most important of all the inexhaustible meanings that lay in the word "Lord" for early Christendom.

FIRST TIMOTHY
Introduction

The Pastoral Epistles

The two letters to Timothy and the letter to Titus are often called "the pastoral epistles." "Pastor" means shepherd. That something is "pastoral" means that it has to do with the work of a pastor in the congregation. These three letters are directed to leaders of the church and give them counsel and directives for their work. They have been called pastoral epistles since the beginning of the eighteenth century.

So, they are directed to individual persons, and not to any particular congregation. However, they are not really private letters of the same type as Philemon. They certainly contain their share of personal counsel, for example, that Timothy should not drink just water for the sake of his health, but most of them are intended to come before a congregation's attention and realm of understanding. Certain parts of them are reminiscent of a church order.

The Genre of Pastoral Epistle

In style and content these three letters are very similar. At the same time, they distinguish themselves plainly from all the other letters of Paul that have been preserved. Every reader of the Bible notices this. Sometimes there are differences of approximately the same magnitude as between a rector's letter of agreement and a Biblical meditation—that despite all differences can admittedly be written by the same bishop, even in our own day.

The differences show themselves in a characteristic matter in the polemics against false doctrine and false teachers. In the congregational letters, Paul enters the melee with the opponents and refutes them with the word of Scripture. He knows that the false teachers have been heard. He appeals and argues, sometimes even from a disadvantage that he is aware of. He speaks personably and passionately. In the pastoral epistles, argumentation only appears as an exception. The matter is settled. It is calmly established with apostolic authority that the false teachers are wrong and that a person should not have anything to do with them. That which is true teaching—"the sound doctrine" as it is called—continues to be confessed and commonly recognized.

This secure consciousness—that there is a recognized apostolic teaching and order that is important to hold on to—gives the pastoral epistles their stamp. In the congregational epistles Paul fights to make the true doctrine known and recognized. Here it is so well known that essential parts of it, not the least in questions of the cross and redemption, hardly need to be mentioned but in passing. The tone is also different, calm and factual, instructive and full of practical details, often a typical "ordinary prose" sometimes with a touch of constitutional text.

Question of Authorship

At the beginning of the 19th century, it was for the first time seriously questioned whether Paul himself could have written these letters. Since then, the question has been discussed endlessly without reaching any unified consensus. One group of scholars seriously regards all three of the letters as "deutero-Pauline," written a generation after Paul's death. Others hold the so-called "fragment-hypothesis" and think that fragments of true letters have been blended together with new material. A third group, that has many from the historical-critical school, maintains that they originate from Paul, even if some figure that he used a coworker as a secretary.

The discussion touched earliest of all on the question of whether the conditions that the pastoral letters witness to really existed already in the 60s. Many scholars thought that there had been no established congregational organization before the post apostolic period, and neither any established doctrine of the church. The gnostic heresy, that the letters address, is dated by some to the 2nd century. However, it has now been shown that gnosticism is as old as Christendom. It was contested already in Colossians. As far as the "doctrine of the church" is concerned, the congregational letters clearly witness that there was a "paradosis," a firmly developed apostolic tradition that Paul with great emphasis claimed everywhere in the congregations. The Acts of the Apostles show how congregations designated congregational leaders already at the very beginning. To declare all such information as a-historical, as some sought to do, is completely arbitrary, especially when a person can with good reason assert that Luke wrote Acts around the year 62. In a passage of First Corinthians (4:17) Paul says that he now plans to send Timothy to Corinth. He says: "He is my beloved and faithful son in the Lord. He shall remind you of my rules for a Christian life, as I have taught them everywhere in every congregation." Already here around the year 54, we have a situation that reminds us of the pastoral epistles: Timothy is sent on behalf of the apostles to help with the establishment of congregations according to an apostolic order that shall apply to all congregations.

Furthermore, if a reader analyses the style and language in the pastoral epistles, then he will conclude that they really could be written by Paul. Some have put in endless effort in studying the vocabulary. They know exactly how many words in the pastoral epistles have no counterpart in the congregational letters. They have attempted to show that many of these words only began to be used after 100 A.D. The counterargument has put in just as much effort to show that most of them were found in circulation already in Paul's day and particularly in the Septuagint, (which is about a century older). It is hard to prove anything exactly with such word statistics. It can be convincing when a person observes that there are 306 words in the pastoral epistles that are otherwise not found in Paul's letters. However, the argument is less convincing when a person hears that in Romans there are 261 words in the same category. Yet it is still possible to ascertain certain facts with the help of such statistics, for example that the words in the pastoral epistles on average contain more letters and so are longer than in the congregational letters. This is a sign that the style is "heavier," less immediate and personal, more official and fiscal. It is this impression a man gets with a friendly read through.

Now a person must remember that both the vocabulary and style shift according to the subject that is being handled. If a person writes concerning the appointment of ecclesiastical ministers or the pastoral handling of false teachers, then a person has to use different words than if he writes about justification by faith. Still the impression remains that the pastoral letters speak their particular language. However, the scholars are deeply divided concerning how this fact should be interpreted.

The Three Theories

As we already mentioned, there are three theories here.

According to the first, the pastoral epistles are so-called "pseudepigrapha." This means that they are written by some unknown person who made use of Paul's name. A person usually considers that this happened around the year 100, in the face of countering a looming gnostic threat within the congregations and consolidating the church upon an apostolic foundation. Many naturally ask if it is reasonable to believe that an earnest Christian, because the author had to have been that, would have made himself guilty of such a deceit. The objection is usually answered saying that a person is not right to talk of deceit. In antiquity it was regarded as fully admissible to publish writings under the name of a deceased teacher, if a person was convinced that he correctly reproduced what the great teacher had taught. The pastoral epistles would have come to fulfill a function that we in our day regard as completely legitimate: to interpret and congenially render the Bible's message in a new era. Before this argument a person still asks if it could have ever been regarded as legitimate to insert small fictitious greetings and errands (as in the question of the coat and books in Troas) to give the appearance that it really was a true book from Paul himself.

The second theory, "the fragment hypothesis," has an answer to give to that objection. It essentially says that here we have fragments from Paul's actual letters, perhaps very personal and untheological, which were expanded and provided with commentary on the actual problems of the day, in the firm conviction that this was what Paul would have said if he had lived. The difficulty with this theory is above all that the adherents of this theory are not united concerning what they should regard as true "fragments." It is also difficult to understand why they are so unevenly distributed, with a great many of them inserted in the second epistle to Timothy and hardly any in the first.

So, the third theory remains and proposes that here we are dealing with an actual letter of Paul. The adherents maintain that the letter's veracity was never questioned in antiquity (aside from possibly Marcion) and that already in a letter from Bishop Polycarp (around 115) we find a series of allusions to them (however, without it expressly saying that it is Paul who is cited). Further, a person emphasizes that the differences with the congregational epistles have a natural explanation. In the pastoral epistles Paul writes to his nearest and most faithful coworkers. Thus, he can speak calmly and with obvious authority. He does not need to fight for the truth. The recipients know the apostolic doctrine thoroughly. What they need is concrete counsel and instruction. This instruction consists in large part of rules that Paul does not need formulate when he writes. On the contrary, it is a question of whether accepted instructions apply in cooperation with others, often repeated and so not originally Pauline.

Some have also emphasized how original that congregational order still is. Around the year 100 the development was in full speed toward the "monarchical episcopacy" with a bishop in every congregation, but in the pastoral epistles it is still obvious that there are many "bishops" in every place, as the order was in Philippi when Paul wrote his epistle to them.

The gnostic heresy that was fought is also of an earlier type. The Gnostics are still found within the congregations. They even appear to be teachers. They could hardly do that by the turn of the century.

If a person adheres to this theory, he must explain the distinctive style in these letters. It can partly be explained by the subject matter and by the fact that a church order is never the work of one man. However, a person must also figure that Paul used a coworker or secretary of the type that not only writes according to dictation but can be given a commission to work out a whole epistle after more or less receiving detailed instructions from his commissioner. There is reason to believe that Paul had such a coworker during his imprisonment, for example, when he wrote Colossians. Those who work out such a letter must obviously be very familiar with the subject it deals with and know the commissioner's train of thought. The contents of the pastoral epistles are in large part precisely that which a coworker to the apostle ought to know inside and out. The many enumerations that are so typical for the style of the pastoral epistles often seem to be taken from some tutorial for Christian instruction.

So, when a draft has been completed Paul would have gone through it and made additions and changes. Then it could have been written out and the letter sent in his name. So, it has rightly been regarded as apostolic and gradually found its place in the canon.

In any case, everything indicates that it was the same coworker who carried the pen in these three letters. We do not know who it might have been. Some have guessed Luke because in one place (2 Timothy 4:11) it says: Luke is the only one who remains with me. However, for reasons of language it is extremely unlikely that Luke would have held the pen. We can only guess that it is a question of one of their faithful coworkers who knows and orderly renders the apostolic instruction and the commonly applied rules without any personal originality, and for precisely that reason was a well-suited secretary.

Some have asserted that some of the characteristics in the language of the pastoral epistles is reminiscent of language from the Christian writing from the time around the year 100 (the letters of Clement and Ignatius). If it were a young coworker of Paul's who held the pen in the pastoral letters, it can very well have been a certain stamp of this language that had begun to be spoken by the second-generation Christians, those who came to characterize preaching and instruction a century later.

Characteristic Key Words

The pastoral epistles contain their share of characteristic theological terms that are otherwise not found in Paul. Here he often speaks of "the sound doctrine" or sometimes "the sound word." This corresponds approximately with what we would call "true doctrine," though it also encompasses a way of life and all the rules that form it. The sound word comes from Jesus Christ (1 Timothy 6:3). It is sound, healthy, and wholesome, in the same way as everything that comes from God. False doctrine is then something that makes a person sick, skewed, and distorted.

Another such typical word used to be translated with "God fearing" (in Greek *eusebia*). A man could also render it with "religion" or with "piety." In the same way it then had the meaning and use for all sorts of piety. Among the heathen it had a good sound. Christians seem to have avoided using it for their own faith from the beginning. However, here it is used without a second thought concerning Christianity. Perhaps it had begun to be used in mission work so that it was conceivable and accessible.

Time and Place

Proceeding from the last mentioned of the three theories, as the following commentary does, we are immediately confronted with the question of where and when these letters could have been written. Can a person fit them into some particular point in Paul's life, as is described in the Acts of the Apostles?

Attempts of this manner have been made. One of the last, by the, in many regards, radical critic John A. T. Robinson—posits that First Timothy was written when Paul was on his way from Ephesus to Corinth (according to Robinson's dating in the fall of 55) while the letter to Titus came about around the year 57 during the trip to Jerusalem, and Second Timothy during the imprisonment in Caesarea in 58.

Already in antiquity people had a different theory that is still common among those who believe the pastoral epistles are authentic. There are many old records—the oldest already from the year 96—that Paul was released and continued his mission work even over to Spain. In the year 300, the church historian Eusebius believed Paul made further trips through Greece, and the pastoral letters came about during this time, so sometime shortly after the year 62. We will return to this matter.

Timothy

Timothy is the coworker of Paul that is most often mentioned in the New Testament. He is mentioned no fewer than twenty-five times, six of those in Acts. His father was Greek and his mother a Christian Jew from Lystra in Galatia. Paul learned to know him there on his second missionary trip, perhaps around the year 50, and took him with him. From that day he seems to have been an inseparable coworker, who only left Paul when he was sent on the apostle's behalf. So, he followed him to Europe, through Macedonia and to Athens. There he was sent away to learn how it stood with the newly established congregation in Thessalonica and came back with good news. Then he was the Apostle's faithful coworker in Corinth. There he was later sent on an important task from Ephesus when Paul ended up there during his third missionary journey. Some years later he is sent from the same city to Macedonia, and when Paul finally travels to Jerusalem, he was with him on the trip. During the imprisonment, he apparently remained with Paul because he is mentioned in the letter to Colossae, Philippi, and Philemon. During the years he was sent to Philippi, and in this context, Paul gives him the testimonial, "For I have no one like him, who will be genuinely concerned for your welfare." (Philippians 2:20)

According to early church tradition, Timothy was the first bishop in Ephesus and suffered martyrdom there. At least the first mentioned record seems to be true to the extent that he was the apostle's replacement in the city, according to what this letter says. As such he had a place approximately corresponding to what the bishop would later be.

1 Timothy 1

1-2 Heading

The superscription shows us already that this is not a private letter that we have in front of us. Rather it is an official letter in which Timothy receives obligations that he will forward and enforce on the basis of the Apostle's orders. In a private letter Paul would not have needed to remind him that he had his commission from God and from Christ Himself. However, here he writes on behalf of the office and what he writes reaches men who perhaps need to be reminded of who it is who speaks.

Paul calls Timothy his "true son." He called all whom he had helped to faith his children. That Timothy is a true son means that he really follows his spiritual father in everything. So, the congregation ought to follow him.

The greeting is for the most part formulated as they normally are with Paul, especially in his later letters. That God is called "Savior" is however something that only comes about in the pastoral epistles. Otherwise, Paul uses the word for Christ. To his customary wishes for grace and peace, Paul has here added "mercy." Perhaps this is because an old Christian usually thinks that the greatest of all miracles is God's mercy. A little further on Paul speaks about just this mercy he himself experienced.

3-7 Timothy's Commission

Without any introduction Paul goes straight to the matter and gives Timothy his directives. He repeats what he has said before. Here we have the only hint regarding the context in which the letter was written. Paul had been on the way to Macedonia and enjoined Timothy to remain in Ephesus. The text does not make it clear whether or not they were both in Ephesus at the time, only that Paul was traveling in Macedonia as a goal and let Timothy stay in Ephesus. There is no such situation described in Acts. This is one of the reasons that one assumes that this deals with a trip Paul made later when he had been acquitted in Rome.

That Timothy should stay in Ephesus has its particular reasons. There were some who spread false doctrine. Paul literally says that they "teach differently," meaning differently than Paul does. So, they were heterodox, like those "preaching to you a gospel contrary to the one you received," as Paul says to the Galatians (1:9).

We receive a hint about what the matter meant. They came with "myths," perhaps of the same type as is spoken about in Titus (1:14), namely "Jewish myths," and therefore "endless genealogies." Most likely it is a matter of an early form of Gnosticism that uses the Old Testament for fantastical speculations concerning the world's origin and the essence of existence. It was a matter of a misuse of God's

Word that distorted it so that it was no longer law and gospel, but only gave rise to theories and speculations that could seem new and interesting enough but neither led to repentance or faith. This is not the Word's purpose, Paul says. So, the Word's office is not exercised. Here Paul speaks about an "administration" that God ordained, and which shall happen in faith. Because he speaks of teachers in the congregation, it ought to be their exercise of office he thinks of.

The injunction that Timothy is now to give the false teachers has the same purpose that all preaching should have: it is to result in the love that comes from a true faith, faith in Christ, that which alone can give a clean heart and a good conscience. It is just this that a person pushes away when he begins to use the Word for other purposes than that which God has set. It was this that happened in Ephesus.

8-11 The Right Use of the Law

Paul has called the heterodox chatterboxes who orate wide and broadly but do not grasp the essential. As always, this touches on the relationship between law and gospel. Our human reason takes it for granted that the law is the right way to God. Apparently, the heterodox have taken this for granted. However, the law is not for the righteous, Paul says. A person becomes righteous through faith in Jesus. Then he receives the Holy Spirit, and the whole of life comes to rest on a different foundation than that of the law. The law is to expose and condemn sin. So it shall also be preached. We shall know that there really are things that God condemns. Paul gives a long account, on such as is distinctive to the style of the pastoral epistles. He follows the order of the decalogue, in each case when it applies to the commandments of the second table, and lists sins against the different commandments in turn and order: parent abuse, murder, fornication, theft, and false witness. That "enslavers" here seems to stand as an example of breaking the seventh commandment can be because slave trading and kidnapping were so often connected. That all this that Paul lists is really condemned by God, indicates that it belongs to the gospel that Paul received his commission to preach. The gospel does not consist in all that can be allowed, but in all that can be forgiven through faith in Jesus.

12-17 The True Gospel

The true gospel is that for which Paul received his commission to preach. He himself was a living example of what it meant. Grace flooded over the brim. He who was the worst among all of Christianity's enemies met undeserved and inconceivable mercy. Here it showed that Jesus really had come to call sinners, not the righteous. Paul is very well conscious that he is the chief of sinners. He hints that it was just his false belief in the law that made him into a persecutor. Then he encountered Christ and the truth about Him, that he calls here "the firm word." "Firm" means reliable, worthy to build the whole of your life upon. With Christ came faith and with faith came love. Paul could have declined to receive the firm word. Then he would have remained in ignorance and unbelief and hopelessly lost. However, Paul would not consider it a virtue that he received the gospel. He knew that it depended on God's mercy that he was saved, and he breaks out into a "doxology," one of these joyous cries of thanksgiving that time after time breaks his train of thought in these letters, just as certainly broke forth during the early Christian worship.

18-20 To be Faithful to your Ordination

Now Paul proceeds to that which we call a church order. So, he reminds Timothy of the commission that he has received. He has been sent to Ephesus in order to lead and organize the ecclesiastical life on behalf of the Apostle. Timothy has been ordained to this commission. (We will hear more about this matter later.) Here Paul only names one of the most important elements in such a rite which corresponds to that which we would call an ordination or installation, namely the prophetic word. It happens that the prophet directly pointed to some particular person with a particular commission (so as it happened when Paul and Barnabas were sent out on the first mission trip, Acts 13:1f). It can also be a question of a prophetic admonition and encouragement that reminded the ordinand of his duties. Here it seems closest to dealing with something in this way. Timothy had been encouraged to "fight the good fight," to do it in faith and to keep his conscience clean. Paul mentions a warning example to men who apparently had been close coworkers to him and Timothy, (they are also named in 2 Timothy). They have lost their faith since they began to do such as the conscience had warned them against. This must have dealt with serious things because Paul says that he "handed them over to Satan," in the same way as he once did (and enjoined the congregation to do) with the coarse sinner in Corinth (1 Corinthians 5). We do not know exactly what this means, but it ought to have touched upon some form of excommunication and expulsion from the congregation.

That Paul mentions Hymeneus and Alexander by name is one such detail that indicates that we are dealing with a true Pauline epistle. It is hard to see what function such a mention should have had one generation later.

1 Timothy 2

1-7 Concerning the Prayers during the Divine Service

Now there follows instruction for life in the congregation. That they should begin with the divine service was so obvious that Paul does not once say that it is this he is now thinking about. The one thing he needs to bring forth is that a person may not neglect the common prayer and that it should include thanksgiving and intercession. The intercession should apply to all people, even the heathens, first and foremost the Caesar and all who govern. This prayer is also needed for the congregation's sake. The heathen state had God's commission and kept order with power. If it did that then the church could also live and work in peace and tranquility. However, the prayer also applied to the salvation of those in power. Of course, God wants all people to be saved and learn to know the gospel. There is only one God, and the only way to Him goes through the one mediator, Christ, He who Himself became man to atone for our sins. As a Christian, it is impossible to comfort oneself saying that perhaps there are other ways to God, and that one should leave everyone to believe as they want. However, Christians know that before a person speaks with a man about God, it is best to speak to God about the man.

If Christ's unique standing in the world should be witnessed to "when the time was right," it was now. Christians knew the answer. Paul knew it better than anyone else, and he reminds them one more time of the commission he received. He is the herald that was sent with the Great King's message and shall cry out that it was he who draws out. He is the "teacher" and the "instructor" of the gentiles. It is the same word that is used in the gospels for Jesus and is usually translated "Master." It was something incredible to be made a representative of Jesus, His fully authorized envoy with a commission that applied to all gentiles. It could sound like arrogance, and his opponents said that it was. However, Paul swears he is speaking the truth. He did not need to say this to Timothy, but rather to those who "taught others."

8-15 Men and Women in the Divine Service

They shall thus pray everywhere, or "in every place" as the word essentially means, where Christians are gathered for divine service; men shall "lift their hands" according to the custom of the time. The prayer is really not something "purely internal" as one often hears among us. Before God, the whole man is engaged, and gestures are as completely natural at prayer as when we speak to one another. However, the heart shall also take part. So, Paul says, as it is literally translated, that men should "lift holy hands," an expression that approximately corresponds to what we mean by praying devotionally, from the heart, righteously and without trying to sweep certain sins away and keep them in peace. A person also prays without old grudges in the heart, and "without doubt" (or as it might also be translated "without disagreement").

The women should do the same. Paul gives some instruction concerning the outer appearance. Certainly, a Christian woman can adorn herself, but she does it in a manner that "befits women who live piously." They who do not believe have their eyes upon her. They will notice that which is essential for her.

Then Paul comes to an issue that he first dealt with already in 1 Corinthians (14:34ff). Can women serve as the congregation's teachers during the divine service? We may remember that "to teach" in the New Testament means to bring the gospel forth for the congregation. So it is not a question of instruction in school, but to speak of God's ways in the congregation as their "shepherd and teacher" (Ephesians 4:11). The instruction during the divine service could take the form of a conversation. We have many examples of this in Acts. It is closest to the form of instruction that Paul thinks about here when he says that women shall listen to it quietly and themselves not "step up as teachers." She shall do this in "all submission," as it says literally. The word "submit" is used (as usual in the New Testament) concerning God's good order that a person submits to with joy when one believes. It is not a question of propriety or human rules, that a person so easily connects to the English expression "submit yourself." In order to translate the New Testament meaning, a person can best translate it with "enter into God's order."

What then follows ought to be seen against the background of gnostic teaching and thought that Paul time and time again turns against in his pastoral letters. We have received a good picture of these thoughts through a remarkable find that was made in 1945 by a few poor farmers in Upper Egypt. It was an entire little library that was hidden in clay jars in a cairn sometime around 400. When all came to daylight, there were over fifty writings, more or less damaged that then ended up in the Museum in Cairo.

Here we have a far fuller picture of Gnosticism than we had before. It was that age's ecumenical movement of the world that gladly borrowed from other religions. From Judaism it had taken a variety of concepts like the story of man's creation and the fall into sin, but the Old Testament belief in God had been changed entirely. Essentially, Gnosticism says that the true God is unknowable, nameless, hidden at an unreachable distance. From him proceeds a lower divinity that is conceived as bisexual "mother-father" or as feminine. The feminine deity has many names: Pistis, Sophia, Epinoia, Ennoia, Barbelo. There is a variety of variants from the myth of the first mother to everything. She was mostly conceived of as that which through some mistake gave birth to a new god, a creator god, the demiurge, Yaldabaoth, or whatever he is called. (The Gnostics loved to stack up strange sounding names on heavenly powers.) It is he who is the god of the Old Testament, an imperfect and often evil power. With the help of his evil angels, he created the human body, but he was not able to give it life. Life came first when the feminine divinity breathed in some of her force of light into it. The first man came forth and was "androgynous," man and woman at the same time. Yaldabaoth and his evil assistants will come to the feminine light power and carve out a piece of Adam and create the woman. So Eve certainly received a great part of the heavenly light power, but the demiurge manages to seduce her. He awakened the sexual drive and institutes marriage. Then comes death, who enslaves the people. Salvation now consists in that a feminine deity opens man's eyes so that they understand what a tragedy happened when they became man and woman. The deliverance already begins in the moment that the Bible calls the fall into sin. It was namely the delivering goddess who hid herself in the tree of knowledge and spoke through the serpent getting Eve to eat so that she received understanding. Then the same divine power worked to open the eyes of men so that they see what misfortune lies behind the difference between the sexes and say no to it, and thereby also to marriage, sexual life, and fostering children. Then they are on the way back to the primordial state where there was neither man nor woman. The Gnostics ascribed special significance to Mary Magdalena. She loved Jesus more than any of the apostles. She was the one who constantly followed Jesus. The apostles took offense, but Jesus said: "I will lead her to make her a man. For every woman that makes herself a man shall enter into the kingdom of heaven." Among the newly-found writings there is a "gospel of Mary" where Mary Magdalena instructs all the apostles concerning the revelation she received from the Lord. Andrew doubts that Christ really has said all this, and Peter begins to ask her if the Savior really said this to her individually, this that he had not said to them. However, Levi rebukes him and says: "If the Savior considered her worthy who then are you to reject her? And so, Mary is right."

These thoughts are, as was said, encountered in many different variations within Gnosticism, but permeating throughout is that the heavenly Epinia-Pistis-Sofia, or whatever she is called, is actively teaching men to free themselves from the false creator god, and from marriage and fostering children so that no man needs to be born into this world any longer. Women who have been illuminated in this manner are "The Mother/Father seed." They can step forth with authority before both men and women and teach them the truth.

Against the background of such thoughts, what Paul means becomes understandable. The Gnostics said that Jesus had overturned the order of creation and gave women full authority to rule over men. Paul answers that precisely this is something that he, as Christ's apostle, cannot permit. When he speaks about "ruling over men," he uses a very unusual word (authentein) that also occurs in Gnosticism. It means to exercise absolute authority and to provide laws with authority against which it does not do to resist. Christian men know that there is one such authority, but it comes only from God. When God's Word is brought forth in the congregation according to God's commission, it has this authority. In the early church a person knew that apostles and prophets and true servants of the Word could speak with this authority. Now the Gnostics argued that women too could do this. Paul answers that it is not God's purpose. A woman shall not step forth as teacher and thereby "rule over men." Some translations say[1] "rule over her man," but the context shows that this is a question about the divine service and the expression seems to mean to step forth as one sent by God to teach and lead. To "listen in silence" also seems to aim at the instruction during divine service. Here Paul uses the same word as just now (where it is translated "in silence"; the Greek word *hesychia*, means calm, quiet, attentive).

Then Paul reminds them of how the Gnostics turned the gospel narrative upside down. It was a fact that Adam was created first and Eve carried out no deliverance in Paradise. On the contrary, she was deceived. Otherwise, Paul usually describes the fall into sin as "Adam's" fall. A person cannot reasonably draw the conclusion from his word in this place that he would regard Adam to have been without sin. Rather, the true meaning is that Adam consciously trespassed God's commandment, but that as Eve was deceived with some unsustainable argument. What Paul wants to get at is the Gnostic claim that Eve represented the divine wisdom and proved how well suited she was to mediate it to the men. The truth was that she was impressed by a false teaching.

Then follows a few words that are often regarded as disparaging to women, but in actual fact will assert her value against the gnostic disparagement. For Gnostics, a woman was precisely as woman and mother a despised and unclean creature. She must be like the man to have any worth. On the contrary, Paul says. Salvation comes to the woman not by her ceasing to have children, but, on the contrary, while she does it, if she really possesses a faith that shows itself in love and holiness. The cause is the same for man and woman. Before God, the man and woman have the very same value with the same opportunity for salvation by the same means.

In some foreign translations it says that the woman shall be saved "through" childbearing. This has awakened great pondering and many discussions, but it really is just a question of a bad translation. The construction that is used in the Greek text can actually also denote a concomitant (not a cause). Paul uses it, for example, when he says that we (in the hope of that which we don't see) wait "*with endurance*"—not on the ground of—(Romans 8:25) or when he speaks of the danger of eating "*with* a bad conscience"—not on the ground of!—(Romans 14:20), or he tells of writing a letter "*with* many tears" (2 Corinthians 2:4).

This section reminds us that there are two different ways to read the Scriptures. For Jesus and the whole apostolic church, it was God's Word. The decisive thing today is not if one reads early history, that which Paul here invokes, as exact history or as stories that in symbolic form give us a message from God about us and the world. In both cases there is something common and inviting

---

[1] The Swedish translation of 1917.

in that which the narration says. On the contrary, it is if one dismisses them as an expression of incorrect performances that do not come from God, then a person is on the path of Gnosticism.

What Paul says here is only a bit of what the New Testament has to say, but this bit fits within the whole picture. Our value is not that we are the same. We are as different as limbs in the body and just this difference lies in God's good purpose. Man and woman are not similar and do not have identical tasks. The apostolic church had nothing against a woman doing an independent job (like Lydia from Thyatira who dealt in expensive dye), or that she witnessed to or instructed others about Christ in her home (like Priscilla). However, when it came to stepping forth as a teacher in the congregation and thereby as a shepherd for God's flock and housefather in God's family, a person had one of God's given orders that he knew he must not overstep.

1 Timothy 3

1-7 The Demand of Bishops

Now follows a list of the conditions that must be met by the man who would become a bishop or deacon. These offices are already mentioned in Philippians (1:1). We still use the Greek names in Anglicized forms, but they don't quite designate the same thing. In Greek, a bishop is called *episkopos*, and the word essentially means supervisor or director. There are many of them in every congregation. Not before around the year 100 did one begin to find a lone bishop as leader of a church in a certain area. The congregations' "angels" in the Book of Revelation could have been such leaders. Around 110 the martyred Bishop Ignatius claimed in his letter that it is the right order. The word bishop had thereby received the approximate meaning it has since retained. However, in the era of the pastoral epistles the matter was completely different. So, a person usually does not translate the Greek *episcopos* with bishop when we encounter it in the New Testament but says "congregational director" or something that hints at what the matter is about.

It is a "noble task," Paul says. Perhaps this is for the sake of the heterodox that he emphasizes this. When we then hear what would be demanded of a bishop's candidate, we can hardly escape being surprised by how elementary the demands are. He may not be weak for liquor or money, he may not be a troublemaker nor violent, which can go straight to tangibility. He may not have a bad reputation among those who "stand outside," those who are not Christians. Here, as in many other places in Paul's letters, we receive a reminder of what sort of life many of the Christians had beforehand, and how a person constantly had to fight with that which they carried with them from paganism. Every missionary who has had the experience of forming a congregation from purely new converts knows what this is like. We should be cautious of believing that an early Christian congregation consisted completely of dedicated people. Rather it was a collection of firebrands taken from the fire and among whom several still smelled of smoke. So, it is important to see to it that the men in the positions of leadership were able to show just how old the past really was. They would be "irreproachable" so that no one would have good reason quarrel with their behavior. In this context, it is also mentioned that an episcopus should be "a one-woman man." Even here it is enough to ask about an elementary Christian demand. Roman law permitted a man to have concubines. Loose relations were not seen as offensive. However, a Christian was to live in strict monogamy and not divorce. To divorce in order to take a different wife could be seen as a type of polygamy, and a congregational director was not to be guilty of that.

Among the positive characteristics named, most are common: respectable and wise, sensible and moderate, just as the ability to oversee his own house and children. Here the same word as was used in the question of a "director" of the congregation is used intentionally. The congregation was God's family. Should a man be able to direct God's family, so must he be able to direct his own. The director may not be newly converted. The congregation in Ephesus had at this point (if the letter is written after Paul's emancipation) lasted so long that there were experienced and tested men. If a person placed a new convert in this position it could go to his head.

It is interesting to see what is not mentioned. There is the personal faith in Jesus. There is the willingness to witness, suffer, and sacrifice for their faith. Such must have been assumed as rather obvious to all who belonged to the congregation. So the only one mentioned in particular is the ability to teach. This is not found with everyone. To instruct was one of the most important and most demanding tasks that the congregational director would engage in.

8-13 The Requirements of Deacons

Deacons did not simply have what we would call "deaconate" tasks. They were coworkers with the bishops, and it is striking that it largely poses the same demand on their personages and manner of life as on the bishops. We may hear that they too should be tested before they are appointed. Bishops must have also been subjected to such tests. This does not mean a probationary service but an examination of properties and character. Women are also spoken about here, perhaps deacons, though some believe that the word points to the deacons' wives, because the women coworkers in the congregation are dealt with in a particular chapter later.

A decisive Christian qualification is mentioned here: the mystery of faith in a pure conscience. Faith's mystery in a pure conscience. Faith's mystery is the gospel, the great mystery of God that was hidden through the centuries but is now revealed through Jesus Christ. The deacons must have grasped and received this, and they shall have preserved it in a pure conscience so that there is no occasion for double-dealing or carrying unresolved sins. Even in where deacons are concerned, it is emphasized that it is an office that has authority when it is carried out in the right manner.

14-16 The Church's Confession of Christ

Paul justifies why he writes the letter, though he himself plans on coming. He might be delayed, and it can be good for Timothy to have these rules in black and white. It is a question of something so infinitely important for life in "God's house," God's temple on earth, the Christian church because this is "a pillar and buttress of the truth." By truth he means the truth that God wants all to come to knowledge of

(1 Timothy 2:4). This truth is the whole of God's salvific work. It is the truth that the church is to proclaim and embody here in the world; Christ Himself is head of the church. So, the Church is far more than an association of men who have the same faith and the same goal for their work. She is the foundation upon which the truth rests here in the world, the pillar that holds it up. For just this reason her members have a great responsibility. They shall stand as witnesses concerning the great mystery that they may look into. And then there follows a citation from a hymn that was sung during the divine service. It is obvious that it deals with Christ, but the exposition goes quite wide. In any case, a person can on good grounds perceive that it is built on three parts, each consisting of two lines that contrast with each other. In the first it is said that Christ stepped forth in the form of man, or "in the flesh," as it literally says. He comes in lowliness. He was rejected. Yet "in the Spirit," it showed who He was. This is the same as Paul says in the beginning of Romans (1:3f): According to the "flesh," He was of David's lineage, but of the Spirit, He has been shown to be God's Son, "clothed in the power of God, finally raised from the dead." The other part deals with how this mystery of Christ is known and proclaimed to the whole universe. The angels behold it with their eyes, but here on the earth it is proclaimed as a message that must be heard and believed. The third part means the response to God's great proclamation. We here on earth, who "walk by faith and not by sight," we believe the message. However, Christ Himself has entered His glory. No faith is needed there. It is likely that there was more to the hymn. If not, then in any case those who sang it knew that Christ would come back in glory and that the faith would be turned into sight.

1 Timothy 4

1-5 The Danger of False Asceticism

A warning against the great apostasy that must come then follows. Jesus had prophesied it (Matthew 24:10f.). Luke says how he heard Paul speak of it (Acts 20:29f). "The Spirit" had expressly said it, likely even through the mouths of the early church prophets. Paul certainly means that the false teachers that Timothy has to contend with in Ephesus are children of this same spirit. The history of the world has entered its last epoch. The great final showdown between God and Satan has begun. No one knows when the end will come, but already now the powers are active, which will come to define the end of time.

All false teachings that draw men away from Christ have something demonic about them. Those who proclaim them do the devil's bidding, even if they speak about God. The picture of false teachers that is described here has certainly been drawn from the contemporary. It was a question of strict asceticism with powerful demands on people. A person was to live in celibacy, and there were many types of food and drink that a person was not allowed to taste. It may have been a matter of Gnostics. As we have already heard, there was a gnostic doctrine of salvation that rejected marriage. It could also have been a question of Judaizers who held to the purity laws in questions of food and drink, and like the monks of the Qumran thought that true fear of God required celibacy. Perhaps it touched on a blending of both. Gnosticism had an almost limitless ability to soak up other religions and deform them.

Paul—as a congenial teacher of Jesus—answers that everything God created was good. Certainly, there is much in creation that has been stained and adulterated by sin. (The meat that a person bought in the square may have been offered to idols.) However, this was of no importance if a person received it in faith, with "thanksgiving." Here Paul uses the word "eucharist" and things about the table prayer that Jesus and all the pious Jews prayed. A person blessed God for His gifts and received them from His hand. Most often there was a recitation of a psalm too. So, everything was sanctified "through the word of God and prayer." Those who tried to make themselves pure through asceticism were to know that they still were not pure. They must be "burned in their conscience." This was the worst form of hypocrisy, that which a person encountered with the pharisees.

6-11 The Blessing of True Doctrine

Again, we hear the sharp condemnation of the "godless myths," against which Timothy shall place "the good teaching" and "the word of faith." The opponents did not understand what faith was. They trusted in their lavish works and their great sacrifices. They loved to speculate with the help of reason, so as "religiously minded" men so often do. Against this, Paul places faith in the gospel. A person should train himself for godliness. The word "train" is the same for that which we have in "gymnastics." It was a Greek word for the physical training that they valued so highly. Paul knows that such can be beneficial, but only in a limited and relatively meaningless domain, namely for this life. Another interpretation says that Paul points to the ascetic "practices." In both cases, it is the same contrast to the "training" that applies both in this life and that which comes. This training consists in holding oneself near to Christ in faith and to receive help killing the old Adam and living in joy and thankfulness for forgiveness.

12-16 A True Shepherd

Timothy is still young. If this letter is written around the year 65, he ought to have been around thirty-five years old because he was very young when Paul took him into his service in Lystra, perhaps in the summer of 50. Now he would instruct (and perhaps correct) those who were twice his age. Paul reminds him that he can do it boldly even though he is much younger. A Christian proclaimer does not receive his authority through the maturity and experience we all receive through the years. The authority lies in a commission that he received from Christ. However, he shall be faithful to Christ not only in his word but also in his manner of life. The most essential is in his work, what he is to take time for and expend energy on, above all is the study of Scripture, to admonish and instruct, meaning to lead the divine service, preach, and care for souls. Books were expensive and scarce, so the reading of Scripture at the divine service was very important. First and foremost, a person read the Old Testament. However, as we shall see immediately, (1 Timothy 5:18), a person could already at this time speak of Jesus's Words as "Scripture." We know that even Paul's letters could be read during the divine service. With "admonition" can be meant both preaching and individual soul care. Even "instruction" can point to preaching but also encompasses all the instruction that was otherwise needed, for example, for those who would be baptized.

So, we learn that Timothy possessed a gift of grace, a charisma, that he received when he was ordained to his office. We do not know what charisma it may have been. Paul calls such gifts as the ability "to admonish" or "to instruct" or "to be a representative" charismas. In any case, if it was a gift then it was not to be left aside.

Here we also receive a glimpse of how it could go when someone was given a commission in an early congregation. It happened during the laying on of hands by the presbytery, thus a collegium of "elders" who led a congregation. Obviously, Paul also took part in the laying on of hands (2 Timothy 1:6). It went approximately the same way a Swedish ordination is done today, where the bishop and his assistants together lay their hands on the ordinand. Moses had already installed Joshua into his office through the laying on of hands (Numbers 27:18f) so that he became "filled with the spirit of wisdom" (Deuteronomy 34:9). Next to the laying on of hands came the prophetic word, perhaps in the form of Scripture reading, perhaps as a particular message through some of the prophets. Paul admonishes Timothy to always consider what he has been ordained to. This is to characterize his whole life. He is to give attention to two things: himself and his instruction, so to both his heart and his innermost relationship to God, that which no one sees, and to the practice of his office, his preaching, and his instruction, where all shall notice how their teacher himself grows in the spirit. This means to be saved and to save others. That a man can "save" others (naturally by leading them to Christ, the Savior), Paul says also in other contexts (Romans 11:14, 1 Corinthians 7:16).

1 Timothy 5

1-2 God's Family

The church is God's family. So, Timothy should treat all the elders as parents, the younger as brothers and sisters. There is no mention of any "middle-aged." Antiquity could hardly recognize the concept. In his best years a man was still young. Afterwards, he belonged to the old.

3-8 Care for Widows

Jews knew that it was a religious duty to take care of a widow, but there was no regularized provision by them. The mother congregation in Jerusalem took care of widows who could not provide for themselves. This demanded an extensive work that was first managed by the apostles, but which was quickly allowed to be handed over to particularly trustworthy men (Acts 6). In approximately the same way, it seems that this was done everywhere there was a new congregation. It was something new among the gentiles, and it certainly aroused attention. For the poor congregations it could be a very heavy task. Paul also gives the prescription that the congregation should only take care of those who really are alone. In the original it says, "true widows," and immediately thereafter is given the explanation that they are all alone. The others should be taken care of by children and grandchildren "as God would have it," according to the fourth commandment. It is thus a Christian duty to care for one's own, so long as it is possible, and not let others take care of them. This thankfulness that a person is obligated to towards his nearest kin is not something a person can just unburden himself with via the tax system.

However, now it was not only a question of taking care of widows. They could also have a task in the congregation. There were some among them for whom singleness had become a gift and a commission. They had been filled with God Himself. This gave them more time than before for prayer and intercession. They no longer desired anything else, approximately like the widow Hanna, who had been alone for more than fifty years and never left the Temple but served God with prayer and fasting, night and day (Luke 2:37). It is of such widows that Paul now speaks.

9-16 The Congregation's Widows

Here the original text speaks of to "be recorded as widows." This cannot really be a question of listing those who were entitled to support. A person did not place the demands on them that are listed here. They may have been a much greater crowd.

We know that the congregation in Rome around the year 250 had approximately 1,500 widows and others needing support. However, among these there was a small, clearly demarked group of particularly appointed "widows" who worked in the congregation. We hear a lot about them during the three centuries that then followed. It is apparent that it is the beginning of this ecclesiastical service that we encounter here, even if a person still does not strictly separate them as only for the congregation's support and those which also have a commission in this service. The later usually we call "congregational widows," but in the early church they were called as here—simply "widows." We would most commonly call their office diaconal. However, their foremost task was and remains to pray. An intercessor was considered to be at the very least as beneficial for their fellow men as those who were engaged in practical activities. These women had taken intercession as their calling when they became single. When they were received in the congregational service they promised to live completely for their commission and not marry. This appears from Paul's words that those who married had denied their faithfulness to Christ. Otherwise, young widows were advised to marry, but "the congregational widows" had obligated themselves with an oath. That they also had practical tasks is seen from the qualifications they would have. They would have fostered children and kept a guest house, where they received other Christians and did not hesitate to "wash the feet of saints" (as it literally says). In antiquity to wash feet was just as urgent as it is for us to wash hands. Usually, a slave or child helped with the matter, but Jesus had shown that no one is too great for such small services. Later we hear that just such tasks as to take care of children and of traveling strangers was entrusted to "widows."

Those who received this ministry would have lived in a true marriage (been a man's housewife, as it literally says). It can possibly also mean that she did not marry when she became single but took a new life situation as a calling. That she would be at least sixty years old is later adjusted to fifty or less, this meant a "question of order" of the type that both can and should be adopted for the situation.

It is noticed that a person had a share of irksome experiences with younger widows. They are recommended to get married. Earlier Paul had given the counsel that a person would rather remain unmarried (1 Corinthians 7), because the time was short and with thought of the "hard oppression we live under," but with the ensuing years, he had come to clarity that Christ could tarry before coming again, and it was God's will that life should continue.

17-22 Rules that Concern the Elders

Already during the first mission trip the Apostle had appointed elders everywhere in the newly established congregations (Acts 14:23) that would lead the congregation. They were responsible for preaching and instructing but also for administration and the economy of the congregation. So, they corresponded to both pastors

1 TIMOTHY 5:17-22

and the church counsel for us. The pastoral tasks quickly came to dominate. Our word "priest" comes from that Greek word for "elders" (*presbyteros*). It is the pastoral office that presbyter's office has continued.

The development from "elders" to "priest" is already on its way when this letter was written. There were "elders" who proved to be good congregational leaders, meaning good shepherds. This applied in particular to those who "made an effort" with the Word—so through diligent study of the Scriptures—and instructing. They should now be regarded worthy of a "double honor." This is a matter of some form of compensation, in money or in kind. Certainly, all the "elders" had secular work, and they were able to enjoy some minor compensation, approximately as elected stewards in our day. However, the more time that was occupied with congregational work, the greater reason there was to pay them for it, and this is what Paul demands here. Though he himself did not want to receive pay for his apostolic work, he strongly defended the right of pay for other apostles (1 Corinthians 9). We hear him now for the first time saying the same about the Word's servants in the local congregations.

A person can take notice that a word of Jesus (Luke 10:7) is cited as something that "the Scriptures say." There had long been written collections of Jesus's words, and there is reason to believe both the Gospels of Mark and Luke existed at this time. However, it would be a while before one commonly called these "Scriptures." On the other side, there was a question of "a word from the Lord" with uncontested authority. Some think that Paul here happened to use an expression that really only fit with the first citation. In such a case, the development would soon show that he still chose the right word.

As the Apostle's representative, Timothy had a place that approximately corresponds to a bishop's. To his tasks also belonged oversight of the priesthood. It was to him that a person would report complaints against the pastors. In such a case, they must be supported by two or three witnesses, Paul says. If they show to be justified, the sinner shall be admonished in the presence of his colleagues (or the whole congregation?) so that all see that a person does not go unreprimanded. Then Paul adds a very serious reprimand to Timothy to seriously denounce that which needs to be denounced and do it impartially and without letting personal sympathies or fear of discomfort be an obstacle to take issue with abuses.

To not "jump to conclusions" can mean to not be too quick with absolving sinners. It is likely that this indicates the ordination to the ecclesiastical offices. Timothy should know who he ordains. If the man is unworthy, he himself is responsible for that which this can lead to. And he who will lead others and correct their mistakes must see to it that he does not have anything to reproach himself for.

The "chosen angels" are archangels. That they are invoked here as witnesses together with the Father and the Son can be because on the day of accounting they shall be in the Son of Man's entourage.

23 Health Advice

As a reminder that we are dealing with living men, quite like ourselves, we learn in passing that Timothy was often sick and that it was the stomach that troubled him. Paul gives the very wise advice that he should be cautious about the water he drinks. He also ought to drink wine. Wine belonged to the daily diet. It was only ascetics that abstained from it. However, we have already seen that Christians disliked every abuse.

24-25 The Responsibility that a Person Does Not Escape

Amidst these admonitions, there comes a reminder that everything finally comes into the day. What people think plays a minor role. There are people whose faults hang out. These are so obvious that they come before sinners themselves when he shall be judged. This may now be by God or men. However, even the hidden sinners receive their deserved reward. They follow the guilty like a shadow. It is the same way with the good we do. Sooner or later, it comes into the day.

1 Timothy 6

1-2 Christians who are Slaves

Many Christians were slaves. When they were called "Slaves under a yoke," it likely pointed to their hard lot. Yet the word "yoke" can also indicate the yoke that Christ wants to put on all of us. In such a case, the expression means only "as slaves who have become Christian." There are two groups of these. Some serve under masters who are not Christian. They shall remember to behave that they do not shame Christianity. Others have Christian masters. They should see to it that they do not act carelessly, and not take their duties seriously enough because they have been treated as brothers and equals.

In an earlier letter Paul has also directed admonitions to slave owners. Here he apparently takes it for granted that they treat their slaves well and care for them as siblings in God's family. It gives us a hint at how Christianity began to influence societal relationships. A person could not yet consider abandoning slavery. Individual slaves could be emancipated, but it was not without further ado a benefit for them. A well-treated slave had approximately the same place as a member of the family. All social security was dependent on belonging to a family. For many slaves, to be emancipated only meant to be made penniless.

3-10 False Doctrine, Quarrelsome Disease, and Greed

Now for the third time there follows a warning against those who "teach otherwise." This is important with true teaching. The true doctrine "follows from the fear of God." That men are drawn to false doctrine shows that something with them is not right. On the one hand, false doctrine shows that they have not understood the gospel. They are inflated and eager for discussion. Their religion is of the type that the old man can thrive quite well with. He gives them occasion to dominate, to step up as debaters, to intrigue. That gives them status and economic benefits.

Here Paul engages the danger of the love for money. When he just spoke to the slaves about their duties toward their masters, a share of modern men would have certainly classified him as a typical product of a capitalist system. Here we can now see how much a mistake such a classification can be. They proceed from a scheme that does not fit the reality. A person cannot classify humanity as oppressors and the oppressed, and the gospel cannot be set on either side of a class war. We all have an oppressor within us. We have a natural inclination to transfer burdens and inconveniences on others. We would rather enjoy and receive than serve and work for the best of others. Christ shows us that this is sin and godlessness, but He offers us forgiveness and a new life that, along with a lot of other things, means to serve instead of being served. It is this lifestyle that Paul recommends to both slave and rich here.

So, Paul warns against this lifestyle that proceeds to be rich and get as much as possible. He does not idealize poverty in any way. People need food, clothing, and shelter, and they should have it. For "clothes and a roof over your head," there is a single word in Greek that means "something to cover you with" and which is used both for dwellings and clothes. That which plunges men into misery is the demand to constantly receive more. Here Paul uses an expression that the stoics also use and that is already found in the Old Testament. "Naked I came from my mother's womb, and naked shall I return," as Job said when he lost everything (1:21).

11-16 Appeal to Timothy

Finally, there comes a ceremonial and penetrating appeal to Timothy personally: "You servant of God…," essentially it says, "man of God." It means a man whom God has taken out of the world, into His kingdom and His service. What then follows can point to Timothy's baptism, but also, and probably more likely, to his ordination to his office. He has made "the good confession before many witnesses." The witnesses could have been presbyters who laid their hands on him (1 Timothy 4:14), and the congregation that was present. In actual fact it was a confession "before the all-knowing God and the great day of accounting that is before their eyes" (as it says in our ordination rite). And now the Apostle admonishes his spiritual son before God and before the Lord Christ who Himself once stood fast to "the good confession" when it meant life or death, namely that he was God's Son, the Savior, the King of Truth. He admonishes him to "fight faith's good fight." The word for fight that is used here is that which the Greeks used for sporting competitions. It means to go all in, like an athlete, to win. This means to preserve "unstained and free from reproach" that which Christ has commanded. Christ's Word and command can never be changed. In them hangs the church's future and the salvation of the church leader himself.

The appeal ends with a "doxology," a tribute to God's power and glory. It seems to be taken out of the liturgy, and some have believed that it is a part of the ordination rite that is cited here as a reminder of the seriousness it is to be set apart for God's service.

God's majesty is described here in a way that word for word could have been in the Old Testament. The Gnostics maintained that the God of the Old Testament was different than Jesus Christ's God and Father. However, the New Testament agrees in all that the Old says about God's exaltation and majesty, His holiness and zeal that is as a consuming fire for us sinners. What Christ has given us is not a new picture of God, but a new opportunity to stand before the Holy. God has not changed but He has created a changed situation, where through Christ, the Mediator and Redeemer, a sinner can be God's child.

17-19 Admonition to Those who are Rich

What now follows seems to be an addition to that which came directly before about the dangers of wealth. Perhaps it was added when the letter had already been completed. Here we learn that wealth is not evil in all circumstances. If a person himself belongs to God body and soul, so one's earthly possessions are also His, and the person himself becomes merely a steward. A person escapes the danger of making money the fundamental basis for life and that in which a person finds security, or as a measure of worth that makes it that he himself receives status among men and in his own eyes. Instead, a person can use them in God's service to the benefit and joy for other people. The man can both have them and be without them. A Christian lays everything in God's hands and escapes anxiety. He lives in faith and thereby wins what is "truly life."

20-21 The Final Reminder

In many of Paul's letters there is at the end a handwritten added greeting. Often it is a last warning for something that is wrong, and then Paul usually does not mince his words. He does not mince his words here either. First comes a positive admonition that gives a final summary of what Timothy may hear in this letter: Guard the deposit entrusted to you. "The deposit entrusted to you" is expressed in Greek with a single word that lacks any correspondence in English (*paratheke*). The best a person can do is the word deposit. It means something that has been deposited, an entrusted treasure, that shall be guarded with love and preserved for coming generations. Even in the congregational epistles Paul talks about this holy tradition that comes from Christ through the apostles, but there he uses the word "*paradosis*." So, Paul emphasizes yet once more that Christianity stands and falls with faithfulness to that which once and for all has been given to us through Christ and His apostles.

Then follows the warning. Now it is said in clear text what is the great danger: "what is falsely called knowledge." In the Greek this knowledge is *gnosis*, and it is Gnosticism that has been pointed out and characterized as "irreverent babble and contradictions." Timothy shall turn away from the Gnostics. There is no talk about any dialogue. Certainly, Gnosticism wants to pose as a modernized form of Christianity, but Paul means that it does not deserve the Christian name and that it does not deserve to be taken up in debate.

As all letters in antiquity, it also finishes with a little farewell wish. It sounds strange that a letter to a single person ends: Grace be to you (all). But there are examples of the matter in other preserved papyrus letters. And it is not excluded that here Paul intentionally includes all of them who in some way or another should participate in what he has written.

SECOND TIMOTHY
Introduction

Paul's Second Letter to Timothy contains a series of notices concerning named individuals, over twenty passages. Eighteen of them are coworkers, either faithful or fallen. Half of these are mentioned in other letters of Paul or in Acts, in some cases both. The rest are unknown to us. This information concerning mostly uninteresting people and their movements has often been set forth as evidence for this letter's authenticity. A person can naturally posit that they have been positioned there in order to give the appearance of authenticity but then a person must explain why nothing like it appears in the First Letter to Timothy. And why has the imposter not seen to it that the information could fit simply and painlessly into the picture of the Apostle's travels that we received in Acts and the epistles?

It is namely this that a person cannot do. The difficulty is so great that even in the early church some thought that it must touch upon a letter from a second imprisonment and not that which is talked about in Acts. Some have assumed from this that Paul was acquitted when his case was finally taken up in the highest court in about the year 62. It is also possible that the case was set aside because the Jews did not show up within the given time frame. They essentially knew that they themselves could be punished if the accusations were false. After the acquittal, it seems Paul had realized his old plan to travel to Spain. He mentions it already in Romans (15:24). That it became a reality is at least very likely. In First Clement (written in Rome in 96) it says that he went "even to the furthest west."

Some have assumed that thereafter Paul made one or two trips eastward through his old mission field. It works to fit together the pastoral letter's notices into a conceivable travel route (though a person should remember that these are guesses and that many other combinations are conceivable). According to this theory, Paul should have worked in Ephesus and the province of Asia, partially under strong opposition from the gnostic circles who had influence in the congregations

(2 Timothy 1:15, and 4:14). Then he returned to Macedonia after he left Timothy in Ephesus. First Timothy is dated to this period. Thereafter Paul may have visited Crete together with Titus. While Titus stayed in Crete, he turned back and met Timothy in Ephesus as he had promised (1 Timothy 3:14). It was approximately at this time that he wrote Titus. After he separated from Timothy, he visited Miletus (2 Timothy 4:20) and gradually travelled the usual path to Troas (2 Timothy 4:13) back to Macedonia in order to winter in Nikopolis by the Adriatic Sea, apparently on the way to Italy (Titus 3:12). Then he was imprisoned again—where we do not know—and from prison in Rome he writes the Second Letter to Timothy, which would thus have been the last we have from his hand.

There is, meanwhile, a possibility that the pastoral letters appeared during the time Paul lived as it is described in Acts. This has been posited by modern scholars (among others the Swede Bo Reicke and the Englishman John Robinson) with great acumen. They think that Second Timothy was written during Paul's imprisonment in Caesarea, perhaps about the year 58. There are several who argue for this theory, one and another against it. We will return to this in the commentary.

When it comes to dating Second Timothy, we have at least three theories to choose among. Some think that it is a question of a "deuteropauline pseudepigrapha" from around 100. Others think that the letter was written by Paul during a second imprisonment in Rome sometime between the years 64 and 67, and some assert that it was written by him in Caesarea, around the year 58. This commentary proceeds from the thought that one of the two later theories is most likely, but to choose between them must be left open.

The style and language are the same as in the other pastoral epistles. A person might also perceive that Paul had a coworker who had a meaningful responsibility for the development of these three letters, and that it is a matter of the same man in all three cases.

2 Timothy 1

1-2 Greeting

The superscription for this letter reminds us of First Timothy so much that a person can surmise that this was a formula that could be used just as naturally as a contemporary church leader uses his letterhead or a secretary forms a greeting according to a particular model even when a person writes to close coworkers.

3-12 The Apostle and His Disciple

After the formal greeting the letter takes on a very personal tone. What shines through is how warmly attached the Apostle is to his spiritual son. The separation has been painful, and he longs to see him again. At the same time, he is deeply thankful to have such a son in the faith. We are told what a good inheritance Timothy received from his mother and grandmother. Paul mentions them by name. It is one of the many small details that speaks to the authenticity of the letter. A person might wonder if the grandmother really would have been able to be a Christian, or if she was dead when Paul came to Lystra. It isn't impossible that Paul speaks about her as a pious Jew. Of course, he says of himself that he serves God "just like my fathers." They lived in faith in the Messiah who would come. Paul had been able to see him come. For Paul it was one and the same faith. The difference was only that the fathers lived in the time of the promise, he himself in the fulfillment. He and they had worshiped the same God "with a pure conscience," and the same sincere faith in His word. Paul had said just that when he first answered before the Procurator Felix in Caesarea (Acts 24:14), something that is emphasized by those who think this letter was written shortly afterwards.

Paul reminds us that it was he who once ordained Timothy to the office he now works in. It happened during the laying on of hands by the elders (1 Timothy 4:14) and by Paul himself. At this time, Timothy received a spiritual gift (a charisma) that Paul does not name, though he hints that it was a spirit of power, love, and mortification. Timothy shall renew this gift, or "fan into flame" as Paul usually says. A charisma doesn't work automatically. It must be awakened and kept alive like all other aspects of Christian life.

Just now it means to not lose heart because Paul sits in prison. Unfortunately, we do not know where. It could have been in Caesarea on the coast of the Mediterranean far away in the east, somewhere in the residence of the Roman procurator as a prisoner on remand, accused by the Jews for revolutionary activity but still being respectfully treated as a Roman citizen. In such a case it ought to have been about 58 A.D. However, it could also have been six or nine years later in

Rome. In the first case, it could not have been so long since he was separated from Timothy. He had actually followed him on his journey to Jerusalem in 57, which for Paul ended with the tumult in the Temple where he had almost been lynched. Many believe that Timothy then came to Caesarea and helped Paul with all the work he could manage from prison. They think that it was during this time that the letters to Colossae, Philemon, Ephesus, and possibly also Philippians came about. Timothy is mentioned as a coauthor in three of them. He must have been sent to Ephesus shortly afterwards, all this provided that Second Timothy was written in Caesarea.

Now Paul asks him to be of good cheer. For the Christians it was naturally bothersome that one of their leaders sat in prison accused of high treason. Yet Paul reminds him that he suffers without shame. It is for the gospel. In a few short statements he reminds him of the chief points of this gospel: not for the sake of our works, only through God's gracious determination, conceived from eternity and realized through Jesus Christ who conquered death. Paul knows in whom he believes. He knows what the message is that he shall carry forth. He has received something that he has been entrusted with. He uses (as in 1 Timothy 6:20) the word "*paratheke*," a deposit, a treasure that he shall invest and give account for on "the day." However, he is certain that it is finally God who preserves the treasure and is responsible for making sure it doesn't go to waste, independently of Paul who sits in prison.

13-14 Faithfulness to Confession

For Timothy it now means to safeguard this "*paratheke*" (Paul uses that word again). He should not seek to be original. He is to repeat what he has learned from the Apostle. Yet it is not a question of reading a lesson. No one can reproduce the sound teaching properly without the help of the Holy Spirit. He should trust that he has access to this help. The Spirit lives in us who are baptized and believe. He who has the Spirit does not find new teachings, but he can lay out the apostolic truth "with the faith and love that Christ Jesus gives." The gospel is something firm, that can never be changed, at the same time it shall be brought forth with personal conviction and with love for those who listen.

15-18 Faithful Coworkers and Unfaithful

Paul makes an aside and pauses upon a few personal experiences that have deeply affected him. Many friends have betrayed him in "Asia," which in the New Testament means the province of Asia, the most western part of Asia Minor. Concerning Phygelus and Hermogenes, nothing more is known. We perceive that Paul expected something better from them. All the more he rejoices over Onesipherus—he too is one of the many for whom we know little more than a name. When this is written it seems he was dead. He probably came to Rome on a business trip. This information is normally regarded as evidence that it was there that Paul sat in prison. They who believe it was Caesarea think that it is misunderstood that Onisephorus expected to find Paul in Rome where the Apostle planned to travel as soon as he carried out his errands in Jerusalem (Acts 19:21, Romans 15:25 f). When he was then unable to find him there but heard that he was in prison, he made the effort to seek him out all the way in Caesarea.

2 Timothy 2

1-13 An Exercise of the Office in the Apostolic Spirit

Now Paul gives instructions to Timothy that can apply for all bishops and church leaders. Paul knows that even the leaders of the church are sinners. There have been many times in which it has appeared that the faithful Timothy easily loses heart. However, Paul does not ask him to step up. Instead, he admonishes him to find power in the grace that is only found in Christ, thus in the forgiveness of sins and in his atonement. Then he reminds him of his duty to preserve the apostolic doctrines as he received it from the apostles. Paul refers to the many witnesses who knew that Jesus did so and had said so. Now it is Timothy's duty to see to it that the message is carried further through capable men who fundamentally know the apostolic faith and can instruct others in it. The apostolic era suffers towards its end. Now others shall step into their wake as bearers of their message. The pastoral office is taking form.

In the wake of the apostles, a person must be prepared to suffer. Paul emphasizes it with pictures that we recognize from his earlier letters, the picture of a soldier, an athlete, and a farmer. The last picture also means that the laborer is worth his hire. He who proclaims the gospel also has the right to live from it (1 Corinthians 9:14). In order to bear his suffering properly a man must have Jesus before his eyes. Here Paul seems to cite a couple of lines from an early Christian confession: "…risen from the dead, the offspring of David." He reminds him that he himself in this hour suffers for the gospel where he sits in chains, and he says trustworthily: God's Word bears no chains. He knows just how the Word goes forth throughout the Roman Empire. He himself, even as the prisoner he is, helps and carries out his share of the work with his suffering. A person can really suffer in blessing in the world when he suffers in communion with Christ. Paul has said it before: the measure of Christ's sufferings that he shall endure, he fulfills it for the good of Christ's body which is the Church (Colossians 1:24). He knows that when he is struck by distress then it happens with comfort and salvation for other Christians (2 Corinthians 1:6). It has always been clear for him that life with Christ means both to suffer with Him and to be glorified with Him. He also says this here with words that a person supposes are a passage from an early Christian hymn. We die with Him in order to live. If we share His humiliation, we shall also share His royal authority. However, he who denies Him, he will also be denied by Him before His Father. And if we are faithless, so… here the thought suddenly turns to the opposite of that which a man expects and it says: He remains faithful; He cannot deny Himself. It is the most extreme reason for our security. To the end it does not depend on our faithfulness, but on His.

14-18 The Meaningless Spirit of Debate

Now Paul transitions to the congregation's problem. The most burning is apparently the false teaching that has gained a hearing within the congregation and is presented by trained speakers and debaters. Paul names two of them: Hymenaeus and Phygelus. We know nothing more about them, but it is obvious that they were influenced by Gnosticism. They maintained that the resurrection had already happened. This exact same teaching is presented in three different manuscripts from the Gnostic monastery library discovered in 1945 at Nag Hammadi in Upper Egypt.

Otherwise, we do not know anything about their teaching, and Paul does not waste any words refuting it. On the contrary he warns against all attempts to debate with the false teachers. It will only cause harm. There are cases where a conversation concerning divisions are meaningless. The gospel cannot be motivated and defended from the values and experiences of unbelief. Faith in Christ depends upon a stance on Christ Himself. Either a man is gripped by Him and follows Him, or he does not understand what it is about. Then it does not help that a person uses Christ's name. The Gnostics did that. Some of their writings speak continually of the Son of Man and about Christ. Yet it is not a matter of the Jesus Christ of the New Testament, but a fantasy figure made to fit in an already finished system. In such a case, no real dialogue is possible. The only thing that can then help is to proclaim Christ, and now Timothy is admonished to do this as a faithful steward of a message he has been entrusted with. He should do it "without swerving." Here Paul uses an unusual word that Luther literally rendered with "rightly divide." The real meaning seems to be to do something without wavering, without detours and slinging bolts. Even in the proclamation a man should be direct.

19-21 Many Opinions but One Truth

Because the false teachers have apparently appeared within the congregation, Paul makes it clear how it is with God's church. It is like a great house where there are vessels of all sorts, both better and worse. Not all who have the Christian name measure up. However, "The Lord knows His own." God knows where He has His children, and a sure characteristic of them is that they not only carry Christ's name on their lips but also avoid all unrighteousness. On this point the Gnostics burst open. We also hear this in John's letters, in Revelation and in Peter and Judas. To be a useful utensil in the Lord's hand a person must keep himself pure from both false teaching and a false living. So, the many opinions are not a treasure but rather a test that shows what is true and what does not measure up (1 Corinthians 11:19).

22-26 The Relationship to False Teachers

So for Timothy, it means keeping the right course also in his manner of life. Paul lists the most important points: righteousness, faithfulness, and love. To this he adds concord, but he makes it clear that this has its limits. It is only possible with those who call on Christ with a pure heart. If anyone preaches a different gospel, then no concord is possible. Where a person passes over the firm word and gives themselves to empty speculations, there a man cannot follow. Paul repeats the warning to not enter discussions about such things. They only lead to strife. The congregation is not a place where a man invites discussion around religious problems. A true servant of the Lord is not a debater but a witness and a proclaimer. He shall be this with all patience, without letting himself be provoked to bitterness and contentiousness, but with a firm conviction that Christ is the truth. It is not arrogance but obedience to acknowledge Christ is right and to trust in Him completely. To this truth also belongs that those who reject Christ are trapped in the devil's snare and need to be set free. So, a man shall meet them with love, but without pretending that their opinions can essentially be as true as the true gospel.

2 Timothy 3

1-9 The Great Apostasy

In the last days there will be a great apostasy. The entire New Testament says this, from the words of Jesus in the gospels to the book of Revelation. However, that which comes to happen then happens on a smaller scale time after time. Here Paul first describes what is to be expected when the course of the world comes to an end, that which Jesus briefly expressed with the words: "Because lawlessness is increased the love of many will grow cold" (Matthew 24:12). Then he continues to say that Timothy has already dealt with such men. They are also found within the congregation; some of them appear as coworkers. They nestle themselves into homes and appear to come with the name of Christ on their lips. They gain an audience, and it is worth taking note what sort of people fall for them most easily. They are those we sometimes call seekers—people who have a religious interest and appear eager to hear, but constantly want to hear something new and be present where interesting things seem to happen. However, they never come to faith, very simply because they constantly draw away when it means reckoning with sin and without reservation coming to Christ in order to be incorporated among His members and thereby also be a faithful member of the congregation.

According to Jewish tradition, Jannes and Jambres are the Egyptian fortune tellers who did the same miracles as Moses and Aaron before the face of Pharoah and in that manner hardened his heart (Exodus 7:11 and 22). In the same way, false teachers now hinder people from receiving God's message when He comes with His invitation and liberation. But they will not be successful, Paul adds. He is right. The Gnostics failed to remake Christianity. Their irrationality became really apparent. Yet it required a long hard fight.

10-13 The Apostles' Disciples

Timothy received fame because he took Paul as his example. Paul never hesitated to point to himself and those who lived like him. Something new came with Christ. Such a manner of living was different than anything seen before. Examples needed to be made, and models to follow, both when it meant the way to believe and the way to live. Now Paul notes that Timothy has been a true disciple who took his apostle as a model, and then he adds: so shall it be even during persecutions and suffering. He reminisces about all he himself suffered in Timothy's home environs. In Lystra—which in all likelihood was Timothy's hometown—he had been literally stoned. This must have happened when Timothy was a teenager. Like Jesus, Paul says that this is what all Christians shall deal with. The world does not come to be more civilized. On the contrary, men will become more and more evil. This is what Timothy ought to deal with—just like every Christian.

14-17 The Mystery of Scripture

It is, however, naturally not the case that some man shall be the final norm for those who believe. It is Scripture. By Holy Scriptures, Paul means the Old Testament. Timothy was fortunate enough to know them even since childhood. Now Paul says that it is just this Old Testament that can save a man if a person actually reads it with faith in Christ and in the light that comes from Him. Then Paul says something that is foundational and essential for our faith in the Scriptures and our experience of it. Something that declares the central place it has within Christendom. It is "permeated by God"; God has breathed His Spirit into it. It is a living Word, in which God comes to encounter us people. The Word does not deal only with God, but it is God who operates in the Word. It is therefore this Word that can essentially give instruction concerning God in a way that nothing else can, and about something that we otherwise could never know about Him and His intentions for us, concerning reproof, or as the Word can also mean, a disclosure of evidence that reveals our sin and examines us, and concerning restitution, so that the right relationship to God is restored, and finally education in righteousness that means holiness. In this way, God carries out His work with a person so that she can realize her provision to live as His child and be a blessing for others.

When Paul wrote this, the New Testament was still in the making. In First Timothy (5:18) we hear for the first time how a word of Jesus is counted as "Scripture." So gradually, it became clear that both the evangelists and the apostolic Scriptures belonged to "the holy Scriptures that save." What Paul says here concerning the Old Testament, the Church today confesses concerning the whole Bible.

2 Timothy 4

1-5 Faithful to the Word in The Time of Apostasy

Now Paul gives his spiritual son one last admonishment. He does it completely with thoughtful seriousness concerning the great day for the eyes the Christ comes in His kingdom and shall let His steward on earth give account.

The first and most important thing is to preach the Word. A steward shall be faithful. He shall do what he has been enjoined to do. And it is particularly a clear, formed message, which the Word's servant shall bring forth. This he shall be prepared to do in season and out of season, whether the moment is convenient for him or not. He shall always "stand ready." The expression is occasionally given "be prepared," but the meaning is hardly that a person shall force the message on people at an inconvenient occasion even if it is very convenient for you. And the proclamation shall "reveal" (the word is from the same stem as the just mentioned "reproof") and rebuke, but also comfort. This should be done with great patience, not bitterness and stinginess, and with thorough examination. The preaching shall also give objective knowledge of God and the way to Him. It happens that men will want to have something else. Paul predicts what will happen. Some want variety and entertainment. They want to hear something new, something exciting, stories about strange things or "myths," such as peculiar and colorful descriptions of other worlds and unknown powers in the universe of which the Gnostics were masters at presenting. Such men want to call foreign speakers that are known for being able to captivate itching ears with such things. The great temptation for a servant of the Word in the congregation is to try to compete with those who offer spiritual entertainment. Here it means to "be sober in all things," to know his duty, to not let one be blown about by opinions and winds. It means a suffering that one may not escape. Paul calls Timothy to "do his duty as an evangelist," for example, to preach the gospel clearly and purely and fervently, but not anything else but the gospel. It is his task and his office.

6-8 A Christian Before Death

Paul figures that his verdict is "guilty," and that he will encounter martyrdom. It can also happen that he does not have long to live. Before martyrdom he does not feel any bitterness toward his judge. He knows that he is an offering upon God's altar, and that the offering will in some way benefit the gospel. He is prepared to depart. Death is not just an end but a portal into the real life, at home with the Lord Christ. His life has been full of fight. He has invested everything, like a runner in the last stretch. Now he will quickly reach the goal. He knows that he possesses the one thing needful. He has prepared faith. All that lies behind him is put under forgiveness. Before him he has the victory crown, that which demands a wholehearted contribution as if only one person could win it, though it is for all who believe in Christ and the longing lasts after encountering Him.

9-15 Personal Instructions

Before his death, Paul still wants one more meeting with his beloved coworker, and now he asks him to come as soon as possible. He has sent Tychicus to Ephesus, probably to relieve him for the time he stayed with Paul. Now Paul is alone. Of his closest coworkers, only Luke remains. One of the others, the otherwise unknown Crescens, he has sent to Galatia (which can also mean Gaul), while Titus has travelled to Dalmatia. They probably both had commissions as missionaries. And Demas has gone to Thessalonica, apparently on some private errand that Paul thought he ought to have returned from for the work in the gospel.

In Colossians and the letter to Philemon there are greetings from Demas, Luke, and Mark. In Colossians, Tychicus is also mentioned. It may be that the letter was written at approximately the same time as Second Timothy. Those who believe that this has happened in Caesarea can cite many good reasons. We know that Tychicus was sent with the letter to Colossae and Ephesus (Colossians 4:7f, Ephesians 6:21). That there was something off about Demas, a person realizes in Colossians where Paul sends a greeting from him but does not, as in the letter to Philemon, receive him among his coworkers. Timothy himself and Mark must have been with Paul, when he wrote the letter to Colossae and to Philemon. At that time, Mark was ready to travel to Colossae and perhaps other places too. When Paul writes the letter to Ephesus, he no longer mentions Timothy, and it is also possible that he was sent to Ephesus. In such a case, Paul now asks him to come back and bring Mark with him.

As for the coat and books in Troas, Paul could have left these during his trip to Jerusalem in the year 57, thinking he would get them when he travelled back through on his way to Rome. Now he needs the coat when winter closes in. The books that were written on parchment (and not papyrus) were particularly valuable. Most often these were in reference to portions of the Bible.

So far, these tasks fit the theory that Paul wrote this letter during the time he sat in prison in Caesarea. However, in the next section we come to encounter details that speak against it.

We do not know in what way Alexander the coppersmith injured Paul. It is tempting to believe that it was through some false testimony. When Paul says that God shall repay him, it means that no one else should do it, neither Timothy nor the congregations, even if they should find occasion.

16-18 Paul's First Defense before the Hearing

We do not know what Paul hints at when he speaks about the first time he defended himself before the court. For those who believe that he is now writing from Caesarea, it is clear that it must be a question of a hearing in Jerusalem or Caesarea. They who prefer to think of Rome as the scene have to choose between the year when the case was finally taken up in Caesarea's highest court or the first court hearing in a different imprisonment. A person may remember that what Paul mentions here ought to have been news for Timothy. This presents some difficulties for the theory that the letter was written in Caesarea because the first trial ought to have taken place while Timothy was still with Paul. Those who believe in a different imprisonment have often put this in connection with the persecution under Caesar Nero (sometime in the fall of 64 or in the year 65). It is, however, improbable that during this persecution, when all rights seemed to have ceased to function, an ordered process should have proceeded in the case of Paul. It seems impossible that during the persecution he would have asked Timothy to come to Rome and take Mark along. This imprisonment must have begun before the persecution or occurred a few years later. It is possible that the trial happened before the persecution broke out, and that one then made the process short for Paul.

In any case, what Paul has to say is that no one came to his defense by standing up and testifying on his behalf. That the matter still had a somewhat good outcome, Paul sees as a confirmation that God still wants to let him carry His message. It is precisely this that is said about his dealings with the Jews and the Roman authorities in Jerusalem in the summer of 57 (Acts 23).

19-22 Greetings and Messages

Paul particularly greets his old friends Priscilla and Aquilla. As so often, he mentions Priscilla before her husband. She seems to have been the more important of the two. He then greets the family of Onesiphorus, possibly because the housefather who did so much for Paul and the congregation had just died.

Two short messages then follow. Erastus may be the same coworker who had been sent from Ephesus to Macedonia with Timothy, when Paul held back to finish his long stay in Ephesus (likely the year 56). Timothy also should have been interested to hear news from him. He may also be the same man of whom we hear in Romans (16:23) who kept the city's accounts. As so often, we are left guessing.

The information concerning Trophimus is a problem for those who think that this letter comes from Caesarea. We actually know that Trophimus followed Paul up to Jerusalem (Acts 21:29), and so did not remain in Miletus when the great travel company passed the city. If a person should fit this together, a person must perceive that here Paul speaks as a director of missions, which accounts for the personal transfers he has just received. Those who think this letter must come from a different imprisonment have a strong argument here.

Finally, there come greetings from four named Christians. Three of the names are Latin. This too is an argument for those who think that Paul finds himself in Rome. Linus is the man who, according to tradition, was Rome's first bishop after the death of Peter.

Despite all the concrete details that we receive in this letter, the question remains. Those who think like the early church tradition that the pastoral epistles come after the time that is described in Acts have very good reasons to invoke. Uncertainty can give us a new reminder that such questions have no decisive meaning. The essential is not when and where a book of the Bible came to be, but what it says. All questions concerning authorship and dating finally receive the Christian answer that the message comes from God and are meant for every era.

TITUS

Introduction

Titus is mentioned twelve times in the New Testament (eight of those times in Second Corinthians) but strangely enough—nowhere in Acts. We know that he was Greek. He also accompanied Paul when he travelled with Barnabas to Jerusalem sometime in the 40s. Paul says that there were some who demanded that Titus should be circumcised, which Paul particularly objected to going along with "because we want the freedom [truth] of the gospel to be preserved" (Galatians 2:1-5). In Second Corinthians we learn that Titus was sent to Corinth (perhaps in the fall of 55) to feel out the situation in the congregation that had caused Paul great worries. Paul waited uneasily for news when he was on his way to Corinth the next spring. When he had not met Titus in Troas as he had hoped, he continued to Macedonia. There he met Titus, who came with very good news, and full of joy for the reception he received. It was because he received this good news that Paul wrote this letter that we call Second Corinthians (2 Corinthians 2:12f, 7:5f, 13f). In this letter we also hear that Titus was again sent to Corinth, among other things, to lead the final push for the great collection for the poor in Jerusalem that he had already prepared. In this context Paul calls him "my partner and fellow worker for your benefit" (2 Corinthians 8:23).

Now we learn that Titus finds himself in Crete, once again on an errand for the Apostle and with full authority to operate on his behalf. The date is uncertain. We will come to deal with this matter more closely in the commentary (1:5). In this letter we also learn that Paul intends to find a replacement to take over the work Titus is doing and wants him to meet up with the Apostle (3:12). One last time we hear him mentioned in Second Thessalonians (4:10); there it is mentioned in passing that he has travelled to Dalmatia. According to later tradition, he ended as bishop in Crete, but that may be just legend. In any case, he belongs among Paul's most trusted coworkers, and showed himself useful in hard and delicate tasks.

There are striking similarities between this letter and First Timothy. The demands that are placed upon ecclesiastical office holders are literally the same in places. This is a strong argument for the authenticity of both letters. Had they been written in the post apostolic era it is hard to understand what this repetition would have served. However, if it is a question of letters from Paul to two different coworkers in different places but with similar tasks, then the similarities are natural.

The question still remains, who carried the pen on behalf of Paul? The speech and contents of the pastoral epistles—as we have seen in the introduction to First Timothy—are so distinctive and so similar that a person has reason to believe that Paul left most of the work to a coworker. Who he was we cannot know. The coworkers we know by name are all excluded. If those who believe that pastoral letters were written during the third mission trip and in Caesarea during the years of 56-58 are right, then there is still one coworker who could have been present during all the occasions when the letters were written, and that is the Macedonian, Aristarchus. We know very little about him, but Luke mentions him as a faithful disciple who followed Paul even to Rome, and in one place the Apostle calls him "my co-prisoner." In any case, he can serve as an example to show that there were faithful followers concerning whose contributions we know nothing. However, if the pastoral epistles came to be after Paul was emancipated, he may have had new coworkers, whose names we never learn to know.

Even if Paul used a coworker who put his stamp on the linguistic formation, he has then in any case sanctioned the contents. Thereby, the letter received apostolic authority. In the early church, the reputation of the apostles did not depend on their talents or eloquence. They had their authority as Christ's fully authorized envoys. They were bearers of the tradition from Jesus, entrusted with the gospel. It was this message that had authority. The apostles would watch it so that it was not distorted. What they approved was then binding. The pastoral epistles show us how binding this apostolic inheritance is for the church of every age. It is possibly their most important message for our time.

Titus 1

1-4 Letterhead

As usual the sender and recipients come first, and as in many other letters, Paul specifies the commission he received as Christ's apostle. He does it with particular consideration for the recipients. It is precisely through Titus that the letter shall reach the congregations, and they should know that Paul, precisely because he is Christ's apostle, cannot speak or teach otherwise than he does. He shall speak in accordance with "the faith that God's elect confess" and an "insight into truth" that is better than the false "knowledge" of the Gnostics. The Gnostics made claim to possess secret writings that were preserved since times eternal and contained truths that only they could teach. Paul says that there really is an eternal plan of God that has long been hidden. But through Jesus Christ, it has now been revealed. So, Paul does not come as the Gnostics with a secretive mystery wisdom that only the initiated can know. He comes with a message from Christ that can be confirmed by men who still live.

So, Paul is an apostle "in accord with" or "in faithfulness to" this message. A person could also translate it "in service to" or "in order to promote." Here in the Greek a two-syllable preposition is used (*katta*) that has many meanings. It is not impossible that the recipients of this letter read both meanings into the word: an apostle would promote this faith and at the same time he would be unquestionably faithful to it.

5-9 The Appointment of Elders and the Heads of Congregations

Titus finds himself on Crete on behalf of the Apostle. Paul himself could have been there on some mission trip since he had been acquitted. This is the common thought among those who believe this letter was written in the mid 60s. However, some believe that it was written already in the year 57 when Paul was on his way up to Jerusalem. They think that the expression "left you" only means that Paul did not take Titus with him. It would have been natural for Paul to take him along given how much Titus had to do with the ingathering of the great gift that now would be handed over. However, during this time Titus had been sent to Crete, and there he was to remain to finish his task. According to this theory, Paul would have anticipated leaving from Jerusalem to start for Rome and winter in Nicopolis on the Adriatic sea on the way where Titus would meet up with him (Titus 3:12).

Now Titus has the commission to organize the newly founded congregation on Crete and see to it that they are placed under the best possible leadership. He is to appoint "elders" and "overseers" (*presbyters* and *episkopos*). The Greek words continue to live in our language in the form of "priests" and "bishops," and it is even a question of the same offices though the functions at that time were not shared in the same manner as now. As we have already seen, the presbyters also had administrative tasks, and there were many bishops within every congregation. Here Paul speaks of a congregational leader as if they obviously belonged to the presbyters (or in any case must be taken from their circles).

In large part, the demand is seen as the same as for bishops in First Timothy (Chapter 3). However, it is just this that makes it so striking that it is a question of elementary moral demand. The congregational leaders must have a good reputation. He who represents the congregation has the same place as the administrator of an estate. He represents his lord and shall take care of all the people of the house. As a particular demand, it is mentioned that he shall "hold firm" to the Word as he has learned it. "The sound teaching" remains not in personal interpretations and original fancy. It has a particular and clear content, and it must be preserved.

10-16 The Treatment of False Teachers

To a right proclamation also belongs "refuting those who contradict." These are also found within the congregation. Paul does not mince words when he characterizes them. They are insubordinate, empty talkers and deceivers. We learn almost nothing about what they teach, which is assumed to be known. Yet it appears as if it touches upon a Jewish/Christian influence that deviates. This does not exclude it being a question of Gnosticism. In the bizarre speculations of Gnosticism, there is a massive amount of Old Testament material interwoven.

Such fantasies seem to have fertile soil in Crete. The Cretans are seen to have trouble holding to the truth. Paul cites a verse (a hexameter) from one of their great prophets, Epimenides. He had lived long ago—just as far back as St. Birgitta lived from our time—and he enjoyed a great reputation as a miracle worker and seer. Paul calls him a prophet, perhaps because the Cretans regarded him the same as the Jews looked at their great prophets, or perhaps because Paul means that he really spoke as a prophet when he characterized his compatriots. So, Titus should know what sort of oil one needs for such leather. He shall not put fingers in between. Yet neither shall he lose hope that one or another of the misguided shall sober up and recognize the truth.

That "to the pure all things are pure" is a sentence we know from Romans (14:14 and 20). That Paul emphasizes it here indicates that the naysayers have declared some things to be unclean, as the Jews did with all sorts of food and certain Gnostics did with the sexual life. For those who believe in Christ and live in communion with Him, everything is clean. But "all that does not happen in faith, that is sin" (Romans 14:23). Where faith is, there it is made visible through works. The Gnostics prided themselves in having a deeper knowledge of the divine than others. Their way of life showed that they lied, Paul says.

Titus 2

1-8 A Sound and Proper Daily Life

Again, we hear talk of the "sound" teaching. A Christian shall be "sound" in faith, hope, and love. The sound is that which fits with God's good will for creation. Where God's will happens, life functions as it should. Sound teaching makes man sound. It preserves the life of faith from exaggerations and its own inventions, ascetic parading, and all sorts of weirdness while invoking the Spirit. A Christian is to be sober, not only in that he does not drink too much, but also that he preserves a sound balance in everything. Here Paul uses a concept three times that was a cardinal virtue for the Greeks: "*sofrosyne*," the right measure in everything. We have no directly corresponding word in English. Here it is rendered with self-control, to be wise, to live honorably, to show understanding.

There is much in Christendom that always appears to be foolishness to the world: to not assert yourself, not to dish back, not to take the opportunities a person has to enjoy and serve money. The offense cannot be avoided. Such things allow a man to be a fool for Christ. However, there are also such things that the world understands because it reflects the good forces that the Creator has embedded in the nature of man: a sense of justice, helpfulness, love for parents, the desire for a good and happy family life. When it comes to such things, a Christian shall show that a sound teaching creates a sound daily life. He who first and foremost should show this is the proclaimer himself. Titus is reminded of the matter, and Paul gives him good counsel for proclamation. First and foremost, he shall give people "the sincere teaching," the apostolic message, without addition or subtraction. It shall be presented with dignity because it is a message from God, and it shall be a "sound" word, that no one shall have cause to condemn—if he really has the gospel of Christ as the measuring stick.

9-10 Good Servants

As in First Timothy Paul speaks in particular about Christians who are slaves. At that time abolishing slavery appeared to be just as unreasonable as the thought of abolishing all taxes today. Only when Christianity conquered the western lands could a man begin to take on such a pervasive reform. Here instead there are rules for how a Christian should carry himself if he is a slave. Slaves were not only manual laborers and servants; they were artisans, business representatives, clerks and officials, even in positions of responsibility. So the rules that are given here can apply for all service in all times. A person should be faithful and reliable, not surly or bad tempered, but be loyal in everything and submit to the rules so that the work functions—in any case, so far as a person can do this without breaking God's command. In our day, there is the opportunity for discussion and co-determination. This means a responsibility and sometimes a duty to "object." However, applicable rules shall be respected. As a coworker, a man may not sabotage that which does not suit an individual.

In this way a Christian becomes an ornament of the gospel. This is our great task when encountering people who do not believe: to show what Christ means in all our dealings.

11-15 The Effect of the Gospel

Essentially, the gospel has an educational effect that shows itself also in everyday life. Negatively, this education means a no to the world's whole way of thinking and evaluation when it comes to money, sex, and prestige. Positively, it means that a person lives wisely and righteously in a manner that even the world can understand and appreciate. However, a person also lives piously in a manner that is folly to the world. Essentially, it means that a person expects Jesus will come. A person builds upon a hope that seems unreasonable to the world. However, it is just this hope that daily causes a man to take up duties that the world appreciates though it would rather neglect them. The basis and driving force in this manner of life is faith in this "Great God and Savior" Jesus Christ, who died to make it possible for us to be His own people. Christendom is really a new Israel, a continuation of the people of the covenant in the Old Testament. To hear this means to be full of eagerness for good. Here the word "zealous" (*selot*) is used, that which the Jews used of their fight for freedom and of others who were unconditionally devoted to some particular thing. Thus, the Christians are an oath bound crowd. However, the goal is to do good.

So shall Titus then preach. Naturally this also applies to other preachers in all times.

Titus 3

1-3 Summary

Now a short recapitulation of the chief thoughts of the letter follows. A Christian shall be an example for fellow citizens and his fellow man. He shall be loyal to the state and to the authorities. Here there is no hint that this loyalty can be a problem. It appears just as obvious as when Paul wrote the 13th chapter of Romans. It seems that this was written before the persecution of Nero from 64-65.

Furthermore, a Christian shall be a good fellow man. This applies to what we would call common decency. In actual fact, it was not at all "common" at the time. We get a description of the life that these newfound Christians had lived previously. Paul references the fact that all recognized. It was a world where "common decency" was something completely unknown, an environment where it was expected to assert oneself with all means, an everyday life full of conflicts and intrigue, envy, and malice.

4-7 The Importance of Baptism

In this evil world the gospel came and made everything new. God intervenes, and He did it very noticeably and openly through baptism. Here we see how clearly a person saw that all depended on God's intervention. Certainly, a person had decided and repented. However, he knew that this could not save anyone. A person is saved by what God has done, and God acted in baptism. Here baptism is called a washing of renewal. A word is used for renewal, a word that would otherwise only appear in a single place in the New Testament (Matthew 19:28), where Jesus speaks about the powerful intervention of God through which the world will be born again. So here it is a question of being born to a new life, a life that belongs together with the kingdom that shall come. Through baptism a man is taken up into God's kingdom and renewed in the Holy Spirit. The Spirit belongs namely with God's kingdom: It is given "through Jesus Christ our Savior," to all those who through baptism are incorporated into Him. It is the same thought that Paul develops in the sixth chapter of Romans. Through baptism we are "grown together with him." This means that we may share in His righteousness; we are made "righteous through His grace," and thereby we are also "inheritors of eternal life."

We people are inclined to believe in our own experiences and feelings. It is those that are supposed to give us certainty. Early Christendom built upon God's promise in Christ and His Word. It was baptism that saved, not something we felt or performed. So, there was never any discussion about the baptism of infants. If God could save an old sinner, then He could also save a child. However, the gift—salvation and the Spirit—would naturally be cared for and used in faith the whole life through.

8-11 Faith and Works Contra Speculations and False Teachings

So, a person should believe in this work of God through baptism. It is a firm word, Paul says, and Titus shall witness to it powerfully. And it is precisely this faith—that God takes man from this world and gives him a share in the new kingdom—that should drive us to a new manner of life. So, works come from faith. All these are thoughts we recognize from Paul's earlier letters. Here they are now consciously placed in opposition to what is not faith but human speculations, and not good deeds but self-appointed contrivances with which a person wants to show his fear of God. Neither do we here find any clear picture of what false teachings stand for. "Disputes concerning the law" indicates that this can be a question of Judaizers that wanted to force Mosaic provisions concerning the Sabbath or circumcision or forbidden foods upon Christians. In such a case, "genealogies" (the Greek word is "*genealogier*," which we also have as a loanword) may mean Jewish family trees and genealogies, from which a person can draw fanciful conclusions. However, "foolish speculations" fit excellently into the wildly developed gnostic myths concerning creation and the many eons and all their divinities that also formed a sort of family tree. Such speculations with their mysterious names have had a great attraction for the people of antiquity. For example, gnostic writings mention the children of the creator god, which we already spoke about (see 1 Timothy 2:11f): The first is Athoth. The second is Harmas, which is the evil eye. The third is Kalila-Oumbri. The fourth is Yabel. The fifth is Adonaion, who is called Sabaoth. The sixth is Kain, whom men call the sun. The sun is Abel . . . and so further with a particular blend of Biblical and gentile names. Such teachings could be proclaimed with a great certainty by men who asserted they had access to heavenly writings of venerable elders. We can understand that Paul considers all discussions of such things as useless and meaningless. If a person comes with false teachings, a person should not seek any dialogue with him. A person should warn him "one or two-times." Perhaps here Paul thinks about the instructions of Jesus (Matthew 18:15f). The first time it can happen between four eyes, next time in the presence of witnesses. Then the false teacher shall be rejected. He has condemned himself when he does not want to recognize the right of truth. Early Christianity did not have any thought concerning "pluralistic" truth. Jesus Christ was truth, and a person must accept this truth.

12-15 Instructions and Greetings

The letter ends with a couple of practical instructions. Titus is promised to receive a replacement soon. We do not know who Artemas is. Concerning Tychicus, we know that he followed Paul to Jerusalem, and that later he was the one who travelled with his letter from Ephesus to Colossae. Paul calls him a "faithful servant and coworker in the Lord." When Titus receives the replacement, he should seek Paul out in Nicopolis where the Apostle plans to winter. There are many cities with that name, but the most likely means a harbor city on the Adriatic Sea from which a person could sail over to Italy.

Later, Paul gives instruction that two coworkers should be provided with what they need for a trip that they are apparently undertaking in service to the mission. The one is called "Zenas, the lawyer." Concerning him we know nothing. Apollos, however, can be the learned Jew from Alexandria who knew Scriptures well and is spoken about in many places in Acts and First Corinthians. Paul emphasizes that the congregations must learn to recognize their responsibilities for mission work and bear the cost for it. To do such is to "really do good works." If they fail on that point, then their Christianity is without fruit.

The letter ends with a short greeting. No names are mentioned. This could be a sign that those who believe Paul never went to Crete himself are right. (See the commentary to 1:5.)

At least the last sentences ought to have been written by Paul's own hand, according to his custom to in this way approve a letter where someone else carried the pen.

With that the pastoral epistles end, in the order they now have in our Bible. Whenever they may have been written, they give an insight into the early Christian congregational life that shows how the gospel already at that time was threatened by radical attempts to change it and fill the original word with new content. Against all such attempts, the pastoral epistles place the apostolic inheritance with their demands for a faithfulness that does not compromise. This is their message to all coming times.

THE LETTER TO PHILEMON
Introduction

The letter to Philemon is placed last among all the letters of Paul in our New Testament. Because it is a letter to a particular person and because it is the shortest of all Paul's letters, it has been placed together with the "Private Letters" and last in the series.

If a person looks at the time and the situation in which it was written, it belongs together with Colossians. It was sent "with the same package," which at the time meant that it was brought by the same traveler. In this case, it was a matter of two people. The one named Onesimus, and it is him with whom this letter deals.

It is really a letter of recommendation. We have many such letters among the papyrus sheets that were more or less damaged or preserved from the desert sands of Egypt. This recommendation is of a special type. It is regarding a slave who has escaped, but now returns to his master. The letter does not speak of his history, but the main facts are clear, and they are remarkable enough.

Onesimus, the slave, has escaped from his lord, Philemon, who lives in Colossae or the area around there. Such was not uncommon, but very risky. If a person was taken in any raid, he was sent back to his owner, who had lawful right to do to him precisely what his anger inspired within him: whip, beat, put on starvation rations, or execute. The slave was his property and, without rights, left to his mercy.

In some way that we know nothing about, Onesimus has developed a relationship with the imprisoned Paul, who during his time as a prisoner was fully active as a missionary. Onesimus had been converted. Apparently, he has helped his spiritual father and now runs errands for him. So, they have come to the agreement that Onesimus, as a Christian, must make things right with his former master. It has also been discovered that his master belongs to the Apostle's spiritual children too. Because Paul was never in Colossae, Philemon must have moved or perhaps converted to faith in Christ during some trip, possibly to Ephesus. In any case, Paul knows him relatively well. And when Onesimus now takes the risk to turn back, he receives a letter of recommendation that apparently has the goal to get Philemon to ponder his duty as a Christian and not just react as a slave owner of antiquity would have seen as natural.

From there we can figure that the letter did the trick. Otherwise, it is not likely that it would have been preserved. A person can ponder how such a highly private letter has been able to avoid corruption. Someone must have put some value in it that he spared it. Could it have been Philemon? Or perhaps Onesimus? We happen to know that at the beginning of the next century there was a bishop in Ephesus named Onesimus. One guesses that the slave Onesimus, that Paul calls a faithful and beloved brother in Colossians (4:9), was a servant of the church and finished as a bishop in Ephesus. Age wise it could fit. In such a case, it would be conceivable that this little private letter was gathered into the collection of letters for Paul that with great probability must have come into existence earlier among the congregations founded by Paul in Greece and Asia Minor.

In any case, it is in all its brevity an extraordinarily illustrative letter that gives a living picture of what faith in Christ meant in everyday life of antiquity, and still means. However, that will be illuminated in the commentary.

1-3 Greeting

As in five other letters, Paul writes together with Timothy. Though, as a rule, he speaks in his own name, the co-author's role, as here, is only to give his assent and endorse that which Paul has to say.

Of Philemon, we only know that which is revealed by this letter, which has already been said in the introduction. The legend says that he was a bishop in Colossae, but that is uncertain. Appia is an unknown Christian, perhaps his wife. (The name's Greek form is Apfia, but from old custom we give the names in their Latin form. We say BARnabas and not barNABas, PhilLIPpus not PHILippus, etc.).

Archipus is also mentioned in Colossians, and there he receives a greeting through the congregation that he shall be careful with the office he has received so that he carries it out in everything. Why he is named here we can only guess. Perhaps he was the leader for the Christians in Colossae since Epafras left. Perhaps he was the only one in the group that normally met at Philemon's. (The "house congregation" receives its share of the greeting.) In both cases it was his obligation to help Philemon to act as a Christian now. Perhaps the admonition to do his duty in all was specifically meant to give him a shot in the arm. If he was pressed to come with inopportune admonitions, it could be good for him to have Paul's commission to point to.

Though Paul also names a whole series of addressees, it is in actual fact a question of a letter to Philemon personally. It is him who Paul speaks to the whole time. That the rest are named hardly means more than that they receive a particular greeting. This is even more emphasized by being placed first and not last in the letter. Possibly, Paul has also thought that they have the right to read what Paul has written to Onesimus, if it should be needed.

4-7 Thanks to Philemon

As usual, Paul begins with a thanksgiving where he recounts what he is thankful to God for and at the same time has occasion to show his thankfulness to people. It is educational to give attention to how Paul forms these thanksgivings. Paul usually reminds his fellow Christians about how important it is to act and speak wisely and to know how a person should apply his word so that they are friendly and create confidence, at the same time as they have some salt and say what must be said. He himself was a master in the art, and here we have evidence of his ability to unite wisdom and goodness. He begins by giving Philemon praise that he surely deserved. However, it is so formulated that before Paul takes up the delicate question of Onesimus, Philemon is reminded of the most important aspects of Christianity. It is a faith in Christ that shows itself precisely in his relationship to other Christians. Paul also reminds Philemon that the communion that faith creates must continue to work in constantly new situations! And that in such a case, we should recognize more and more what we possess in Christ. Neither does Paul neglect to emphasize what a joy he himself has received from what Philemon has done. All this must be a strong motive for Philemon to not disappoint Paul now.

8-14 Paul asks Onesimus

Finally, Paul comes to the point. However, he goes forward wisely and carefully. He has still not mentioned Onesimus, and we can assume that Philemon, when he receives this letter laid out—by Tychicus or someone else (it's a given not Onesimus)—still does not know what it touches upon. Paul also notes that it applies to something where he as an apostle with complete emphasis could decree what a Christian should do. However, here he would rather speak as a friend and fellow Christian. (In the greeting Paul does not, as he otherwise does, call himself apostle, but only prisoner.) He is the old Paul that now sits in prison, and who now comes with a request for his Christian brother.

Then comes the request. He still does not mention the name of Onesimus. He speaks about having a child, a spiritual child, brought to life during his imprisonment. For this child he now asks. And it is—Onesimus! The name—a common name for slaves—means "the useful," and Paul plays upon this meaning as he continues. (This is why it is best to give the meaning in the English translation.)

Paul knows very well that Onesimus has not at all been useful. Perhaps he had been a great waster. In such a case, he has confessed this to Paul together with his other sins. Yet now he is really "the useful." He has been this for Paul, and he comes to be this for Philemon—this Paul says in good order. He would gladly have kept him, and he could have good need of him. He is also certain that Philemon would have allowed it and considered it a friendly service to Paul. However, Paul has not wanted to act arbitrarily. Philemon shall not continue in a forced position, where he has no choice. He should do what is right of his own free will.

15-19 A Slave Becomes a Brother in Christ

Now Paul peers into the deepest connection in all of history. He means that there lies a purpose of God behind Onesimus fleeing. He was brought into Paul's path so that he would be changed and return as a new man. Philemon shall be thankful for this. He has been returned more than what he lost. (A slave was such a precious possession that it was a painful loss to suffer.) When now Onesimus comes again, he is something better than a slave. He is a beloved brother. If Philemon retorts and reacts according to his natural feelings, then he may immediately hear Paul's voice: In any case, that is what he is to me . . . And then comes the soul-searching question: Ought he not to be even more than that for you? Both as a fellow man for whom you, before God, are responsible? And as a fellow Christian, one of the other limbs in the body? So, Paul appeals to all that binds him and Philemon together and comes with his final request: Receive him as if you are receiving me! Has he caused you injury and does he owe you money? Then I will gladly pay it. Here Paul cites, half-jokingly, the conventional formula for a promissory note, of which we know from innumerable papyrus and pottery shards. So, he makes his application that must blot out all concerns that Philemon might still have: remember that you also have a small debt to me. You have me to thank for your new life, that which means everything to you.

What then does Paul want Philemon to do? It is typical that he doesn't give any particular provision. He trusts that Christ will come to speak to Philemon in his conscience and that Philemon will follow that voice. So, he only says the essential: remember that you are dealing with a Christian brother and treat him accordingly. (We notice that it is the basic rule that Paul gives to all Christian masters and employers in Ephesians and Colossians.) Philemon has different courses to choose from. He can release Onesimus and let him look for a job. He can retain him as a "house slave" and give him a place that would in reality correspond to a member of our family. In any case, he shall see to his best.

It is in this way that Christendom has recreated the social relationships, abolished slavery, and given women and children a completely new position in society: by overcoming the old orders from within and giving people a new way of looking at each other. In a case such as this, it meant more than formally freeing your slaves, which in antiquity often meant tossing them out into the slums. It meant to take them on and be responsible for their best.

20-25 Final wishes and Greetings

When Paul finally emphasizes his desire that he shall "benefit" from Philemon, he plays again upon the name Onesimus. There lies a fine little example in the allusion: it is not only slaves that shall be useful! When Paul finally asks Philemon to receive him as a guest, it is meant as a show of confidence. To be able to receive the Apostle in his home when he came to the congregation for the first time must have been something remarkable. Here Paul wants to show that he is serious with his estimate of Philemon.

Then follows the greeting permeated by the same persons who were sent greetings in Colossians. This is yet another sign that the letter was written and sent at the same time.

Then the letter ends with a customary expression of desire for the grace of Christ. This remarkable little letter thus gives us such a concrete and realistic example of what it means to live by Christ's grace, in the kingdom of forgiveness, where one receives forgiveness without limit and gives forgiveness without reservation.

HEBREWS
Introduction

The Author

Concerning Hebrews, we do not know much more than we can guess as we read it. In antiquity a person knew nothing certain about the author. Among the church fathers in the east many believed that it was Paul, and so gradually that notion prevailed also in the west, and the letter was commonly accepted as Holy Scripture. It accompanies all the oldest manuscripts from the New Testament that we know. However, it is placed after the letters of Paul that were already accepted from the beginning, and the content gives no information about the author.

Some of the later church fathers (around the year 200) already pointed out from both speech and method that Hebrews is so distinctive that it had to have been written by someone other than Paul. (Some guessed Barnabas or Luke.) Both Luther and Calvin thought the same, and after the reformation, people of evangelical persuasion have commonly been convinced that the letter must originate from one of the Apostle's coworkers or disciples.

From the letter itself we can see that the author must have been a Greek speaking Jew. He is very familiar with the Old Testament in its Greek translation. It is that which he cites throughout, especially when he diverges from the Hebrew text. He is very familiar with the scribes' manner of reading and use of the Bible, and he uses their manner of interpretation and arguing. At the same time, he writes as a cultured Greek who received an academic education. He seems to have been acquainted with Philo, a learned Jew in Alexandria and a contemporary of Jesus, who in his writing attempted to make Judaism feasible for philosophically interested Greeks.

As mentioned, in antiquity some guessed, among others, that Barnabas was the author, a theory that has received currency among modern exegetes. Barnabas, Paul's perennial coworker, was a Levite and a citizen of Cyprus (Acts 4:36). As a

Cypriot, he spoke Greek and as a Levite, he ought to have had in-depth knowledge about the temple and temple service, which play a great role in Hebrews.

Luther proposed that the author was the learned Apollos, who is spoken about in Acts (18:24f) as well as many places in First Corinthians. Even this theory has received new credibility among contemporary exegetes to be "not so bad either." Of course, Apollos was a citizen of Alexandria, the city of Philo, "a cultured man, very knowledgeable in the Scriptures," and he "emphatically rebutted the Jews and proved with the help of the Scriptures that Jesus was the Messiah." According to First Corinthians, some were also impressed with his Greek education and eloquence. All this fits well with the author of Hebrews. However, here we only guess. The church father Origen (around 200) came to the often-cited judgment that God alone knows who the author is. So, we learn to be content with that.

The Addressees and Purpose

A person can ask if Hebrews is really an epistle. It does not begin like letters did in antiquity, but the conclusion is done in the style of a letter. Rather, it could be called a sermon. It intends to give Christians instruction and edification, and it was certainly read during the divine service, broken up into smaller pieces.

The actual name "Hebrews" (or more literally translated: "To the Hebrews") is regarded to be a rubric that was added later, that does not have any direct support in the letter itself. By "Hebrews" a man meant Jews who spoke Hebrew (or rather Aramaic) to differentiate them from those who had Greek as their mother tongue. However, the letter is written in Greek and addresses itself to people who are used to reading the Scriptures in Greek. It may be a question concerning Jewish Christians, but the matter is disputed. Some think that the author addresses a group of lawfully faithful Jewish Christians, perhaps a fraction within a congregation that began to falter in their Christian faith and may have been in danger of returning to Judaism. Others think that it is uncertain if the author was chiefly thinking about Jewish Christians. Perhaps the truth is that he writes to an average early Christian congregation with a core of Jewish Christians and such gentiles who "feared God," i.e., who were influenced by Jews and very familiar with their religious use of Holy Scripture. We may remember that the Old Testament was the Bible of early Christendom that was always read and explained in the divine services. Paul makes diligent use of it in his letters, and he exposits it according to the methods that he had learned from the rabbis in precisely the same way as the author of Hebrews does.

In any case, the point of the letter is clear. The author wants to show that no one can compete with Christ. He is greater than the angels and greater than Moses. He has carried out a work that has decisive meaning for all people in all times. All that God has similarly made with Israel has only been a preparation and a foreshadowing.

Time and Place

Hebrews has much to say about the temple service in Israel, and sometimes it sounds as if it were still being performed. In any case, it does not say anything indicating that the Temple has been destroyed and that sacrifices can no longer be offered, which otherwise could have been a strong support for the author's train of thought. Of course, he emphasizes that there has come a new order for Christ that makes the old temple service superfluous. So, it appears as if this letter appeared before 70 A.D. However, this is not certain. Neither can we draw any conclusions from that which we know about the addressees. They have already been Christians for a considerable period of time, but they can remember when they became Christians. They have been exposed to persecution; they have been harassed, mocked, and robbed of their possessions. However, it seems none of them have suffered death for their faith. All together these conditions fit in a long series of congregations, but not Jerusalem, and in the question concerning Rome only up until the great persecution under Nero, 64-65.

It is just as hard to form an idea as to where the letter may have been written. There is essentially only one concrete bit of information, namely a greeting at the end from "those who are in Italy." In all likelihood, this means that some Italian emigrants, who settled down somewhere in the immense empire, send greetings home to their compatriots. A person has therefore guessed that the letter had been sent to Rome. It was known there already in the middle of the 90s, because it is cited in First Clement (written around 95 A.D.). That which was said about the recipients can fit very well with the congregation in Rome, if it was written immediately before Nero's persecution, perhaps when it was already under full sail.

Many of these questions will be treated in more detail within the commentary. In conclusion, it can be said that there is reason to say that this is written to some congregation in Italy, perhaps the one in Rome. In such a case, it must be written before the year 65. But we know nothing for sure.

The Scriptural Exposition of Hebrews

Hebrews largely consists of expositions of scriptural passages that the author uses to prove what he wants to say about Jesus Christ. As we already said, he uses the Septuagint, the Greek translation of the Old Testament. If a person compares these passages with our Swedish (or English) translation of the Old Testament, there are often great discrepancies. This also shows that the author sometimes gives them a content that does not seem to fit with the context. The whole work can then be very puzzling, but it is because here we encounter a manner of expositing Scripture that was adopted among the Jews and commonly practiced by the rabbis. They were convinced that the scriptural word could contain more than one meaning. Behind the immediate meaning that anyone could ascertain lay additional truths that a person could find if he dove deeper into the text. A person read it in light of other Scripture passages; a person tested all conceivable meanings that a word could have; a person took into consideration different reading styles and different ways to add vowels to the Hebrew text, which only consisted of consonants. So, a man found hints, foreshadowings to that which would later be the reality and teachings that applied to the time the man himself lived in. A person often interpreted the text figuratively and allegorically.

According to modern scientific methods, a person does not read the Bible in such a way. Instead, one uses an historical approach and reads the text as a document from a foregone period. The people a person meets there are assumed to think and speak so as one according to other sources can be thought that people thought at that time. The text shall thus be understood exclusively from the conceptions of that time and the common cultural background. If a person measures the interpretation of Scripture in Hebrews with this measure, it appears lacking.

Here we have to make it clear that it does not depend only on two different manners of interpretation but of two different conceptions of reality. Modern science limits itself consciously to the "objectively ascertainable," thus to external facts. It observes everything as an event within this world determined by such causes that anyone can ascertain. A man counts nothing with causes that lie outside the material world, for example, God, if such things do not express themselves scientifically. It does not belong to the reality that it studies. This means, for example, that a person does not count that God would have spoken through an Old Testament prophet or Psalm writer or that which was said long before the Babylonian captivity would be able to say something essential about that which happened centuries later and be a message to men in coming generations.

However, according to Jewish and Christian conceptions, it is just this that is the essential, that which gives Scripture its meaning. It is that which motivates us to engage it. In the Old Testament we have prophesy, foreshadowing, and allusions that shed light on the works of God, even such as would happen much later. According to both Jewish and Christian conviction it is the Messiah who is the central figure in the Old Testament. He is the goal and the meaning of all God's operations. According to Christian conviction, the deepest dealings of the Old Testament deal with our Messiah, Jesus Christ. It is full of foreshadowings and allusions that speak of Him. Therefore, a correct interpretation is an "interpreta'tio christia'na," a Christian interpretation. This is what Hebrews gives us.

One such interpretation can appear arbitrary, but it is not. It does not interpret the Scriptures in whichever way, but it reads it in light of what has actually happened. It has found the key to the right interpretation in Jesus of Nazareth. It proceeds from God, who speaks to the fathers and through the fathers, knows what He plans to do, and lets the picture of His Son be woven into the description of Israel's fate, in the message of the prophets, in the temple service of the High Priest, in the sacrificial rites, and in the mysterious figure of Melchizedek.

If there really is a God and if He has dealt in such a manner, it is a question that science does not undertake to answer. In such questions there is no "objective" answer because it touches upon a reality that is inaccessible to instruments of measure. This is also true concerning the question of who Jesus really was. It is this question that Hebrews wants to answer.

Hebrews and Our Time

Hebrews is often experienced by contemporary readers as fanciful and strange because of its manner of expositing the Scriptures. We have already seen that this manner of exposition asks the most serious questions of us modern men. This is not the only point where Hebrews is relevant for our day.

Above all, this is true of the chief theme, Christ's unique place in existence. This also applies to the exhortations in the letter. They direct themselves to people who can already look back a long time as Christians. The first love belongs to the past. Everyday life and inertia are noticeable. Now it means to hold out, to take seriously what a person received and be renewed by it.

There is also a noticeable similarity between the situation where Hebrews came to be and the situation that a person often encounters in an old state church. Here Hebrews has a particular message to our day when it so pervasively and constantly points to Christ and says that that which He did once and for all is the remaining basis for all Christian life. It seems to be more and more relevant even when it points to the persecution that some must deal with and should prepare to encounter. We all have reason to read this letter, of whose sender and recipients we know so little, as a message directed to us today.

Hebrews 1

1-3 The Son is Without Parallel, Greater than All Creation

Hebrews begins as a sermon or a tract, not as a letter. With a long sentence that encompasses the first four verses in Greek, we learn what this sermon is about: the Son's incomparable place in the world. So, it takes up a subject that is just as relevant today as in the first century: Why just Christ? How can our position before Him have such a decisive meaning?

Hebrews answers: something decisive for history has happened here. God has intervened in a manner that has an all-pervasive meaning for us all. What He has done cannot be compared with anything that has happened before. Before God spoke through prophets; now He has spoken through His Son. At that time the message applied to the fathers; now it applies to us. At that time God spoke for a long time and in many different ways. Now He has spoken a final and decisive Word. The world has entered into the last era of its long history. Naturally, the "fathers" means the Jewish people. The expression indicates that the author speaks to Jews. However, he could say the same thing to the gentile Christians, for whom it was clear that the Church was God's new Israel and that they were the spiritual heirs to what God had done since the days when He had Abraham depart from his father's house.

So now God has spoken through His Son. The Son is far greater than all earlier witnesses. He shares in God's being. In Him, God's glory radiates. The phrase "imprint of his nature" can mean an impression, an authentic picture of the true reality. (The word that is here translated with "nature" more often means "reality.") The Son is not only an instrument. He is "heir of all," partaker of all that God possesses. He has a share in creation, and He holds it with power. His particular work is that He carried out a purification from sins. All this is now developed in detail.

4-14 The Son is Greater than the Angels

The Son is totally unique. He cannot be compared with the angels. His name already shows that He is someone far greater. The author ponders the name "the Son" or perhaps "The Lord," *Kyrios*, the name above all names, that was God's own.

The author now shows this with a long series of citations from the Scriptures. He reads it in the same way as we speak about an introduction. Here God speaks. The word does not only deal with those who lived long ago, but they have a message for all times and deal with important things that God plans to do. The most important thing it speaks about is the Messiah and His kingdom.

Three of the Psalms that are cited here were regarded as messianic psalms. This applies to the citation that begins "you are my son....", "Your throne, O God..." and "Sit at my right hand..." (from Psalms 2, 45, and 110). In our era it has been made applicable within exegetical circles that from the beginning such psalms were "royal psalms," which in oriental fashion hailed the king as a god. If this was the original meaning, then in any case, it lost all meaning among the Jews in the days of Jesus, where people read and sang these psalms thinking of God and His Messiah. This is why Hebrews uses them to show that the Messiah stands far above all angels—something that was not always obvious to the Jews.

It is harder to understand how the author thought that the other citations can deal with Christ. It is conceivable only if a person remembers how He viewed the Scriptures. The word "I shall be his Father, and he shall be my Son" is taken from Second Samuel (7:14) where God speaks to David and promises him a descendant on the throne. On the one hand, the word clearly points to Solomon. However, his name is not mentioned. It speaks only of an offspring whose throne shall remain "forever." So here a person could see a promise that reached beyond Solomon, and also applied to "David's Son" whose kingdom would have no end. The cited verses find their final application in Him.

The verse "let all God's angels worship him" is taken from the Psalm (97:7, so as the verse sounds in the Septuagint). In this Psalm the LORD is praised as the great King, who steps forward in glory and power. However, Christians read it as a psalm about the Lord Christ. We see this from the introduction to the citation: So, God says when He brings His firstborn into the world (perhaps through the resurrection, perhaps at His return, in any case as victor, King, and LORD). So, a person reads these words as a proclamation from God who invited all the world to praise His Son.

The citation about the angels that God can make into winds and flames of fire (and thus so are changeable according to His will) is also taken from the Psalter (104:4, even here according to the rendition of the Septuagint). As a contrast, the already mentioned verse from the messianic psalm (45:7) is given first place to be followed by a passage that deals with God's eternal immutability (Psalm 102:26f). The latter can appear strange because the passage deals with God and not about the Messiah. Yet a person has clearly determined that here we are talking about God's intervention, then He shall "reveal his glory" and "free death's children," then "all people shall gather to serve the LORD." So, a person also saw a prophetic indication of God's work in Christ—and thereby also a proclamation of the eternity and power that Christ took part in.

So, the conclusion is: All other spiritual powers are no more than servants. However, the Son shares in God's own being. He is God.

Hebrews 2

1-4 A Person may not Despise such a Salvation

So here something happened that is outstanding and inescapable. If a person has been able to hear of it, then it is important to pay close attention to it and not just let it "float by" as it literally says. To apostatize or fall away is seldom the consequence of a thoroughly well thought out decision. For most, it happens that they are just driven along by the stream. This is what the author warns against.

He reminds them of how Israel's children had to face their infidelity to the covenant that God made with them at Mt. Sinai. Yet this covenant could not even be compared with that which was prepared by Christ. The old covenant was mediated by angels, according to the established Jewish faith that we encounter in the New Testament (Acts 7:53, Galatians 3:19). However, it is different with this new covenant. It was the Lord, Christ Himself, that proclaimed it. Then it was confirmed by those who heard Him, meaning the apostles, His fully authorized envoys and spokesmen, and in turn their word was confirmed by God Himself who allowed signs and miracles to happen and gave His Holy Spirit to them who received His Word.

A person can take notice of two interesting facts here. First, that the author of Hebrews clearly counts himself among those who did not receive the gospel directly from Christ but through the mediation of His apostles. So, he himself was not an apostle. Then he speaks of miracles and signs as a well-known fact that could apparently be confirmed by a series of witnesses. Even Paul speaks about them in the same way (2 Corinthians 12:12).

5-18 The Son's Humility is Part of His Greatness

That Christ is the Lord of everything will be revealed in "the world that shall come," that which the gospel speaks about. Yet it does not look as if "everything is in subjection to him." However, the Scriptures say that it shall be so. We have already heard a passage quoted that says this (in the last citation of the preceding chapter, Psalm 110:1). Now there follows a similar occurrence, a long citation from Psalm 8 that concludes with the words "you laid everything at his feet." It is this that is the main thing in the citation. The author emphasizes that: Here everything is subjected to Him. So, we know that the kingdom that comes belongs to this.

In the meantime, there is now more in this Psalm citation that has been of meaning for the author of Hebrews. As we read it in our Old Testament, this deals with the sublimity of man. It says that God made him "little lower than heavenly beings." It is a clarifying translation of a Hebrew expression that literally means "someone a little less than gods." Those who translated this passage into Greek also made a clarifying translation and wrote "you made him someone little lower than the angels." This "someone lower" can also mean "for a little while." So, the author of Hebrews understood it, and saw a reference to the Son of Man in the phrase "a son of man." So, he found a deep and clear truth about Christ. A method of interpretation such as this was established among the Jews. They were convinced that below the surface meaning of God's Word, that which a person immediately sees, there is more to discover, if a person tests the different meanings of the words and sees them in light of other Bible passages.

So here the picture of what used to be called Christ's "humiliation" and "exultation" appears. For a short time, the Son operated in humility, "lower than the angels." He suffered death. However, it is precisely for that reason that He has "been crowned with glory and honor." Normally, a person assumes that the word points to His exultation at the Father's right hand. However, in Hebrews this has a special meaning; Christ's exultation means that He has been inserted as the great High Priest, the atoner of our sins, He who brings forth an eternally applicable sacrifice and remains the great intercessor. A little later it says that it is precisely as the high priest that He received "glory and honor." In the Septuagint, they used the word when it speaks of how Moses clothed Aaron in the robe of a high priest (2 Moses 28:2).

To Christ's exultation, His glorification and honor, belongs first and foremost that He is the Atoner. That He received all power, means first and foremost that He has the power to forgive sins and can remove all guilt. He has received this power and glory "by suffering death." He has received His place of honor as high priest "through God's grace," as a link in the saving work of God, so that He might taste death so that everything might come to good. Essentially, it is written: "so that He would taste death for all." He receives His place of honor as high priest to die for His people.

It is in this connection that the name Jesus is first mentioned in Hebrews. Then it reappears almost as often as "Christ." However, Christ is seldom called "Lord": Here the language of Hebrews diverges markedly from Paul's letters.

In what follows we get to hear more of how Christ's suffering belongs together with His exultation. It was necessary that He suffer. God who is the Creator and Lord of all things could not save His lost children in any other way. They were helplessly separated from Him and could not be taken up into communion with Him without first being purified. It was the Son's task to carry out this purification. He would be a "chief" for those who would be saved. The word for "chief" could also be rendered leader, guide, pioneer, one who opens the way for His people. In order to do this, He must first be "made perfect" through suffering. This does not mean that the Son was imperfect before. The word "perfect" is used here—and a couple of other places later—concerning the consecration of the high priest to His service. What was lacking in the Son was not any characteristic or ability. But there remained a part of the work that would be completed—that which He said in the hour of death: it is finished.

So, it is the Son who sanctifies sinners and makes it possible for them to meet the Holy. They themselves can only receive. Though there is such a fundamental difference between them and the Son, they still have the same Father, and it is wonderful that He knows them as a brother. Again, there are a couple of Bible citations that show this. We can perhaps think that this is strange, that the author of Hebrews does not give examples of how Jesus, in fact, called the disciples His brothers. Instead, He goes to the Old Testament. However, for Him the scriptural word is the most sacred of all. So, he cites the 22nd Psalm (which begins "My God, My God why have you forsaken me" and which in so many places cause us to think of the suffering of Jesus). To this he adds a citation from Isaiah (8:17f), taken from a chapter that fits the Christian situation precisely and that which now happened in Israel.

Then there follows a final passage that deals with the incarnation, about the great miracle that the Word became flesh (as John says) and that He who was in the form of God assumed the form of a servant and became like us men (as Paul expresses the matter). Hebrews tells us that it was necessary so that He would be able to be our high priest. Here the word is mentioned for the first time, though the author has long had the thought in mind. In order to overcome death, He Himself must die. So, He must become man. Death is our enemy, a tyrant and destroyer. At the same time, he has power over us. No one can escape it when it desires to strike. It is completely natural that men fear it. The Son wants to free His brothers from this fear. Therefore, He must become like them. How His death could rob death of its power is only said later. Here instead is mentioned a different side of the incarnation: as man the Son could not only suffer but also be tempted. Even this belonged to His task as a faithful high priest, and so to His glory and honor.

Hebrews 3

1-6 Jesus is Greater than Moses

An appeal to the brothers is made again. They are "holy," which does not mean moral perfection, but set aside for God. They really have received a "heavenly calling" and are taken up into the kingdom of God. So, they shall now perpetually look to Jesus. He is our "apostle and high priest." "Apostle" is called an envoy with full authority, who can deal and speak in his lord's place. It is just that which the Son has done. It is Him whom we confess. We know that He faithfully carried out the task He had received.

There now follows a comparison with Moses who was also faithful in the task he received. For the Jews, Moses was the greatest that ever lived. God had shown him a confidence that not one prophet had received, and he had been "faithful in all of God's house" (Numbers 12:7)—he, like Jesus. And still—what a difference! Moses was faithful as a servant. He served in the house that God created. What he did was not something final, but only a witness to something that would come. However, Christ is the Son who is rightfully ruler over the house He Himself created. His house is the new Israel, that which shall remain, and where we are received. If we . . . once again, the admonition. This means to hold fast to that which we have received, a bold victory and certain hope. There is no question about feelings and moods or of personal characteristics. It is a question of a reality that gives us a fundamental reason to be bold. It is a "victory sure" hope . . . once again, an expression that is hard to translate, that speaks about "hope's pride" (or "fame"). It is a question of the certain victory in the arrogant joy of the opposition's eyes, and security that the gospel gives.

7-19 A Warning Against Unbelief

Again, there follows an admonition that is a consequence of that which has just now been found. Jesus is far greater than Moses, the greatest man who lived on Earth. To be able to hear the gospel of Jesus is to be placed before an offer and a possibility that spreads over all else and places us before a choice with eternal consequences. Here it means to listen and not harden your hearts. We stand in the same situation as those who are described in Psalm 95. There God reminds His people of what happened during the sojourn in the desert during the time of Moses, when people opposed God and forwent the promise to enter into the promised land. As usual, Hebrews follows the Greek text called the Septuagint. In the Hebrew text there are a couple of place names (Meriba and Massa) that the Greek translators circumscribed according to the meaning the names had (2 Moses 17:7). The author of Hebrews has read the text so that the forty years came to apply to God's deeds in the desert instead of for the time God was angry with His people, which of course did not, in fact, play a great role.

This time it was God's own people on the journey to the land where they would enter into God's rest. So, it was now also with the Church, God's new Israel, which had been called out of the darkness of unbelief, the spiritual Egypt, and were on the way to the promised kingdom. Everyone had the experience that this was the matter of a desert journey with dangers and privations. It was easy to begin longing for Egypt. It is that which Hebrews now warns against. The heart of unbelief within us can take the ground. We must encourage one another. It is still called "today." The call from God reaches us every day anew. It means to hold fast "to that which was really already begun for us." This used to be translated as "at our first confidence," but this translation seems to be lacking any basis. It touches upon a word that was earlier translated as "being." The basic meaning seems to be "reality," something's true essence. The reality in question here is that which encounters a Christian from the beginning, Christ Himself.

Who was it that never arrived? The trembling tragedy lies in the answer: Just those who once gathered around Moses for the great departure from Egypt, those who were able to see God's great deeds. Would this same tragedy now be repeated? Here a person had gathered around Christ, had seen God's powerful deeds and had participated in the great departure. Should a person in the end be found lying in the desert? What was it that should be decisive for the end?

Hebrews answers: that it is faith, faith in Christ, the chief gift that God sent us to lead us in His will.

Hebrews 4

1-11 The Promise to Share in the Rest of God

The Israelites in the desert are also put forward as a warning example (as Paul also does, for example in 1 Corinthians 10). The new Israel can learn from their fathers in the old. All have been given to hear "the joyous news." Here it means so much as God's promise, His call, the message of His salvation. Yet it does not help to hear if a person will not receive the word in faith so that it becomes "involved" or "interwoven" in those who listen (as it is usually written). There is a risk of falling behind and never entering into God's rest.

Which "rest" is this a question of? The author of Hebrews has naturally seen that in the beginning it was a question that applied to coming to rest in one's own land, that which God had promised to His people. However, it must mean something else here. Essentially, Joshua did not bring all the people into this rest, which it is a question of. In such a case, God would not have established this promise later ("through David"—it is here said in accordance with the information in the Septuagint that is not found in the Hebrew Bible). Essentially, the words of Scripture are directed to those who hear it. So long as the Word speaks and says "today," this promise still applies. It is this conviction that lies behind the textual exposition we encounter here. Just as behind all real proclamation.

The conclusion is that this is a matter of the same rest that is spoken of already in the creation story when it says that God "rested from all his work." The author does not say how he imagines this rest. It is a matter of something that we cannot really imagine: God's eternal peace, security in a world where everything is as it should be, a world without unrest and fear, without hustle and stress, without danger and disappointment. This rest has been since the world's beginning. In the deepest sense, it is the rest that God wants to bring His people into. However, this time the people trespassed. Still the promise remains. And now it is serious. There is a "Sabbath rest," which we are called to enter. We can participate in God's own rest with all its beauty and security.

And then the admonition comes again: Let us strive to enter into this rest. Let us be warned by those who spoiled their chance.

12-13 The Living Word

The author has allowed the Scriptures to speak, and now he reminds us of what separates this word from others.

It is a living Word. It does not only say what someone else has said or done. Here it is God who speaks and operates. He comes with a demand and a comfort with judgment and forgiveness.

So, this Word is powerful. It is a teaching "with power and authority" as the people said in Capernaum. It can burn like a fire. It can be a hammer that crushes rocks. It can give birth to a new life.

It is like a sharp sword; it penetrates mercilessly. It uncovers and reveals even such things in our spiritual life that we are hardly aware of ourselves. This means there is enough content to the Word that it separates soul and spirit, bone and marrow, (or "joints and marrow," as it actually reads). It exposes our innermost intentions and is a judge over them, a power that tests in order to accept, justify, or condemn.

The Word does all this because it is the living God who speaks. We notice that the continuation of the text seems to deal with God Himself: all is exposed before His eyes. It is before Him that we must give account, even when He comes in His word.

Some have rightly called both these verses a summary of the New Testament's "Biblical view" if we may now use such a misleading word. It is peculiar because of course this "view" is precisely that we cannot put ourselves at God's side and look at it to form an opinion of it. On the contrary, in the Word it is God who looks at us, speaks to us, questions us, and lets us know how we look in His eyes.

14-16 Conclusion, We Have a Great High Priest

The author of Hebrews is now finished with the first part of his letter. He gives a summary that is at the same time a transition to the main theme of the letter: Christ is the great high priest. We have already heard that the Son is far greater than both angels and Moses, and that His greatness reaches its highpoint in His work as our high priest. We are now reminded that He "ascended through the heavens," this wants to say that He "sat at the right side of the Majesty" as it says already in the introduction. We are reminded that He suffered and was tempted and that for just this reason He can help those who are tempted. He can "have compassion with our weakness." The word "com-passion" shall be taken very literally. It does not mean a cheap overlooking, that costs nothing. On the contrary: He has really suffered with us and for us. He shares His sibling's difficulties in everything—only with the exception that He remains without sin, "obedient unto death on the cross" as Paul says. So, His royal thought is a throne of grace, where sinners dare approach to receive mercy and help "in the right time," when it is needed most, when it looks most hopeless. It is this faith we confess, and we shall hold fast to this confession—even through daring to approach the throne of grace.

Hebrews 5

1-6 The High Priest's Commission

We have now come to the chief theme of this Scripture: Christ who was our great High Priest. The author begins with a reminder concerning the High Priest's commission. For a Swedish reader (The Swedish Church and people never stopped calling their pastors priests after the reformation, but it is also helpful to note that there is a difference between a priest in the Old Testament and a pastor today), it is important to first understand that "priest" here means something else than it does in our daily speech. Our word "priest" comes from a New Testament word, "presbyter," (this is also true of the English word priest often used in Episcopalian circles) that means a congregation's leader. Actually, the New Testament pastoral [priestly in Swedish] office has its beginning in the apostolic commission to be shepherds and teachers in the church. We usually speak about "the preaching office" with the "administration of the means of grace." This gives a good description of the contents. Here it is the question about something else that the original text has a completely different word for. It means namely the Old Testament cult servants of the temple, thus, a sacrificial priest among whom the chief priest was the foremost.

It is this the author makes clear for us. The chief priest is a man who received the commission to serve before God by offering gifts (bloodless gifts) and "sacrifices" (slaughtered) all to atone for the sins of the people. "Priest" here means also "sacrificial priest" (in Greek *hierevs*). One can express differences so that the sacrificial priest is the representative of the people, who in their ways step forward before God, while he who has received the preaching office is God's representative who steps before the people.

Both of these commissions presuppose a call from God. The chief priest would not have been able to sacrifice if God had not instituted his office. It is this sacrificial office that Christ has taken over and fulfilled. Aaron's and all the old chief priests' service was a picture of that which would come. To the prototype also belonged Melchizedek, the venerable priest of whom we catch a glimpse in Genesis and another place in the Psalms (Genesis 14, Psalm 110), and who is here mentioned for the first time.

We may also remember that when Christ is called "chief priest," this is because of both His sacrifice, and His role as intercessor. Therefore, the author does not think about His teaching (that which one usually calls His "prophetic" office").

7-10 A Man Like Us

The chief priest represented his people and was himself taken out of their midst. So, Christ must also be a man, like us, and be our brother, to carry out His work on our behalf. We have already heard how He was tempted in everything. Now there follows a reminder about how He had to struggle anxiously and prayerfully. It is probable that the author has Gethsemane in mind, but the word can also have a wider view, both on the cross and at an earlier occasion Jesus could say "now my soul is in anguish" (John 12:27). In early Christendom a person knew that it really had cost Jesus something to bow to His Father's will. He Himself went under the general rule in God's kingdom, which is to submit. It was not easier for Him than for anyone else, to the contrary. However, this belongs to His "perfection." We have already encountered the expression (2:10) and seen that it does not mean that there was something Jesus lacked, but that there remained something that He must carry out. In this case, it meant the perfect obedience that He would test with suffering to become a blessing and salvation for humanity.

It is hard to escape thinking of Paul's words in the Letter to the Philippians (2:6f) about Christ who emptied Himself and became obedient to death on the cross and who for just that reason has been exalted above all things. Hebrews' author says the same thing but gives the thought a particular configuration: the exaltation means that Christ has become our chief priest. Again, he uses a citation from Psalm 110: "of the order of Melchizedek." However, he pauses for a moment before explaining what he means by that.

11-14 The Danger of Remaining on Baby Food

Again, the author interrupts his investigation and submits an admonition. We are reminded that he is writing to real people with special problems. He asks if they really understand the deep truth he wants to set before them. He gives them a rather sharp scolding for having become so sluggish. Apparently, they have been Christians for a long time. They ought to have been able to grasp basic knowledge. There is a Christian instruction, an apostolic *paradosis* that every Christian ought to know and be able to tell others. Apparently, this point has been lost among those to whom Hebrews is addressed, or in any case, among some of them. Perhaps the author wants to anticipate any objections that he is too learned and deep for their simple understanding. This happens even today when talk of the atonement, the major theme of Hebrews, is dismissed as incomprehensible "theology." The author allows the remark to return like a boomerang. He who says such shows only that he has been too sluggish and too superficial to receive which he ought to have known by this time.

There is a time when one is a "child in Christ" and needs milk. Paul also says this (1 Corinthians 3:1f). This is not anything bad. However, if a person remains on baby food, then something has gone wrong. Then a person can never understand "the word of righteousness." There is doubt about how this expression should be understood. It possibly means the deep truth concerning the new righteousness in God's kingdom that which the Sermon on the Mount deals with and that is indissolubly connected to faith in Christ. However, it is more likely that the author points to the Jewish conviction that a child could not distinguish between right and wrong but must grow up to "know how to refuse the evil and choose the good" (Isaiah 7:15). In either case, it is the matter of a serious reprimand, or even a warning, because the author still dares to come with solid food.

Hebrews 6

1-3 We must go further

So, it is high time to hurry on and not constantly stay stuck on a few elementary truths. The author gives us a short hint of what belonged to the first foundations of instruction. It begins with the call of Jesus: "convert" (or "repent," the same word as in the gospels, *metanoia*, change of mind). The dead deeds are all the sins of the gentiles. So, conversion means first to believe in the one true God. It touches on an instruction for gentiles, not for Jews. Then follows instruction about baptism. Strangely enough, it is written here in the plural ("baptism" in plural or "purifications," as the word literally means) as if it meant different types of baptism. Possibly this meant to distinguish Christian baptism from that of John the Baptist, or the baptisms that proselytes received or from the Jewish rites of purification. The laying on of hands can be that which preceded baptism or was used when praying for the sick—we do not know for sure. And finally comes the resurrection and the great judgment, certainly in connection with the instruction concerning the return of Christ. All this has been developed into an instruction about the work of Jesus and His work in the church.

So, these ought to be well known things. Now it means to go further—if possible. There is really an insurmountable obstacle.

4-8 The Irreparable Apostasy

There is an apostasy that is final. But what does it deal with? There are those who believe that the author of Hebrews means *every* apostasy, whenever a baptized person gives up his Christian faith. That some church fathers had reservations against Hebrews was because they interpreted this text this way and found that it did not fit with the gospel. However, the text can be interpreted differently. This depends on what a person reads into this that is listed here, that which one such apostate Christian has experienced. A person can interpret it as "normal" Christian experience. However, a person can also see it as an expression for an experience that is so deep that there is something more extreme to add. It would then be a question of having tasted "the heavenly gift" and "the powers of the age to come" in a manner that cannot easily be outbid here in time. He who then apostasies must consciously choose the dark. It is that he loves. He belongs at home there. He has his place among the enemies of Christ and crucifies Him again—"to themselves" as it says in the original text, with his own hand, complicit in the desire to get rid of Him, with cold blood, or however a person can best render the meaning.

A person ought to take notice that it does not say that the apostate may not return. It says that it does not happen. It is a matter of an impossibility that resides in his own being. The parable of the bad field also says this. Rain falls upon it, but the field does not absorb it.

9-12 Hold Fast to the Promise

Now the author hurries to say that he does not mean that it is so bad among those to whom he speaks. It is apparent that he wants to give them as powerful a warning as possible. He has noticed signs of laxity and laziness in their Christianity. However, at the same time, he gives them confirmation that they have "served the holy," which must mean that they helped other Christians, perhaps their own poor, or other fellow Christians, the way the Pauline congregations gathered money for the mother church in Jerusalem. God does not forget such things, he says. Apparently, he means that God will preserve their faith even if it must happen through his chastisement of them (12:7f).

It is now important to hold fast to the promises and preserve their hope. To this belong both faith and patience. The faith knows that Christ comes and that the victory is His. Patience knows that we can wait. God determines the point in time and not us.

Instead of the expression "to preserve a steadfast hope," some translations read "to have the full assurance of hope until the end" or something like that. This is because the original text contains a word (*pleroforia*) that can mean both "full certainty" and "fulfillment." Because both meanings fit in the context it is hard to know which a person should choose in a translation.

13-20 The Unwavering Promise of God

As an example of faith and patience, the author presents Abraham, he who hoped when there was no hope to speak as Paul (Romans 4:18). It is precisely this promise to Abraham that will have particular meaning in Hebrews. God bound Himself with an oath when He gave it. When men take an oath, they do it before a higher power. There is no one higher than God, and therefore He gave His oath before Himself. God's Word is already unwavering in itself. Here there is a double confirmation. A little later the author will show why we too have such a promise. Here he summarizes that which is familiar and only urges to faith and perseverance. We have an unwavering firm hope. He likens it to an anchor that holds firm. (It is this comparison that makes the anchor a symbol of Christian hope.) It has its foothold "before forgiveness," namely in the Temple, even in the holy of holies, with God Himself. Christ has entered there as our High Priest and opened the way for us, so that we can be certain of salvation.

Thereby we have been brought back to the main theme. For the third time it says: Christ is a high priest forever after the order of Melchizedek.

Hebrews 7

1-3 Who was Melchizedek?

There are only four verses in the entire Old Testament that speak of the mysterious Melchizedek who became so well known for both Jews and Christians. We first meet him in Genesis (14:18-20), in a chapter that has caused headaches for scholars in every generation. This chapter tells the story of foreign kings who invaded Canaan and carried off great booty, among other things Lot and his family. However, Abraham chased the intruders down, liberated Lot, and retrieved the booty. It was on the return home that he meets Melchizedek, the king in Salem who was a priest of God, the Most High. He blessed Abraham and received a tenth of his booty. We learn no more. However, this king and priest who lived in Salem (that is regarded as the same as Jerusalem) came to appear as one of God's great servants and witnesses before Moses. That is why he is called a different king (Psalm 110:4); you are a priest forever in the manner of Melchizedek. In Jesus's day this Psalm was commonly believed to deal with the Messiah. Jesus Himself invokes its first verse ("The Lord said to my Lord") to show that the Messiah is something more than an earthly descendent of David.

The author of Hebrews now references these two passages. He emphasizes what all Bible expositors at the time were agreed upon: Melchizedek must be a type (foreshadowing). His name had a deeper meaning. Both "the King of Righteousness" and "the king of peace" fit for the Messiah (Zechariah 9:9, Isaiah 9:6f). Even that which is not said has this meaning. It belonged to the principles of that era's Biblical interpretation that a person gave attention not only to all that was said but also that which was left out. Now this was the remarkable person here that received the blessed Abraham—The man who received a greater promise than anyone!—had stepped forth out of nothing, without any task concerning father or mother, family or style of life. He was a prototype of the real Messiah, Jesus Christ, He who was God's Son. He had stepped forth into humanity in a manner like no one else. He possessed eternal life. He was really a "priest forever." The psalm verse receives its deepest and truest meaning when it is applied to Jesus Christ.

4-10 Greater than Abraham

Now the author shows that Melchizedek must have been greater than Abraham. First, he received a tithe from Abraham. Otherwise, the sons of Levi received tithes, and they receive it only by the authority of the express regulations in the law. Melchizedek had no law to invoke and neither any lineage from Levi. Levi was not yet born. Abraham was his great-grandfather, and according to Jewish conception, he represented his descendants because he carried them in his body and was their origin. In this sense, Levi was present to give the tithe to Melchizedek. And further: he blessed Abraham, though it belongs to whoever is greater to give his blessing to he who is lesser. And for the third: all men who were able to receive a tithe have been mortal. However, this Melchizedek is a priest forever.

Here we notice how this whole time the author has Christ in mind. Melchizedek is the prototype but what is said of him also applies to Christ and receives the fulness of meaning only when it is applied to Him. So Christ is greater than Abraham, just as He is greater than angels and Moses.

11-19 The True High Priest

So, the Messiah should be "a priest forever in the order of Melchizedek." With that, God has already made it clear in the Old Testament that the whole of the temple service and the way of salvation that it instructed would only apply for a time. It is this thought that Hebrews now presents and illustrates. The old temple service, the whole of the Levitical priesthood and all the daily sacrifices were only a preparation, something that would apply for a time. They could make "nothing perfect" by taking sin away and carrying people home to God. This was why God promised to send a different high priest. Something pervasive would happen that upset the foundation for Israel's relationship to God. Israel's whole existence, the whole of its legislation, rested in the covenant in the people's worship of God and its center point in the temple. The law could not change without God, and He changed it in such a decisive point as the temple service, so the whole of the old system was revoked. It was just this that God prophesied that He would do when He called His Messiah "a priest forever" of another type than the old high priest. "The one hinted at here" was essentially Jesus Christ. The author gives a reminder of something commonly known, that Jesus was of Judah's tribe and so did not have the earthly lineage that was otherwise necessary for a priest. Instead, He received His office "through the power that gives indestructible life," God's sovereign power that creates new life and new orders. So, with that, that which was the old order was relieved of authority. Instead, something better had come, a new way to God, the one that the true High Priest had paved when He entered into the holy of holies.

20-25 The New Covenant

The guarantee for this new covenant is Christ Himself. Of course, God had confirmed it with an oath, that His Messiah should be a priest forever. The author of Hebrews had explained earlier what it means when God confirms His promise in this way. The priests of the Old Testament had never received such a confirmation. They would, of course, only exist for a time. However, Christ was a High Priest for eternity. The new order that has come with Him can never be changed. He is and remains the Savior for all eternity, who can save all of them who come to Him to be carried to God. He can save them, "completely and wholly" (or "for all eternity," as the verse can also be translated). He is also the High Priest in the meaning that He is the one who prays for His people. That He is a priest for eternity means that He is always an intercessor who is ready to bring forth prayers for others when they need them most.

26-28 A High Priest Such as We Need

Now the author can draw deep, constructive conclusions from his long and learned exposition. This was God's good intention, which He testified too so long in advance. It was this that Israel's sacrificial high priests were able to foreshadow and depict without knowing it themselves. They were all sinners who were able to sacrifice for their own sins also. However, when the fulness of God's time had come, the true High Priest offered Himself (so as the author will describe later). He was without sin, holy as God Himself, innocent and unblemished in all matters of evil. And He has not entered into God's heavens, into a kingdom where He is "separated from sinners" (for all their sins are atoned for and removed). All this is His for eternity, in a perfect manner. His kingdom shall have no end.

Hebrews 8

1-5 Christ does a Priestly Service in Heaven

Now the author has come to the main point of that which he wants to say. He emphasizes this. He has found a key word when it comes to interpreting Christ's work in all of its fundamental meaning for the world: Christ is our High Priest. This does not only mean that He "sits at the right hand of Majesty on the throne in heaven." All Christians knew that. It belonged to the foundational instruction that everyone learned from the beginning. No, Christ also does a "priestly service" in the real temple, that which is found in heaven. In the original text there is a Greek word that is used that we have as a loanword: Christ is "liturgy" in heaven. He served in the "true tent of revelation." Of course, God had commanded Moses to erect a transportable tent during the desert exodus, which became a prototype for the temple in Jerusalem. However, this was only "a copy and a shadow." The true sanctuary is found in heaven, and a divine service takes place there, a heavenly liturgy, that has decisive meaning for our salvation. Now Hebrews will describe what Christ does in this temple service as High Priest. However, there is one more thing that must be said before we can understand this properly.

6-13 A Better Testament

Through Christ, God has completed a new testament with His people. The Old Testament was made at Sinai. Its foundation was the law. In the law was also included all that which regulated the temple service and the priesthood in Israel. It was the highest and best that God had until then given the world. And yet it was only a foreshadowing of something better. It could not achieve something that really freed people from sin and brought them to God. In such a case, a new testament would be needed. However, already in the era of the prophets' time God had spoken of the New Testament that He would make with His people. Here Hebrews cites a long passage from the prophet Jeremiah (from the important and content rich chapter, 31:a). There God promises a New Testament. He rebukes His people who broke His testament but promises a better one in coming days.

    The author naturally knew that when Jesus instituted the Lord's Supper, He had said that now this New Testament had been created. However, he does not remind them of it. It was more important to remind them that God said it in Scripture. For both Christians and Jews, the Scriptures were the Old Testament. No one could deny that God has spoken about a New Testament there, just as He had promised to send His Messiah. The gospel, the joyous news, that the Messiah had come just now and brought the New Testament with Him. To this New Testament also belonged a new temple service.

Hebrews 9

1-5 The Temple in the Old Testament

As a background to Christ's priestly service, the author now paints a picture of the tent of revelation in the desert (that which the old bible translation called "the tabernacle"). So, it is not the Herodian temple in Jerusalem he describes. Neither Aaron's staff nor the jar with manna were found there not even to mention the tablets of the law, as they had been lost long ago. However, it was the temple of the wilderness that was made according to a heavenly prototype. So, it had something to say about the invisible temple where Christ was High Priest.

The description is taken from the Greek Bible. A person can see this because instead of the jar it is called the "golden urn." In the Hebrew text it only speaks of a jar (Exodus 16:33). That it speaks of a "second curtain" is because there was one also at the entrance to the "Most Holy Place." The incense altar stood before the inner curtain but was considered part of the "Most Holy Place" (1 Kings 6:22).

"The Mercy Seat" (the place of atonement) was the lid on the ark. It had a name that has commonly been translated "seat of grace." Paul uses the same word as Christ when he says that God presented Him as a "means of atonement" (Romans 3:25). It was here that on the great day of Atonement the great high priest would sprinkle the blood of an animal that was sacrificed as an atonement for the sins of the people.

All these details could be laid out allegorically as pictures of Christ and His salvation. However, the author says that he does not want to. He wants to concentrate on the "main point" that he now returns to.

6-10 The Retiring Service of the Priests

We receive a picture of the first temple. Now the service that the priests did there is described. This picture is simultaneously a picture of the most important and most profound in Christ's work.

The tent of revelation had two rooms. The outer is where the daily sacrifices took place. The priests constantly entered and exited there. However, their service was not sufficient. There was a more important sacrifice on the great day of atonement, that which only the high priest could carry out when—only once a year—he was able to enter into the Most Holy Place and sprinkle the blood on the lid of the ark of the covenant.

Now this is a foreshadowing and "parable" (the author uses the word parable) that points to the whole of Israel's history which now reached its fulness. All these sacrifices were incomplete. Why they were still commanded by God is something the author explains later. Here he only points out that they could never "perfect" the sacrifice so that it actually was free of their sins. The daily sacrifices were insufficient, as then the great day of atonement would not be needed. However, even this was only a prototype to the great and decisive day that would come. "The Holy Spirit indicates" this. He is really the one who speaks in the Holy Scriptures, meaning through the stories of what happened in Israel. In their history and their legal statutes, there is interwoven a picture of Him who would come. Even the "external prescriptions" only applied for a time—"until the time was ready for a better order"—where some of the prophets who pointed forward let what was coming be understood.

Here it is said that the priests "enter" the temple. So, it sounds as if they were still doing it, and thus, Hebrews ought to have been written before 70 A.D. That which was said in the previous chapter also points in that direction, when it says that Christ if He now—when the author writes—lived on earth would not even be a priest "because there already existed those who presented the sacrifices" (8:4). Or when it says that the old covenant "is soon ready to disappear" (8:13). Had the temple really fallen and the old temple service ceased, the author would have at least hinted at that. It would, of course, be a convincing confirmation of what he now said.

11-14 Christ's High Priestly Service

So, all the prototypes were such. Now came the fulfillment: Christ. He is the real High Priest who presented the atoning sacrifice that really applies. He came as a high priest "of the good things that have come" or (according to a different way of reading) "for the good things that we now expect." These "good things" mean both something that we have already received: forgiveness and sonship, and something that comes: the perfect service with God in heaven.

The real temple, the most holy place, where God Himself lives, is found in heaven. It is there that Christ has entered, not as the earthly high priest "with the blood of goats and calves" but with His own blood. The sacrifice is forever applicable. It has attained an eternal redemption; it does not need to be repeated but has happened once and for all. It has been presented "through an eternal Spirit." It has certainly happened in a visible way, through the events of history that took place in Jerusalem and Golgotha. But at the same time, something happened in eternity, outside of time and space. That which appeared was that evil men committed a miscarriage of justice. Yet at the same time, it was God with His Spirit who worked. Something important happened that must happen before God and within God Himself, something that could make children of God from sinners. Christ entered into the most holy place and offered Himself as a sacrifice to God.

In the old sacrificial service, "the blood of goats and bulls" was presented. (In the great Day of Atonement, the high priest sacrificed only "one bull and one goat.")

Or one blended the ashes of a red heifer with water and sprinkled it on those who were defiled, for example, by coming in contact with the dead. This gave an "external purification." It worked as a cure for ritual impurity and other blemishes, even for moral guilt, but only until later and only in an external way. It could not give real purification of the conscience and real peace with God. However, Christ's blood has the ability to "purify our conscience" by giving us full and perfect forgiveness.

15-28 The Meaning of Christ's Blood and Death

Greek has the same word for "covenant" as for "testament" (*diatheke*). In the translation here, we have used both words. Perhaps we think it touches upon two completely different things, but a testament is also an agreement concerning two parties. Certainly, the one party, he who establishes the testament, is completely sovereign, and he alone can prescribe the conditions. Yet this was also true of the covenant between God and Israel. It was a covenant "that God prescribed for you." As it says a little further on, God's covenant contains specifications for an "inheritance" that should come to materialize. It was also natural for the author of Hebrews to speak of a "covenant" that was at the same time a testament. We even do the same in Swedish when we call the writings of the new covenant "The New Testament." [This is just as true of the English language as it is for Swedish.]

Now the author has brought attention to yet another similarity with a testament that he will bring forward. A testament is not put into present effect if the one who established it has not died. This is also with both covenants. The new is put into present effect through Christ's death. However, even the old was put into effect through a vicarious death. At that time sacrifices sufficed. The bloody sacrifices had their deepest meaning in this—that they with trembling seriousness explained how serious sin was. He who violated God's law would surely die. However now in the time of the Old Testament, a sinner could come with a sacrifice that would remind him that he deserved to die, but that God allowed him to offer an animal instead. Through God's consent, the blood received a purifying power until the time was ready for a better order. Then the old covenant was sealed with the blood of sacrifices, and according to the law, the blood was used as a means of purification and a path for the forgiveness of sins until later. In this manner, there came the possibility for sinners to live in the presence of God despite everything.

However, all of this was just foreshadowing. The real temple was in heaven, and should sinners ever enter, a better sacrifice was needed. It was this that Christ brought forward when He sacrificed Himself. "He himself entered into heaven in order to step before the face of God for our sake." That the sacrifice happened once and for all is emphatically emphasized. The old high priest must enter into the holy of holies every year anew. However, Christ's sacrifice suffices to atone for the sins of the world once and for all and take away their guilt. The author is reminded of a parallel for us men. There are two things that shall only happen once for us: death and judgment. In the same manner, Christ died one single time, and then He comes, once, finally and irrevocably, for judgment. The difference is that we are judged while it is He who judges. There are mutual differences between the two events in Christ's life. He died to take away sins. When He comes again, nothing more can be done about the matter. Then He comes for the salvation of those who have already received the forgiveness of sins.

It can seem strange that "the heavenly archetypes" should need to be purified by sacrifice as it happened with their images on earth. However, the author is here thinking of something closer to an inauguration for a means of purification rather than a purification. In both cases, it means to open a path to God and create the possibility for a sinful man to live in communion with God. Both cases demand an atoning power that only God can give, and in both cases, the power is found in the offering of sacrifices. In the old covenant, they were only a preparation, a solution for the interim in expectation of something better.

Hebrews 10

1-18 The Eternally Valid Sacrifice

The author can now give a summary of what he calls "the chief point" of his message. The chief priest and all the others who belonged to the priesthood and the service of sacrifice in the old Israel were only a shadow of "the good thing that would come." He who would come cast a shadow before Him, but it was still not His real form that a man saw. The sacrifices did their service in expectation of Him. There was a perpetually renewed reminder of sin in them, a reminder of the most serious type. Of course, they said: you deserved to die, you who broke the Lord's law. This confession made the sacrifice his. The sacrifice also meant that he paid with his willingness to make good what he had broken, even if a person never could do it in full. Even in Israel the pious knew that no sacrifice could make good what a person broke.

Then the Messiah came, Christ. The Psalm that was just cited (40:7-9) says why. The Christians essentially read the Psalm as a book, where they heard Christ speaking again and again. They were more right in doing this than we usually understand. As a pious Jew, Jesus had time after time sang and prayed all these prayers. These words had also passed over His lips, and so they had received a deeper content than when normal men took them in his mouth. Now Christ says here that God who does not demand sacrifice has given Him a body. In the Hebrew text it speaks here of "ears," but in the Septuagint the text changes between the readings "the ears" and "body." In continuation, the meaning depends upon how one carries the word. As they are taken here, they receive a clear meaning that points to Christ: God gave Him a body, so that He would be able to fulfill God's will and offer it as a sacrifice. About Him it was written in "the book," also in Scripture.

When now Christ says this, it means that God abolishes the old order and establishes a new one. Christ offers the perfect sacrifice, He who really can take away all the sin and "for all times perfects them who are sanctified." This forgiveness is really whole and perfect. He who has a share in this work, which he has performed as a great high priest—his sin is wiped out forever. Before God he now stands as pure as if he neither had nor has the least sin.

There are two things that are assumed to be so obvious that they did not need to be said. It says nothing directly about how Christ's sacrifice receives this atoning power through Him, making the world's sin His own and taking all of these consequences on Himself so that He suffered death in our place. It hardly says anything about how we receive a share in this atoning work through faith in Christ. There is something glimpsed many times as something obvious, but that which dominates is the word against apostasy. The letter to Hebrews directs itself to men who believe. Faith is the obvious continuation. However, faith may not be so obvious that a person does not guard himself about it.

19-25 What it Means to Believe

The author is now finished with what he wanted to say about the basis for our faith. A forceful admonition to take advantage of what we possess in our faith now follows. First and foremost, this means to dare to believe that you may be a child of God. A Christian cannot say: "I know not if I dare to call myself a Christian." Christ has opened a "new and living way" to God Himself. A "living" way (as it is normally said) can mean that it is He, the living Lord, who is the way, but more probably, a man ought to translate it, "a way to life." We can go "in through forgiveness." This picture too is taken from the temple. The sinner is not even allowed to look into the Holy of Holies. However, Christ has opened the way for us all through forgiveness, "it is through His earthly body." The comparison can seem strange, but a person understands it better if he thinks about that which was forgiven, that which was a hindrance, has now become an open gate. It also means Christ's body. He has borne the great hindrance, our sins, upon the cross, upon it they were reconciled. Therefore, there is the one perfect forgiveness and way to God that lay open.

We also ought to go upon this way straight to God "with upright hearts," so that we do not squirrel away any of our sins, and "in full assurance of faith" so that we dare to believe that we may come for the sake of Christ. Our hearts are cleansed from all the accusations of the conscience, and we have been baptized. The words point to our baptism. That is where our bodies "have been washed with water that purifies." In the New Testament, baptism is the sure ground for both faith and life as a Christian. Baptism is not a single event in the past. It is something that a man lives in and trusts in, something that seals and gives the assurance of faith.

This faith shall now also be confessed before the world. A Christian is not ashamed of his hope. The Christian hope is certainty that Christ comes again and that all will ultimately depend on our position to Him. We have His promise that we believe Him on His word, and then the world may say what it will.

To faith belongs finally the responsibility to the congregation. As a Christian, a man is a member of Christ's body with responsibility to all the other members. So, we are to "encourage each other in love and good works." We cannot stay away from the divine service. Incidentally, we hear that this happened at this time. By continuation, we see how serious a person took the matter. What now follows is a warning for that apostasy that cannot be healed. Instead, we shall encourage each other, first and foremost in that we do not stay away but faithfully be present. And then follows the reminder that the day approaches: the great day when Christ comes. Perhaps the author had seen a sign of its nearness just in this that there were so many who seemed to tire and stay away. For such it comes and goes when the time approaches its end.

26-31 Yet Another Warning Against Apostasy

Yet again, the warning against apostasy is repeated. There is an apostasy that can never be cured. It is not a matter of a single fall for sin, and neither many sins that a Christian must also confess and confesses every time he prays the Lord's prayer. Here it is a question of consciously and intentionally sinning, though a person has been able to test and receive all that Christ can give. It is a matter of a decisive choice where one finally passes over to God's enemies. It means an attitude where one "tramples the Son of God under foot" and consciously insults all that comes from Christ, knowing well what it is a matter of. The gospel is not a message that says that everyone finally comes to God. All can do that by following Christ, the great High Priest, even in the Most Holy Place. However, a person can also say no and stand outside. Here one is completely carried there and sees what it means, and then leaves again, finally and clearly indicating that he does not want to be part of this, then the matter is decided. And the author reminds us, not the least us modern men, that it ends badly. He takes two verses from the Old Testament (Deuteronomy, 32:35f), of which the later reminds us that God's own people stand under His judgment. (In the 1917 translation, it is written that God will gather judgment to His people, but the original text, both the Hebrew and Greek have the word "judge," which for the Jews meant to sit for judgment, whether a person was condemned or freed.)

32-39 Persecution and Perseverance

Now the author does the same as previously when he gave his readers a powerful warning (6:1-9): he comforts them saying that he is sure it will not go so bad with them. He believes he has good reason for this. He reminds them of how it was "the first time," when the light came to them through the gospel, and they became Christians. It is apparent that this era lies sometime in the past, but if it is a matter of a few years or decades no one can say. In any case, they in this first time withstood persecutions. No one seems to have been killed, but it can still be rather hard. Many received public ridicule; they were mocked, abused, and plundered. It may have happened in connection with riots and uproar, but even the authorities had to have been involved because some had been put in prison. It was a common punishment to declare the possessions of the accused to forfeit, and perhaps this was what these Christians suffered. They received fame for their courage. They had stood fast during all abominations. Without complaint they were plundered, and they have—which perhaps demanded the most courage—without consideration put themselves in solidarity with those who were attacked for their faith.

We would really like to know more about these events. Then we could perhaps say where and when and to whom this letter was written. However, the sort of suffering and persecutions spoken about here belongs to the ordinary in the period of the first missions. We encounter them time and again in Acts. The description could particularly fit Thessalonica or one of the congregations in Galatia. It has often been thought that the addressees are in Rome. As a matter of fact, severe unrests appeared among the Jews in connection with the Christian mission in the 40s. However, the hints do not fit with the bloody persecution under Caesar Nero following the burning of Rome in 64. Some have thought that here the author—many decades later—reflects back, but the details in the picture do not fit. Rather the letter could have been written when the great persecution was getting under way. The serious warnings against apostasy could easily fit in that situation.

So, the author encourages boldness. He uses a word that has a double meaning of courageously stepping before those who have power. This courage would be needed now. He also emphasizes that perseverance is needed if a man shall be able to do God's will. The hour of testing has come—or rather the time of temptation. It is not certain if the matter is of just a short and decisive test. The time is still short. The Lord is near. Thoughts of the return of Jesus live, as always, in early Christendom. "He shall not tarry." And it would show that the Lord was, in fact, near even if He tarried. The certainty that He comes to be victorious and that every day brings us closer to that day has given Christendom a power to endure horrid fates and survive bloody persecutions in all periods of distress.

The word about the righteous shall live by faith is also cited in an important context in Paul (Romans 1:17). It is taken from the prophet Habakkuk from a context that is here rendered according to the Septuagint and diverges greatly from the Hebrew text. In Paul, the important point is faith in Christ who died for us. However, here it is applied to faith in Christ who will return. The one does not exclude the other. This hope meant that a person always lived before His face. The wait time became filled with His presence. For this reason, the time was short, and a person received the ability to tough it out that he otherwise would not have had. So, Christendom could also endure when a person gradually discovered that they were wrong to believe that only a few years were left or possibly a couple of decades. That which bore and gave meaning to existence was the faith that He would come, even if a person did not know when. The promise remained, and a person still lived with the same expectation under the same hope and in the same faith.

The author speaks of this faith in the next chapter.

Hebrews 11

1-3 What Faith Is

The entire chapter that now follows is devoted to a description of faith illustrated with pure examples from the Old Testament. All these heroes of the faith that are presented here trusted in God's promise, and the whole time the core of God's promise was that which would come: Christ and His kingdom. The context with the preceding is then clear. Before the threat of persecution and temptation to apostasy, faith in the promise is needed.

The passage begins with something that a person often conceives as a "definition of faith." Since Luther's day a person has usually translated: "Faith is a firm confidence in that which a man hopes for." And this expression can now apply to a religious faith—and several others. A modern man happily draws the conclusion that faith is something "purely subjective," a personal conception that requires no basis in reality. However, the author of Hebrews thinks the exact opposite. He speaks of the Christian faith and how it differentiates itself from all other faiths and private opinions. He uses a word that we encountered twice before (1:3 and 3:14) and that means "reality." It literally says: "faith is the reality in which a person hopes. It is the evidence of something man does not see." The author wants to say that where there is true Christian faith, there is the reality itself—God with His eternal kingdom—that enters into our world. It is this that causes faith to exist. "That in which we hope" is thus not an acceptance or an unsure thought. It is something real: Christ and His kingdom. Faith is evidence and a guarantee for this reality. He who himself does not believe does not let himself be convinced by such evidence. He cannot understand that faith can be anything but such an acceptance and expectation that he himself can have. But for he who has faith—thus communion with Christ—it is an overwhelming proof. He has a certainty that is just as firm as the certainty concerning the external reality.

Therefore, faith is something decisive. Through faith "the people of old"—the patriarchs of the Old Testament—God's "commendation," God Himself has confirmed that they walked the right path.

As a first example, the author takes faith in creation. It is not a theory concerning the origination of the world. It is something that we "understand in faith." And faith consists in that the reality Himself comes to us and opens our eyes. Then we see that God is present in all that He created. Behind the visible stands the invisible. So we see and understand what the Scriptures mean when they teach us that God created all this through His word.

Then there follows a long series of examples from the Old Testament. The early church—like the Jews—loved such enumerations. We have examples of them in Stephen's defense (Acts 7) and in Paul's preaching in Antioch (Acts 13). We can ponder that the fathers' faith is here compared to faith in Christ, but for the early church it was clear that even for the fathers it was a matter of faith in God's promise that from the very beginning had the Messiah and His kingdom as its center. In this sense, the Father had believed in Christ.

4-7 The Faith of the Primeval Patriarchs

The first three examples are taken from primeval history. First comes Abel. For the Jews, that God "had regard for Abel and his offering" (Genesis 4:4) was a clear proof in his faith. God sees the heart. Such a man of faith can be killed, but still continue to speak. The words can indicate that Abel came to stand as an example for all coming generations. Perhaps they indicate that his blood cried to God from earth.

The second example is Enoch, the seventh of the primeval patriarchs, of whom it says that he "walked with God" (Genesis 5:24) and that God took him away so that he was no longer seen. As a third example, Noah follows. Here the similarities between the primeval patriarchs and early Christendom are revealed. Noah was told that the end of the world was near, and he believed it. He built an ark and was saved. Christ has said that the world proceeds to its end. He Himself has built the ark where we can be saved: the church with baptism (1 Peter 3:20).

8-22 Faith of the Patriarchs

Then Abraham, who was the original picture of a man of faith even for Paul, follows. He departed without knowing where the path led. He lived in the promised land as a stranger without the right of residence. He neither grumbled nor doubted. He was willing to sacrifice Isaac though he knew that it was upon this, his only son, that the fulfillment of the promise depended. He could "not see and yet believe" (John 20:29). His faith protruded from the reality, from God Himself. And in Abraham's sacrifice there "lies a prototype," namely of Christ, the only Son who was offered on Golgotha to then come back from the dead. Here we have a hint that even Jesus had to believe without seeing. His suffering was a true suffering with all the anfechtung and angst that man can know and suffer. Yet his faith was a true faith. It had its basis reality, in God.

Abraham, Isaac, and Jacob all died without seeing the promise fulfilled. They only saw the promise from afar. They greeted it. And they saw that it not only meant a land on earth but something far better: "the city with firm foundations," God's kingdom, the city that God built for them.

So, they died. But they saw the future from their death beds. The confirmed their faith in the promises. They spoke about coming times.

23-29 Faith's Great Work through Moses

The greatest in the series was Moses. His faith was also a faith in the impossible. Already his parents risked everything for a hope that seemed unreasonable. And when Moses grew up, he did the opposite of what normal people would have seen as obvious. They would have thanked fate or their lucky stars or perhaps just God for the chance they received in life. Moses went the way of faith—against all odds and all that men would have called wisdom and reason. Yet it was precisely because of that, that he became a savior of his people.

It says that Moses took upon himself "the reproach of Christ." Christ was namely present in the events the Old Testament describes for us. Paul says that the rock that gave water in the desert was Christ (1 Corinthians 10:4). Everything pointed forward to Him and His kingdom, even when the ancients did not understand it.

The author wants to say that to the world the Christian faith looks like a gamble on something unreasonable and impossible, while in actual fact, it is the only true reality, the only thing that gives expression to reality itself. Faith does like Moses: it sees the invisible, or more correctly, the Invisible. Thus, it can hold out; it does not wear and break. And finally, it is proven right. Israel is saved through the Red Sea, but the Egyptians expire when they try to take the same path without faith.

30-40 Faith Makes the Impossible Possible

The author continues his journey through Israel's history. He remembers the walls of Jericho that fell and the prostitute Rahab who was saved because she joined God's people. However, the narrative then breaks off. It is too much for him. There are so many men of faith to speak about that he gives up. He lists off some of the judges; he mentions Samuel and David, but then he transitions to a summary account of such remarkable events that his people's history witness to, events that are all an expression for faith's unreasonable connection with God's reality. Several of these examples point to specific events in history; others mention what time after time has been repeated. That "they stopped the mouths of lions" could be said of Samson and David, but also of Daniel in the lion's den. That they "quenched the power of fire" may point to the three men in the burning furnace. That women had received back their dead speaks of the widow in Sarepta and the pious women in Shunem. Even war and victory are constantly spoken of in the Old Testament—to the wonder and offense of many. However, we have seen how obvious it is regarded that even military exploits could be a manifestation of faith. It meant to secure Israel's existence, and the whole of God's plan for humanity depended upon Israel.

However, these great works that were done in faith did not make life easy for those who believed. Even for the greatest among them it meant to believe without seeing and to trust in the promises without yet being present for the fulfillment.

To believe meant to suffer and be persecuted. There follows a new enumeration longer than before. It only consists of examples of suffering that people of faith had to endure. Some of them are taken from Scripture, others from Israel's later history, that which only went two hundred years back in time and is described in the books of Maccabees. Then it happened that whole families were tortured to death. They could have bought their freedom if they just renounced their religion, but they would have rather died. In Jesus's day a person in Israel had a long and bitter but faith strengthening experience of what it cost to confess the only God in a heathen world.

In many manuscripts there is a word after "they were stoned" that means to "be tempted" but also to be "subjected to interrogation under torture." In some translations it is rendered "they were martyred."

"They were sawn in two" refers to a late Jewish writing according to which the prophet Isaiah fled his persecutors and hid himself in a hollow tree which the persecutors cut down.

Of all these, none of them "saw the promise fulfilled." Individual promises could well be fulfilled, as with what has just been said. However, the great and essential thing to which the promise applied meant the Messiah and His kingdom, and this, the most important, they only saw in the distance. The fulness of time was not yet, but now it had come! The author and his contemporaries had received the great privilege of living in a time when God did what His faithful waited thousands of years for.

Hebrews 12

1-3 The Course, Witnesses, and Goal

Now comes the conclusion. We have so many witnesses, a whole cloud that surrounds us. They can teach us endurance and we need that. To live as a Christian is to have started a race that demands an "all in." Paul also used this picture. He could also speak about how a person must refrain from all that hinders. However, a new detail appears here: "the great cloud of witnesses." The picture must not be pressed. It is hardly they who look upon us. Rather it is we who should look to them. They are witnesses in the meaning of the New Testament: witnesses who testify that the promise holds, that the Lord is faithful, that it pays to endure.

We shall also despise every weight and particularly the sin that "ensnares us," as it says in some translations. A word is used here that is not in any other passage in the whole of Greek literature. It means "something that is easiest (or much easier) to snare." It can only point to the sin in general and its ability to ensnare us. It can also be a question of some particular sin that for us is a besetting sin. Both translations have good reasons behind them.

It also means to race and keep your eye firmly on the goal. And the goal is Jesus Christ, the founder and perfecter of our faith. "The founder" can be translated "chief" or "leader." In such a case, the meaning is that Jesus is who leads the whole cloud of those who believe that which has just been described for us. However, the former translation is perhaps the best because the author then says that Jesus is the faith "perfecter." Here again, he uses a word that is not found in any other place in Greek literature, and which he himself seems to have coined. The meaning is clear: one who fulfills and finishes a work. Jesus Christ, He who is the true reality, is He who wakens and perfects the true faith, so that He vouches for the truth and reveals the reality.

Therefore, Jesus is also the archetype and model for all faith's heroes, who now have passed in review. Even they refrain from the joy that lay within reach for them: Abram from family and home. Moses from the place of glory in Pharoah's house, the martyrs from the freedom they could have received by denying their faith.

The word "in place of the joy..." should also be translated with thought "of the joy..." Even then Jesus is a picture of the faithful witnesses, who had their eye firm on the joy that would come.

The example of Jesus shall also cause us to endure. He encountered an unceasing enmity (or opposition, as it can also be translated). A fight can be hard but if it is short, it can still be harder. It can be far harder to stand fast if a person is perpetually exposed to reviling and harassment. It is the daily attrition against a hostile and unsympathetic environment that usually cracks faith. For just this reason we are urged to look upon Jesus in order not to tire and give up.

4-11 God's Fatherly Discipline

"Still you have not yet resisted to the point of shedding your blood." Other Christians had had to do that. In Jerusalem, Stephen and James, the brother of John, suffered martyrdom. The first congregation to endure a bloody persecution with many victims was the congregation in Rome (during the reign of Nero 64-65). The word also fits in only if a person believes that Hebrews was written before the year 65. Undeniably, there is a premonition of an approaching storm that will put the Christians before a previously unknown test.

But how can God put His faithful to such a test? Faith in God's fatherly love seems to collide with that which actually happens with His children. This seems to have been the situation among those to whom the epistle of Hebrews is directed to. The answer is: have you forgotten what God says to His children? For just the reason that they are His children, they receive His discipline.

That parents should chastise their children was at that time self-evident to both Jews and the heathen. It belonged to a good and responsible upbringing. If a person did not discipline a child, then the man felt no responsibility for him, and neither did he have any real love for him. However, this is not some instruction concerning corporal punishment and discipline of children that is given here (though in any case, a person has the right to draw this conclusion; spanking is not something that can be considered reprehensible in all circumstances). Here it is only stated that discipline is received as a natural thing, and that everyone knew that it could be an expression of a parent's love and concern. Then it is stated that we have far greater reason to look upon our heavenly Father in the same manner when He disciplines us. He does it out of love, for our best.

This is an important part of the Christian view of the suffering that even affects those who believe. They are never a penalty. For Jesus's sake, all sins are forgiven. The guilt is paid, and a penalty does not factor in. However, as children we can receive Fatherly discipline that always points to something good and is one of the proofs that God loves us and that we are in His hands.

12-17 Waste Not the Grace of God!

Everyone has to help bear the weakness found in a congregation. Again, the author takes a pair of citations from Scripture (Isaiah 35:3 and Ecclesiastes 4:26). They speak about giving help to them who have difficulty making it. There are those who put themselves forth, even in the narrow way. They may not raise faults and sculling so badly that they cannot be bothered further. There are bitter roots, another expression from Scripture (Deuteronomy 29:18), but they may not be permitted to push away and grow so that they spread their poison. As a screaming example, Esau is mentioned. He is put forward as the prototype for a man who "took the joy that was set before him," a joy that did not last long, and thus wasted the precious thing that he possessed. He destroyed everything before him, precisely on this decisive point. He did that which could never be changed. Still, he hoped to receive his inheritance. He prayed about it with tears, "but he found no opportunity for repentance" (or "change of mind," as it says in Greek). Here again the dark mystery that met us twice before in this letter peeks out. There is a definitive no to Christ, an inner hardening, that never goes to the other. Perhaps a person can undo something stupid he has done. A person can try to get the provision to keep on going. Yet the heart has become unreceptive to repentance and faith that make it possible to live together with God. A person "does not find the way to repentance."

18-24 Sinai and Zion

Time after time we encounter in Hebrews the thought of the unfathomably great thing that is offered to us in the gospel, that which Jesus has hinted at in the parable of the Treasure in the Field and the Pearl of Great Price. Such an offer had never been given before, and it can never be outdone. It is important to grasp it.

Now this thought receives a monumental connection when the author sets Sinai and Zion against each other as symbols for the best there is before and the overwhelming new that has come.

We have not come to Sinai, he says. The Jews had reason to be proud and joyous that they were able to stand at Mt. Sinai and to receive the law from God, He who gave them more than any other people on earth had ever received. And still, it was the law they received. They had encountered God's majesty in all of its crushing power and supremacy. There was fire and dark clouds, storms and trumpet blasts. It was too much for them. They asked to not hear anymore. This is apparently what the author wants to posit, what he knew as a Christian: so, the law in its majesty is something that man must fear, something that can cause us to tremble. God is not to be played with. The outlines of this picture are streamlined here and emphasized with the freedom in the exposition that we have encountered many times before.

However, now God has led His people from Sinai to Zion. Zion was the rock upon which Jerusalem sat. It played the same role for the Jews as the Acropolis for the Athenians and the Capitol for a Roman. For the Christians, Zion was the symbol of God's kingdom and the new people of God, the Church. Now what this new Zion means is described here. It is God's city, that which before was called the city with the firm foundations. It is at the same time something coming and otherworldly, the heavenly Jerusalem, and something that already has a port and forecourt on earth. To Zion belongs the heavenly hosts of innumerable angels, but also an assembly and congregation of firstborn sons who have their names written in the heavens. This assembly, a joyful congregation that celebrates a joyful feast, is both in heaven and on earth. To it belongs "the righteous who have received full communion" and all the heroes of the faith that reached the goal. Yet even on earth, there are firstborn sons who have their names written in heaven. This Zion is the living God's city where the Almighty Judge reigns. However, the leader for the new covenant that poured out blood like rain sits there. It is called in the basic text, "a splash of blood," after the foreshadow in the Old Testament where a person splashed the blood of the sin offering as a means of purification. Christ's blood "speaks louder than Abel's." His blood cried to God and with the accusation of fratricide. However, Christ blood speaks with a powerful voice about an atonement who can let even blood red sins become snow white.

This has also come to us. What do we do now?

25-29 The Risk and Security

Yet one more time Hebrews warns its readers to take advantage of the salvation that is now offered to us. There is a risk that God's people will once again act as at Sinai and will "escape hearing." At that time, it applied to a voice heard here on earth. Now God has spoken from heaven. He has sent His son from heaven and then lifted Him there once again, and from the right side of the Father He now speaks to the world through His gospel. God has nothing greater and better to offer. This is God's supreme message. We should not wait for anything else. He who rejects this, he rejects God. What we then have to wait for is the last great settlement. When God finalized the covenant on Sinai, the earth shook. Through the prophet (Haggai 2:7) He gave the promise of a far greater upheaval. For Christians it was clear that this was that which Jesus spoke of. Heaven and earth shall pass away and give room for a new heaven and a new earth.

And this is the great security, says Hebrews. We have the promise of a kingdom that cannot falter. All else is perishable. However, that which has received a share in the kingdom of Christ shall never perish. Here is the foundation for a boundless thankfulness and security, but not for the satisfied security that changes the gospel into a colorless truism of a well-meaning God that no one needs fear. On the contrary, "our God is a consuming fire" (another citation from Deuteronomy 4:24). The God who spoke at Sinai was the living God. He has not changed. However, He has carried out a miracle of mercy that makes it possible for sinners to live as His children. The gospel speaks about this matter, and it is the gospel that Hebrews so urgently asks us to heed.

Hebrews 13

1-6 Three Ethical Ground Rules

As so often with Paul, there now follows a series of rather loosely assembled admonitions in a brusque and succinct style that is strongly reminiscent of the apostles. First comes a reminder of three ethical ground rules that we also encounter time after time with Paul. It begins with love for the brothers. Hospitality is mentioned as a special but important application of love. The inns of antiquity were often places with dubious reputation. It meant a lot for traveling Christians to be able to receive Christians in the home.

The second chief rule applies to the honor of marriage. Among the heathen this issue was in a bad state. It belonged to the greatest actions of Christendom that it created good homes. A person was very conscious of how strictly Jesus had taken the indissolubleness of marriage.

The third rule deals with money. Greed and immorality were counted as the sins that were most devastating to faith. The love of money excluded love of God. This view of money was completely religiously motivated: a Christian man can trust in God. He need not build his existence upon a foundation of money. The author emphasizes this with two scriptural citations (Joshua 1:5 and Psalm 118:6).

7-8 The Significance of Shepherds

The congregation should think of those "who spoke God's word" there. They are called "leaders." The original text uses a word that otherwise represents rulers, men of high office, and military commanders, but as in Hebrews and the 1 Clement, here is used for leaders of the congregation, such as otherwise are called shepherds and teachers, presbyters and bishops, or something else. Here it touches upon such as is already dead. It can be those who first lead the gospel to the congregation (so as is told in 2:3) or perhaps, more faithful, such as in the congregation which of the apostles or their coworkers were designated as leaders. The congregation shall have them in mind and believe as they did. For Christ is the same yesterday and today and in eternity. This well-known word seems to stand here a little unmediated, but the meaning can be that the gospel and the apostolic Christian faith, as the congregation from the beginning has received from their leaders, never can be changed. It is confirmed by the immediate continuation where it was warned by new teachers.

9-14 Nothing May Be Placed Next to Christ

"Diverse and strange teachings" have apparently exercised a certain allure for some in the congregation. The situation reminds us of that which we meet in Colossians or the pastoral letter, but it is hard to say which teaching it touches upon in any particular case. As a contrast to the true Christian faith in grace, also in Christ alone, a reference to "sacrificial meals" is placed here. In the original text, it is only written "food." Some believe that it touches upon Jewish regulations concerning clean and unclean food. However, it later speaks about that which comes from the altar, and therefore, it is rather a question about sacrificial meals. Both Jews and heathen could point to their sacrifices as a proven way to communion with God. Here the answer is now given that even we Christians have an altar. It must be a question about Christ and His sacrifice in Golgotha. Perhaps the author thinks particularly about the Lord's Supper. He mentions that something comes from this altar that can be eaten. "They who serve the tent of meeting" may be the Jewish priesthood. In such a case, it means that the temple still remains, and that the high priest still carries forth the blood of the sacrificial victims. However, the word can also point to "Judaizers" who still hold to the old ceremonies.

The author has found yet another detail of importance in the Old Testament foreshadowing: The bodies of sacrificial animals were burned outside the camp. So, Jesus was lead outside the city gates, outside the holy city, ostracized by His people. It made it that His own blood, and not that of goats and calves, cleansed the people. So, we shall follow the reviled one who is our Savior out there. Some have wished to interpret this as an admonition to Jewish Christians to no longer sit on the fence but understand that something now has come that in the long run is not compatible with Judaism. How much they then endeavor to remain faithful to the law, they will not be accepted. So, the Word surely has reality even for the gentile Christians. Even they are tempted to try to be tolerated by adapting to the religious practices observed by the environment. However, a Christian could not live like others. The offense was unavoidable.

15-16 Our Common Priesthood

Every time the text above has referred to "priests," it has meant sacrificial priests—they who served in the temple and were one of the foreshadowings of the great High Priest, Christ. Then Christ once and for all offered Himself; now the old sacrificial service in the temple was superfluous and meaningless. Yet there is a sacrificial service that continues. All who believe in Christ are called to carry it out: a spiritual temple service that remains partially to carry forth the sacrifice of thanksgiving and partially in sacrificing your strength, your time, and money in service to your neighbor, even a sacrifice of worship and service. For "such sacrifices are pleasing to God." Nothing else. It is this that is called "the common priesthood" and to that we were all ordained in baptism.

The word "priest" is here used in its Old Testament meaning and has nothing to do with those we normally call "priests" (pastors) and the "priestly office (pastoral office)." This Christian "pastoral office" is really something new that came with Christ, a commission to proclaim the gospel and be shepherds and teachers for the congregation. So it is not a sacrificial service but a teaching office.

17 The Respect for the Teaching Office

"The Leaders" are mentioned again; this concerns those who speak God's word to the congregation. Here we may hear that they "watch over our souls." They have their task from God, and before Him they shall once give account. A person should listen to them and abide by them, of course, when they speak God's word. It continues as we can see of the pastoral letters, that the shepherds shall faithfully keep to the gospel and carry the word forth just as it was given to them. When they do it, a person shall also receive it and abide by them. And the author of Hebrews adds what is a shocking reflection for many modern men: if a good shepherd has worry over his flock, then it is worse for the flock.

18-25 Final Wish and Greetings

The letter writer prays a prayer as Paul also normally does. Then follows a solemn final wish that conjures up the picture of the great shepherd and reminds one of the chief thought in the letter, the New Testament and the blood that sealed it. The conclusion is a typical "doxology."

The letter could have ended here, but a couple of more personal lines follow, such as Paul adds in many of his letters. First comes some usual disarming words where the author asks the addressees to forgive if he has spoken too boldly. Then follows some personal information, the only such information in the whole of this letter: Timothy has been released. This gives us no evidence for dating because we do not know when or how Timothy ended up in prison. If a person attempts to combine this information with that which can be taken from the letters to Timothy and Titus, a person cannot say more than that Hebrews ought to have come after these.

The greeting from "he who is from Italy" does not say much either. As we saw in the introduction, it is very likely to be thought of as a greeting from a relocated compatriot whose home was Italy, where the addressees are also to be found. Among the addressees the "leaders" are particularly greeted. They form a group next to the remainder of the congregation, "all the saints." As in the New Testament, the saints are a name for the Christians.

HEBREWS 13:18-25

There is much in this chapter that is reminiscent of Paul's language and style. The similarities are so great that some have proposed a theory that Hebrews must have been written by a coworker of Paul's, more or less at his commission whereby Paul would have added a postscript in his own hand. Another theory says that from the beginning Hebrews is a sermon or tract that by request was sent to another congregation—perhaps Rome—and that the last chapter or a portion of it is added as a sort of afterward from he who arranged for the transmission.

Such theories—more or less likely—can find endless variations without us coming any closer to the truth. In such a case, it is rather meaningless if we know of whom and to whom this letter has been written. The remarkable thing is that even if it would be written to Jewish Christians in a very special situation, so it has meaning for Christians in all times. It presents Christ as the absolute one off in the world's history. It admonishes His confessors to take the consequences of their faith and makes it clear for them that the gospel is an offer from God so overwhelmingly great that everything else takes a back burner. It consists of a new settlement with all half-hearted Christianity that regards it as more or less obvious that a person is a Christian but at the same times expects a variety of other forms of faith and morals that can also have their justification. Opposite of this, and in true apostolic manner, Hebrews sets the gospel of Christ as the revealed one, the inevitable and for all times applicable truth.

INTRODUCTION TO JAMES

The Catholic Letters

The letters that come after Hebrews in our Bibles have been called "catholic," meaning "the general," since antiquity because they do not address any particular person or congregation but direct themselves to the general (catholic) church. The name is slightly misleading. As the introduction to First Corinthians shows, Paul's letters too could be intended for a wider audience. Ephesians was most certainly a circular letter sent to many congregations in Asia Minor, in the same way as 1 Peter, and John's third letter is directed to a particular person though it is counted among the catholic letters. In their deepest sense, all the letters in the New Testament were written to the whole of Christendom. Otherwise, they would not have found a place in the canon.

The Place of James in the New Testament

A Swedish reader of the Bible is accustomed to finding James right after the letters of John. In the English Bible, it comes directly after Hebrews and stands as first among the catholic epistles. This is the old order that is found in almost all the Greek manuscripts. It is Luther who caused the relocation. He regarded it as uncertain that four of the New Testament books, namely Hebrews, James, Judas, and Revelation, originated from any apostle. So, he placed them last in his translation of the New Testament, and they still remain in this order in certain German Bibles. The same order has also been followed in Sweden, though Hebrews quickly found its way back to its accustomed place while James remained in its relocated place until the new translation of 1981 restored the original order.

A Tract

This letter is essentially a little tract that does not address any particular congregation but all Christians. It contains a short series of admonitions that are apparently influenced both by the Old Testament and by the instruction of Jesus. There is no question of what we call dogmatics or doctrine, but of ethics (morality), thus instruction concerning Christian morals and way of life. The epistle gives us fragments of an early Christian "parenesis" (an edifying admonition), collected without any visible plan. Such parenesis also appears in Paul's letters, as a rule toward the end, but the difference is striking. Paul uses admonition with reason of special conditions in a particular congregation. However, with James it is a question of general teaching with address to men in widely different situations.

The Author

Concerning the author, we do not know much more than that his name was James (Jacob), and he was a "servant of Jesus Christ." No one from antiquity knew who he was. Many thought that he was the brother of Jesus; others contested that. Even in the fourth century, the matter was discussed, and only at the beginning of the fifth century was it commonly accepted that the author was the James that the New Testament mentioned as first among the brothers of Jesus and apparently was the eldest of them. During the earthly life of Jesus, he does not seem to have been a disciple. Paul says that Jesus appeared to him after the resurrection, and in Acts we encounter him as one of the pillars of the mother church. When the other apostles left Jerusalem (likely around 40 A.D.), he was the obvious leader. In later sources, it is said that he received the appellate "the righteous" and for the sake of his piety was held in honor even among law believing Jews. In the year 62 the high priest Ananus saw to it that he was executed during a period when the Romans did not have a procurator in Palestine. Josephus says that James was brought before the great council, condemned to death, and stoned. The matter woke indignation even among orthodox Jews who complained to the newly appointed procurator and had the high priest deposed.

Could he then have written this epistle? That the author is a Jew appears obvious. Some scholars have proposed to show that it is a matter of a purely Jewish writing that received a Christian label, but there are so many reminisces of the words of Jesus and so many Christian thoughts in it that the theory might not be quite right.

The author writes in Greek that contains some "hebraisms," but is otherwise error free and otherwise witnesses to a rich vocabulary and a certain care for unusual words with a literary ring. The congregational life that the letter reflects shows many ancient features. It does not take notice of any tension between Jewish Christians and gentile Christians. He does not take any notice of a gentile environment. For example, it does not mention anything about servants who have gentile masters or about Christian women whose husbands do not believe. Such problems as socializing with gentiles or eating sacrificed meat are conspicuously absent. It only speaks of "elders" in the congregation, not about bishops or deacons. It could fit excellently in the mother church of Jerusalem during the 50s. There are also scholars—even of the higher-critical school—who regard the epistle of James to be the oldest among New Testament documents, appearing already at the end of the 40s. In such a case, "James the Just" could be its author, so long as one dares believe a Palestinian Jew could be so at home in Greek, or that in the mother congregation James had access to a coworker who had Greek as his mother tongue.

Meanwhile these same facts can now be interpreted in two contradictory ways. The absence of the problem that Paul wrestles with (the law, circumcision, clean and unclean food) could be because these were not yet relevant, but the reason can also be that they had long lost their relevance. In the latter case, the epistle must have been written long after that period, sometime before the close of the century. This is also the common dating among those who think that the author was a Greek speaking Jew in the second or third generation, and that the letter is a little collection of such material as was traditionally used for instruction in Christian ethics. In such a case, this material ought already to have had a very firm form. For understanding, it plays no great role if we date this epistle sometime before 45 and 62 (thus during the life of James) or a generation later.

James and Paul

Luther had reservations of a theological sort against the epistle of James. He saw it missing the essential in the apostolic message: proclamation of Christ's death and resurrection. Further, he thought James's teaching on the relationship between faith and works in chapter 2 clearly fought with Paul and the whole New Testament in general. So, he thought that James, especially in comparison with Romans, Galatians, and Ephesians, was a "proper epistle of straw." The picture is taken from First Corinthians (3:12) where it says that a person can build on the foundation of Christ with gold and silver but also with hay or straw. So, Luther did not want this book to be counted among the New Testament's "true chief books" but would not "hinder anyone from valuing it as high as he wants, because the remainder still says many good things."

In our day, we are more inclined to see the epistle of James as a piece of true early Christian parenesis. That it does not speak about Christ and His work of salvation does not hinder it from being for James and his readers an obvious assumption, though it was not repeated in precisely this context. Had Romans been missing except for chapters 12 and 13, then this would have still consisted of almost pure parenesis.

Concerning the relationship between Paul and James in the question of justification, we will return in the commentary on chapter 2.

James 1

1 Letterhead

The introduction to this letter is shorter than otherwise in the New Testament. It is a typical letter opening for antiquity that very shortly says who the sender and recipients are. Concerning the letter writer, we learn that his name is James (Jacob) and that he is a Christian. As we saw in the introduction, already in the early church people discussed who this James might have been. The addressees are "the twelve tribes in the dispersion." The dispersion (diaspora in Greek) was the usual name for the Jews who lived outside Palestine. However, just as in the beginning of First Peter the word here points to the members of the new Israel, which are also found spread about the Roman Empire.

2-4 The Persecution Can Bring Good with It

The first thing James speaks about is the "trials of every kind" that the Christians encounter. To be persecuted was something that every Christian had to figure. It was evidence that he was on the right path. Jesus had praised the persecuted as blessed. When for the first time the apostles were abused, they rejoiced that they were regarded as worthy to suffer for the name of Christ (Acts 5:4). So, James admonishes the tested to rejoice. They can rejoice in their trials. The trials could have the same effect as training for an athlete. It strengthens and develops. A person learns to endure and is brought closer to the goal: to be a complete and fully matured Christian. The word translated here as "complete" can also be translated "perfect." It is the same word Jesus used in the sermon on the mount when He says: be perfect as your father in heaven is perfect. It is possible that James has precisely this exhortation in mind.

5-8 Wisdom from God who Answers Prayer

Even an upright disciple can lack "wisdom." In the Christian sense, wisdom can be taken from God's revelation in the Word when the Spirit gives it life so that we understand how to apply it to ourselves and our contemporary world. The result is a mature Christian discernment that understands what God's will is. Wisdom is thus a gift from God that assumes prayer and communion with God. When a person wants to take on a problem, the knowledge and methods a person can learn from unbelieving experts are not sufficient. Their point of departure is often faulty. A person has to learn the right foundational view and the decisive values from God.

However, it is necessary to pray in faith so that a person is certain that God really has something to give that no one else has, and He gives it "willingly." A person could translate "generously," as free and without reproach. So, He does it without remembering how little we deserve His gifts. He who doubts that God really can and will give wisdom and guidance, he is exposed to all the opinionated winds that drive and toss him in whatever direction the wind chooses to blow.

9-11 Exultation and Humiliation

The next admonition follows immediately. It is characteristic of James. He has gathered teachings and proverbs that he has lined up without any obvious order of content. Sometimes he begins with some words or expressions that he has just used—a so-called "keyword"—but then he speaks about something completely different.

Here there is a warning against building on that which the world sees as the best in life: money and status. The real greatness is seen as poor in the world's eyes. He who has received what men would so like to have, he shall boast in his humiliation. Some believe this is meant ironically, and that here humiliation means a deprivation and impoverishment that waits for the kingdom. Others translate it "humility" and think that it means the humble insight that wealth is not of much worth. In any case, James wants to establish that the only thing the rich man knows for certain about the future is that he himself is as perishable as the summer green. James says it with apparent allusion to a word of Isaiah (40:6f).

12-18 God Tempts No One

The New Testament uses the same word for testing and temptation, though a person must (as in verse 2) say testing in English [Swedish]. Though it is, as here, closer to talk of temptations, the whole time we must still remember that temptation is at the same time a test that has something good with it when a person withstands the test. What James wants to say now is that temptations—like such tests, for example, in persecutions—never come from God. They have their origin in evil. James does not directly say "the evil one." He does not want to give people the slightest opportunity to blame either God or Satan. It is of their own evil desires that a person is tempted. We bear the evil within us, and if we yield to it, we will not escape our responsibility. It is as when a child comes into the word. The desire is nourished and becomes pregnant so that the evil grows within us and finally is born as mature sin; we have only ourselves to blame for this. And what the sin in its turn gives birth to is not joy and a meaningful life, but death, eternal death. Such does not come from God. No one should fool themselves here, James says. Perhaps he has encountered the gnostic propaganda of that day, where it was maintained that the God of creation was in fact pernicious. The opposite is true, James says.

Nothing but good comes from God. He is the Father of lights. Literally, it says the light's Father, and it points to the stars and all that gives light in the heavens. God's light is unchangeable. Here the text is uncertain, but the meaning is completely clear. With God there is only light and goodness. Nothing evil and no temptation can come from Him. On the contrary: it depends completely and wholly on His good will that we are born anew through the mighty Word that He has allowed to go out. And they who believe are only "first fruits," the first beginnings of a great harvest that will be gathered in when God creates new heavens and a new earth.

19-25 To Hear and To Do

A Christian should be quick to hear. On the one hand, it may mean hearing the word of truth, that which gives new birth. Proclamation and instruction often happened conversationally. Then, as now, there may have been participants all too eager to talk. They could need admonition to be quiet and listen. However, the word certainly has a wider purpose. Here, as so often, James uses an already formulated phrase that very well could have been taken from Jewish wisdom literature. It means that a person should think before he speaks and watch that he does not erupt. Nothing good comes from the wrath of man.

The admonition that then follows is, however, typically Christian. Because we have been born again, we should lay aside all filthiness with a daily fight against the Old Adam and humbly receive the Word. It is "implanted" in us (literally translated), so sown in our heart according to Jesus's Parable of the Sower. It means both to open oneself to it, bow before it, and to let it work. James adds something that is a matter of the heart for him: It means to do the Word. There is a dangerous self-deception that consists in only hearing and participating in the divine service, to seek moods, feelings, and experiences, perhaps human fellowship, but does not let it come to deal with the points where one is allowed to overcome himself. The Word can be compared to a mirror, James says. What good does it do to look in the mirror if a person immediately forgets that he has a soot stain on his chin? A Christian constantly looks anew in the "perfect law of liberty." For James, this probably means the whole of the Christian message, that which frees a sinner from all guilt through faith in Christ and at the same time makes us into Christ's willing servants. Such servants do not forget their Lord's will; it is a joy and happiness for them to put into action.

26-27 False and True Service Before God

James takes an example that is just as relevant in all times. Worship participants are back to their everyday lives—or perhaps just on their way home. Prattle returns, the gossip begins, and people criticize in a completely different spirit than the gospel's. What was the divine service worth? Others translate the gospel into action. What we call social care at that time functioned first and foremost within one's family. For the Christians, who were God's family, this applied to the whole congregation. It was a continuation of the divine service, not a replacement for it. The divine service was something obvious for James. He has already said that this meant to receive the Word. This alone can bring rebirth and keep the faith with power, the faith that is then active in love.

James 2

1-7 To Treat Everyone Equally

James gives us a picture of an early Christian congregation that could fit well with the mother congregation in Jerusalem. Most who came to the divine service are poor, insignificant people. However, there were also a couple of rich lords like Joseph of Arimathea. Now the risk is that a person does not take the brotherhood of faith seriously but classifies God's children according to their social position.

James speaks about the divine service as "your synagogue." It seems very Jewish, but in fact a gentile Christian could use the word for their divine service. Usually there was a lack of seating; most had to stand during the divine service. James lets us understand that a person could even sit on the floor.

James asks some rhetorical questions that do not require answers. Everyone knows that Jesus had praised the poor as blessed and said that the kingdom belonged to them. Already in the Old Testament, "the poor" had been named as pious Jews, "the quiet in the land." Mostly they were insignificant people like John the Baptist's parents who lived 'righteous before God, walking blamelessly in all the commandments and statutes of the Lord.' (Luke 1:6 ESV) The rich often belonged to the party of the Sadducees. They were the Temple's high priesthood, and to them belonged many of the council lords and capable businessmen. They were those who in the beginning appeared as the hardest opponents to the mother congregation, and who caused the first persecution. They would also be guilty of the death of James. With the good name that is pronounced over you, James means Jesus. The Christians were baptized "to Jesus" or "in Jesus's name."

8-13 The Law of Freedom Has No Holes

The "royal" law most likely means the "most important" or "the greatest." The words of Jesus concerning the greatest commandment immediately comes to mind. Every Christian must have known that the commandment concerning loving your neighbor, that James cites here, was included in a double command that according to Jesus was the most important in the law. Now James says that the law does not know any loopholes. It seems as if he met some men who made it for themselves by reducing the whole law to the only commandment and then interpret it in their own way. One such wrong interpretation is revealed when a person in some concrete point sets himself over the law—as, for example, to 'make a difference in people.' As a good Jew, James knows that he who broke one commandment is guilty of all of them because he offended God's law and set it aside. As a Christian, he knows that he stands under 'the law of freedom.' We have already heard that he means the whole of the Christian message who on the one hand makes a man free from all guilt and on the other hand a servant who of their own free will sets themselves under the law of God's kingdom. Here it does not do to cheat. The love of love has no gaps. James takes a drastic example. It may seem strange that he chooses adultery and murder, which cannot have been common in pious Jewish Christian circles. However, perhaps here, like so many times before, he assumes his audience knows Jesus's word in the Sermon on the Mount. Adultery is also looking at another man's wife with lust, and murder is also to be angry with his brother and cuss him out.

Without clear context but with clear reference to the words of Jesus, James reminds them of the meaning of mercy. In judgment, it shows that he "triumphs." Here Jesus uses a typical New Testament expression for the Christian boldness that can lift his head with joy when others hang their heads down.

14-26 Faith and Works

A person can comprehend this passage as an open polemic against Paul. James seems to interpret the word concerning Abraham's faith, which was counted to him as righteousness, in a completely different manner than Paul does (Romans 4:3). Luther had this comprehension and thus drew the conclusion that James must have been wrong, and that on this point he did not stand for the apostolic truth.

However, now it is obvious that James does not turn against the doctrine of Paul at all. A faith without works is an absurdity. Faith unites a man with Christ. He who believes becomes a member in Christ. Therefore, faith is active in love. Deeds are a proof that there is faith. Paul can even say that it makes no difference if a man is circumcised or uncircumcised but still keeps the commandments (1 Corinthians 7:19). If James has Paul in mind here, then it would have been easy to answer that Paul never taught anything like that. However if James is not thinking about Paul, what can it be that he then hints at?

A person can resolve this problem in two different ways. The one is common among exegetes who favor a late date for James. They think that the author opposes a distortion of Paul's proclamation that appeared after his death among people who had never heard him themselves. That such distortions appeared is not unbelievable. We can already see from Paul's own letters that his opponents distorted and caricatured the doctrine of justification. There are many examples in Lutheran history of Paul being misunderstood and becoming an excuse for lazy and comfortable worldliness, which confessed the true doctrine with their lips but never possessed it as an active power in the heart.

However, there is now also another possibility, namely that here James describes pious Jewish Christians who have not yet heard talk of the doctrine of justification as Paul has formulated it. Scholars who favor an early dating of James have given reason for this view. The reformers themselves had already pointed out that James uses the word "justification" in a different meaning than Paul. For Paul it means an unmerited reception of Christ's righteousness and thereby to also be born again. However, the same word can also literally mean to be declared innocent. The word can be used this way concerning the judgment God gives when He examines a person. This is what Paul means by the word in Romans 2:13, and Jesus in Matthew 12:37. People are declared innocent because they have faith, a faith that also shows itself in deeds. Thus, James does not mean that a sinner can earn God's grace by good deeds and be reborn as God's child in this manner. He had just said that it is through the gospel that we are born again (1:18) and thus not through deeds.

The dead faith that James opposes here is thus simply a cautious attitude, a dead knowledge concerning God. James points out that even the evil spirits have this "faith." But it did not help them; it just filled them with horror, something that the disciples themselves had heard and seen when the possessed encountered Jesus in Galilee. When James attacks this faith, he only does what the prophets, the Baptist, and Jesus had done before him. Even among the Jews there was this faith that accepted all that Scripture taught about the one God, but that did not bear "such fruit as bears in keeping with repentance" (Luke 3:8). It is thus against this that James turns, even as Paul had done.

There is a passage here, verse 18, that is hard to interpret because the old manuscripts lack punctuation. Literally it says, "but someone comes to say you have faith and I have deeds. Show me your faith without deeds and through my deeds I will show you my faith." This is a matter of someone coming with an objection. In some translations, it was thought that the objection only consisted of the words "you have faith?" and that the answer would be "Yes, and I also have deeds, show me an example." However, the division does violence to the text. If on the other hand one allows the objection to say, "you have faith and I have deeds," then there is hardly any objection to the argumentation of James. For this reason, new translations suppose that "you" and "I" have a common meaning here that corresponds to 'the one and the other.' He who would come with this objection maintains that he who can come out: some have faith, others have deeds. Then James answers that faith without deeds is a delusion, something that cannot exist. If there is faith it is marked by works.

The Biblical word "Abraham believed God and it was counted to him as righteousness" seems to be interpreted by James in a completely different manner than Paul. Paul sees it (Romans 4:1f, Galatians 3:5f) as evidence that it is faith that justifies. James seems to contradict this interpretation and offers as evidence the obedience of Abraham and his willingness to sacrifice his own son: So, faith and works work together. Paul maintains that Abraham was justified by faith long before circumcision and the law were given, or Isaac was even born. His faith was a faith in God's word and promise. James was certainly aware that Abraham's faith was counted to him as righteousness long before he was put to the test and received the order to offer his son. So, he says that faith "is made perfect" through his obedience. Here, there is enough explanation of the apparent contradiction. Paul thinks of what would happen in this moment when a man comes to faith in God's promise (which today means faith in Jesus Christ). Then it is this faith alone and without works that means something. However, James considers the life of faith and then deeds must accompany it; otherwise, faith is a delusion, a dead cerebral faith. A person could say: Paul thinks of what happens when the new faith is kindled. James thinks about the continuation and the final judgment. Then deeds rightly enter the picture. They are proof that faith is there. Even Paul can without thinking say that every one of us must "receive what is due for what he has done in the body, whether good or evil" (2 Corinthians 5:10).

Rahab the prostitute seems to be a strange example of justification. The fact is that she was often mentioned in the early church. Matthew mentions her in particular as one of the ancestors of Jesus. In Hebrews she is counted among the great witnesses (11:31). In the First Clement (from around the year 95) a motivation for this is provided: she confessed her faith in the one true God. Perhaps James wants to give a reminder that even this faith showed itself in her deeds.

James 3

1-12 To Restrain Your Tongue

For the third time now, we encounter a continuous piece in which James strings together expressions and admonitions that touch upon a particular theme: use of the tongue. He begins by warning those who want to be "teachers," which in the New Testament means to be teachers in God's word and thus "shepherds and teachers" for the congregation (Ephesians 4:11). James reminds them that "teachers" will be judged more harshly than others. It alludes to the servant "who knows his lord's will" and therefore shall be punished harder than others if they have not done it (Luke 12:47). The warning applies to both priests that have not taken their commission in full seriousness and layman that want to enter into the spotlight and hear their own voice.

Essentially, bridling your tongue belongs to the hardest of all self-disciplines. If a person controls that, then a person can believe that he has the rest of his life under control. He is "perfected" (essentially "complete"), as far as a Christian can be. It is strange, James says, that such a small part of our body can determine so much, but it is like a horse's bit or a rudder on a ship. It determines the direction. Therefore, so much depends on who holds the reins or the tiller. Now he is dominated by the world's manner of thinking, and life has in its tongue a piece of this evil world with all this rudeness and selfishness. Therefore, the tongue can cause so much evil. A few mocking, denigrating, or challenging words can be enough to trigger devastating conflict. Many of the masterpieces of world literature deal with this, both in Greek tragedies and Icelandic sagas, and this describes our own experience. A few drops of poison from a mischievous tongue can cause enmity for years. So the tongue sets "the wheel of life" on fire. Most likely that expression was intended for our daily life and the course of our life. The tongue has the ability to constantly light new fires and make the water hot for both us and others.

James now deals with his fellow Christians seriously. They reveal themselves through their words. In the divine service, they bless the Lord Christ and his heavenly Father. The expression is meant literally. "Bless you the Lord" was the most common introduction to a prayer of thanksgiving. The same lips that formed this blessing could, and still can, not even a minute later, form a hard condemnation of people, perhaps even a scolding that their spirit is tantamount to a curse.

So may it not be. James clearly alludes to Jesus's words in the sermon on the mount about false prophets. A bad tree cannot bear good fruit. A person cannot pick grapes from thorn bushes or figs from thistles. The evil word must come from an evil source. As long as the spring is allowed to flow freely, a person cannot be a true Christian.

13-18 True and False Wisdom

In the Hellenistic world, wisdom (Sophia) was something of the highest man could imagine. Paul used to say that a person must be careful of that which the world called wisdom. James says the same thing. If someone has the wisdom and formation that is deserving of the name, then it must appear in all his life. Above all it makes its mark in this, that he does not make himself noticeable and look down on others. The point here is directed at the type of scribe that would talk disparagingly to the crowds who did not know the law (John 7:49). It could just as well be directed against the wise Stoics with their disdain for common people, or the teachers of gnostic wisdom with their conviction to rise above the great masses of Christians. This teaching and formation has brought the self-assertion, mutual envy, and struggle for their own prestige that James opposes relentlessly. Such a "wisdom" does not come from God. It is at home in this fallen world. It is "selfishness" as it is normally called. It has nothing to do with the Spirit of God. On the contrary, it is worked by an evil spiritual power. It is nothing to be proud of. If a person carries it to conclusion, he injures the truth. It only brings disorder, schisms, fighting, and all sorts of evil. It is the opposite with the wisdom that comes from God. It is free of self-assertion and the demand for prestige. For this reason, it can be objective and not bother itself with small personal slights. It can remain above the fray where others are bogged down in personal quarrels. It is "impartial." The translation of the word is not certain. The basic meaning has to do with "not making distinctions," but it possibly touches upon not hesitating or faltering or preserving concord.

Finally, there comes a passage that is a reminder of the seven beatitudes in the sermon on the mount. Those who make for peace sow a seed they themselves can harvest. Jesus says: they shall be called children of God. In fact, James says the same thing: they reap righteousness; they enter into a right relationship with God.

James 4

1-10 Repentance

James's letter does not reflect the conditions of any particular congregation. Instead, we receive words of warning and admonition that take aim at entirely different situations, though a person might wonder if James turns to his fellow Christians or if this is a question of a mission sermon. The powerful message and preaching of repentance that now follows could be directed towards outsiders. The description of their prayers fits well with that which is common among heathens. A person comes with their sacrifice in order to obtain the help of the gods in private matters that could be completely immoral. The principle is *"do ut des"* (I give that you might give). However, it is probable that this call to repentance applies to people who claim to be Christians. Even Paul sometimes had to deal with congregations in which there were found members who fought and sued one another (1 Corinthians 6:1f). When James speaks here about what causes quarrels and wars among you, it is not meant literally, but it touches upon private conflicts or possibly even quarrels among different groups within the congregation. This is also meant with the expression "you murder." A person might be able to take it literally if he thinks that James is speaking to heathen here. Others explain that it is a copier's mistake. From the beginning, there should have been a word here that means "you envy." However, it can also be explained as an application of Jesus's Word in the sermon on the Mount, where He says that he who is angry with his brother breaks the commandment "you shall not murder."

All such fighting happens because "your passions are at war within you." Even Paul speaks about "the law of sin in my members," which "is at war with the law of my mind" (Romans 7:23). It is the old ego within me. It loves "the world," the epitome of all self-interest could desire: money, pleasures, success, and power, and freedom to do what one wants. It is this drive that lies behind all the conflicts of everyday life. However, he who loves the world is on a helpless collision course with God, who has a completely different plan for our life.

Those who love the world are "unfaithful people." Essentially, it is written "adulterers." Behind this expression lies the old thought of God who is the true bridegroom, who has Israel as His bride. Apostasy also constitutes adultery. When James warns of it, he cites a Scripture that has been lost, unless the "citation" is a summary of what Scriptures say about the jealousy of God, who does not tolerate any idol beside Him. The cited word can be translated in at least three different manners. It possibly says that the Creator who breathed His spirit within us has unconditional claim to us. He loves us and will not share those He loves with an idol. A person cannot serve both God and Mammon. He who tries to do that must repent—in the words of the original meaning in the Old Testament: make an about face and approach God. He has every reason to silence his laughter and stop their happy partying. For us, "mourn and weep" are not natural expressions for remorse and shame. It was for the Jews. Different people at different times can have different expressions for their experiences. However, remorse is basically the same.

11-12 Obey the Law—or Judge It?

If James had wanted to write a systematically ordered collection of admonitions, then he ought to have set this passage with what he said about sins of the tongue. However, now he does have Proverbs as an example, or some other collection of words of wisdom where the audience's attention is held in tension precisely through the constant alternation.

Here he gives a short admonition to not speak ill about a fellow Christian. He who does this simultaneously slanders God's own law. He shows that he can neglect it. He suggests—indirectly—that a person does not need to take it seriously. So, he has put himself in the place of legislator and allows himself to change that which the Almighty has said.

13-17 The Future is in God's Hand—Not in Ours

The Jews were an enterprising and entrepreneurial people. They had established colonies all over the Roman Empire and even far outside its borders. They were merchants and artisans who kept abreast of the best opportunities for work and profits. What James reproduces here can be a conversation overheard between good friends and business associates. What he turns against is the obvious conclusion that a man can make such plans on the one hand, just what the secularized West regards as obvious. Men have taken their lives in their own hands. A person can calculate on the basis of facts that a person considers more or less obvious: peace and health, wages and prices. Most have not thought of God. Some pray a prayer for blessing over their plans, in particular when there are uncertain factors that a person has no control over. For others, thoughts of God awaken only when a serious concern appears in their calculations. However, then he has a problem. A person ponders how he steers when such things happen.

Against this, James places true faith that knows its total dependence and takes every new day as a gift from God's hand. God is not there to watch over our plans. It is we who should insert ourselves into God's plans.

As a conclusion, there is a proverb that has a wider meaning but fits here too. It is this negative formulation of the truth that Jesus has positively formulated with the words: if you know these things, blessed are you if you do them (John 13:17).

James 5

1-6 God's Judgment Concerning Rich Oppressors

James takes hold of the sledgehammer again and preaches a merciless sermon of condemnation to those who have made wealth their God. A person can ponder whether they belong to the congregation. Rather, James seems to speak to rich compatriots who oppress and persecute the weak Christians. Here there is no admonition to repentance, only an inescapable condemnation for their unrepentant worship of mammon. The prophets of Israel had spoken just as strictly to the godforsaken upper class of Gods' people (Isaiah 5:8-12, Jeremiah 22:13f, Amos 8:4-8). God's judgment would strike them by suppressing their land and shrinking their wealth. James looks ahead to something even more serious: the great and final judgment. In actual fact, it has already fallen. All that the rich trust in, it is corroded from within. Before God, there are no noble metals that do not rust. There are no stable, valuable assets that guarantee a comfortable future. He who builds on such poor ground heads toward a certain downfall. Even more serious is that these rich men in their hunt for money have oppressed the rights of the poor. This sin cries to heaven, as Abel's blood once did (Genesis 4:10). Right now, the oppressors have power. They have judged and murdered the righteous who dared to assert their rights against them. They believe they sit secure. It is the height of hubris. Their "success" is the greatest conceivable misfortune. James does not even need to say it but breaks off and is silent. However, it is a loaded silence, like the silence under towering thunderclouds, just before the first lightning strike.

7-11 Patience in Expectation of Christ's Return

Three short admonitions now follow; all three different sections are marked by the repetition of the word of address "brother." Here James speaks with fellow Christians, and there is no connection with the preceding paragraphs, which have a completely different address. Again, we see that James's letter is a collection of short texts for different occasions that could be read and laid out according to the law.

From these three short paragraphs, the first two have the common theme of Christ's return. In the original text, the word "*Parousia*" is used in the first paragraph, this early Christian word for the return of Christ in glory, His coming as it says in the old translation. In the second part, it speaks of how "the judge is at the door."

Between the first and the third piece there is similarity in that they both speak of patience. In the first it means having patience even if it seems that Christ's return delays. In the early church a person expected Jesus every day and was convinced that the time was short. Paul also gives the admonition to some Christians to have patience. James uses the picture of a farmer in Palestine. He has sown in the fall and now only has to wait for the harvest. However, he knows that it takes a while. First come the fall rains, and then the spring rains. These are the two decisive periods of rain in Palestine—in November and March.

The admonition in the second passage to not grumble (actually sigh) at one another seems to have no direct connection with the preceding. The nagging dissatisfaction and the ability to see the mistakes of others and lay the guilt on them indicates the characteristics of the old man.

In the third piece, patience is what is needed during the suffering and persecutions that every Christian should count on. Jacob asks us to think of how it goes for God's servants and witness in past times. They may suffer, but God had not forgotten them.

12 No Oaths

The prohibition against salting your language with oaths goes back to the words of Jesus (Matthew 5:34f). Jesus's words also mention examples of oaths against heaven and earth, and even there, it says that a simple yes and no will be sufficient.

13-18 To Pray in All Life's Circumstances

Tradition describes James as a great intercessor, as kneeling so diligently and long in prayer for his people that his knees finally became calloused like a camel's.

Now here he gives some soul care and counsel that says to take refuge in prayer in every situation. A person should do this during persecution and difficulties just as much as when everything is going well. A person should do it even when sick. Even in this case, it is a matter of soul care and counsel, not an order. The sick received counsel to call the elders, the shepherds of the congregation, and ask for their intercession. Perhaps it is assumed that the sick were too weak to pray for themselves. The presbyters may also pray "over him," gathered around the sick bed. They can also anoint him with oil. It is said that when Jesus sent the apostles out over Galilee they "anointed many sick with oil and cured them." To anoint kings and priests was an old custom with religious contents. According to James, in this case, its effect was due to "prayer in faith," so a prayer to the Lord Christ in faith in His ability to—if He wanted—cure the sick.

This passage can be misunderstood in two ways. On the one hand, it has been perceived as an instruction concerning preparation for death. It has been referenced as the Biblical basis for the last anointed sacraments, according to evangelical conception, a sacramental action that Christ instituted and connected with a promise of grace. However, here it is apparently not a question concerning an institution of Christ. If a person wants to conceive of this as a preparation for death, a person must interpret the wording as if it meant to save the sick person and give him the forgiveness of sins, and therefore a firm promise of Christ to allow him to resurrect. The word can really have this meaning. The Greek word to "save" (*rädda*) can also mean to "save" (*frälsa*), and "rise up" also means "to resurrect." It is not impossible that there is an intentional double meaning. The closest and most true meaning is that the sick shall be healthy again and get up from his sickbed. However, behind this there may be the thought that if Christ does not choose this manner, so He takes the sick home.

The other misconception is that here we have a particular promise that faith's prayer and anointing with oil would always cure the sick. There is no such promise. Here it speaks of the presbyters. It is they who should pray. They were the leaders of the congregation, often appointed by the apostles (Acts 14:23) who equipped them with particular gifts of the Spirit (1 Timothy 4:14). Here it is assumed that they have the gift of healing, and this gift does not work without exception, but only where God wants. Perhaps this is the reason that Paul says that an individual believer receives the gifts of healing (1 Corinthians 12:9), as if it were a question of a gift that must be constantly given again and not once and for all. What James gives here is a counsel of soul care. So, a man can do. It shall then be done in faith and in the spirit as Jesus taught us: Not my will be done but yours.

James emphasizes the power prayer has when it is prayed in faith. It is in complete accord with the instruction of Jesus. Here, "a righteous man" means a man who is righteous through his faith in Jesus, but perhaps the word also has the Biblical meaning of a Christian that has particular gifts and tasks: an apostle, prophet, or martyr.

19-20 Responsibility for Those Who Stray

James proceeds from that "someone of you" can wander from "the truth." A man must consider this. "The truth" was both teaching and life. To depart from it was just as serious in both cases. So, a man would feel responsibility for those who wandered. To carry him back was to save his life. And he who was successful with it, he could be said to have "covered a multitude of sins." This expression also appears in First Peter (4:8) where it says that love covers a multitude of sins. It seems to mean that it draws a veil of mercy on them. Here the meaning can be that he who returns to the true faith receives all forgiveness, no matter how bad he had been. His sin is covered, and therefore he is blessed, as it says in Psalm 32.

So ends James's epistle. The end is just as abrupt as the transitions from one theme to another have so often been. This is yet another sign that what we have here before us is not a letter to a particular congregation, neither a little thesis or sermon, but a collection, intended to be read and used in selection according to the congregation's shifting needs. The whole time it is a question of admonitions. The foundation—Christ and His work—continues to be confessed. Should a person build upon this basis only with James, then a person could as Luther says that the reality was a building of hay and straw and that this letter is "a true epistle of straw." However, if a person puts the admonitions rightly, the picture becomes something different. For admonitions also belong to the full harmony of the gospel.

FIRST PETER
Introduction

The Author

The name of the sender, which is normally the first thing in a letter, is "Peter, Apostle of Jesus Christ." That it really was Peter himself who was the author of this letter was never under any doubt in the early church. The letter has been known and read since the oldest of times. It is cited with certainty by Polycarp, who was born in the beginning of the second century, and allusions to it are found in the oldest of manuscripts we have outside of the New Testament. It is obvious that people from the oldest times were convinced that it came from Peter.

Doubt concerning the matter first appeared in the West with the enlightenment, and since then the questions of authorship have been in lively debate for over a hundred years. The doubt concerning authenticity is based first of all on the language. The letter is written in good Greek, more groomed and literary than either Matthew or Mark and a richer vocabulary than we find in John. Some have found it inconceivable that Peter would have been able to write in this manner. He was a fisherman, who spoke Aramaic with a rural Galilean dialect that immediately betrayed him. Among his learned compatriots in Jerusalem, he was seen to be an unlearned man of the people (Acts 4:13). Further, it is apparent that he who wrote this letter has been very conversant with Paul's manner of thinking and speaking. That Peter was really so Pauline has been doubted.

Now, however, there is a notice at the end of the letter that can give a resolution to the problem. We know that the letter was written "by Silvanus" (or "through Silvanus"). The same expression is used at times by those who convey a letter or write it upon dictation, but it can also point to a coworker who prepared it at the commission of the sender. Here it is probably a matter of the latter, because Peter emphasizes that Silvanus is "a faithful brother as I regard him," saying that he wrote "this briefly" with the help of Silvanus, which of course could not be said if Silvanus only served as a mailman.

Now Silvanus is the same name as Silas, and we know one man with this name very well from Acts and the letters of Paul. He was a Greek speaking Jew, one of the leaders in the early church, who traveled with the Apostle and delegates of the early congregation to Antioch to bring the decision that was made at the "Apostolic Council" in Jerusalem (probably in the year 49). In Antioch he worked for some time as a prophet and preacher, and Paul took him with him as a coworker on his second mission trip. It was Silas who sat by the side of Paul in the stocks of the prison in Philippi. He also followed along to Corinth. Paul mentions him in 2 Corinthians (1:19), and he writes as coauthor in both letters to the Thessalonians.

Suppose now, as many exegetes do, that this is the Silvanus who has his hand with the preparation of this letter as an aid to Peter, then the problem resolves itself concerning the language and "Paulinism." Silvanus has apparently, as Paul and the author of Hebrews, and many other Greek speaking Jews, possessed a certain education and could write Greek like educated men did at the time. So many years as Paul's aid had familiarized him with Paul's world of thought and used his pictures and language without needing to quote or cite his writings. At the same time, Silas had been one of the leaders in the early congregation of Jerusalem and at that time must already have been a close aid to Peter. Peter also pronounces his full confidence in him. There was a series of tangible comparisons between this letter and the letter we have of Peter and his preaching in Acts.

This commentary proceeds from the adoption that this letter is written by Silvanus at the commission of Peter, according to his instructions and with his final approval.

The Time and the Addressees

The letter is written from "Babylon," which most certainly is used here as in Revelation as a pseudonym for Rome. We know that Peter lived in Rome at the end of his life. If he is the one behind this letter, it must have been written in the 60s. Because it is stamped by the great seriousness that precedes a threat of persecution, some have wanted to place it at this time, when it comes together with the great persecution under Nero, under whom Peter suffered martyrdom according to tradition. In such a case, the letter must have been written during the fall of 64.

Those who doubt that Peter is the author would rather place it around the year 100. At that time, Christians lived under the perpetual threat of being indicted and punished if they did not sacrifice to Caesar. There is an interesting correspondence from around the year 110 between the governor Plinius in Bithynia, one of the areas mentioned in 1 Peter, and the Caesar Trajan, precisely concerning the application of the laws against the Christians. Against such a date speaks, above all, the fact that the letter was already at that time known and read in Asia Minor and was taken for granted as being a genuine letter of Peter's. The attitude toward the Roman state is also positive, as we know from Paul. It seems the sacrifice of blood had not yet been demanded. It appears to the contrary as something new and also shocking for many. After that which happened under Nero and later under Domitian, the attitude became something different. The Book of Revelation testifies to this. That 1 Peter would have been written right after the Book of Revelation and addressed the same people in Asia Minor appears highly unlikely.

Yet one more reason against the later dating is an often-established fact. This letter, like Hebrews, Ephesians, and other letters that are claimed to be written after the time of the apostles, stands both spiritually and literarily higher than the Christian literature that is preserved from the time around the year 100 (Clement, Ignatius, Polycarp, and so on). A person has to wonder how there would have been such significant writers so filled with the spirit and power of the apostolic era whose names and fates would later have been totally forgotten.

This letter is addressed to the Christians in Asia Minor. These are areas in the north, central, and western parts. No congregations are mentioned in particular. Apparently, there were small groups round about the land. It has been doubted that the mission at this time could have reached as far as Pontus and Bithynia, but we might remember that every Christian carried Christianity with them wherever they went. So, we also encounter Christian groups in places where we have not heard any talk of mission. This applies to both great cities like Rome and Alexandria and small villages like Pozzuoli in the neighborhood of Naples (Acts 28:14).

The Purpose

There are two motifs that perpetually return in this letter. The one is the unavoidable persecution for the sake of Christ, which means that a person who shares His suffering will also share His glory. The other is, once again, the thought of a new life, the sanctified life, to which all men are called through the gospel and consecrated through baptism. Baptism plays such a meaningful role that many scholars want to see this letter as a sermon and instruction for the newly baptized, perhaps purely as a ritual with prayers and admonitions to be used in connection within the ceremony of baptism. But now there is the fact that this letter addresses itself to all sorts of Christians, newly converted as well as veterans. This is not hindered at all by the fact that it speaks of baptism. Baptism is the basis for the whole Christian life. It is a constantly repeated motif for a sanctified life, a consecration to something that a person daily realizes. It is a later misconception that baptism should be a single treatment, something that one left behind him. It is possibly the misconception that some want to see this letter as an admonition only to the newly baptized. In actual fact, it applies to all the baptized. A person could even call it a sermon on the art of living in one's baptism.

1 Peter 1

1-2 The Letterhead

As always, in antiquity the letter begins with the "undersigned's" name, which always comes last for us. Peter presents himself as "apostle of Jesus Christ," thus, an envoy with full authority (power of attorney) who can speak with authority on the ways of Christ. The receptors are the Christians in Asia Minor. "Asia" is the Roman province with the name, a part of what we now call Asia Minor. This lies far in the west. Bithynia and Pontus lie on the north coast, Galatia and Cappadocia in the inland. The Christians are "elect exiles." That they are the elect means that they are God's chosen people, the true Israel, His own people who inherit all the promises and benefits that God has given His people. At the same time, they are "strangers." The Greek word means sojourners in a foreign land, people without the right of domicile. They live "scattered" or in "diaspora," as it says in the original text. By *diaspora* is meant the Jews who since the time of the Babylonian captivity had been dispersed in the world and in the time of Jesus were more than double the Jews in Palestine. Here the word is given new use for Christians. They are God's people, dispersed throughout the whole world. They are chosen by God. They have become His people, "through the sanctifying work of the Spirit," that the Spirit performs through the Word. They have received the gospel in obedience and "to purification through the blood of Jesus Christ."

So, Peter, in a few short lines has summed up that powerful event that happened with these people. God has given them an exceptional position, the highest that can be thought of. And at the same time, they have become strangers to the heathen environment in which they live. What that means concerning benefits, risks, and obligations the letter will come to deal with.

3-9 The Inexpressible Joy

Now the letter begins with a thanksgiving, a real fanfare of jubilee and joy that can allow us to imagine what it was like when an "an early Christian" prophet, like Silvanus, at the celebration of Holy Communion praised God from his inexpressible benevolence. Those who interpret this letter as a sermon on baptism propose that it is there that a person "is born anew to a living hope through Jesus Christ's resurrection from the dead." This is precisely what Paul says in (Romans 6:3f). We are baptized into Christ's death in order to rise with Him, "even as Christ was awakened from death by the glory of the Father." Some will even see this section as an introductory prayer to a baptismal ceremony, something that it could undeniably pass for. At the same time, here we hear a personal tone. In the mouth of

Peter, the words take on a particular meaning. He had literally been born anew in the living hope through the resurrection of Jesus Christ. For Peter, the denier, all had become hopeless until the moment when the Resurrected One came to him, as the first among all apostles (Luke 24:34, 1 Corinthians 15:5).

Salvation is called an inheritance. It is something that one has a right to and possesses, though it still has not been distributed in full. It is well kept in heaven, and even the heirs are preserved by God Himself when they believe. So, they rejoice in jubilee. They have greater reason for it than anyone who has hidden a treasure in a field, or has gotten thirteen right on the tip, to speak contemporary Swedish.

However, with this jubilee comes the reminder that it is a joy even amidst "various trials." A person can even be thankful for those. They give us an opportunity to show the genuineness of our faith. It is like gold that is refined in the fire, where it rids itself of slag. Even faith has its refining fire (we find the same expression later, 5:12). And that one stands in the test is a guarantee for the glory and honor that comes.

The deepest essence of faith is caught in the word: You love Him though you have not seen Him. Again, we hear a personal tone in Peter. He loved his Lord, and he knew what a privilege it was to see Him, both before and after the resurrection. Now he rejoices for the many thousand who love Jesus without having seen Him. Perhaps he thinks of the Savior's words to Thomas: "Blessed are those who do not see and yet believe." In a respect he is like them: He is on the way to reach the goal of his faith, the salvation of his soul. So, it is with salvation. It is at one and the same time something we possess and something that comes. A Christian can say they have been saved. This happened to him on Golgotha and in his baptism. However, at the same time, salvation is something that lies ahead of him, a goal that he strives to receive but still has not reached.

10-12 God's Hidden Plan Revealed

So there is something inconceivably great that has occurred. God had had it in preparation already from the beginning. However, it was His secret, His hidden counsel. "The mystery of Christ, which was not made known to the sons of men in other generations" (Ephesians 3:4-5). Not even the angels knew what would come. The prophets only received a dim conception of it. Yet they had to struggle with His message and often could not understand the content themselves, though they knew that they spoke for the coming generations. But now it had all happened! Christ has come. He had suffered and been glorified. Now the message of Christ is preached, clearly and intelligibly to all, in the power of the Spirit who was poured out upon the witnesses of Christ. This too is something inconceivable, something that can never be outdone, this to encounter the gospel. We come to think of the words of Jesus and John the Baptist, who was greater than any of the Old Testament prophets but still poorer than the least in Christ's kingdom. It was through the church that the great mystery should "be made known to princes and powers in the heavenly places" (Ephesians 3:10). The angels had longed to see it. We have seen it with our own eyes. It is not strange that Jesus has said: "blessed are the eyes that see what you see."

13-21 A New Way of Life

Now the consequences follow. We have received a share in this inconceivably great thing. So, we shall live in a new manner. This is early Christian logic. God's work, the gift, that which is already done, comes first. We respond to this with a new manner of living. So, the admonitions often begin with a "therefore."

At the beginning, the foundational text sounds ordinary: gird your minds. To gird yourself was to tighten your belt and roll up your robes so that you could walk and move freely while at work or on a journey. It corresponds somewhat to rolling up your sleeves and spitting on your hands. Peter adds: "stay sober." In the New Testament the word "sober" always has a greater meaning than it has in English: reality, facticity, clarity. A person should see the reality, not as any superstition does in its nearsightedness, but with a view of the real context so that a person knows what is coming, or better, who is coming. We shall be "obedient children." Just because we are children and may call God Father, we shall be "holy." In the language of that era, this means something that was separated for God, God's possession, consecrated for His service. When Christians called themselves "the saints," it meant that they were God's people, God's own. Now Peter reminds us that God is holy, also in a moral and ethical meaning. Because we shall live in "fear," not as heathen who run away and want to keep themselves away from God, but as children who are afraid to make their Father sad and leave Him.

Again, the reminder comes from the basis and motivation for a Christian life: We are redeemed, just as slaves or prisoners of war could be redeemed from their misfortune. The misfortune was a purposeless, empty, and misspent way of life, a life that lacked meaning in life. The price was "the precious blood of Christ." Just as in Hebrews the Old Testament sacrifice was seen as a foreshadowing. The sacrificial animals that had to die in the place of sinners had to be flawless. It was a foreshadowing of Christ. He, the Righteous One, died for us, and, therefore, we unrighteous people can be children of God. That Christ would die to atone for the world's sin was determined already before creation. And now it has happened "for your sake," Peter says, and reminds us again of the inconceivable event that happened. It is thanks to Christ that Peter now gets to have true faith in the real God, He who awoke him from the dead and made Him the Lord of the Church. So, faith is also "a hope in God." It is not, as among heathens, an opinion about God, a belief in His existence or faith in a moral ordering of the earth, but something much more: a hope. In the New Testament, hope means complete certainty about

God's last great intervention, when Christ comes, and God creates a new heaven and a new earth.

22-25 Born again

Between this passage and the previous passage something important has occurred: Baptism has been instituted. This is what those who read 1 Peter as a collection of prayers and admonitions used at baptism in the mission of the early church believed. The previous passage was directed at those who would be baptized. Now they are baptized, received in the church, and now they are reminded of what has happened and what they are obligated to.

There may be something to this theory. However, it is at least just as likely that it has something to do with an admonition to both new and old Christians. Baptism is something real that a person should have perpetually before his eyes. In baptism, a person has been purified "in obedience to the truth." This does not say "in faith to the truth" or "in insight of the truth." In the Bible, truth is a summary of God's will and His meaning for the whole of our existence. A person should do truth; it is not only a collection of facts but also a program for life. The first admonition to them who bowed before this truth, therefore, is to love one another, "earnestly from a pure heart." They are "born again." Faith does not just mean a new bit of knowledge and having a different view of all of existence, nor a determination to live in a new manner. It means that a person receives a share in a new life that comes from Christ Himself. This life, unlike our biological life that came about through "a corruptible seed," has come about through God's Word, who Himself is living and life giving. So, the Word is not only a listing of certain facts; it is a power that can create faith and give life because it is eternal. It remains and gives a life that does not die. Peter cites a word from Isaiah (40:6f) that speaks about "all flesh." Here it means all mankind, but only as it applies to the life we possess from nature. It is likened to grass that dries up. Few regions on earth can illustrate this word better than Peter's home region by the sea of Galilee. During a few short weeks of spring, the grass grows fresh and high on the slopes, the flowers bloom in unbelievable colors, and the mountains turn blue in the distance like they do in the northern lands. A few months later and everything has changed. It crackles under foot as a person walks across the ground, the slopes are white, and the mountains on the horizon are consumed by a red colored haze in the sunlight. So it is also with all of humanity that is only born once. We must be born again through the Word, which remains—who created this life that never dies. And Peter says, this is the Word that shall come to us in the gospel.

1 Peter 2

1-10 Our Common Priesthood (The Priesthood of All Believers)

What now follows is one of the most important consequences of baptism. We are ordained to the priesthood of all believers. Initially there is a call to put aside "all malice and deceit." This could mean criminal behavior and heavy vices. New Christians could often look back on such things. But typically enough, it also touched upon sins that sit deeply rooted in our nature and that a Christian will always have opportunity to combat: envy, lust, and speaking ill of others, or putting oneself in better light. You are newly born children, Peter says. You need the pure milk of the gospel. There is a strong argument right here for those who would read this letter as an admonition to the newly baptized. But the picture of the newly baptized that need milk instead of substantial meat is used in both Paul (1 Corinthians 3:1f) and Hebrews (5:12f), even of Christians who have long since been baptized and ought to have left childhood behind. Here in Peter the emphasis is on the thought of the gospel as the true food, the necessary requirement for the necessary growth. Every Christian needs "to grow up into salvation," as the word can be translated. Salvation is not a onetime experience. It is a process in which a Christian is drawn in but is not completed. The expression "tasted that the Lord is good" is a citation of Psalm 34:9.

Growth happens through communion with Christ. Here Peter switches to another well-known picture: the church is God's temple, built upon Christ, the living stone that also changes us into living stones. And again, the image shifts: in this temple of the Spirit, we are a holy priesthood. This word that Peter uses has nothing to do with preaching and the pastoral office in the Christian church. It is not a question of apostles, pastors, teachers, or "elders" (*presbyters*, the word that lies behind our "priest"). Peter uses a completely different word that means "sacrificial priest" and what is used of the Levitical priesthood in the Old Testament, those who offered sacrifices in the Temple of Jerusalem. The sacrifices were now abolished by God. They had only been a foreshadowing. Since Christ offered Himself, they have no function. Now there is only one type of sacrifice that remains: the spiritual offering of praise and the sacrifice of ourselves in service to God and our neighbor. The sacrifice that all Christians offer. Such sacrifices are never perfect and cannot extenuate any sins. It is only for Christ's sake that God receives them. However, the baptized Christian is wholly consecrated to this, our "spiritual temple service," as Paul calls it (Romans 12:1). We Swedes too easily blend the concepts because we have come to use the word "priest" for both the pastoral office of the New Testament and of the sacrificial ministry of the Old Testament. However, the

Bible uses different words for these two things that are completely differentiated. The priesthood of all believers has nothing to do with the pastoral office.

Peter puts forward two biblical words that speak of the precious cornerstone—the one is taken from Isaiah (28:16), the other from the Psalter (118:22). The latter about the stone that the builders rejected, Jesus Himself had used in the temple square as a warning to His opponents. Peter had repeated it as an accusation before the Sanhedrin (Acts 4:11). Now he combines it with yet another word from Isaiah (8:14) that speaks of the stone that was a stumbling block. It was precisely this that had happened during his lifetime: Christ has been both a rock of salvation and a stumbling stone. So, it was determined by God. Here the roads would part ways, and "the hearts of many would be revealed" (Luke 2:35). They who believe are now "a chosen race" and "a royal priesthood," even priests who have a share in the kingdom of Christ and may share His power. To their holy ministry of sacrifice also belongs that they "shall let the world know what wonderful deeds he has done, he who has called you from darkness to his wonderful light." To this common priesthood also belongs the duty to witness to that which God has done for us. The world should know that we are Christians and that we are happy to be so. We are God's people. We know what it is to have garnered His mercy. Again, Peter applies a few words that were said of Israel (Hosea 1:6f; 2:23) to the Christian church. It is we who are His people.

11-12 To Live as Christians among the Heathen

The text continues with a long series of advice and rules that illustrate what it means to live as a Christian and aims at different groups and situations. The introduction applies to all. They are reminded, as in the very beginning, that they are strangers on earth. They are different. They can say no to a lot that goes without question for others because they have grown out of the desires of our Old Adam. So, they are also unpopular. That the Christians were accused of monstrous vices is evidenced by Roman writers. A Christian should refute such slander with his dealings. Let them see your good deeds, Peter says. Then they will come to praise God for them. Perhaps not now, but "in the day when he seeks them." God's work with men can take a long time. He breaks down opposition and ignorance bit by bit. The agent is often good works that are done by those who have been slandered or dealt with harshly but respond with small kindnesses and service or by still doing their duties as if nothing happened.

13-17 To Live as Christians in Society

With "to every human institution," Paul means all the powers and authorities that allow society to operate. The basic idea is as positive as with Paul (Romans 13). God wants there to be a society. The state carries out God's will when it upholds what is right with power. Up until the great persecution under Nero, Christians had a mostly good experience with the Roman administration of justice. A person has reason to ask if something like this could have been written later. There is expressed here the firm conviction that a Christian has nothing to fear from society if he lives an honorable life. The persecution seems to have come from ignorant people in the general public, and a Christian should refute them by the good that he does. To this good also belongs that a Christian fulfills all his obligations to society. Certainly, a Christian is free, but not in a worldly manner. He is free as a child of God, free from guilt and punishment, free from fear, and from the compulsion to think of himself, always looking out for number one. However, he is free as God's serf who belongs to God and serves Him. This freedom is not a means to assert themselves and their own interests, neither is it an excuse to dodge difficult duties.

18-20 To Live like Christians When a Person is Subordinate to Others

Now Peter turns to servants, or "house people," as the word actually means. They were the subordinates in a household or craftsmen. They could be free, but most often they were slaves. Now they receive the same admonition that we encounter all over the New Testament: to submit. This means to place oneself within God's order, and as a rule, it applies to the whole of Christian life. A person was quite conscious of what that could mean. A person could be unjustly treated and could suffer, though he had done the right thing. Yet even here, it means to overcome evil with good. Jesus had drawn up the ground rules already with the sermon on the mount. A person should not fight with those who do them evil but turn the other cheek and reward evil with good. It is the rule that is consistently applied in I Peter. The answer to slander and persecution is good deeds. A Christian doesn't go toe to toe. A Christian suffers rather than returning in kind. And in the midst of all this, a Christian may be prepared to suffer even for that which a Christian did that was right and good.

21-25 Christ as Example in Suffering

A Christian is also called to suffering. Christ Himself is the example. He gave us an example to follow when He took suffering upon Himself rather than slaying His opponents—which he could have! He had committed no sin, in contrast to the rest of us. He said nothing when He was reviled. He was tortured but never threatened His executioners. And His suffering became an infinite blessing. It was our sins He bore, actually bore them in His body, even upon the cross so that now everyone can look upon the picture of the crucified and think: There, in His suffering body are all my sins. This means two things: by His wounds we are healed. All is atoned for. Yet precisely because of this we now live for righteousness with Him and let the sentence of death fall upon our old man with all his selfishness. This is the meaning of baptism, and it is what a Christian may realize daily. This also means a willingness to suffer without returning in kind.

In the deep exposition of the meaning of Jesus's suffering that Peter has given, he has insightfully used citations and glosses from the 53rd chapter of Isaiah with the description of the Lord's suffering servant. We can consider whether or not he used expressions and pictures that are taken directly from the passion history instead or from his own memory. However, this is typical of early Christendom. The Scriptures were God's own Word. It witnessed to Christ. A person could not describe the Savior's being and work better than with the words of Scripture.

This is also true of the citation from Isaiah that closes this passage. Like sheep we have all gone astray. *You* did it, Peter says. He speaks to converted gentiles. Yet he can also add *now you have turned around*. And then comes a characteristic of Christ that is not easy to use because it has a double meaning. This means that He is the shepherd of our soul and "*episcopos*," which has become bishop in English. In older translations it also says that Christ is our soul's "shepherd and bishop." However, the word really means "overseer" or "superintendent." In the early church it was used for the man who led a congregation (for example, Philippians 1:1). Here, Peter is thinking first and foremost of Christ who is the good shepherd, who is a caretaker and guardian of the sheep. But at the same time, the word receives its color from the language of the early church. In the early church there were both "shepherds" and "overseers," and here we also get a picture of Christ as the church's use of shepherd and episcopos.

1 Peter 3

1-7 To Live as a Christian within Marriage

Next group are housewives and their men. The instructions given are the same in substance as those Paul gives in Ephesians (5:22 and following). Together they give a good picture of the early Christian view of marriage. It is an order of God. The family is a world apart where God has given husband and wife different roles. The man is the head. Finally, it is he who carries the responsibility. A Christian wife enters into this order of God.

If the man doesn't believe, serious problems naturally arise. These are taken up here. It is hinted that a Christian wife could suffer threats. Still, she should go the Christian way, not to answer harshness with harshness, but overcome evil with good by being a good housewife to a difficult man. In this manner, he could be won over. It is obvious that some had experienced this. However, then it is not helped with clothing, jewelry, and outer beauty. This does not mean to win the husband for yourself but for Christ. That which then convinces is something that is found in the heart, "the imperishable beauty of a gentle and quiet spirit." Paul could have said: the love that believes all, hopes all, and endures all things.

The wholly domineering consideration here is thus to win her husband for the gospel and save him. This is not a question of common advice to a housewife in a problematic marriage. This is rather understood to be the case of a Christian who is willing to follow Christ also in suffering.

With the man it shall be "in the same manner." This sounds wonderful because it has now been said that the wife shall be subject to her man. Yet in the world's normal way of seeing things, this applies to two opposite roles: to subject oneself and to be the head. However, the early Christian viewpoint is essentially the same thing: to enter into God's order as a servant of Christ. In Ephesians Paul gives the man the task to love his wife as Christ loves His church and gave Himself for it. Here Peter gives a reminder of the man's duty to show: "prudence and respect." In the Greek, there is a word here that indicates the good opinion that a Christian should take through the knowledge gained. With "live with" in the Greek is also meant the sexual side of marriage. That the woman is the "weaker vessel" points out that the man as a rule has a stronger body than a woman. The man shall show his wife honor. She has the same standing before God as he does and the same worth in God's eyes. They are coheirs with the same access to the good that He gives. The division of roles between them does not imply differing values. The role that the man received he has received as a commission to be a help to his wife and give her security and joy.

8-12 Summary: To live as a Christian in the Church and in the World

There now finally comes a word that applies to all in the congregation. This applies to the interrelationship: concord, compassion for those who suffer, brotherly love between all the members of God's great family. This also applies to the opponents who taunt and harass. Here the Christian way is inculcated: to not return what you get but meet evil with good, curses with blessings. And here he repeats what has just been said to the servants: we are called to this. And it is precisely this way that is the way in which a person is blessed.

There then follows a long citation from the 34th Psalm, the same Psalm that has been cited once before (2:3). It places particular emphasis in the order that turns from evil and does what is good, to seek peace and hunt for it. Here the Christians have seen a proclamation of the way that Christ would go and there His faithful would follow in His tracks.

13-17 Before the Threat of Persecution

Peter takes up a particular problem that became real: a threatening persecution casts its shadow before it. We don't know which persecution this is a question of, but Acts and the letters of Paul show us that the young congregations were able to suffer for their faith time after time. The counsel that they now receive says: let no one shame you. Only continue to do that which is right and good. In the end, who will do anything evil against those who only do good? But Peter counts on the possibility that the Christians will still suffer. In such a case, they are blessed. Jesus had said this in the Beatitudes. The heart shall keep him holy, and they should see to it that they can answer those who want to know what it is they believe and hope in. This could possibly mean before the judge, but Peter is probably thinking about everyday life, where coworkers or relatives come with their questions. A person should know how to answer them. Perhaps they are not successful the first time, but every Christian knows this from personal experience. However, in all these questions where a person is asked or feels uncertain, a person should seek answers afterward with the help of instruction that is given in the congregation. And when a Christian answers, it shall not be aggressively, as it is so often in discussions, but gently "with respect," with the humility that has its place before God (thus, "not cocksure," as the expression says). And a person shall have a good conscience because he has not shirked his daily obligations. They who vilify Christianity shall not bring water to the mill by what you do.

18-22 Even Christ Suffered, and Became Salvation

Again, Christ is put forth as the great example. However, here all the weight lies in the meaning His salvation had for our salvation. He suffered for the sins of others. He did it once and for all, with consequences that apply for all time. Then He can carry us sinners home to God. The work of His atoning death extends to the dead, or at least to some of them. What is meant by "the others that are held in prison" is unclear and very contentious. It must have been something known to the Christians of that era. A person has to try explaining it with late Jewish notions (in Genesis 6:2f) of fallen angels who were captured in the underworld. Others meant that what is here, as in 4:6, applies to the dead and that "they who did not obey in Noah's day" stand as representatives for the fallen humanity before Christ. That Jesus came to them in the spirit must mean that this happened when He was "dead in the body." That He preached to them cannot mean anything except the gospel so as it expressly says in the next section, where they may return to the matter.

That Noah and the ark are mentioned here is because they are seen as foreshadowing of the wonderful salvation through Christ. In the water Peter sees a foreshadowing of baptism. The water carried the ark and lifted it out of destruction. So the waters of baptism also save us. Baptism cleanses, not the body from external dirt, but the conscience from guilt, and binds us for all time with God. Here the translation is uncertain. In the original Greek text, a word is used that has previously been translated as "prayer" or "petition," but actually seems to mean an action through which a person is committed to something, an assurance or a guarantee. That baptism works "in power of Jesus Christ's resurrection" shall be understood well enough in light of what Paul says in Romans (6:2f). We are baptized in Christ's death in order to be resurrected with Him, "just as Christ awakened from the dead through the Father's glory."

1 Peter 4

1-6 To Suffer with Christ is to Die to Sin

Christ has also suffered. When we suffer, we shall see a purpose to it. It shall help us to "die to sin" (2:24). The train of thought is so compressed that we must fill out what is implied. It is the thought of communion with Christ that is established in baptism when we become members in His body to both suffer and be glorified with Him. We are called to share in His suffering. When we do that, we disclaim all that our old man desires. We say no to sin and all that it has to offer.

This applies to a high degree to those to whom Peter writes. They have been heathen and lived just as the great masses of the heathen lived, naturally not invariably but still to such a great extent that it was counted as normal, of which even contemporary authors like Petronius, Ovidius, and Juvenalis witness to. In such an environment, it attracted attention if anyone became a Christian and began to live in a completely different manner, precisely as it does in the milieu of secularized western society. A person was slandered and mocked. If this happens, a person may leave the matter in God's hands. It is He who judges, and this He comes to do with both the living and dead. So then, here there is a little digression that does not belong within the same context. When it is spoken about them who are already dead and so may never hear the gospel, we may know that they also, in fact, have been able to hear it, apparently after death. It is certain, as it is with all men, that they fall under the judgment that sins drag with it: the judgment that they must die. However, they too have received the possibility of eternal life through the gospel.

The opinions have been very divided about this last piece. Some have attempted to interpret it in many different ways in order to escape the thought of a conversion after death with the questionable consequences that a person fears it could bring. However, the wording hardly allows any other interpretation than the one we have given here, and they are probably right who say that the text just wants to emphasize that Christ's death applies to all generations, even those that lived before Him. So, it does not say, nor in any other place in the Bible does it say that there would be given the opportunity for salvation after death for those who in time have said no to God's offer of the gospel.

7-11 To Serve Each Other, Each with His Gifts of Grace

Then follows some penetrating admonitions against the background of the Parousia. The time is short. Christ can come any day. A person expects Him within the near future. Even if we realize that we know nothing of the timing, so it still belongs with Christendom to know that this world goes to its end, that Christ comes and that He commands us to watch. So, we are to be "sober-minded," wise, keeping everything in proportion and with clear sight for that which is essential. Most of all it means to persevere in love for each other. That "love covers a multitude of sins" means, just as in the Old Testament passage cited (Proverbs 10:12), that it draws a veil over the sins of others. It forgives; it does not speak about them; it does not harbor a grudge for the sake of a wrong. Later, hospitality is mentioned, which means so much for other Christians when they were traveling or perhaps fleeing, but who could be quite a burden for those who practice it. However, before all is spoken here of the gifts of grace, charisma, and again we can note the spiritual relationship with Paul. As for him, it is assumed that every Christian has received some particular charisma. He has received it in order to serve with it, not to flaunt it and be regarded as an elite Christian. He is only a steward of God and what he receives is not his own. As an example, he mentions preaching, which should be done according to God's Word. If the congregation has a task, that is also counted as a gift of grace, so a person should not take it in his own power, but with the power that it is assumed God gives an upright Christian. And everything shall serve so that God is glorified by Jesus Christ.

So, a "doxology" comes at the end with a solemn Amen. A person may have the impression that the letter writer had thought to finish here.

12-19 Comfort and Counsel to the Persecuted

That which now follows works closest as an addendum. Paul's letters give us many examples of such things. When his dictation was finished, he came to think of something else he wished he had said. Here a person can guess that Silvanus had finished the letter, but that Peter let him add a few addendums. Much of it had been said before, but now it receives a new emphasis.

First, it concerns the persecution. We receive the same picture of that as before: It does not mean a bloody martyrdom; it does not speak about sacrificing to Caesar in order to live. They who persecute are the great masses rather than the authorities. Had this been written in the post apostolic period, the picture ought to have been different. It is apparent that the persecution comes as a shock. Peter admonishes the Christians to not be amazed. That which happens to them happens to all Christians. He reminds them—with obvious reference to Jesus's words in the sermon on the mount—that they shall rejoice. They are blessed if they are reviled for His sake. Then Peter inculcates the same counsel as he had given before. In the midst of all injustices a Christian should continue to do good and not stain himself. Previously, many had been thieves and criminals of various sorts. ("Meddler" is used here as the translation for a word whose meaning is uncertain.) But now a Christian should be finished for all time with all such things. Peter reminds them that the judgment comes, and that God's own people will also answer for their deeds, just as the persecutors will not escape their punishment. However, God shall mete it out, not us.

1 Peter 5

1-4 Admonition to the Congregational Leaders

The next addendum that Peter wanted to include, "if we have interpreted the context right," is a word of admonition to the "elders" of the congregation, that is, their spiritual leaders, the presbyters. Peter could have spoken with authority as an apostle, but he didn't do that. Instead, he emphasizes that he has the same commission—he is a "co-presbyter," a brother in the office. They all share in the same assignment as shepherd. Peter had received it directly from Christ. The presbyter's commission was mediated to them through the apostles and the church. Furthermore, Peter says that he speaks as a "witness of Christ's suffering." In the New Testament, a witness is not mainly a spectator but rather a person who attests to something. What Peter wants to say here is not that he has been an eyewitness to Christ's suffering (which, of course, he had been), but that he received the commission to witness to them and explain their meaning and purpose (which he had also done in this letter). Then he speaks as "one who received share in the glory that comes to be revealed." Some have wished to see it as an allusion to Peter having seen the Resurrected One and having been present at the Mount of Transfiguration. Rather, he wants to emphasize that he speaks as a fellow Christian and coworker that shares in the same hope and looks forward to Christ's return in the same manner as other Christians. He is certainly an apostle, but above all a Christian brother. This modesty speaks strongly for the authenticity of this letter. If anyone in a later generation wanted to exploit the great apostle in order to receive attention, he ought to have stressed his apostolic authority in a different way.

Then follows the admonition. The presbyters are to be shepherds and leaders. In the Greek form, the latter word means to be a bishop, a congregation's director, who has countenance and watches over it. (The same word is used of Christ, the shepherd and keeper of our soul, 2:25.) Here there is no real difference between being a presbyter and bishop. This is also an indication that we are dealing with a text from the very earliest of the church's history (compare Acts 20:17 and 28). The shepherds shall fulfill this task as servants of Christ, willingly and not from coercion, not for the sake of money and not only at certain hours prescribed in the regulations. These admonitions are still read at every ordination. They must be taken seriously by all who work in the service of Christ. Other norms apply to them that are not negotiated by unions.

Obviously, the congregation's leaders had authority. Authority means power in this world. In Christ's kingdom, power means an opportunity and an obligation to be an example. The shepherds should be this too, and not behave like lords.

5-7 Subordination and Humility

The young receive the admonition to subordinate themselves to the presbyters (or it possibly means they have the elders in common). We have already seen that subordination in the New Testament means to enter into God's order. The presbyters are set as shepherds and leaders, and in the same manner, the young shall subordinate themselves. In both cases, it is a question concerning a willing service to Christ, a manifestation of the same faith. Finally, it means for all that they subordinate themselves. Paul says this expressly in a similar context (Ephesians 5:21). Here it says to humble yourself. A person humbles himself before others, but above all before God, even when He allows persecutions or other misfortunes that befall us. He who places himself under His hand when it seems to weigh heavy on us, he is exalted when God's hour comes. Worries about the future should be left to Him. Again, we hear an echo from the sermon on the mount.

8-9 One Last Admonition before the Persecution

Once again, the admonition "be sober" comes. It means much more than to "not get drunk with wine" (Ephesians 5:18). It is to be spiritually perceptive and realistic, to not let yourself be confused by propaganda and be sucked in by a heathen environment but keep yourself alert and know that Christ is near, always near, even if He does not come in my time. It also means to know that we have an enemy who wants what is worst for us. He is compared with a prowling lion. To be devoured by him is not to be killed, but to apostatize and deny the faith. So we are to stand opposed to him firmly in the faith. Here Peter reminds us one last time concerning the persecution that it is not anything to be amazed by. It belongs to Christianity. This time it hits all Christians in the world. And it can happen again.

10-11 The Final Wish

The final wish that follows, often written on pulpits in our land, takes up the chief thought in the letter. We are called by Christ to share in His glory. This means that we suffer a little while here in this world. However, God comes to complete His work with those whom He called. We can trust in Him. Then follows the concluding doxology.

12-14 Greetings and the Letter's Conclusion

As a last postscript, Peter says that Silvanus helped him with this letter. As we saw in the introduction, we shall believe that it is a matter of Silas who is spoken about in Acts and who is called Silvanus in Paul's letters. That it is not only concerning a writer to whom Peter dictated, or a command to convey the letter is shown in that Peter expresses his confidence in this coworker and says that he with his help wrote briefly. So, he did not send a greeting for Silvanus. A co-author does not need a separate greeting. Instead, there comes a greeting from the congregation in "Babylon," which is almost certainly a codeword for Rome and from "my son Mark." All indications are that this is the Evangelist Mark. He was really named John Mark and was raised in a home in Jerusalem that was a gathering place for the early church. It was there that Peter went on the night that he was freed from prison (Acts 12:12). It must have been well known to him. Perhaps it was he who once baptized Mark. This is perhaps why he calls him his son. From a source at the beginning of the second century (Papias), we know that Peter met the end of his life working in Rome and that Mark was his interpreter at that time, which was the reason he then wrote his gospel where he faithfully handed over what he learned from Peter.

The kiss of peace that could be called the kiss of love (as here) or the holy kiss (1 Corinthians 16:20) was the sign that all in the congregation were siblings in God's great family and loved one another. This seems to be the final thought from this letter. Then follows the apostles' blessing of peace directed to those who belong to Christ or as it is usually said, "are in Christ." Living stones in His temple and members of His body.

SECOND PETER
Introduction

The Problem

The Learned Origen, of the older church fathers (cr. 185-254), says, "Peter has left us one commonly recognized letter, maybe 2, but that matter is uncertain." So, there was already at that time a discussion concerning Second Peter. Origen and many with him personally regarded it as authentic, but even at the beginning of the 4th century there were others—among them the great church historian Eusebius—who counted it as those Scriptures of which the apostolic authorship could be questioned. Only during the latter half of the 4th century was it commonly accepted.

During the reformation, the question flared up again. Erasmus rejected it. Luther accepted it, and Calvin was hesitant. Among the newer historical-critical exegetes it has almost without exception been regarded as "pseudepigrapha," published under Peter's name long after his death, perhaps just before the middle of the 2nd century. Quite commonly it has been regarded as the youngest among the writings of the New Testament, and many think that the contents are stamped with Hellenistic thought patterns that ought to have been foreign to a Galilean fisherman like Peter. On the other hand, qualified scholars defending the traditional point of view have not been lacking.

The Relationship to First Peter

The hesitancy in the early church was not because 2 Peter was unknown in later years. On this point modern scholars have no serious reservations either. The letter was certainly known in the latter half of the second century, and it is possible—though not certain—that we find traces of it even in church fathers from the beginning of that century. We may remember that this is a relatively short letter and that we do not have many Christian writings before the first half of the 2nd century. It would be a coincidence if such a small letter should be expressly cited in any of them. There are important authors of antiquity—like the historian Thucydides (cr. 400 B.C.)—who are not cited in any preserved writing for the first 200 years after their death.

The hesitancy among some of the church fathers had a different reason. Everyone was certain that 1 Peter was authentic. However, every Greek with a sensibility for style could note that 2 Peter was not written by the same person. In contrast to 1 Peter, which was written in a clear and almost classical Greek, 2 Peter is characterized by a rich vocabulary, sweeping prose, with a penchant for vibrant old and particular words that crowd each other like ornaments from a baroque altar piece. Modern research has shown that it touches on a style that was cultivated in Asia Minor in the century just after the birth of Christ and among other things can be studied in a pair of long and pompous inscriptions.

So, the two epistles of Peter cannot have easily been written by one and the same person. However, the question of authenticity is not decided for anyone by this. As we have seen in the introduction to 1 Peter, there are scholars who think that the real author of this epistle is a coworker of Peter who is named in the end as Silvanus, who at the commission of the apostle is responsible for the form. Peter has had many such coworkers. Aside from Mark, we know of at least one named Glaucias. So coworkers could have stepped in when Peter's own linguistic abilities were insufficient. As a modern parallel, there is a Chinese bishop who used many secretaries. One wrote in English, another in classical Chinese, and a third in more contemporary Chinese. In such a case, it is of course not possible to decide if two letters have the same author from purely linguistic considerations. The linguistic differences between First and Second Peter could be because Peter—who himself could have hardly had the linguistic ability enough to have written either of them—has used two different coworkers who were able to work relatively independently.

The Relationship to Jude

As all readers of the Bible notice, there are striking similarities between the short Jude and 2 Peter, especially in the second chapter. Of Jude's twenty-five verses there are no fewer than fifteen of them that in some form reappear in 2 Peter. There is no question of a direct citation, but there are so many similarities in thought and word choice that there must be some connection. Many scholars think that Jude must have been the original text. With him the train of thought is clearer and easier to follow. Peter makes paraphrases and tries to avoid using a couple of late Judaic writings as directly as Jude. From this a person draws the conclusion that Peter had Jude as a source and so must be younger. Against this it has been objected that both authors may have had a common source, perhaps an oral one. It is a polemic against a certain type of false doctrine. The fight against them may have been relevant within a certain part of the church. Some have tried to formulate their argument and so a pattern has been formed that different people have applied in their own forms. Two such forms can be contemporary despite their differences.

Other Bases for Dating

Unfortunately, the polemic against false teachers does not give us any sure reference points for dating. They are common references and do not go into any details. In general, the scholars think that it is a matter of some form of Gnosticism. These followers consider themselves Christians and want to be present in the church. They misuse their Christian freedom for immorality. The picture of them shows tangible similarities with these opponents and misconduct that Paul confronts in 1 Corinthians. There are also similarities with the "Nicolatians" in Revelation. In any case, the picture fits the first century but hardly in the second. And naturally, there is nothing unlikely in that towards the end of his life, Peter fought against the same degenerations of Christianity that Paul met thirty years earlier in Corinth.

Those who want to date 2 Peter to the second century gather their best argument from the content where certain expressions (like "divine nature" or "insight" *epignosis*) and certain thoughts and subjects (like the absent Parousia) are considered to belong at home in the second century. Some of these arguments will be taken up in the commentary. They do not lack counter argument. For example, the absent Parousia (thus, that Christ had not returned). It is a fact that in the beginning the disciples expected that Christ would come during their lifetime. Paul still expected it when he wrote Thessalonians. In "the prison letters," he is no longer sure about the matter. In general, the exegetes figure that the great crisis came right at the beginning of the second century, and that it is where second Peter belongs at home. However, against this, it has been made applicable that the crisis must have happened when the first generation of disciples died off. In such a case, Peter ought to have taken the problem seriously in his last years.

Time and Place

They who maintain that this letter originates from the Apostle Peter, though perhaps a coworker is responsible for the preparation—have a certain reference for the dating in the letter's own information (1:13f). Here an old man speaks as he looks ahead to death. We find ourselves in the midst of the 60s. In such a case, the place would likely be Rome where Peter resided in his last year

They who do not share this theory have commonly supposed that we are dealing with the New Testament's youngest manuscript, which came about in the second century about 140 A.D. at the latest. Here, however, there are many theories. Quite a few scholars believe it was at some point around 80. In such a case, the letter can—as one of the many theories propose—be the work of one of Peter's disciples who were well acquainted with his thought and attempted to render them loyally and faithfully.

Comments on the Question of Authority

No Christian can escape asking what consequences it has for his own reading of the Bible if it would be that this letter has nothing directly to do with Peter.

In the beginning of the century, it was not uncommon for people to speak about a "fraud" or of a "forgery." That even appeared in theological handbooks.

Others claimed that such a person should not see this as "pseudepigrapha." In antiquity it was not regarded as unjust to produce a work under the name of a great teacher if a person was convinced that he correctly rendered his thoughts. This is somewhat true when it comes to profane literature. However, within the church a person hardly looked at the matter that way. In the second century and later, there appeared a series of writings with false designations of origin not the least among the Gnostics, and among them a series of writings asserted to be by Peter (a gospel, an apocalyptic, stories of his life, etc.), but they were rejected as frauds. A presbyter who produced a false letter of Paul was dismissed.

It is also hard for us to accept the thought that a Christian who apparently placed high demands on the Christian way of life and work and takes his Christianity most seriously—for the author of 2 Peter did that—and who, in addition, reproaches the opponents that they come with false claims, would be able to write a letter that presents itself as having come from an apostle, not only in the superscription but again and again in the actual text. Here a person stands before a psychological difficulty so great that every other theory appears more acceptable. He who believes that the whole of Christendom is a single great fraud naturally accepts such a theory without difficulty. However, those who have some idea of what a Christian conscience is find it hard to do that. Only in such a case as a person believes that it deals with a faithful disciple who after his master's death wanted to lay out his thoughts, can one come to terms with the thought that this is a pseudepigrapha that he has in front of him.

However, the problem can also be seen from a different point of view

The synod that finally received 2 Peter in the canon (it was held in Carthage in 397) at the same time rejected the so-called Barnabas and 1 Clement as not apostolic. This shows that they did not proceed uncritically. We can question the early church's historical knowledge; however, we cannot well disbelieve that there was a sense for what in the end was apostolic. As Christians, we have a right to believe that the Holy Spirit could lead to such a determination so that what was received into Scripture also ought to be found there. Michael Green, one of the modern scholars who engaged extensively with 2 Peter and who has claimed its authenticity, said that if it would be shown that it really is pseudepigrapha "then I would for my part believe that we must accept the fact that God used the genre of pseudepigrapha literature to mediate His revelation. I would accept it the same way as I accept history and proverbs, myth and poems, apocalyptic and wisdom literature and other literary forms that together make up Holy Scripture."

Finally, the decisive question is not who wrote what in Scripture, but what God wants to say to us with that which is actually there.

2 Peter 1

1-2 Introduction

The author has chosen to give his little writing the form of a letter. People often did this in antiquity. So, the sender's name is first. However, there is no particular addressee. The Scripture directs itself to all Christians, and that which would be the heading continues into the following presentation without any clear demarcation.

So, the Scriptures direct themselves to those who have "obtained a faith of equal standing (value) with ours." The word "value" is chosen with calculation. Essentially, the risk is that some did not understand how valuable faith is but allowed it to be thumbed on. That which is the most valuable is also said: "the righteousness from God and the Lord Christ, the righteousness that comes from faith." Here a person could also translate it "from our God and savior Jesus Christ." However, the word probably means "God" in Christ.

The desire for grace and peace is the same as in First Peter, but with the addition "through the knowledge of God and Jesus our Lord." Time and again, we encounter this emphasis of knowledge and insight. We may remember that this is not a question of mere knowing but a knowledge of the heart that builds upon personal experience and is seen most deeply in a living communion with Christ.

3-11 The Joy to Believe and the Duty that Follows It

In the Greek language the first sentence is connected to both the preceding and the following. The word flows forth in an abundant wealth. Early Christian words of praise stack up on each other. It is not a matter of a logically disposed educational presentation. Rather it is an attempt to make the addressees conscious of the inconceivably great things that come to them through the gospel. The Word constantly awakens new associations and leads a person's thoughts to important things that the listeners heard or were present for. One of the expressions is new, and we do not encounter it in any other passage in the New Testament: "to become partakers of the divine nature." For the Greeks, it was something well known. Mystery religions often used this concept. It was the inner longing of many pious heathens: to in some way share in the divine. For the Christians, the thought had particular meaning. Christ Himself lives in us. Christ would, of course, live in us. We would be branches in the vine, members of His body. Paul could say: Now I no longer live—it is Christ who lives in me. In the Eastern Church this idea of partaking "in the divine nature" would later become a beloved thought.

However, the gift has demands. He who received it shall summon all his power for it to become visible in their way of life. The author gives an example of it in a "chain," an enumeration where the one word gives the next. Such a "rhetorical device" is not unusual in the early Christian literature. It is not to be read as a chain of cause and effect. The enumerated characteristics do not come the one before the other like stages in a particular sequence of time. Neither is it a question about a successive set of steps in a ladder. Rather, it is different sides of the same thing with an inner context. First comes faith. This is the prerequisite for all the others. Next is named kindness (or "virtue") as the first and most obvious manifestation of faith. Then "insight" is mentioned (or "knowledge," gnosis), self-control, and endurance (or "patience"), all such fruits of faith are particularly necessary in a heathen environment. "Brotherhood" (love among siblings, philadelphia) was essentially a natural love, but is used by the Christians for love between siblings of faith. "Love" (agape) is God's own love that has been poured into the hearts of those who believe. It is hard to decide how the author saw the relationship between this and "brotherhood."

If there is faith and it functions, then it allows us to be effective. The apostles can exhort as if all depended on what we do. However, it is not a matter of being blessed through your deeds. The departure point is always the gift. You are saved, so live as a Christian. We also see it here. First comes joy for the unfathomable gift. Then comes the exhortation to set all sails. However, after the enumeration of all the good fruits of faith, the notification that there is a driving force that does not allow us to be ineffective comes again. If this driving force is not there, then a person has been blind to the essential. The essential thing is the forgiveness of sins, that which a person receives as a completely undeserved gift. So there comes an exhortation to show our earnestness when it comes to "confirming your calling and election." The call came through the gospel. If a person answers yes to this, it is a sign that a person is elect and has his name written in the book of life. It does not mean that God has destined some to be damned, and others to salvation. However, He knows from the beginning who will come to say yes. The call is just as seriously meant even when it comes to the others. They could have been saved but said no. Yet for those who said yes there is a possibility to convince himself that he really is elect. He notices this when a person wholeheartedly holds fast in Christ. Then the knowledge ripens: Christ wills it. He answers me, and then I shall never fall. Then I can be certain to enter into Christ's kingdom. However, it is a gift, "a richly provided" gift.

12-15 The Apostle's Testament

Two passages now follow where the author clearly claims to speak as an apostle. In the first he justifies why he speaks about what he knows the readers already recognize. He wants to give them one last reminder of what they hold fast to. He still remains in his "tent," which according to Paul (2 Corinthians 5:1) is a picture of the body. However, he knows that the decampment is near. Jesus has confirmed it for him. Perhaps this is a reference to the Word of the Resurrected One (John 21:18), perhaps to some later revelation. So, he now writes a sort of spiritual testament in order to confirm that he stands fast with all he has taught before, and so that no false teacher can claim he stood for some new teaching.

16-18 The Apostles as Eyewitnesses

When the apostles came with the gospel, they did not come with "cleverly devised myths." The word is clearly pointed against false teachers who were probably Gnostics. For them it was characteristic that they came with fantastical myths about heavenly powers and their destinies and battles against the creation of the world long ago. The apostles could therefore tell about something that happened in this world in their own time. They were "eyewitnesses." In the original text there is an unusual word here (*epoptai*) that was used in mysteries for those who in mystical revelation saw the gods and thereby belonged to the initiated and were regarded as the religious elite. Here the word also has a polemical point: here it is a question of a real eyewitness, who saw and heard something that happened here on earth. This event refers to Christ's transfiguration. Otherwise, it does not belong to that which played any prominent role in the early church. It is not told in strict accordance with any of the gospels. The heavenly voice is given with its own words. They are cited as evidence that it really is an eyewitness that speaks. A forgery would have reason to give the words as they were known from the gospels. The critics think that such an expression as "the holy mountain" already testifies that this was written in a post-apostolic period. The other side answers that for a Jew such as Peter any place was holy if God revealed Himself there (like Bethel, Genesis 28:16 and following, or the ground around the burning bush, Exodus 3:5).

19-21 The Mystery of the Prophetic Word

"…we have something more sure the prophetic word…" Scripture was the Word of God for both Jews and Christians, but for Christians this meant that it held a power that the Jews did not know. All that God says and does in the Old Testament pointed forward to that which would come, the Messiah and His kingdom. Now the Messiah had come. Thereby, Christians had received the key to the Scriptures. The Christians read it with a new seriousness and a new joy of discovery. When it says that the apostles were completely taken by "the ministry of the word" (Acts 6:4), it did not only mean that they preached but also that they searched the Scriptures to find God's meaning in all that had happened. Then they found how the whole of Scripture witnessed to Christ. It was just that which Jesus Himself had said (Luke 24:27, John 5:39). This manner of reading shed new light on the whole of existence. It is this apostolic experience that they speak about here: The Word shines like a light in the wilderness. It is dark in the world, but "the night is far gone, and the day is near" (Romans 13:12). The light of the coming day already ascends in our hearts when the morning star (Christ) shines upon us. However, the reason is that we give attention to the Word.

Then there comes a very real warning: it does not do to interpret the Word according to one's own thoughts. It can create bafflement with all the different interpretations of Scripture. In actual fact, it is no cause to wonder. The prophetic Word cannot be judged and understood if one does not have the Holy Spirit. It has not come about like other literature. The prophets spoke of an inner force, under the influence of the Spirit, and what they said came from God. However, the message from God cannot be received and not understood rightly if one does not listen in faith, and willingly bow before it. It is always something of the Spirit's work when a man hears God speak in the Word.

For the early church, it is clear that the apostles "preached the gospel in power by the Holy Spirit who was sent down from Heaven" (1 Peter 1:12), and that their interpretation of the Scriptures was the right one. Here there is the obvious answer to someone asking: "who shall we then believe?"

2 Peter 2

1-3 False Teachers Stand Condemned

Just as false prophets were found in the old Israel, so there are false teachers in the church, God's new Israel. Jesus had prophesied it. Paul foresaw it when he bade farewell to his coworkers on Miletus (Acts 20:29f). Even here in 2 Peter the warning is applied to the future, though a person gets the distinct impression that the author himself has encountered this sort of false teacher and is well aware of their modus operandi.

So, there are "teachers," and these most closely correspond with what we would call pastors. They give the impression of preaching Christ but smuggle in false teachers that destroy faith. They deny "the Master who bought them," perhaps by denying that He atoned for their sins. In any case, they deny Him through their lives because they live in such a manner that draws shame upon Christendom. It is, of course, usually the moral shortcomings of the proclaimers that the world disapproves. With the denial of the teaching, one is usually more forgiving. Here it seems to be a question of the sort of false teacher who shows himself at the expense of the congregation. The problem of how they became shepherds is not dealt with. It is only noticed that they cannot escape their judgment.

4-10 Examples of Warning and Comfort from Scripture

Essentially, it ends badly if a person contradicts God. The author takes two well-known examples from the Scriptures: the flood and the judgment that fell upon Sodom and Gomorrah. However, he first mentions a different example that we would hardly understand if we did not know how the Jews exposited a passage in Genesis (6:1f) where it speaks about angels (the sons of God) who were seized by desire for earthly women. According to Jewish tradition, they were plunged into the underworld to be kept until the day of judgment.

So, the judgment fell upon the evil. However, Noah and Lot were saved. They had had pure sin and unbelief around them. Yet they had held fast to God, and He preserved them. The application to their own situations could not have been hard to make for the readers.

The expression "the Lord's power" renders a Greek word that means dominion or rule. It may point to Christ but also to the angels and spiritual powers. Some believe that this concerns the congregation's leaders with the authority they had. In any case, it must be speaking of something that a Christian ought to have respect for.

11-14 The Impudence of the False Teachers

Even the expression that is here rendered with "angels" [Swedish: powers of the spiritual world] is dark. Usually it is translated as glories, and a person gets the content of the word from the context, which unfortunately is not all that clear. Meanwhile, in a similar passage from Jude (v. 9), it is clear that it speaks about evil spiritual powers. It appears as if the false teachers spoke shamefully and provocatively of the devil and his kingdom, without understanding what a serious matter it touched upon. They may have been Gnostics who were convinced of their superiority and who demonstrated their boldness by placing themselves above the elementary commands of Christian morality, not the least in the sexual category. It would fit with the dark picture that is given of them in what follows. They are on the hunt for money and women. They have the word in its power but used it only to live for their enjoyment. Apparently, they still belong to the congregation or are understood to be received there so that they can enjoy communion and hospitality. It fits in the question of Gnosticism, but only in an early phase.

Judgment concerning them is harsh. They are like unreasonable animals. They live a purely animalistic life and satisfy their urges without contact with God, condemned to pass away. As a contrast to their impudence are mentioned the angels who abstain from the blasphemous powers of evil though they really had the power to do so. This likely indicates an episode that is told in a late Jewish edifying Scripture, which is also used in Jude (v. 9). However, here there is only a very common suggestion given. The actual episode is not mentioned, perhaps because it is not mentioned in the Old Testament.

15-22 Apostates Who Become Stumbling Stones to Others

False teachers go astray and lead others astray. They are like Balaam. They present themselves as prophets but are out after money. Balaam was put in his place by a donkey of all things. So, everyone ought to be able to see that the false teachers are unreasonable. They are wells without water. No one can be quenched of thirst with what they have to offer. They are clouds or mists driven by the storm, formless and constantly changing. False teachers come in perpetually new forms. They are torn apart but reform in new shapes—until finally they swirl away into the great darkness where they are at home. They come with pompous words, prestigious words that are relevant for the time. They attract loosely anchored Christians who have recently come to faith and know too little to see through the emptiness in their fashionable sounding words. They promise freedom, but they do not know what real freedom is. For the false teachers, it is the freedom of the old Adam, freedom to decide for oneself, live the good life, get as much out of life as possible, a freedom that is actually a slavery to "corruption." This means both moral corruption here in the world and finally corruption in eternity.

2 PETER 2:15-22

The picture we receive here of false teachers is simultaneously indefinite and sharp. It is indefinite when it comes to what they actually said and taught. It is hard to say with any definiteness which direction they went. At the same time, we have a sharply detailed picture of the essence of false teachers in every generation. They want to claim for themselves that they are a form of Christianity. They want to have their place within the established congregation. They like to use its offices and its methods of work. However, in its essence it is an apostasy, a no to the new life in Christ and a no to the fight against the old selfish ego who demands to assert himself and take advantage of its opportunities to enjoy the new life. Then the false teaching can take many different forms. It can step forth as solid middleclass values in the pastoral office that cares for its rights. It can take the form of radical new innovations that recast Christian ethics and suit the era's demand for freedom, especially in the sexual sphere. The relationship to savage spirits in the early church is still unmistakable.

So, these false teachers belonged to the congregation. It is heavily emphasized that they had been Christians but apostatized—in the heart, though they preserved an external relationship to the church. So, it was really bad. There is more hope for those that have always lived in darkness than for those who have returned to it after they have seen the light and lived in it for a while. Two dramatic proverbs—one from Proverbs (26:11) and one from an old Greek philosopher (Heraclitus)—shed light on this and become the conclusion of this passionate chapter, where one imagines the voice trembling with anger when the faithful shepherd speaks of the harm that is caused by these shepherds of whom one can use the prophet's words: "You eat the fat, you clothe yourselves with the wool, you slaughter the fat ones, but you do not feed the sheep" (Ezekiel 34:3).

2 Peter 3

1-7 How Does it Go with The Promise of Christ's Return?

The author lets us know he has already written a letter that the readers clearly know. This is commonly thought to be First Peter. However, the description does not fit well with that letter. The point of it does not fit with what is stated here, and so a person has to at least figure that there may be a letter that has been lost. The author wants to remind them of what "the holy prophets" have said. Some have wanted to see this expression as evidence that the letter belongs to the post apostolic period, but it already appears in the song of Zechariah (Luke 1:70). Even concerning the expression "your apostles," some have said that it could not come from an apostle. Just as if the pastor of a large parish could not speak to his congregation members and say "your pastors" without including himself! When it speaks about "the message" (in Greek: *entole*) that Christ has given, the word has approximately the same breadth of meaning as when Jesus says "all I have commanded you" in the great commission. (In both cases, the same Greek root is used.) To Christ's "entole" (mandate) belongs all that He commanded His apostles to say and do.

In this case, it applies to the promise of His return. Already in the letters to the Thessalonians we see that faith in Christ's quick return could cause questions and doubt. When this was written, the question was burning. The old disciples had died, and the Lord has not come. The false teachers—like the same ones that they just spoke about—come with their scornful questions. Don't the cold facts show that this is altogether an illusion? Christ does not come, and the world will remain. It has done so since pagan times and will continue to remain. With "our fathers" is meant all past generations back through the ages and not—as some maintain—one or two generations of Christians. It is clear from the counterargument that the author offers. There he says that it is not as the opponents—in true Greek manner—have alleged, namely that everything remains the same and the course of the world is an endless circle that continues through the ages. Here the Christian doctrine of creation is set against this. The world has remained in the power of God's Word and will receive an end by the same Word. World history is not a course of circles where nothing new happened under the sun, but a drama where God acts with His created world. He has already shown once—in the flood—shown that He can draw a final line and let judgment fall upon the world.

It is hard to say how the author thought about the role of water in creation, and here the translation is uncertain. Some think that, according to late Jewish conceptions, God created a new heaven and a new earth after the flood, but this is uncertain. In any case, what he wants to say is that the world we now live in shall disappear on Judgment Day into a cosmic fire. This the prophets had already said:

"The Lord will come in fire" (Isaiah 66:15), and "in the fire of my jealousy all the earth shall be consumed" (Zephaniah 3:8).

8-13 The Lord has not Tarried

Now the answer to the mockers' question follows. For Christ a thousand years is like a day. He has not delayed. His manner of measuring time is different from ours. If He still gives the world time, then the time is a time of grace. He sees that there are still people to save here, and He does not want any to be lost. One of His days of grace can be like a thousand years for us. If He wants to give the world more days such as this, it is His prerogative. However, we should know that He comes, and He comes suddenly and unexpectedly, like a thief in the night. Then the universe shall pass away, "with a roar." So, we have normally rendered the Greek word, which with its own sound tries to paint the sharp, whining sound of an arrow or whip, the crack of thunder, or the crackling sound of a flaming fire. A modern picture that would fit here in this case, could be the igniting of matches that light up in the blink of an eye. A hundred years ago people laughed at the thought that the stable material, which was regarded to be eternal and consist of unchangeable atoms, could suddenly be dissolved. Modern nuclear physics has taught us to look upon this matter with new eyes.

The word that is translated as material here is the Greek, "*soicheia.*" Sometimes it can be used for stars (and in old translations was rendered "heavenly bodies"). However, it is usually used for fundamental elements (earth, water, fire, and air) that all things were thought to be made of, thus, what we call material.

For the Christian, the conclusion will not be to try to figure out when the day comes but to be prepared to meet Him every day. To this comes a thought that might surprise us: we can speed it up. The meaning is probably that the sooner the church completes its task of proclaiming the gospel to all people and the better we use the time of grace, the sooner Christ comes. This day is something which every Christian eagerly looks forward to. Of course, this means that God really brings an end to all evil and creates a new universe "where righteousness dwells." Finally, the world shall be such as the Creator in His benevolence wants to have it. It is unbelief that speaks of the world as "passing away" and "the end of everything." In actual fact, it is the matter of a beginning. A new world comes, and the real life begins.

14-18 Summary and Conclusion

Then there comes one last summary admonition. In true apostolic manner, it is emphasized that what we are to do is presented as an answer to what God is doing. God shall make everything new; thus, we shall let ourselves be renewed. "To be found... at peace" means to have peace with God through Him who is our peace, Christ. So, the basis is forgiveness through faith in Jesus. However, in

Biblical manner, peace is also perceived as a good order of God (*shalom*), where all functions as it should. So, peace means to "strive to persevere without blemish and at peace." Every new day the world receives is an invitation to salvation, and the invitation also includes old Christians.

Then there comes a reference to Paul's letters. Many perceive this reference as conclusive evidence for the late arrival of 2 Peter. A collection of Paul's letters seems to have not existed before around 100 A.D. and, in the best case, not before 60 A.D. Luke did not use them when he wrote Acts (approximately 62 A.D.). Here they are placed next to "the other Scriptures," which apparently points to the Old Testament and possibly the gospels. On the other hand, it can be said that in his travels, Peter must have been familiar with Paul's letters. There is reason to believe that he resided in Rome during the years when the "prison letters" came to be, and he and Paul were both attended to by men like Mark and Silas. There can hardly be any doubt that Paul's letters had already been written, spread, and were read in the divine service alongside of the Old Testament texts. When here there is talk of the "other Scriptures," it can quite simple mean "the other Scriptures that are lectured upon at the divine service."

That Paul was misinterpreted and that he is invoked by false teachers with lax moral ethics and a worthless way of life can be seen by his own letters. This happened during the Apostle's lifetime. This is not the only time that the doctrine of justification through faith and the freedom of the Christian has been abused.

This sigh of complaint that Paul is sometimes difficult to understand has often been repeated through the ages. Many Bible readers have felt comforted that we also encounter it in an apostolic letter.

The last word in the debate about the appearance of 2 Peter is not yet said. He who is disturbed by these debates can comfort themselves that the old undivided church, the martyrs, and the great fathers of the church agreed that this letter was a true expression for the apostles' teaching, and that it says something that is and remains fundamental for Christianity in all ages, when it admonishes us to faithfully hold fast to all that which the apostles told to us, which came from Jesus Christ, but to let us be free of those who teach or live differently.

FIRST JOHN
Introduction

The Author

Every student of the Bible notes that John's Gospel and 1 John are similar in language, manner of expression, and thought. It was considered a given in antiquity that the same man had written both of them, and the majority of modern scholars are in agreement with that. Certainly, there are some small circles that contest this, but their arguments have not been persuasive. Most of their arguments are actually quite different. A person who has wrestled with authorship cannot avoid thinking that with those methods a person could show that several of his own letters and essays could not have been written by himself.

If now a person should, as is laid out in the introduction to John's Gospel, believe that the fourth evangelist is the apostle John, the son of Zebedee, then it must have been him who also wrote this epistle. It is apparent that it is written by a Jew who learned to speak flawless Greek but had a limited vocabulary and still thinks like a Semite in short straight main clauses. Just as apparent, it is noticed that the man speaking has precisely the same place in the church that an old apostle ought to have had. He speaks with personal warmth and unmistakable authority, like a true father in God to his spiritual children.

1 John spread throughout the church in which it was regularly read very early. It is frequently cited by the older church fathers (according to Eusebius already by Papias at the beginning of the 2nd century).

The Background and Purpose

There are differences between John's Gospel and First John that indicate they came about in different situations. In the gospel, we are still moving on Palestinian ground. The great issue of debate is if Jesus of Nazareth is the Messiah, God's only begotten Son, and John defends this by digging out of his own personal memory and meditating upon that which Jesus said and did. In John's letters we are carried to the congregations of Asia Minor to a Hellenistic milieu, where the debate is whether the Son, the revelation of God (whom even the opponents believed in) was really identical with the earthly Jesus.

The opponents seem to have been Gnostics. One of their leaders, Cerinthus, lived in Ephesus at the same time as John, and it is possible that it is he and his followers who are referred to in the letter (2:19). In actual fact, Gnosticism may have been older than Christianity. It had borrowed a lot from Judaism and other religions and had a great ability to use religious concepts that appeared relevant. When Christianity began to spread, it clothed itself in Christian costume, though on almost every point had the direct opposite conception. It taught that the world was not created by God, but by a "demiurge," an evil spiritual power. Therefore, material and so also the body were something evil. The soul, the spirit of man, therefore had its origin in the true God who lived in an inaccessibly distant place. Salvation consisted in that the spirit liberated you from material, and this happened through "gnosis," that is, through an enlightenment of reason that gave true knowledge. According to the gospel, on the other hand, the border is not between spiritual and material, but between evil and good and runs throughout body and soul, depending on our faith and attitude toward life; salvation consists in that through repentance and faith the whole man returns to God. The Gnostics tried to hide all these contradictions by using the same words as the Christians. They thought of themselves as the intellectual and religious elite who had been initiated into a higher wisdom. This caused them to look down upon normal Christians with arrogant contempt. This is behind John's constant reminders that he who really knows God also loves his brothers.

On one point the Gnostics had apparently shown that they meant something different than the apostles, though they used the same words. They spoke about "Christ" and about the "savior," but they meant one of the emanations (divine effluence) from the highest God who gave rise to new divine beings. They could not possibly accept that such a spiritual being could really become man and that Christ really had "come in the flesh" (4:2). Even when it came to morals, they showed their contempt for the material. This could happen in two different ways. The one possibility was a strict asceticism that rejected the bodily, such as Paul polemicizes against in 1 Timothy (4:1f), where he speaks of false teachers who forbid marriage and different kinds of food. However, a person could also show contempt for the body in a directly contrary way. Because the material was worthless, it did not matter what a person did with his body. A person ate and drank to excess and took sexual liberties, while at the same time claiming to have a higher insight that gave him true spiritual freedom. It is such "libertinism" that is fought against in, for example, 2 Peter and Revelation.

FIRST JOHN

Gnosticism is the original type for the form of Christian counterfeiting that uses Christian expressions but fills them with a completely new content. As parallels in our time, a man could mention the attempt to present Jesus as a social revolutionary who was most concerned with reforming society. Another parallel could be the theology that regards it as inessential who Jesus was and is content with the fact that there is a message that has gone out in His name. The Gnostics did the same. The man Jesus was irrelevant to them. Against this, John places the historical reality, that which really happened, that which he saw with his own eyes and can witness to.

In his showdown with the Gnostics, John takes up three chief points with which a person can test the content of their asserted Christianity. We encounter them again and again. They have their validity as litmus tests even today, and John understands how to use them in a way that confronts believers with soul searching questions.

It is not without reason that 1 John is recommended to unfamiliar readers of the Bible. The language is profoundly simple. There are no Old Testament citations or allusions that demand prerequisite knowledge. At the same time, this letter is in its simplicity so profound and universal that it finds constant relevancy in new situations.

It is hardly a real letter. It lacks the normal superscription as well as concluding greetings. Perhaps it was sent to congregations with some coworker who first presented a greeting from the apostle and then read his message. In any case, it was intended to be read in many congregations, a sort of apostolic "shepherd's letter" that takes up questions that were relevant at this time and have ever again found relevancy through the church's long history.

1 John 1

1-4 A Jubilee

There is no superscription of the normal sort for this letter. This may be because a personal representative for the apostle had it with him, or that it was sent together with an accompanying introduction that could have looked something like second or third John (if it was not actually one of them as many believe).

Instead, this letter begins with something similar to a jubilee, an outbreak of overwhelming joy. Because "the joyous message" has become a worn-out expression, here we get a glimpse of how fantastic and overwhelming it actually was. John had experienced it. From childhood he had known "that which was from the beginning," the God of the fathers and the whole world, who lived in a light where no one could come. Now it had been revealed; He entered into our world! John had been able to see it with his own eyes, he had touched Him with his own hands! He knew that he had encountered the Word of Life. "The Word" is precisely the name that John uses in the prologue to his gospel as an expression for the mystery of Christ. Most likely it also points to Christ here too. In his Word, God Himself stepped forward, creating, and operating. There we could encounter Him—just as it was with Jesus. Therefore, He is called the Word. He who stepped forth here was "the eternal life, which was with the Father," which was otherwise hidden and inaccessible. Here he had been revealed and found among us. No wonder the words pile up for John, already from the third line when he came to "the word of life…". The meaning is never complete (the word "is what we speak about" has been added in translation). He begins again to say that life really has been revealed. Nothing like this has happened before; he must testify to it. He says the same as Peter said to the Sanhedrin when they commanded them to be quiet: "we cannot but speak of what we have seen and heard" (Acts 4:20).

So now he writes. Through Christ "we"—thus, the apostles and all those who received the joyous message—have received a fellowship with the Father that would otherwise not be possible. And now he will draw all others into this fellowship. It is clear that John is writing to Christians. So, they already have this fellowship. However, as we will see immediately, it is threatened by false teaching. So, John wants to fortify it and give it depth—"so that nothing shall be lacking [may be complete]" in his joy—or perhaps "theirs" as it says in a few manuscripts. To this great joy over the great wonder also belongs that one shares it with others. Otherwise, it is not complete.

1:5-2:2 The Truth of the Light, Three Ways of Denying It

So, John goes directly to his subject. He summarizes the apostolic message in the Word: God is light. This may surprise us, but we immediately receive a clarification. This fundamental sentence—that many heathens could agree with—has particular meaning for a Christian and has particular consequences for the whole of our way of life. And it is precisely these consequences the false teachers do not want to recognize. The showdown with the false teachers already begins here. It will continue throughout the whole epistle. John has developed this introduction with a deeply edifying presentation of a series of core Christian truths. There is reason to believe that the false teachers were Gnostics. However, what they said is in large part such as is said even today. John initially specifies three false propositions. He introduces all three of them with the phrase "if we say," then he establishes that they are false positions, and finally he sets up the opposite, true Christian dogma.

The first false teaching is that a person can have fellowship with God even if he wanders in the dark. There is no true religion if it does not have moralistic consequences. If a person believes himself to be "religious" on the basis of moods, experiences, and feelings, without it having any effect on his daily life, then a person lives a lie. However, if a person walks in the light so that it really permeates both heart and deed, then a person lives in both forgiveness and sanctification in the power of that which Jesus did for us when He died. His blood "purifies us." Here John uses the Greek verb form that marks that it is a matter of something that continues to proceed. We need purification day by day.

The second false teaching is the proposition that we do not have any sin. This means that sin does not sit within our nature and that we can then be completely free of it so that a Christian should not really need any confession of sin. The Christian truth is that we always have sins to confess, but also that there is always forgiveness for Christ's sake. He is "faithful and righteous." Both words have for John the same meaning that they have in the Old Testament. There God's faithfulness and righteousness emphasize all this, that He stands firm on His testament and keeps His promises.

The third false teaching is that we in fact do not sin (even if we admit that there is sin in our nature). Here John makes an interjection for soul care that gives the third point a partially different form than the two previous intros (this caused confusion for the person creating chapter divisions in the beginning of the 13th century so that he put one right here in the midst of this passage). John does not want to be misunderstood. He does not excuse sin. No one shall believe that he can take it easy with it. What he writes about forgiveness he writes so that we will not sin. We shall know both that there is an opportunity for forgiveness and what that opportunity cost our Savior. He was allowed to die in our place. It is His blood that purifies us. He is the propitiation for our sins. The propitiation is with Him. It is something He has won, not just something that happens with us. In the power of this He can "carry our case before the father." In the original text it says that He is our *"paraclete,"* our advocate. It is the same word that Jesus uses in His farewell speech in the Gospel of John concerning the Holy Spirit. So, the word can be used for both Christ and the Spirit. Of course, Jesus also says that He shall ask the Father to send "another paraclete," when He Himself has departed (John 14:16).

Jesus can be our advocate with the Father because He is righteous. Here the word can also point to His faithfulness, but it is also possible that John thinks of the righteousness that He actualized when He became man and fulfilled God's law. "He completed what we should have and become our righteousness."

1 John 2

3-6 A Test of Truth: Obedience

"By their fruits you shall know them," Jesus had said of false prophets. Now John presents the test, but he does it so skillfully that it simultaneously becomes an introduction to self-examination for everyone. He allows us to meditate. The same questions and thoughts return. He constantly approaches the great truths from different angles. Yet we come to find that the question of truth continues to return, and that truth is constantly tested anew from three points of view: obedience, love, and faith.

The Gnostics claimed to know God. Their name came about because they believed they had gnosis, knowledge. Yet the claim shall be tested by whether a person keeps his commandments—or "holds fast" to them. The Greek word means both that a person keeps (that is, fulfills) them and that he recognizes that they are correct and stands fast by them even if he is only partially successful in fulfilling them. If a person does that, love for God has done what it should. Here the original text says, "God's love"; in Greek, this can mean both "our love for God" and "God's love for us." It is often hard to say which is meant, but here it is fundamentally a matter of the same thing. We love God because "God's love has been poured into our hearts." (Romans 5:5)

7-11 The Second Test of Truth: Love

Now John engages with his most loved theme. The readers have heard it many times before. The false teachers have probably said that he has nothing else to come with but the old nagging for love. They made a claim to come with something new, bold truths that would carry Christianity further. John gladly admits that he does not come with anything new. He writes what they have heard from the beginning. Yet it is something really new, this thing with love, Jesus Himself had called it a new commandment (John 13:34). He had proved that it was something new in His own life, and the Christians—and even their contemporaries—could note that there was something new here that the world had otherwise not known. John says this is because a new day has dawned, and a new age is breaking in. To be a Christian means to live in this new light. The Gnostics also knew this, and they made claim to be more enlightened by this divine light than the common Christians. Here is the test, John says. Those who look down upon their "unenlightened" fellow Christians without any love for them, they must remain in the dark. He does not figure in any grey area between light and darkness. Either a person is with Christ and then everything is forgiven, or that person does not have the right place and so remains in the darkness. In the same way, he does not speak about any grey area between love and hate. If a person does not love, then there is something wrong on the decisive point. However, he who loves his brother, he walks in the light and does not risk stumbling, neither to go astray—as the false teachers did. The point of the apostle's word is directed against them, yet at the same time he sets his fellow Christians before the same questions and gives them reason for self-examination.

12-17 Two Counter Points: The Church and World

Here John includes some words of admonition and warning, without any apparent connection with the preceding. He turns to the church's faithful members. Some think that he divides them into three groups that correspond to the three spiritual stages of maturity. However, in such a case, these do not come in mutual order—the father's ought to, of course, come last. It is likely that here John, as everywhere else, uses "children" as an address for the whole congregation. Then he turns to the elderly and younger in turn.

Strangely enough, he repeats what he has to say. First, he says, "I write" and then "I have written." In Greek it says again "I wrote," and it can mean precisely the same thing as "I write" because a letter writer in antiquity would imagine himself in the moment when the recipient received the letter. There are many explanations to this repetition: that John had to take a break here and then repeated himself, that he dictated a draft and tagged on a paragraph, that he wanted to formulate something else, which then accidentally remained in the final draft, or that he pointed to a preceding letter or only what to give the greatest possible weight and emphasis to that which he wrote. We have no certainty. We can take the text as it stands.

John now says to the whole congregation that they all have the forgiveness of sins for the sake of Jesus. Thereby, they are true Christians. They know the Father—precisely what the Gnostics maintained only some of the chosen did.

Then John speaks to the elderly (fathers) and says that they "know him who is from the beginning," which should well mean that they are firmly anchored in faith in the Son who was of eternity, through which and to which all has been created (Colossians 1:16). To the youth (young men) he then speaks of their struggle and victory. In the Greek it is a lively slogan: *neaniskoi nenikekate* (you young have won). They all had to fight. They knew whom they fought against. They also knew how they had been able to win: they held fast to God's Word.

Then comes the admonition: "do not love the world." Yet does not God love the world? It is precisely John who preserved the great word of Jesus: God so loved the world . . . (John 3:16). How does that fit together?

Here it is a question of two different types of love. The one is the divine love that desires the salvation of the fallen world. The other is human selfishness that wants to get their share of the enticing fruit of the fall. Here "the world" means all that is hostile to God, all that which opposes God and is inspired by Satan. "That which is in the world" is thus the evil that does not come from God. It is not the things themselves, but the whole evil context in which they are abused. John gives examples of this. He literally says: desires of the flesh and the desires of the eye and boasting in the good a person has. "The flesh" is the world within the individual person, not the body but the egoism, the selfish will that enjoys others and satisfies the needs of the body in a manner that God does not desire. "Desires of the eye" is the lust that can light up the eye before something that a person wants to have and perhaps can have but does not need and perhaps does not have a right to. What a person would live on becomes instead a status symbol that one boasts in. It is to love the world and that which is in the world. And this love excludes love for God. "You cannot serve both God and Mammon."

18-27 The Third Test of Truth: The Apostolic Faith

Jesus had said that before He returned "false christs and false prophets will arise" (Mark 13:22). Something like this seems to have happened, and John draws the conclusion that the last days are here. Essentially, he says "a last hour." Some believe that he means the final act of a world-drama (that had begun when Jesus came to earth) has now begun its last scene. So, he would have made hasty conclusions concerning the signs of the time which can be a timely reminder for us all of how easy it is to do that. Others think that he only wants to say that there comes a time of decisive meaning, a testing by fire for the Christian church.

The word "antichrist" is only used by John, but the matter is found also in Paul and Revelation. In the great final settlement between God and Satan, evil sets up a competitor to Christ, a false savior. Jesus also speaks of pseudo-christs, who make themselves out to be on His errand. However, John apparently means by "anti-christs" men who do the work of the anti-Christ. It is the matter of men living now who have membership in the church where they seem to have been active as teachers. However, at heart they were never at home there, John says. And now they have gone so far that they left the church and openly showed that they deny the apostolic faith.

This is the third test of truth: The apostolic faith. He who does not whole-heartedly believe as the apostles is no true Christian. He does not belong "to us." John does not hesitate for a second to draw a line. He is sent out into the world with a particular message that creates true communion with Christ. Christ is who He is. Here there is no other. The gospel is not "pluralistic." Within a congregation, there can be found those who do not believe in the Christian way. So, there can be different opinions. Through disagreements, it shall "be revealed that not all belong to us." As Paul says: "there must be factions among you that those genuine among you may be recognized" (1 Corinthians 11:19).

John is quick to say that he trusts in those to whom he writes. They have, of course, "been anointed" (essentially, "received oil") by the Holy Spirit. He seems to mean: Christ has given them the Spirit. Of course, Christ means "the anointed." He was anointed with the Holy Spirit, and He gives the Holy Spirit to all of them who believe. So, they have all "received knowledge." They are not—as the Gnostics said—ignorant, in need of a new and higher anointing that only a Gnostic can give.

Then we receive a short insight into the false teaching in concern. A person denied that Jesus was the Christ. This means: a person denied that the man Jesus really was the Son, He "who was from the beginning." Some said that He was only a man in which for a time—from baptism to right before the crucifixion—the divine had had his dwelling and worked. However, he who denies that Jesus really was the Son, neither does he know the Father and so he has no real communion with Him. He "is the anti-Christ," John says. Anti-Christ can thus work in a series of men before he himself steps forward.

Against this false teaching, John now sets a double shield: the Word and the Spirit. "That which you have heard from the beginning," just that apostolic message that you shall let "abide in you." So, a personal effort is demanded for the matter. A person should open himself, continue to listen, remind him of what a man heard, and imprint it on the heart. "Anointing" is the Spirit who brings the message to life and helps us apply it to ourselves. All Christians have received this anointing, John says, in an obvious polemic against the false teachers. They made claim that the individual possesses it. Therefore, they could instruct others. They boasted that they came with something new, an interesting and profound interpretation, something no one had heard before. Yet no Christian needs such instruction. The Spirit has taught him what is the truth and not a lie. He has said it from the beginning and says it again now. You shall remain in Christ—implicitly: just as you learned to know Him, and you do that when you hold fast to that which you have learned from the beginning. So, there is no question about that which depends on the Spirit to come with his own interpretation and new teachings. The false teachers did that. The Spirit's true anointing brings the true Word to life and keeps us in a true apostolic faith.

1 John 3

2:28-3:10 A Life of Obedience

John is finished with the three tests of truth, and yet not finished. He has hardly hammered in the last nail, and once again he states that we shall remain in Christ to be able to endure when He comes. So, he returns to the point of departure. It belongs to his meditative manner of thinking. He loves to return to the same foundational thoughts in order to see them from a new angle.

So once again, he takes up the theme that a Christian lives a righteous life. The new thing he has to say about the theme is that the righteousness is an important consequence of a Christian being "born by him." According to the context, "him" ought to mean Christ, but apparently John means God because he otherwise always—and also in what follows here—says that we are God's children. We are really that because we are born again and have partly received a new life that comes from the Father.

When John speaks about "he who shows himself righteous in his life" neither does he think concerning common societal honor. This a man can show without being born again. Here he once again applies the test of authenticity for a Christian. If his faith is genuine then it will show in a true Christian life.

He who makes us Christian is someone that the world does not see and does not understand, just as little as they understand who God is. Yet John repeats it: we are God's children, already here and now. What we will then be, this John acknowledges that he does not know. It is worth remembering. Not even an apostle could answer all questions. Christendom rests upon revelation, not upon philosophical speculations. We know what God has let us know in His Word. There is a limit and beyond that limit we must answer as John: It is not yet revealed. However, we know this much: we shall be like Him, our Resurrected Lord. We shall be able to see Him such as He is. And for just this reason a Christian purifies himself and takes care with his life.

Thereby, John is back with his theme, that he now varies in two similarly built-up sections, both of which begin: "all who does [practices] sin." A person notices that "it does not say that in English." However, the expression is so purely Johannine that we ought to maintain it. Namely, he distinguishes between having sin and doing sin. We all have sin. He who says that he does not have sin, he deludes himself (1:8). Yet it is just as certain that a Christian does not consciously and purposely do such things as God forbids. All sin is essentially a break with God's law. They who sin are "of the devil" as it is normally said. They are governed by him and belong to him. Here, "sin" does not mean to commit a particular sin but to live in sin and continue in it. The Greek language has an ability with its different verb forms to cause a verb to refer either to a particular operation or some regular continuation. Here it is a question about the latter. So, a person could render it "live in sin."

However, now Christ is revealed to take away sins and thwart the devil's deeds. Two times it is said, and two times is drawn the logical conclusion: he who remains in Christ and is born of God, he cannot be at peace with sin. He does not sin, and does not live in sin, not so long as "God's seed remains in him." "God's seed"—it is that which kindles new life. This can be the living Word or the Holy Spirit or both. So long as the new life works in a Christian, he cannot be at peace with sin. He cannot set himself above God's commandment. And it was just that which heresy did and has done in all times.

11-17 A Life of Love

To obey means to love. The love command comes first among all commandments. John now goes over to the other authentic requirement: love. Once again, he reminds us that he doesn't come with anything new. Those who need to hear something new gather around false teachers. Yet John also gives a new aspect to love. He who loves is hated. Those who obey God are not tolerated well. This is illustrated already in the story of Cain and Abel. So, we should not be surprised in the least if the world hates us. It is connected to the fact that we have gone over from death to life. He who does not love, he remains in death, just as he wanders in the darkness. Here there is a double connection: life-light-love and death-darkness-hate. Whoever hates his brother bears the mark of Cain on his forehead, and the mark shows to whom he belongs, "He was a murderer from the beginning" (John 8:44). The opposite is Christ who rather than destroying the evil people gave His life for them. We have learned thereby to love and so we know what we ourselves are obligated to do: not go the way of hate; that only leads to death, also for others, but the way of love is where a person is prepared to give his life for others. John only gives love a highly concrete application so that it would not be conceived of as a romantic feeling that believes that it ought to embrace unknown people, whether they live far away or here at home in the Christian family circle among the brothers and sister who do not have what they need. Christian care for the poor, sick, and old was something new in the world of antiquity that awakened the heathen's wonder and even admiration in some.

18-24 God is Greater than our Conscience

John gives yet another exhortation to love. The real love that does not consist of phrases, resolutions, and protests but in concrete action toward living people. Thereby, he seems to have gone over to the third requirement of authenticity, by speaking of to "be of truth." However, he first makes a digression. Like the good seelsorger he is, he knows that a Christian looking at himself always finds deficiencies in his love. On this point our conscience always has something with which to accuse us. John uses the word "our heart," but he means precisely that which we call "conscience." We must remember that God is greater than our conscience. The conscience is not everything. It only knows the law. However, God has a place in His fatherly heart for more than the law, holiness, and righteousness. There is also His will for salvation, His self-giving love that offered His most beloved to save the lost. The gospel speaks of this. The conscience does not know the gospel. Of the truth of the gospel, a person can only be convinced "before Him" when he hears of talk of Christ. Then the conscience can finally come to peace. God "knows all" and when He says that He forgives for Jesus's sake, I can believe it. Then we can boldly step before God. We are His children, and we receive what we ask of Him, if we namely hold fast to His command and will that His will should happen in everything. Then we will neither have anything but what He gives.

John summarizes again. The chief thing is: Believe in Christ and love one another. Hold fast to His commandments even if they condemn us. We may not have another law by which we can imagine we are righteous. We must give Christ the right, take upon ourselves His command and trust in His forgiveness. Then we have the communion that John speaks of already in the introduction. We remain in God and God in us. And this we know because we have received the Spirit. John does not mean that we can note this by referencing any particular experience. A person cannot feel whether or not he has the Spirit. Rather, a person recognizes that which was just mentioned. He believes in Christ. He cannot be without Him. A person has entered into a cohesiveness of love, with responsibilities for other men and communion with them. He also notices the conscience's warnings and accusations when they drive us close to Christ. The whole Christian life is a life in the Spirit, and it is the sum of the Christian's life experience that gives us certainty that we have received the Spirit.

1 John 4

1-3 Testing the Spirits

The spirits that shall be tested are the "spirits of prophets" that Paul also speaks about in 1 Corinthians (14:32). The prophets had a highly treasured charisma (gift). They could speak according to the Spirit's inspiration. The problem was that a person could encounter false prophets. Jesus had warned of them. A person would know them by their fruit, that is, by their lifestyle and the result of their work within the congregation. Here, John has already commanded the same test of authenticity. The false prophets can be exposed by their unrighteousness and lack of love. Yet to this he adds still one more test that he now makes use of again. How does their word fit with the apostolic proclamation? John puts his finger on the decisive point that is always up to date. What do they say about the divinity of Christ? Most false teachers can be exposed upon this point. The Gnostics teach that the true God did not create the world and had nothing to do with the material. The savior He sent could not possibly have become man. The heavenly Christ had only temporarily made use of the man Jesus, from the time of His baptism to the time just before His crucifixion. Against this, John places the Christian faith. Jesus really was "Christ, come in the flesh," as it is literally said. God's Son really became a man of flesh and blood. He who denies this is not a Christian who happens to have a dissenting opinion. No, John says, he is a mouthpiece for the anti-Christ, who is already operative in the world and uses his tools to hinder and destroy Christ's work.

Therefore, the prophets must be tested according to the apostolic message. He who says something different than the apostles is a false prophet. John is just as relentless on this point as Paul (Galatians 1:8).

4-6 We and the Others

There is a necessary line between those who belong to Christ and those who do not, even if they want to be called Christians. Therefore, John says "you" (concerning his spiritual children) and "we" (meaning himself and the apostles as well as the other proclaimers of the gospel) and contrasts them with "they" (opponents and false teachers). "They" have not had any success among "us." Christ's spirit is stronger than the anti-Christ's. In other areas they can have success. They belong to the "world" (the fallen world that is in opposition to God). They speak such as the world understands and wants to hear. They are popular. Yet among those who belong to God, (normally John says "who are of God"), they have no success, and this is just as sure a sign of those who are of God and those who are not. It can sound like insufferable arrogance to say something like that. However, John is Christ's apostle. He has met Christ and been taken into His service. He knows what Jesus said: my sheep listen to my voice (John 10:27). He who is of God, he listens to God's Word (8:47). The road forks where the gospel is preached. John does not doubt for a minute that a position is taken here that reveals where a person is at home.

7-10 God is Love

Now John returns to the other sign of authenticity: love between God's children. This is not a matter of natural love, he who we all can show to someone who is close to our heart and is good and friendly in return. There is nothing noteworthy about that, Jesus says (Matthew 5:47). Here it is a question about something new, something of God's own being, that is revealed before us when He offered His only Son and let Him die that we should live. Christians did not use the normal word for love when they talked about God's love and how we should love. Instead, they had taken up an unusual word (*agape*) that showed that this was a question about something new.

God is love, John says. He is love. (We usually say, "the love," but in the text it says "love.") Otherwise, it can be said about God that He is "spirit" (John 4:24), "light" (1 John 1:5), and a "consuming fire"(Hebrews 12:29). The heathens could also say all this. This belongs to the revelation of God that is possible without Christ. However, what God's love really is, that is revealed before the world, when God gave His only begotten Son to atone for our sins. God *so* loved the world . . . .

To really learn to know God is to encounter this atoning love. It means to be born with a new life. God's love is "poured into our hearts."

11-16 The Connection Between Love and Faith

This also ought to be obvious that we love one another because a life in communion with God is a life in love. For the Gnostics, as for so many others, divine communion was something else. It consisted in "seeing God." A person could do this through a strong emotional experience, perhaps ecstasy, or perhaps through some type of deeper "knowledge" or "illumination." However, no one has ever seen God, John says. We do not get a true picture of Him through our thinking and our speculation. Neither do we possess Him in our emotional experiences. The only manner in which we receive communion with Him is to let ourselves be filled by His love, so that it may "reach its goal within us." Here John uses a Greek word that is usually translated with "be fulfilled." The basic meaning is to reach completion and come to the prescribed goal, and the goal for God's love is that we who are loved should love one another. That we reach the goal is when we notice "that He has given us His Spirit." John does not think of any single experience in the past, but of that which a Christian day after day may have: a life that is filled with The Holy Spirit's comfort and admonition (Acts 9:31).

No one has seen God. And yet there are those who did see Him, namely in the Son. This "we" have done, John says, we apostles and disciples. And "we" have witnessed that God really sent His Son for the world's salvation. He who receives this message and confesses Jesus as God's Son, He has received communion with God. This we have seen and come to believe in; this is God's love that came into the world when Jesus Christ came to us.

17-21 Love Makes us Bold

Now John begins to summarize. To be a Christian is to live in God's love. This brings with it a boldness before judgment. As a good child, a Christian may be afraid to leave his father, or to grieve him, but he is not afraid of God Himself and does not fear the day of judgment. He knows that he is "such as he—Jesus—is." He has shared in His life and His righteousness, already now, though He lives and remains in the old world in His old body and with His old man. Still, he belongs to the siblings of Jesus and has the same access to the Father as Jesus. Because God loves us with this inconceivable love, so we love—both God and our siblings. A person cannot love God over the heads of your siblings. Some believe that they do this and perhaps also that they love people in other parts of the world that they have not seen. But true love shows itself in the relationship to the people that a person has before their eyes and with whom they are brought together in everyday life. John gives a reminder of the double commandment to love what we received from "Him"—from Jesus. It cannot be halved. A person cannot remove love of the neighbor and satisfy himself that he loves God. Neither can a person remove love for God and believe that it is enough to love people.

For the third time John says who is a liar though he maintains that he is a Christian. It is he who does not keep the commandment and does not live righteously (2:4). It is he who does not have a right confession of Jesus as God's Son (2:22). And now finally: it is he who does not love his brother. So, John has also applied his threefold test of truth here.

1 John 5

1-4 Summary

From perpetually new viewpoints John had meditated upon three important expressions for a true Christendom: the true faith, love, and obedience. Now he shows how all three have their meeting point in the same fact: that we are born of God. Through faith in Christ, a person becomes a child of God, born again. He who loves his Father, also comes to love His children. "It is clear to us" that it must be so. John uses the same expression that—with small variations—return incessantly in this letter. A person can say "Thereby, we know" or "We understand," but in this place "it becomes clear for us" fits better. When we love God and want to live according to His will, it becomes inescapably clear to us that we shall love our brothers and sisters in the faith. This love is not primarily an emotion. Love for God is actually a love in action (3:18). A person obeys His commandment, and His commandment is not heavy when a person loves Him. Then there is a power that means victory over the world. This victory is won by all who are born of God. John does not say "all" or "each and every." For it is essentially not we men who win the victory, but something in us that comes from God. It is not our intentions, not our will or our intelligence, not our organization nor activity, but our faith.

5-12 The Importance of Faith

This world conquering faith does not receive its power from he who believes but from Him in whom we believe. It must be a faith in Jesus, a true faith in God's Son. John gives us something decisive in the faith, so concentrated that we find it hard to understand what he means. He says that Christ came through both water and blood. It is tempting to think of His baptism and death. However, John then says that the blood and the water witness together with the Spirit. How shall it be understood?

We may take our point of departure in baptism and death. We have already heard what the Gnostic Cerinthus, who at this time worked in Ephesus, taught: that the heavenly Christ only occasionally took His dwelling in the man Jesus. It would have happened by His baptism in Jordan. The Gnostics too could say that Christ "came through the water." However, they denied that he was upon the cross. So, John emphasizes that Christ came "both in water and with blood." Jesus was really Christ during His whole life, at once man and God. It was so He through His death was the atonement for our sins. John has already emphasized twice that He is that (2:2 and 4:10). What John says here against Cerinthus has its application in later attempts to restrict the divinity of Jesus and the meaning of His redemption.

When John then says that the water and the blood witness, it seems to have some connection with what he relates about the witnesses, possibly himself, as in Golgotha say how blood and water flowed from the open side of Jesus. For John, it was apparently a meaningful sign, and it is presumed that he afterwards saw as a continuation of the stream of life from the heart of Jesus as in baptism and the Lord's Supper that it would flood out over the world. The interpretation gives a good meaning to His word here in the letter. He says that there are three who witness about Jesus Christ. First the Spirit that speaks when the gospel is preached (1 Peter 1:12) and then also the sacraments where Christ Himself is present and deals with us. It is God Himself who in this manner witnesses about His Son through the Word and sacrament. He who believes and is received, "he has the testimony within him," not independent of the outer means of grace, but as an inner power in them, a personal conviction. However, to not receive the message of Jesus, this means to say no to God Himself and the incredible offer in which He gives us eternal life in His communion. Here there is life, literal life.

The word of the three witnesses has a particular address to the baptized in a people's church. Jesus came not only in the water. So, the Spirit (who speaks through the Word) and the blood (the Lord's Supper) must have its place in a Christian life.

13-21 The Security of Faith

John ends his letter by confirming that he knows that those who receive this have eternal life. So, it follows that they can boldly come to God with their prayers. They know that they already have what they have prayed for, if they actually "pray according to his will." John apparently believes this to be the obvious prerequisite for all Christian prayer. Deep within there always lies: "according to your will, not mine but yours."

Even if someone sees a fellow Christian, a "brother" committing sin, he can boldly pray for him. This can be applied to both small and great, but obviously John first thinks about serious and willful sins that break the relationship with God. He actually says that God who answers prayer shall "give him life." Usually it reads "and he shall give him life." This "he" can refer to the intercessor, and in any case, it means the person (he) who prays is the reason that the sinner receives new life. There is then a qualification. There is "sin unto death," and then prayer is of no help. This does not refer to certain works over which a person should be able to make lists. It speaks not of "sins" but of sin, and it means the state of hardening that comes if a person definitively and consciously says no to Christ, after he has learned to know Him. Jesus also says something of the same thing when He warns against the sin against the Holy Spirit, or what Hebrews describes as a state where there is no longer any possibility for conversion.

Against this background John now pounds firm three lovely truths that a Christian can hold to. They all begin with a "we know"—through God's promise. The first we know is that Christ holds His hand upon those who are born again and keeps Him. Essentially a different reading and translation is that the Christian "gets to be"—for the others, we know that we belong to God, though we live in the midst of a fallen world in opposition to God. And for the third, we know that Christ has come (the Greek verb form means that He "is come" so that we have Him with us), and that He has given us the ability to know God, who is "the truth," the Real and the Only. We have learned to know Him in His Son, who is both true man and true God and who for this reason has the ability to give us the unfathomably great gift: eternal life in communion with God.

Finally, there comes a warning against idols. John probably means all the gods of heathendom, but he can also refer to heretical false saviors or: "sexual immorality, impurity, passion, evil desire, and covetousness, which is idolatry" (Colossians 3:5 [ESV]), or something else that remains just as relevant in all times. The last word in this letter that began with a joyous cry and ends with an assurance of our sonship is also a reminder that no one can be God's child without joining the fight with the world, which is in the power of the Evil one.

SECOND AND THIRD JOHN
Introduction

These two small letters, the shortest among the writings of the New Testament, are typical occasional letters. They are precisely long enough to take up the space of a standard sized page of papyrus. They contain short greetings from the apostle that a traveling preacher could have carried with him. They may have been "accompanying letters" to a greater circular. A person can indeed think that these accompanied First John. In such a case, Second John may be a particular greeting to a certain congregation, where the longer letter, which lacks an introductory greeting, would be read. In the same way Third John could be a greeting to the leaders for one such congregation. All three letters could have been given together at such a place. These are uncertain guesses, but they still give us a notion of how such letters worked when they were written.

For us, they have meaning in that—like Paul's letter to Philemon—they open a window into the everyday life of the early church. We discover that the problems people had to contend with are not so different than ours, and we receive counsel and instructions that are given with apostolic authority and have application for all time.

Precisely because these letters seem so ordinary, there was reason that people in antiquity did not want to keep them in the canon. Even at the beginning of the fourth century the thought was shared, and only at the end of that century were they commonly accepted. There is no reason to doubt their authenticity or antiquity.

Concerning style and contents, they are so closely related with First John that a person can assume that they have the same author. In the introduction to my commentary on First John, the reasons why it is believed this is written by one of the twelve, and the Apostle John more specifically, are presented.

Both letters come from one person who does not say his name but calls himself "the elder" or "the presbyter." In Greek it is the same word. Presbyter was the name for the spiritual leader of a congregation. In certain contexts, this word only means "the elderly." In other contexts, we normally render it with "the elder." The Jewish people already had such "elders" in every synagogue; thus, the Christians received this expression from them.

An apostle could also be considered a presbyter. Peter calls himself (1 Peter 5:1) a "co-presbyter" to the other presbyters, and even with Papias (at the beginning of the second century) we see that an apostle—or in any case, John—could be called a "presbyter." But it is more likely that here the word just means "the old man." Apparently, it was the designation that people in the congregations commonly used for their old apostle, the last of the twelve still living. That the letter writer was a respected leader of the church with great authority in the congregation appears to be very clear by his manner of writing.

There is a theory that aside from the Apostle John there would have also been an Elder John in Ephesus who would have written "Revelation" (as a few in antiquity thought) or alternatively the Gospel of John and the Letters of John (as many in modern times have thought). The later thought has sought support from the superscriptions for both of these letters. However, it is, as it has been emphasized in the introduction to my commentary on the Gospel of John, weakly substantiated.

So, this commentary starts from the assumption that here we have before us two small letters from the Apostle John, who was commonly known as "the old man" in his congregations. They have their particular interest and value for edification precisely as personal, small handwritten letters—the only of their like to be preserved from the twelve.

2 John

1-3 Heading

The letter comes from "the old man" (see the introduction) and is addressed to "the elect lady." Here "elect" means elected by God, Christians. The word "lady" translates the Greek word *kyria* that is the feminine form of *kyrios*, lord. It could be used for the mother of a house in the capacity of a lady in charge of the household by her husband's side. The English word wife[1] says entirely too little. The English word "lady" and the German "Herrin" render the meaning better. It is the matter of a congregation, which is personified in this manner, approximately as we do when we speak of Mother Sweden. Of course, the elect is "a royal priesthood," called to rule with Christ. The church is the bride to Kyrios Christos. So, she could be called kyria.

The children are the members of the congregation. John says that he loves them "in truth." This means that he really does, but also that he—as it says immediately following—does so for the sake of truth. The truth is God's good will and purpose, that which He has revealed in Christ (who is Himself "The Truth"). Those who believe have opened themselves to the truth. It has taken possession of them. It will remain with them for eternity. And therefore, they also love one another. They can do nothing else.

Then comes the apostle's desire concerning grace, mercy, and peace. However, here it is not only a desire, but an assurance. The Christians can be sure to receive all of this because they hold fast to the truth and love. These two are indispensable and simultaneously indissolubly united. The truth is that which faith rests in. Love is a consequence of faith. Faith cannot be found without love, just as love is not found if faith does not hold fast to the revealed truth.

Thereby, John has already hinted at what the contents are in his greeting to the congregation. We cannot know exactly which congregation it is addressed to, but it is very certain to have been a congregation in Asia Minor. It could very well be one of them mentioned in Revelation.

4-6 The Great Commandment

John states with joy that he knows that the congregation has members who "live in the truth" (literally walk in the truth). He does not say that all do this, neither that it is a question of a few. The Greek expression only says that there are those who do it. The truth is thus something that a person "lives" or "walks" in. It is not only

---

[1] Swedish word "fru"

a sort of knowledge but a way of life, a divine order that rules over us and shapes our lives. John can describe it as "the command we received from the father." This does not mean that it is first and foremost a matter of a law. With "command" John means the whole of God's good will—above all, that we shall be saved through faith in His Son. When it comes to what we should do, there is a fundamental command that John never tires of repeating. He knows that he has said it innumerable times before. In the early church tradition, it is said that some listeners informed John that they had heard that enough. However, John cannot help but say it again. He does it considerately—"and now I ask you"—but still searching. This is the chief summary of the commandment that we received: we shall love each other. Love is not a feeling that one must go and wait for. It is first and foremost an unselfish service for the benefit of others. It is something a person can decide to do.

7-11 Warning Against False Teachers

John declares why he has reminded them of both truth and love. It is on these points that Christendom is threatened by false teachers. It is apparently a question of the same false teachers as in First John. They call themselves Christians, but they turn Christian doctrine upside down and destroy Christian love. Like the apostles, they have gone out into the world, and the congregation can be certain of a visit by them. So, it means to look up. They come with a new teaching of Christ, the same as we hear about in John's first letter. They deny that the man Jesus from Nazareth really was God's Son. In it, man can recognize the Arch-deceiver, the anti-Christ. It is his errands they do. Therefore, a person should beware of them. If a person follows them, they lose the "reward," the undeserved reward of grace that laborers in the vineyard receive. They say that they come with something new that goes beyond the knowledge that the apostles shared. They say that a person cannot just stand by the old. A person must make progress, develop themselves and move forward. They draw people in with something new and exciting. However, those who make "progress" in this manner, they no longer remain in the teachings of Christ that come from God and can never change. So, it means to "remain in the teaching." There is, in fact, a Christian teaching that can be expressed in intelligible words, and which has been "once for all delivered to the saints" (Jude 3). If a person remains in it, then he has both the Father and the Son. This means: a person has communion with them; a person has everything they have to give. So, it means that they watch out for those who come as traveling evangelists. Perhaps they present themselves as fellow Christians. However, if they do not "carry" the teaching of Christ's own teaching, that which was shared by the apostles, then a person could not receive them.

So, this is said to the congregation, and it applies to evangelists who come with a demand to be able to speak to the congregation. This does not apply to individuals who might have incorrect thoughts in the questions of faith. A person can receive them and try to correct them. Here it means agitators for a false teaching who consciously want to change the gospel in its main points: the faith in Jesus Christ who is both true God and true man and who died on the cross for the propitiation of our sins. Such a person should not be greeted with a "welcome." It is this that the congregation may not do. To spread false teaching in questions of Christ is really an evil deed not just a little deviation in his way of thinking.

What John says here has its application both in the call and ordination of pastors. The church has often sat over this, which was essential to the early church in a fateful way.

12-13 Final Greeting

Finally, John says that he hopes to be able to come personally to speak directly to the congregation. So, he has written very briefly. He apparently has a position that gives him an obvious authority and a sort of supervisory prerogative among the congregations in a greater area. It fits then that it is an apostle who writes.

The letter ends with a greeting from the children to "the elect sister," so from the sister congregation where John now resides, most likely Ephesus.

3 John

1 Heading

In distinction from the previous letter, this is directed to an otherwise unknown individual named Gaius. Apparently, he has been one of the leaders in the congregation. John calls him "the beloved." In normal usage it may be more natural to say, "the dear" (just as the address "my beloved brothers" could perhaps be rendered "my dear friend" or something like that), but a person forfeits some of the sincerity in John's address. He really means that Christians should love each other, not only be good friends. When he says that he loves "in truth," here it means—as in the preceding letter—not only that he does it honestly, but also that it is a consequence of his faith and that he lives as a Christian.

2-8 A Faithful Coworker Who is a Joy

John begins with a little well-wishing. It is his prayer that when it comes to health and general wellbeing, Gaius should have it just as well as he does spiritually. Then John tells of what great joy he has received from some itinerant Christian preachers who have reported how well they were received by Gaius. They have "testified to your truth" and of "how you walk in the truth," as it says literally. Once again, we encounter a key word for John: truth, which is God's good will, revealed in Christ and mediated through the apostolic message. So, the truth can be found with a person, and it reveals itself in that a man lives in it and "does the truth." And this is essential. Therefore, nothing can make an apostle happier than that he hears that his children walk in the truth. His "children" are members of the congregation for whom he is a spiritual father.

So, Gaius has made himself known as a good and faithful servant when it comes to receiving itinerant coworkers. Hospitality was an important link in missions and in congregational work because this was often driven through unpaid full-time workers, who traveled from one place to the next. In antiquity, there were plenty of these itinerant speakers, philosophers, teachers, and agitators who raised money for themselves and their activity. Now we hear that the itinerant evangelists did not usually receive any money from outsiders. John emphasizes that it is the duty of Christians to receive them and care for them during their stay and give them what they need to make it to the next congregation. Here he does not touch on the problem that arose when it came to false teachers who pretended to be good Christians. It assumes that the itinerant preachers really "proclaim the name," meaning Jesus Christ, according to the true apostolic doctrine. So, we receive clarification that complements the preceding letter, where it mostly speaks of false preachers that a person should not receive.

9-10 Inner Conflicts in the Congregation

The problem in this congregation is not that false teachers are welcome, but that the true ones are not received in certain circles. We learn that John has written to the congregation, but that a certain Diotrephes (otherwise unknown) has seen to it that the letter did not result in any action, or maybe not even read.

So here there must have been a serious conflict between the apostle and a certain group within the congregation. In and of itself, it is not so strange. Even Paul could have difficulties with his congregations. There are times when he did not even know if he was welcome in Corinth. Then as now it must have been local leaders who would rather avoid any involvement from superiors. The concern with Diotrephes is he apparently refused to receive those who came from John. The apostle lets it be understood that he plans to come himself and call the recalcitrant to account. What positions Diotrephes and Gaius held is not clear. Perhaps they were leaders for their own factions. That Diotrephes wishes to put some of his opponents out of the congregation should likely be conceived as he and his party at some congregational meetings have attempted to bring about a resolution for excommunication.

11-12 A Recommendation

Gaius should not follow this poor example. Instead, he should do that which is good and continue to receive those who come from John. This is likely how a person should think concerning the unmediated recommendation of a certain Demetrius. It is conceivable that he is the one that carries this letter. He receives unreserved praise. He has received a good testimony from everyone even "the truth itself" [himself] which likely means Christ or the Spirit through some prophetic message. John personally vouches for him with the apostolic authority he has.

13-15 Final Greeting

The conclusion is reminiscent of the previous letter, but it is not a matter of a stereotypical repetition. The sentences are formed differently (which is more obvious in the Greek than in the English translation). Perhaps the similarities are there because both letters are written in similar situations where John prepares for a trip he is planning.

Finally, John sends greetings from friends in the congregation where he is now and sends his greeting to "all friends" in Gaius's circle. He mentions no one by name. He has already filled the front of the papyrus page, and the backside should only have the address. The paper would be rolled together, and the backside had the same purpose as an envelope for us. However, John asks Gaius to greet everyone particularly "by name," as it literally says.

John is usually called "the apostle of love" with good reason. His letter reminds us that he lays just as great an emphasis on the truth, and for him, the truth is something very particular, that a person cannot change: the apostolic message of Jesus Christ. "The apostle of love" can be impassibly strict when he rejects the false teaching. He does not pull his punches when it comes to a person such as Diotrephes. What he stakes out for us is the narrow path the church must follow: The church must not be asserted at the expense of love, but neither may love obscure the truth. Then it is no longer Christ's love.

JUDE

Introduction

In the heading Jude introduces himself only as a Christian and "brother of James." Since antiquity people have guessed that he means the James who was brother to Jesus and who became the respected leader of the mother congregation for twenty years and is mentioned in many places in the New Testament. We know that aside from James, Jesus had three other brothers, and that one of them was named Jude (Mark 6:3). We also know that the brothers of Jesus did not believe in Him during His lifetime but that in connection with the resurrection they came to believe. They are mentioned among those who gathered days before Pentecost, and Paul mentions them in a passage (1 Corinthians 9:5) that "the Lord's brothers worked as circuit traveling missionaries. According to a source from the middle of the second century, two grandsons of Judas had been Christians and lived as poor farmers with small plots of land during the reign of Caesar Domitian (81-96).

Jude is mentioned by authors from the end of the 1st century and seems to be mentioned already in the beginning of the first century. There were still some in the fourth century who doubted that it was apostolic, first because Jude cites a couple of late Jewish "apocrypha," that were not considered to be Holy Scripture.

It is particularly for linguistic reasons that many in our day doubt that Jude could have been written by a Galilean Jew. It is written in good Greek by someone who had a certain literary education. The author has an apparent predilection for sonorous, often unusual and archaic words. He loves pictures, and his language does not lack rhetorical force. If the letter originates from Jude, the son of Joseph, then he must have had help with the formation of it by someone who had a Greek education.

In the introduction to Second Peter, it has already been emphasized that there are many points of contact between that letter and Jude. People have not been able to find agreement concerning the reason. Those who believe that one of the authors knew the other's work and used it are not unified on who it should be in that case. Both have their own style. What they have in common are not complete sentences but only individual words, expressions, and pictures, but these are so distinctive that a person has to think they had a common source. The same pictures or expressions can be used in different ways; the order can vary, and both authors have some material that others did not use. So, the most likely is that they both have heard at least something that they have used in their own way. It could very well be a question of an oral instruction.

It deals with a sharp account with a distortion of Christianity that was smuggled into the congregation and now developed a serious threat to apostolic Christendom. What the false teachers were saying is only hinted at. We learn that they made a claim to be Christians and participated in worship. But their way of life was anything but Christian, and they used a distorted gospel to defend their immorality.

It is easiest to think that here we are dealing with an early form of Gnosticism, of approximately the same sort as we encounter in John's letters and in Second Peter, partially also in Colossians. Gnosticism was the first great attempt to adapt Christianity to a religiosity that appears more current and to give the Church's message a new content by manipulating the old terms. It was an attempt to reinterpret the gospel proceeding from departure points that were fundamentally alien to it. The same thing has also happened in modern times, and it constantly happens again, something that contributes to the continual relevancy of Jude.

Concerning the age of the letter, the sentences go a long way, and we have nothing certain to hold to. The dating ranges from the middle of the first century into the first part of the second century. Yet all are agreed that here we encounter a document from a period when the apostolic church found its form and became conscious that it possessed a final message that must be preserved for all the future. This too contributes to the relevancy of the letter.

1-2 Heading

The introduction shows that this is a "catholic" letter that does not direct itself to any congregation but to all Christians. The author does not consider himself an apostle but instead cites what they have said (v.17). This has been cited as an argument for the letter's authenticity. Had anyone wanted to give the authority to his writing by giving the appearance of having been written by a brother of Jesus, then he would hardly have let Jude appear so unassuming.

3-4 The Reason for the Letter

The author begins by saying that he really wanted to write about salvation, but then he received an urgent reason to set himself down and take up a special subject.

Essentially, it has been shown that the apostolic faith is threatened by false teachers who are undermining it. They have crept in among proclaimers and teachers who appear to be Christian, but in actual fact smuggle in a new faith and make the gospel something other than it is. This is a mortal danger. The true Christendom is essentially given once for all through the apostolic message. Jude emphasizes just this: *once for all*, this faith has been delivered to the saints. The word "delivered" (or "handed over") is the very same expression that was used concerning the apostolic teaching when it was carried out into the world and established congregations. It had a particular form in which it was handed over to the congregations to be preserved undistorted until the day when Christ comes again.

Now Jude lets it be understood that the apostolic faith is threatened by false teachers that have crept into the church. The Scriptures have prophesied that they would come and draw "condemnation" upon themselves—most likely Jude means the condemnation that the Scriptures pronounce upon false prophets, who pervert God's message. It is just this that the false teachers do. Jude immediately indicates two decisive points from the beginning. First and foremost, they distort the gospel of God's grace so that it becomes a defense for a dissolute life. This danger has followed the gospel through the ages: the unconditional offer concerning forgiveness through faith in Jesus becomes an excuse for unrepentance. According to Luther's[1] catechism, it is precisely this that characterizes a dead faith: that a person "acquires the comfort of God's promise of grace without repentance."

The other fundamental problem according to Jude was that the false teachers denied Christ. They already did this with their lives, but he means that this had its basis in their teaching. Namely, they denied that He "was the only master and lord." Again, this is a danger that follows the gospel through the ages: to make small reservations when it comes to Christ's unrestricted authority and attempt to adapt His word and His message so that it would fit better with thoughts that are current to the day. It was just this that the false teachers did. That is the great danger.

5-7 Three Examples of Warning

Jude presents three examples. First, God's own people Israel. Israel was the prototype for the church. God had saved them from Egypt and brought them through the Red Sea—the prototype to baptism. However, it did not help those who gave up their faith. Jude thinks all the baptized should consider this. It did not even help that the angels had been created for the foremost of missions. (Jude uses a word that can be translated "lordship," "authority.") Those who rejected the call received a relentless verdict. Here Jude gives us a hint concerning the origin of evil. In "the heavenly world," which was created before our universe, there was a rebellion and

---

[1] Swedish Catechism, meaning the commentary on Luther's Small Catechism added by the Swedish state church of the time.

apostasy. So, there are fallen angels. Both Jews and Christians believed this. The fallen angels indulged in fornication. So, a person read the narrative in Genesis 6:4 concerning "God's sons" who began "to go into the daughters of men." In Sodom and Gomora people also engaged in fornication against their nature, which in the New Testament is always condemned as a hard break against God's order. The fire that fell from the heavens over the sinners in Sodom is also a foreshadowing: So, it comes to go with those who contradict God.

8-10 The Arrogance Behind the False Teachers

Despite these warning examples the false teachers do the same thing. We get a description of them—not of their teaching but of the consequences it has for their personality. It is drastic and brief. Jude uses picturesque language that is occasionally hard to translate into ordinary prose. We cannot say exactly what he means by saying they are blinded by their dreams. The foundational word may have been that they sleep the spiritual sleep or that they live in a dream world. Most likely it is perhaps that they cited their dreams, visions, and false revelations. That they "stain his body" (literally: the flesh) points to their fornication. It is an indication that these are Gnostics who taught that what a person did with their body made no difference as long as one belonged to the "enlightened."

Even the phrase translated as "reject authority" (in Bo Giertz's translation: "Do not ask who the Lord is?") can be comprehended differently. Literally, it says that they "overthrow the dominion." Most likely this applies to the authority of Christ, His position as Lord. We have already heard that the false teachers denied this point precisely. In what manner they blasphemed "the glorious ones" is not quite certain. It must have meant some sort of spiritual arrogance that considered itself capable of also judging the truths revealed to us in the Scriptures and cannot know otherwise because it applies to things that are not accessible to our human reason. A Gnostic can in many ways be compared to contemporary "authorities" who set themselves above God Himself and His revealed truths and tests what can be accepted but dismiss that which they do not like or apprehend with an obvious superiority.

As a contrast to this arrogance Jude references the Archangel Michael's example. He reminds them of an episode that is not found in the Bible, but which according to the information of the church fathers should have been in a late Jewish writing called "The Assumption of Moses." The actual event makes no difference for Jude. He only wants to emphasize that while Michael dealt with the devil, he did not once allow himself to blaspheme but left the judgment to God. The false teachers express themselves without thoughtful respect concerning things that they do not know. That which their reason can understand, namely that which has to do with the created world, they use that to their own destruction. This could also be said about modern men, who so often makes use of their God-given reason and their power over material things in a way that is morally devastating and finally threatens the whole of humanity with downfall.

11-16 Woe to the False Teachers!

Jude continues the annihilating judgment over the false teachers and stacks one drastic picture on the other. First, he takes examples from Scriptures. They take Cain's path—he who murdered his brother (which, of course, false teachers also do spiritually). They imitate Balaam who undertook to injure God's people for money. They do as Kora who led a rebellion against Moses and thereby against God. When the congregation celebrated the Lord's Supper (and in connection with that held a true meal, an "agape feast" as it was presented in First Corinthians 11, among other places) then the false teachers are also present without fear. They sit there as hidden reefs (blemishes). The word that Jude uses here normally means a skerry or a dangerous underwater rock that can make a person suffer shipwreck. Perhaps this is just what Judas means. The false teachers really step forward as teachers, so Jude uses an obvious reference to a well-known chapter of Isaiah (Ezekiel 34) to let it be understood that they are false shepherds. What they speak is not God's Word, for the Word is that which rains and snows that does not return empty (Isaiah 54:10f). On the contrary, they are like threatening storm clouds that pass by without giving rain. They are sterile fruit trees that do not bear fruit and stand dead in the fall. It says "twice dead" in the original Greek. Perhaps, Jude thinks the story of the tree is less significant than that of the false teachers who are dead in double measure, both through being born into a fallen generation and through apostasy again after being baptized. They can still have the word in their power and be intrusive and violent as the waves of a storm, but altogether they are finally a froth of flotsam and shame. They are stars that can lose their orbit and are snuffed out by the dark. When Christ comes, they receive the well-deserved reward for their deeds. Jude references a long passage from the Book of Enoch. Enoch is mentioned in Genesis (5:18f) as a pious man in the seventh generation after Adam. A book with his name was circulated in late Judaism and even in the early church. It is preserved, and it is noted that Jude cites it almost exactly (the whole of verse 15). Some think that Enoch was found with his collection of holy Scriptures, but he could just as well have read it as an edifying Scripture, alongside the Scriptures. Later, it is likely because Jude considers it necessary to speak about who this Enoch was and not use any of the usual expressions for Bible citations (for example, "The Scriptures say" or "it is written").

Jude finishes his annihilating characterization of the false teachers with some words that could be used concerning many contemporary men who do not believe as the apostles. They have made their own desires into their lodestars. They want to rule over their own lives. However, it is just that which they cannot do. So, they grumble and complain without ever being at peace. On the one hand they are arrogant and use big words when they speak about that which God alone has the right to determine. On the other hand, they can bow before those who have power on earth. When they have nothing to lose, they can present themselves as prophets for the truth and ones who judge others. However, when they have to encounter true powerbrokers, then they fall away and are cautious about admonishing them.

17-21 Stick to What the Apostles Said!

To this apostolic message also belongs the warning against false teachers since Jesus had said that they would come. Paul had expressly warned against them. Jude is convinced that these warnings apply to those they are now dealing with. Again, we get a little detail that shows they were Gnostics. They drew lines between different sorts of men. They themselves were charismatic, spiritual people who thought they stood on a higher plain than other Christians. On the contrary, says Jude, they are "psychics," people who only have a soul but not God's Spirit. Everyone has a body and soul but only those who have been born again have the Spirit. It is a distinction that we also find in Paul (1 Corinthians 2:14).

For those who want to be Christians, it means to let themselves be edified on the ground that has once and for all been laid by the apostles. There a man shall be incorporated as living stone, united with the foundation and enveloped by the other stones. The foundation is "your most holy faith." So, faith is not just a personal lifestyle and an answer to God's call; it is also the message itself that makes it so that we can come to faith and that we have something to believe in. Jude mentions three basic prerequisites to be able to remain and grow in the faith: to pray in the Holy Spirit, to keep yourselves in the love of God, and to wait for the return of Christ.

22-23 Consideration for Those Who have Strayed

In conclusion, Jude has a few words to say about those who have been led astray by the false gospel. The text is uncertain, and there are variants in the old manuscripts. Obviously, the congregation has responsibility for them all, and a person should be merciful towards them. There are some of them that are not locked in. With them a person should engage with particular care. A person can also help the others though it can be like grabbing an iron from the fire. A person should not be afraid of burning themselves if they are successful with it. To others, a person should show mercy but the whole time with a salutary fear. Even when a person loves sinners, a person should loath sin. Jude says it dramatically: hating even the garment that is "stained by the flesh," as the word is literally translated. It is the same warning Paul gives the Galatians: When you admonish a brother, you shall keep your eye on yourself, so that you do not also become tempted.

JUDE

24-25 Doxology

The end is a practical "doxology," a praising of the sort that early Christendom had learned from the Jews. Here Jude weaves in that which is finally the great comfort in all division and all disagreements that threaten the church. God is powerful to preserve both His church and His faithful to the great day when all discussions fall silent and the great joy for God's glory and Christ's victory breaks out never to be silenced for all eternity.

REVELATION
Introduction

Controversial and Beloved

No other book of the New Testament has been so controversial and at the same time so beloved as Revelation. In the congregations, it was beloved and read already from the very beginning. It was thought to be written by the apostle John. Justin Martyr testifies to this already from the year 150. From the second half of the second century there is further witness to the same thing. Yet among the great Greek theologians the idea was debated. The church father Origen (died in 254) did not like it, and his disciples contested its place in the canon (the holy Scriptures) openly. One of them, the Bishop Dionysius of Alexandria (from around the year 250), did a linguistic comparison with John's Gospel—worthy of reading even today—to show that the two Scriptures could not originate from the same authors. A second person from Origen's school, the bishop and the church historian Eusebius (died in 339), presented the theory that there were two men with the name John in Ephesus, of which the one, the apostle, wrote the gospel, while the other, the presbyter, authored Revelation. They were taught to dislike Revelation partially because of its language that did not at all correspond to what a person considered as good Greek and partially because of its theology, its talk of a millennium and of heaven in the most concrete manner, which philosophically educated Greeks with their abstract thoughts found to be completely naïve and simplistic. In the western half of the empire where people spoke Latin, Revelation was accepted early. In the eastern half of the empire, it was practically accepted during the course of the fourth century, even if the opposition lived among one or another theologian for a couple of centuries later.

We have experienced some of this opposition in our own generation. The liberal theologians with their Biblical criticism did not have much to spare for Revelation. Many thought that it did not belong at home in the canon, and in wider circles people were slightly embarrassed by it. At the same time, it was read and beloved not the least where there was something of the spirit of awakening. This popularity could be partially explained by people's ineradicable desire to give a little emphasis to the forgiveness of the future. However, during the Second World War—not the least in the lands that suffered the worst—it also showed itself to be a *book of revelation* with unsurpassed ability to carry men through awful events and give them a simultaneously realistic and faithful view of the world events. Since then, its topicality has increased rather than decreased.

A Prophetic Book

Revelation differentiates itself markedly from all other New Testament books. At the same time, it obviously belongs in the context it describes. This is because it—alone—is derived from the prophecies of the early church. Paul had already said that the church is built upon the foundation of the apostles and the prophets (Ephesians 2:20). The apostles have left indelible tracks among the New Testament books. However, the contribution of the prophets is surprisingly small, even though next to the apostles they were the most meaningful among the early Christian spiritual fathers and teachers. They admonished and comforted. They interpreted the events of the time and showed the way. Sometimes they prophesied the future, but that was not the most important. They received their message directly from God. So, they were not teachers and shepherds in the same manner as those officials who—through the apostles or in other ways—were chosen, placed, and ordained to lead the congregation through preaching and instruction. The prophets only spoke when the Spirit gave them something to say. They were charismatics.

Of all the prophets that appeared in the early church, there are not a whole lot that were preserved. We get an idea of how it could sound if we read, for example, the beginning of Ephesians. However, only in the Book of Revelation do we have a piece of early Christian prophecy in just the form that the prophet used when he presented it. It is a prophecy that is more directed to the future than prophecies seem to have been most commonly. However, it also shows us clearly how prophecy contained comfort and admonition (as in the seven letters) and how it gave them an illustrative help to understand their own time. There is really no doubt that it had a particular message to just those men who heard it read for the first time at divine service in the home congregation.

The Background of Revelation

The oldest information concerning John's Revelation is completely consistent. It goes back to men who themselves came from Asia Minor (Justin Martyr and Irenaeus). The tradition says that John received his revelations when he stayed on Patmos as a prisoner during the reign of Domitian. Domitian reigned from the years 81-96. He was more particular than any others in his demand to be worshiped as a god, and this led to serious persecutions of Christians, the most serious since the era of Nero. It is in this situation that Revelation came to be. The Christians, even the least and the most unimportant, stood before the threat to be tortured and killed for the sake of their faith.

Around the year 1900, the higher-critical Biblical research was completely agreed that Revelation should be understood exclusively apart from this situation. The great Babylon was the city of Rome. The beast was Caesar Nero, who John believed would return from hell and be reincarnated in Domitian. This was the beast who would let loose a fearful, but brief persecution against the Christians. So, Christ would come and establish His millennium, and it would happen in the very near future. With this message, John would now comfort his fellow Christians and admonish them to hold out. It must also be noted—the critics say—that John had made a capital error. And thereby, the value of Revelation was reduced to a minimum for us and our era.

Now a man can note that there was not a hint of such an interpretation of John by the authors of the second century. A person must also ask how the book would have come to be preserved and read if this really were understood in this way by those who received this message from Patmos. They must have all experienced that the message was false. This commentary will show how many reasons there are for a completely different way of reading John's Revelation.

An Apocalyptic Writing?

The Book of Revelation is sometimes called "The Apocalypse." The word comes from the Greek text where "revelation" means "apocalypse." Among the Jews there was at this time a series of "apocalyptic" writings that had originated during the previous centuries. They dealt with the world's destruction and the great judgment that the prophets had already spoken of. Many presented themselves as the compositions of some great saint in the past (Enoch, Moses, Esra). The contents are often highly fantastic.

Around the turn of the century (1900), there were many scholars who considered Revelation to be one such apocalyptic writing. A person depicted John as a completely clumsy compiler who sat with the work of others in front of him and gathered loosely broken passages without noticing how disunified they were. Then he put together a patchwork, full of contradictions that he presented as his own visions. This way of looking at things is thoroughly criticized today.

When Revelation is called an "apocalypse," the word really has new meaning found in Christendom. This normally means an "exposure" or "revealing" of something that is hidden. In the New Testament it is the matter of God's great mystery, his plan for the salvation of mankind. This plan—God's eternal "plan of salvation"—had been established before the foundation of the world had been laid but was only revealed and realized through Jesus Christ. It was the task of the apostles and prophets to preach this to people. Paul emphasizes how he as an apostle has received insight into it and how he is required to lay it out for people. He emphasizes that it is not only the apostles but also the prophets who have received insight into Christ's mystery (Ephesians 3:5). Every early Christian prophet was in this sense "apocalyptic." What he spoke for comfort and admonishment at the divine service was an "apocalypsis" (1 Corinthians 14:30).

The revelation of God's mystery is not fulfilled until Christ comes again. Christ's return can be called His "apocalypse" (1 Peter 1:7). When Revelation is called an "apocalypsis"—this is the first word in the book—then it is a question of one such prophetic revelation that came from Jesus Christ and which He lets us know that He received in the form of a series of views (or visions as they are usually called in the psychology of religion). So, John tells what he saw and heard "in spiritual rapture," in a state where he was pulled from everyday normal experiences, so in some form of ecstasy. His description also bears the sign of coming from a visionary, who is transported to a world where a person no longer sees and experiences things as we do in an awakened state. Rather, it has its similarities with that which we all experience in dreams. The scenes grow, we are transported, we stand before visions that we do not understand, and sometimes we experience immediately and intuitively who or what we have before us. Yet there is a decisive difference between a dream and a vision. When the visionary awakes, he knows that he has not "merely dreamt." He has encountered a bit of reality. Of course, he can be mistaken. Finally, there is a question of faith concerning what lies behind his vision. It is Christian faith that the prophets really received in their message from God.

This commentary assumes that John describes visions that he really saw. This assumption sets us immediately before the question of how these visions are connected to the prophecies of the Old Testament. Is John not dependent on them?

Revelation and the Old Testament

The Book of Revelation is full of Old Testament words, pictures, and thoughts. There is no question of direct citations. John never cites, as is Matthew's example, what some particular prophet has written. Rather, it is a question of what we call allusions. Perhaps it is just two or three words, but they are so distinctive or so bound to a particular picture that there is no doubt about the origin. Some 350 such allusions have been found in the text. A learned commentator has counted that the book's 404 verses contain 278 kinds of them. John has grabbed most of these from the Old Testament's writing (most from Isaiah, Daniel, Ezekiel, and the Psalms, in that order). He is no compiler who has made an extraction for some certain purpose. It is, on the contrary, apparent that he "cites" from memory, half unconsciously. He uses words and pictures that enter his language and world of thought. He is a Biblically literate Jew who thinks and speaks with the words of the Bible, so that they come to his tongue on their own.

It would not have occurred to his audience to think that he was "dependent" or "influenced" by Scripture like an author that is dependent on his role models. Scripture was, of course, God's Word. It revealed God's plans even in questions of the world's future. When John is now able to see "what must take place" (4:1), then there has to be a connection with what the prophets were once able to see. How a person conceives John's "dependence" on the Old Testament finally depends on what a person believes about God and His manner of revealing Himself. If God has really spoken through the prophets and through John, then the connection between their writings is not just literarily dependent.

Attempts at Interpretation through the Ages

How Revelation should be understood has always been a problem for the Christian Church. In the great mess of interpretive attempts, a man can hit upon certain chief types. As a rule, during the Middle Ages and the Reformation it was read as a sort of prophetic church history where a person found a description of the Church's fate during the course of the ages. In Pietism, a different viewpoint called the eschatological dominated. By eschatological is meant knowledge of the world's last days, the final point in world history. According to the eschatological interpretation, Revelation is a description of the last days. So, then it has nothing to say to our own time. To this there is a third diametrically opposed conception that is called the idealistic. This means that the Book of Revelation in actual fact presents ideas that are applicable in all eras. A person considers that the world shall remain for millions and millions of years. The "last days" are then completely uninteresting. However, in all times there is in progress a fight between evil, destructive powers, and Christ's Church. It is this fight that is described in John's symbolic form. So he has something to say to our day also.

All these interpretations contain something correct; they also have a common error. They start from a view of the Biblical word that has a feature of rationalism. A person takes it for granted that the Bible will give us knowledge that can be expressed in clear sentences with fully comprehensible words. When the Book of Revelation speaks in pictures and uses mysterious symbols, a person asks what these pictures and symbols "mean." A person takes it for granted that they can be translated into normal and conceivable prose with the help of words that have a clear meaning for all. However, there is a way to mediate the message that does not directly turn itself to understanding and cannot be expressed in clearly defined terms. Artists have always known this. A lyricist uses words and expressions that do not follow the letter but should still be taken seriously. Such language works intuitively and mediates a reality that cannot be mediated in any other way, at least not as well. A painter can have something to say without using "apprehensible" pictures. Music almost exclusively uses a language that cannot be directly changed over into normal prose.

A person must have this in mind when he reads the Book of Revelation. If a person reads it like a textbook, then he will go astray. There are three things a person has to clarify for himself.

The Words say more than Words

Our language can also be used to express what really cannot be expressed in words as long as they have their normal meaning. We all know that there are things that "are hard to express in words." This is most true concerning God and the whole of the heavenly word. The Bible uses verse and poetry to such a great extent. The poets have the ability to use language in such a way that it mediates something that really cannot be said in normal everyday prose. The Old Testament's prophets made great use of poetry, great poems and bold poems, when they spoke about God and His deeds. If, for example, a person reads Isaiah 40, then a person reads a series of examples of picturesque and infinitely expressive images that cannot be taken literally and yet still have something essential to say, something that can hardly be expressed in normal prose without distorting and toning down the message they mediate.

The language of the Book of Revelation touches on the border between prose and poetry. It has its own rhythm; it allows itself to be divided up into lines of poetry without difficulty (as some translators have done), and it is, above all, full of expressions that attempt to capture something that will not really allow itself to be captured. John often makes not of this himself by speaking of something as "similar to" or "appears" or "seems to be." A person notices how he looks for words and pictures that describe what he has seen. Often, he stands by hints and enjoys leading our thoughts in a certain direction. Intuition, empathy, imagination, and spiritual affinity are needed to understand him. There can often be double meanings in the words. It has always been so with the prophetic word. It has a depth that a person cannot peel back with the first pass.

Images That Are More Than Images

The Book of Revelation is full of images and "symbols." It is not unusual that the expositor sees his task as to try and find out what they "mean." A person often then assumes from that that the image or symbol is something mysterious or unknown that stands in the place for something we recognize. If a person can just find out what this is, then he has solved the riddle.

This is a bad mistake. The Biblical symbols stand for a reality that can certainly be expressed even in such a manner, but that can never be expressed completely without using the symbols to help. God *is* light. Christ *is* life. He *is* the bread of life.

He is the *true* vine. All such things are more than symbols. This is not the earthly phenomena—that we think we know—that can give us a picture of God or Christ. There is something of God's own being that comes to expression in these earthly phenomena. God has revealed Himself in His creation. The whole earth is full of His glory. Light is not just a movement of waves that we can measure. It reflects something of God's being. Life is not just a complicated function of protoplasm. It is something that comes from God. When we eat bread and when the branches receive their nourishment from the stem, something happens that happens in its fullest seriousness, in its deepest reality, only when we receive life from Christ. So, it is not just a question of earthly things what we use as pictures. It is a matter of a divine reality that also shows itself in earthly things. This is why such things can be used as "pictures." Paul has given a classic expression to this when he says that God is "the Father from whom all fathers receive their name" (Ephesians 3:14).

A person must have this in mind when he deals with the "symbols" in the Book of Revelation. They stand for realities that cannot be expressed or understood without the help of these symbols. A person can express this in another way also, but the symbols are never superfluous. The beast is really a beast, a reality with a monstrous nature. The great whore is a reality, "the mother of all earth's whores and abominations"[Revelation 17:5]—not just a picture of them. There really is a great Babylon even if it is not found on a map. The marriage feast of the Lamb is really held. A person can call these pictures and symbols, but a person may not forget that this is a question of realities that a person distorts if he makes himself independent of symbols.

Events that Happen More than Once

Events in the Book of Revelation gather in circles where the number seven plays an obvious role. Three such circles are immediately at the fore for every reader: the seven seals, the seven trumpets, and the seven bowls of wrath. Scholars say that there are many such circles, but we can occupy ourselves with these three. The interesting thing now is that one and the same event seems to happen again and again when we go from one circle to the next. When the seventh seal is broken, we seem to be at the end. The sun goes dark, the heavens rumble and roll up, the stars fall to the ground. However, after the seventh seal, the seven trumpets follow. The drama repeats itself, and the affliction begins anew, though to a higher degree, worse than when the seal was broken. Now a third of the earth is struck. Now the abyss opens, and the afflictions come and cover all that man has been able to give each other. Here we already encounter the beast who rises up from the abyss and ravages until the seventh trumpet sounds, and victory is declared. But only then does it seem to start in earnest. The dragon, the beast, the false prophet, and the great whore step forth. And concerning the beast, we hear that it has already been active.

A person could give many examples of this. It is as if we touched upon a spiral that carries us upward—or if a person wants: downward, because it is a question of steadily increasing afflictions, harsher apostasies and hardening of the heart. A person believes that he has fulfilled a revolution and is closer to the goal but finds that he has entered into the middle of a new circle, somewhat like the preceding but now on a different plane. From this new point of view a person can see what was before and understand it better. Perhaps he can also imagine what is coming if the spiral continues for a few more laps.

This can give us a conception of something that is essential in the Christian view of history. It is not just a circular course where everything is repeated, as the Greeks used to think. Neither is it completely a development towards constantly better circumstances as some modern men like to believe. It is a fight between God and Satan, where God finally comes to be victorious, but where Satan brings more and more of his resources and in the end total mobilization. Certainly, there is a development of techniques and social apparatus, but evil can use anything that reason can find for its own purposes, and it also does that with these. So, the course of the world runs in constantly worse circles. The war becomes more devastating; the destruction of nature becomes worse. The Book of Revelation also witnesses to all this.

However, within this "development" there is also a circular loop. That which once happened foreshadows that which will come. This is one of the fundamental thoughts in the Bible's view of salvation history. That which happened in Israel is a foreshadowing of that which will happen with the Messiah and His kingdom. What happened to God's enemies in Sodom and Babel shall happen again. Sodom, Babel, and Egypt foreshadow something that repeats itself; there is an exposure of powers that are constantly active in history. In every new circle we catch a glimpse of something that shall appear in its awful reality when the world's last hour is imminent. The beast has already been active and lets us imagine how its kingdom comes to be seen. However, it was not the last time and not the final revelation. The Book of Revelation lets us see how it will look.

Those who attempt to identify the events of the Book of Revelation with that which happens in their own era have always been mistaken. However, there still may have been something true in their thoughts. They saw what was the deepest meaning in what was happening. However, they did not see that there are events that happen more than once, first as a foreshadowing and a premonition, perhaps a general repetition, without thereby being the last and final fulfillment of the prophetic word.

When was the Book of Revelation Written?

The Church Father Iraneus (circa 180) said that John saw these visions "not so long ago, and close enough to our own time, towards the end of the reign of Domitian."

REVELATION

Domitian was Caesar from 81-96, and so the Book of Revelation would have been written in the 90s if Irenaeus is right, which the majority of the scholars regard as likely. There is essentially only one other date that finds any mentionable support, and it is the year closest to Nero's death, the year 68. The Book of Revelation bears traces of having been written during a period of serious persecution. Such a period occurred in Rome from 64-65 under Caesar Nero, who attempted to blame the Christians for the burning of Rome, while people began to whisper that he was the one who started it. The persecution was extremely harsh, but it seems to have been limited to Rome and had nothing to do with the cult of Caesar. Domitian was the first in a series of Caesars who seriously demanded to be worshiped as divine. Caesar worship had appeared even in the last days of Caesar, but it was rather an expression of the spontaneous and servile tribute of the provinces than a demand from Rome. Finally, Caligula had demanded to be acclaimed as God, but this had been regarded as evidence of insanity. Domitian seems to have enjoyed the Caesar cult as a way to secure his power. This put Christians in a new and extremely dangerous situation that they would suffer under for more than 200 years.

There are other reasons to believe that the Book of Revelation came relatively late. The letters to the seven congregations witness that they are not newly established but can look back on their first days as something in the past. "The Nicolaitans," who are mentioned as a well-known party, seem to have not existed in the 60s. On the other hand, none of the people who were active in the congregations of Asia Minor during Paul's days are mentioned.

Who was John?

That the seer on Patmos was named John is presented already in the superscription to his book. That this dealt with a prophet of the early church with a respected place in the congregations of the province of Asia is obvious. According to a unanimous and early tradition from the first century, it is a matter of the Apostle John, one of the twelve.

The old tradition, as we have already seen, encountered objections already in the early church. The reason is that the tradition says at the same time that the Apostle John is the author of the fourth gospel. And the language in both of these writings, the Gospel of John and the Book of Revelation, are so noticeably different that it seems unthinkable that it could be the same man who wrote both of them.

It is certainly clear that both cases are dealing with a Jew who thinks in a semitic manner and must have learned Greek as a second language. The sentence structure is typically semitic with short thoughts, some subordinate clauses, and simple construction. There are few adjectives. New sentences are most often introduced with an "and." All this is typical of Hebrew and Aramaic.

At the same time, the differences are striking. John the Evangelist writes a correct and careful Greek without any lapses towards the whole rather complicated teaching form. In Revelation we encounter a language that must have terrified a contemporary language instructor. Now there were certainly also Greeks who spoke in this manner. Their breaks with the careful rules of speech are called "Soloicisms" after the city of Soli, a neighboring city of Tarsus. It also looks as if here and there in Asia Minor people were known for their barbaric Greek. It is possible that John very simply spoke as he had learned from his Greek neighbors. Yet in an important exception, as a Jew, John was basically at home in the Greek Bible. These words constantly come to his tongue. It must have given his language a ring that differentiated it markedly from his neighbors. We could very well think of him as a Jew of that type that has been found in every age: one who taught himself the language of the land where he struck roots and spoke as those spoke in his environs, with all the characteristics that belonged to his Jewish milieu.

There are many striking differences between John the Evangelist and John the author of the Book of Revelation, whom we can perhaps call the prophet John. The prophet constantly speaks with the words of Scripture; the evangelist does not do that. If a person reads an edition of the Greek New Testament where the Old Testament citations and allusions are printed in a coarser style, then a person finds such references by the prophet in every other verse, while in the evangelist's gospel a person can browse several pages without hitting upon a single one. And actually, the greatest difference is in the basic mood, the actual experience of Christ's communion. The prophet burns with glowing desire for the Lord, who would soon come. He reaches with the whole of his being towards the day when Christ will prevail. For the evangelist, it is a great and wonderful thing that Christ is with him. He lives in the secure certainty that through the Spirit he already now possesses communion with the glorified Christ. This creates a tranquility and gives a peace that the world cannot give, a security that has conquered the world. The prophet is like a volcano erupting. The evangelist is reminiscent of a Swedish forest star that shines in the clear heavens on a summer night, and at the same time hides unfathomable depth under its calm surface. Here we seem to stand before two different types of disciples—both legitimate, both true, and both needful. Yet it is hard to think of them united in one and the same person.

On the other hand, we stand before the difficulty of explaining how both the Book of Revelation and the Gospel of John could have received such an early and grounded reputation as apostolic, originating from the same John in Ephesus. That they have a spiritual kinship and some common "Johannine" essence is commonly recognized. They both talk about Christ as the Word and as the Lamb (though layered with different Greek words). They both speak of the water of life for those who thirst. They lay the same special meaning in a series of words, for example, "to keep" his Lord's Word and commandment.

As has already been mentioned, in antiquity there was already the thought that there was a different John in Ephesus, a presbyter. It is the learned Eusebius (he died in the year 339) who interferes with that hypothesis. He cites a passage in

Papias who, sometime around the year 130, lists his informants in a writing, among them mentioning two Johns (or the same John twice, as many think). Eusebius also cites another church father (the already mentioned Dionysius, who wrote around the year 250), who is said to have heard that in Ephesus there are two graves that are ascribed to a John. In our time, many scholars have held fast to this theory. Meanwhile, they have not commonly followed Eusebius when he posited that it was the Apostle John who wrote the gospel, while the "presbyter" was the originator of the Book of Revelation. On the contrary, they have wished to make the "presbyter" into the author of the gospel, while the Book of Revelation—possibly—is regarded to have been written by the apostle.

Whether a person believes it was one and the same John or two different men, one encounters problems. If it was an early Christian prophet that has given us the Book of Revelation, then a person must ask himself why the apostle, the reputable John, is not mentioned, not even in the letter to Ephesus. The prophet speaks with an obvious authority. It is, in and of itself, natural, for the early Christian prophets had such authority. However, if one of the twelve lived—and according to the whole early church tradition, the apostle John lived into the 90s—then a prophet could not easily overlook him. A person might guess that the prophet sent out his letter in consensus with the apostle, in knowledge of having his full approval. Yet it still seems strange that here the prophet obviously takes that place that would normally have been given to the apostle.

If a person takes the other position—that it is the same John—then a person must try to explain the very deep differences in language and temperament. Some have tried to explain them by saying that there was a considerable amount of time that lapsed between the arrival of both books. In such a case, the Book of Revelation with its unedited Greek must have come first, likely in connection with Caesar Nero's persecution, which for other reasons would not be likely. It has, therefore, usually been assumed that in Ephesus John was surrounded by a circle of disciples that were responsible for the linguistic development of the gospel, while on Patmos he was completely by himself. In such a case, this circle of disciples must have made its impression not only on the language but also on the theology and piety that we encounter in the gospel.

The question concerning authorship of John's Gospel and Revelation will probably be one of the questions that we cannot answer, at least not for the present. And does it really matter? If John was not an apostle, then in any case he was one of the early Christian prophets who together with the apostles were the Spirit's instruments and made up the foundation upon which the Church is built.

The Translation

Translating the Book of Revelation is not easy. Of course, John uses a language that is extremely distinctive and, least of all correct, if a person measures it by the measure of that era's academy. In and of itself, there is something edifying in this, that God has used a man as His instrument who never received a higher education. So, a true message of Christ can also come that is clothed in a linguistic dress that some regard as uncultured. Yet how should a translator render such language? It does not do to attempt to mimic the deviations from the theoretically correct form, especially considering that Swedish (or English) does not have as many inflectional forms as Greek. It is easier to render certain difficulties in the sentence structure, but there is a question of whether it is correct to do that. For the people to whom John wrote these were not difficulties. It did not grate on their ears. Most of them spoke this way themselves. The best thing is perhaps to use an English dialect, which for an average congregation would sound approximately how the congregations in the provinces of Asia had perceived the Book of Revelation when it was first read for them in the divine service.

A particular problem arises from the poverty of adjectives. This is typical for Hebrew. John constantly uses a few adjectives that cover a range of meanings. One of them is "great," which he uses even where we would not. For example, he speaks of a "great voice" or a "great thunder." In such a case, it is obviously justified to choose other words in English. However, in a number of cases a person may need to use the word "great," though the meaning is clearer if a person uses a more nuanced word. This happens often in this translation so that it has received a richer vocabulary than it originally had.

To "Understand" The Book of Revelation

The person who wants to understand the Book of Revelation like a person understands an article in the newspaper will never understand it. The first thing a person has to have clear for himself is that this book deals with such things that we—so far—can only partially conceive. We may be ready—as John himself—to encounter a reality that can only be described partially with words. We may—like him—find ourselves listening to voices that speak in God's stead, without directly seeing who speaks, or seeing visions that we can only partially conceptualize. It is not certain that we shall understand everything. When God speaks about the end times and the last great test, He first and foremost speaks to those who come to suffer it. What He says can never be understood fully and completely before the day comes. When God speaks, He has something to say that concerns those He is speaking to. So, we should not expect a sensational exposure of things that do not concern us. What we can understand and receive is such as we need to know already now.

Here then is the always relevant meaning of the Book of Revelation, that which comes to happen, and which John describes that has its equivalent even now. History is a fight between the same powers, and God has the same enemies that are important to recognize. The final act in the history of the world shows in gigantic, enlarged scale the powers that have always been active.

REVELATION

Because it is a question of spiritual powers, they cannot be described with common, ordinary prose. Means of expression are required. So, The Book of Revelation has a certain similarity with the surrealist painters, such as it is when they are inspired by Christ (as, for example, within the Halmstadgruppen). Such art has a message without being immediately "conceivable." It stimulates contemplation and invites meditation. It demands empathy, and it has something to give even when a person is not quite sure how a person should express it.

The Book of Revelation belongs to books of the Bible that invite meditation. To meditate on God's Word means to try to dive into its depths. God's Word conceals many hidden riches under the surface that a man first sees. What man finds when he meditates is a personal experience. A person is enriched by it; one can help others see it, but a person cannot demand that others shall see it, such as one can demand in questions of the Word's immediate wording and meaning.

In the Book of Revelation, the Word often does not have any immediately comprehensible meaning. So it often is with prophets. It shall be received personally and affect us somewhat like a surrealist painting, or a piece of poetry (though the message in this case comes from God not an artist). If the Book of Revelation works in such a manner, then it has something to say to every era concerning precisely that era. However, this message can only be heard by those who come in the wavelength of the prophetic Word and understand how to decipher the signs of that age.

So, a man can only say what the Book of Revelation means for Christendom in great sweeps. It describes what will happen in the future that can be both distant and very close. That which comes to happen is already now happening. When the visions on Patmos roll up before our eyes, we time and again recognize ourselves and our own time. The meaning is not that we should identify what we see with particular persons and events in today's world—not before the time is fulfilled, and then no one needs to come with any such interpretation because everything will be inescapably clear. Just as slight is also the meaning that we shall try to make up an exact description and schedule for that which comes to happen. We have no way of doing that. We should know—just like the addressees in the seven letters—that we are in a spiritual war that encompasses the world and is merciless. We should know that even where it looks as if all has gone bad, Christ finally prevails. We should know that the world does not have millions of years ahead of it. The time is short. Christ comes soon—he who has eyes to see, he recognizes when the signs pile up.

Revelation 1

1-3 Forward

The Book of Revelation begins with what can be called a forward, a short introduction that says how the book came to be. We learn that it is a matter of a revelation, so something that no man can know or learn for themselves with the help of the knowledge or resources that a person would normally have at his disposal. It deals with something that only God knows, but which He has willed to let us know. This revelation comes from Jesus Christ, which He in turn received from God. Christ has sent a messenger (an angel: in Greek it is the same word) to His servant John. "Servant" can also be translated "slave." Paul also used to call himself "Christ's slave." It is John who witnesses here. What he witnesses to is God's Word, in the same way that what the prophets spoke was God's Word. The message comes from Jesus Christ Himself. It is He who let John see all of this. So, he who reads this message is blessed. It is assumed that this will be read aloud during the divine service, as a word from God. It is a matter of a prophecy. Prophecy played a huge role in the apostolic era. Early Christendom had its own prophets. Their efforts were so important that it was said that the church is built on the foundation of the apostles and prophets (Ephesians 2:20). A prophet spoke with inspiration from the Spirit when he received a message to present from God. It usually happened orally, but here comes a prophecy that John received in his exile. So, he wrote it down, and now he sends it to the congregations. He does it with the certainty that he is dealing with a command from Christ. It is this certainty that the Christian Church shares when it gives the Book of Revelation its place among the books of the New Testament. Because this is a message from Christ, they are blessed who read it to the congregations or sit there and listen to it. A prophecy could deal with something that would happen, and it says here already at the beginning that it is so with this prophecy. However, a prophecy could also admonish, comfort, and give guidance concerning the situation in which the hearers already found themselves. This prophecy will also do those things. So, a person should take care with what is written there. So it is even today.

4-8 Heading

The Book of Revelation has the form of a letter and was once actually sent from the sender, John, to the congregations in "Asia," which here—as everywhere in the New Testament—means the Roman province of Asia, which encompassed the westernmost part of what we call Asia Minor, so a rather limited area. The letter also begins like all letters of that era with the sender's name. The model is well known to us from the letters of Paul. Like Paul, John begins with a wish for grace and peace from God, but it is formulated in its characteristic way. God is He "who is and who was and who shall come." The Jews could speak of Him who was and is and *remains*. John says that He is the one who *comes*. God's work is not finished. There remains something important that He shall do and reveal, and this revelation will be concerned with that. There is something essential in this Christian faith that John has captured here in these words. God is not only the Eternal that remains. He is the living God who operates and intervenes and still has great things in preparation. So, the greeting also comes from Jesus Christ, who has been and is and shall be God's instrument and revealer. John immediately breaks out in praise and thanksgiving and gets in some short words with the most important of Christ's work, that which our fathers summarized in His three "offices": prophet, priest, and king. He is the prophet who has witnessed to the truth. He is the high priest who has freed us from our sins with His blood and was the first to rise from the dead—so that we shall also rise up like Him. He is the king, the exalted who has all power. And He loves us. Truly *loves* us, here and now! He has made us His coregents, kings who share the power and glory of His kingdom. He has made us "priests before God." The word John uses means "sacrificial priests" such as served in the temple in Jerusalem. They were able to step before God (in distinction to the people), and now we all may do this. The way is open even into the holy of holies, and we both can and should bring our offerings of thanks, praise, and intercession, as well as the sacrifice of ourselves with all we own and have and are able. Those we call "priests"[1] today are something else. They have the task to be the leaders and seelsorgers of the congregation. For this the New Testament uses a completely different word: "elder" (presbyter, the word from which our word "priest" comes) shepherds, and teachers, etc.

Yet, what can John mean with "the seven spirits before God's faith"? Otherwise, he speaks about the Spirit, the one in the manner that we are familiar with, but here he speaks about God's seven spirits. A person could believe that it touches on created beings, such spirits that serve God. Yet he mentions it in connection with the Father and the Son and our thoughts are led directly to the Trinity. So, some have wanted to see these seven spirits as revelations of the one Spirit. Everyone knew that the Spirit reveals Himself in manifold and different ways. Paul used to highlight and sometimes he spoke about the Spirit's gifts as "spirits" (1 Corinthians 14:12; it is usually correctly translated as "spiritual gifts").

---

[1] In Scandinavian churches, pastors are called priests as they are in the Episcopal church. This is not a typical designation for these leaders in English speaking Lutheranism or Christianity in general. However, it is sometimes used. And the English word priest actually shares the same etymology as that of the Swedish, coming from the word Presbyter, and not meaning the sort of sacrificial priests a person would find in the temple of the Old Testament.

A person used to also speak about the Spirit's seven-fold being, like the prophet Isaiah had described (Isaiah 11:2-3, so as it was exposited by the rabbis). And it is probable that John thinks about something in this way. He mentions the seven Spirits two times. (We will return to this matter.)

John finishes this passage with a typical word of praise, a "doxology." It culminates in an "amen," where the congregation certainly joined in when this letter was read in the divine service.

The first doxology is followed by two prophetic words. The first means that the Lord comes, reveals Himself so that He is visible for all, to the dismay of those who rejected Him and did everything to eradicate faith in Him—so that they even persecute His church at the very moment that John writes this. Here John cites a word that is cited in John's Gospel (19:37) with thought of the lance that Jesus received. Here John thinks about all that a person has done since and notes how fearful it must be for the persecutors to discover who they have stuck. And again, the congregation answers with a roaring: "Amen."

Again, a prophetic word follows. There the "Lord" speaks. In the New Testament, this usually means Christ, but in the Book of Revelation it points to the Father as a rule. So, it also does here. Alpha and Omega mean the beginning and the end because these are the first and last letters in the Greek alphabet.

9-16 John Encounters the Resurrected One

So, John describes how it goes when he receives his task. He was on Patmos, a little island just off the coast of Asia Minor, southwest of Ephesus, so little that it is normally not even included on the maps in our Bibles. There is a quarry there, and the Romans used it as a place of exile. When John says that he was there for the sake of the Gospel, he probably does not mean that he was there on a preaching tour, but that he was in exile. Then he falls into some form of rapture and ecstasy. He literally says that he "came in the Spirit." It happens on a Sunday. That a person celebrated the first day of the week as a day of worship appears in a couple of other verses in the New Testament (Acts 20:7, 1 Corinthians 16:2), but this is the first place in early Christian literature where we hear it called "the Lord's Day." Of course, it was on this day that the Lord had risen, and then a person encountered Him again in His Lord's Supper.

The first thing that John encounters was a voice, not a vision. It was a mighty voice, that sounded behind him and commanded him to write up what he will see in a "book"—thus a papyrus roll—and send it to those congregations that are named, first and foremost Ephesus (apparently his own city) and a further six cities, all lying within a radius of 120 miles northeast of Ephesus. John must have been well known and accepted as an authority among them all, because he did not need to tell them who he is. He only calls himself a brother, who shares with them the suffering (a person could also translate: "grief" or "sorrow"), which they apparently now find themselves in, just as he has the same share in Christ's kingdom and in the perseverance which Christ has given them.

John turns himself to see who is speaking to him, and thereby begins the long series of visions. The first impression is light, overwhelming light. Seven candle sticks are lit. We might imagine them as seven great lampstands, standing on the floor, hung with small oil lamps. And in the midst of them, John encounters HIM. He does not mention anyone's name. Instead, he attempts to describe what he saw. His first thought must have gone to one of the prophet Daniel's visions: Daniel must have meant this when he spoke about "one like a son of man" (Daniel 7:13). Now every Christian certainly knew who the Son of Man was. So here Jesus stood. He wore the ankle length robe of a high priest and a golden girdle. But He Himself was pure light. John grasps at the whitest thing he knows to find the word. It was like the blinding snow. His hair shone like white wool does in the sun when it becomes luminous. His feet were embodied light like ore coming out of the smelter. In His eyes burned flames and His face was like the high summer sun in its full strength. His voice was mighty like a roar of surf as it breaks against the beaches of the Aegean the day after a storm so that it is heard far up in the mountains. He held seven stars in His hand. We do not need to ask how He held them or how John knew that they were seven. In a prophetic vision a person knows what it is at first glance. Only in a dream can we experience something similar. Neither do we need to ask how a sword protrudes from His lips. We can meditate on this. There is a Word that is sharper than any two-edged sword. It proceeds from His mouth. When He sends out His Word, a sword shimmers in the air. It shoots forth a ray of light, something like shiny steel, something like a surgeon's scalpel. It knows its goal and it pushes through.

17-20 The Commission

With this encounter John experienced the very same thing as Isaiah once did when he was able to catch a glimpse of the threefold Holy in the temple, or as Ezekiel and Daniel and other divines have spoken about. This encounter with God is crushing. There is something in God's being that is at once enchanting and annihilating. And it is worth taking notice that the encounter with the heavenly Christ can be the very same thing, not only for a persecutor like Saul, but also for an old, dedicated disciple like John. It is foolish to believe that we encounter a different God in the New Testament than in that of the Old. God is the same, His white-hot zeal is the same, and it is also found with Jesus Christ, who is the true God.

However, something has happened since the days of the Old Testament. When the Resurrected One approaches John, who lies there as if dead, He has something to say that could not be said in Isaiah's day. John, who lies there, crushed, and knows that he cannot remain before such a God, learns that it is precisely this God, who has died so that no one else should have to perish. And so, he receives a renewed order to write. What he shall write applies to both the present and the future. The seven candlesticks he has seen are the seven congregations. And the stars in Christ's hand are their "angels."

Is this a matter of guardian angels? Some have thought so, but it seems unlikely, when a person then reads what they receive for a message. They seem to be men of flesh and blood with several weaknesses. Now, in Greek the word "angel" means, essentially (as in Hebrew), "messenger," and in the Old Testament, it can be used for prophets (Haggai 1:13) and priests (Malachi 2:7). It is likely that John who knows his Greek Bible backwards and forwards, has used the word in this sense.

It is apparent that each of the congregations had its own "angel." From the beginning congregations were led by a college of representatives who could alternately be called priests (*presbyters*) or bishops (*episkopoi*). However, in the beginning of the second century, we see in the letter that Bishop Ignatius of Antioch wrote around 115 that the church had transitioned to having a bishop in every large congregation, assisted by a college of presbyters. To judge by the letters, it seems that this order had been applied in these areas of Asia Minor already in the year 90. So, we would have evidence for this division of the office between bishops and priests already in this passage of the New Testament. This gives us confirmation of how clearly the Church of Sweden saw this matter during the Reformation. In our first church order—from the year 1571—it is namely noted that at the beginning there was no difference between bishops and ordinary priests as we have today. However, because the order "was very useful and without a doubt from God and the Holy Spirit, who gives all good things, to the end that where she and all Christendom were pleased with it and embraced it. So it has remained and must continue as long as the world remains."

Revelation 2

1-7 The Letter to Ephesus

The seven letters that follow now are all formed according to the same model. First comes a presentation of Him who revealed Himself to John, with different details of His image. There then follows a characteristic of the congregation, first praise and then critique (sometimes only the one). Thereupon follows an admonition, and finally there is an exhortation to hear what the Spirit says together with a promise to those who win the victory.

The first letter is directed to Ephesus, "the diocesan city" with the congregation that was the oldest and foremost. At this time, it ought to have been established for approximately forty years. Of those who were present from the beginning, not many are still alive. According to tradition, its leader ought to have been the apostle John, and here we immediately stumble upon a problem. If the "angel" is the bishop of Ephesus, then this could not have been the John who wrote this on Patmos. However, it could not well have been the apostle John either because it seems unlikely that he would be put on the same level as the other congregational leaders. It remains a possibility that the apostle had a special place as a recognized leader within the whole province of Asia. In such a case, it can be he who now finds himself exiled on Patmos. However, it is also conceivable that he finds himself in Ephesus or elsewhere and that the prophet on Patmos sends this message conscious that the Lord Christ Himself has confirmed what the apostle has already tried to say to his congregations.

Another problem is whether the letters are first conceived as messages to the congregational leaders. That they also direct themselves to the congregation is, in any case, obvious. The praise and glory are given to both.

In the introduction it says—translated literally—"written to the angel of the congregation in Ephesus." The "congregation" can also mean the church. The church was one and indivisible, but this one church appeared visibly in a particular place as the local congregation. He who now sends the message holds the stars—the congregational leaders—in His hand. Their task is to be His outstretched right hand, each in his own place. He walks around the lampstands. This means that He comes to His congregations, visits them and watches over them.

The congregation in Ephesus receives praise for, among other things, that this congregation has functioned both when it comes to life and doctrine. Naturally, the false apostles that are spoken about here do not belong to the twelve, who were all dead except for John. But "apostle" means "fully authorized ambassador," and a person could also be this for a congregation or some other commissioner. We know that such false apostles appeared from the little letter concerning "apostolic doctrine" (*didache*), which was written a couple of decades later.

However, there is one thing lacking from this first congregation: the first love. We can imagine what is meant if we read how Acts describes the first era of the congregation's history (19:10f). Such rich and happy times are also dependent on what the congregation wants and does. So, the congregation may "do the same deeds" again. We will hear more about what is meant by the "works of the Nicolaitans" later. The word of warning about the moving lampstand is in many ways worthy of consideration. Of course, the lampstand is the congregation. Here we see that the essential thing in the congregation is that the Lord Himself is present in the means of grace, the Word, and sacraments. It is, of course, this lampstand that can move, while the dead congregation remains and goes to meet its doom because Christ has taken His hand from it. It is also worthy of consideration that today Ephesus lies desolate, and that there is only an unimportant Turkish town without any Christian congregation but with immense church ruins.

8-11 The letter to Smyrna

Smyrna is forty-eight miles north of Ephesus. It is a large city with an excellent harbor that successively competed with Ephesus. Bishop Polycarp was led to martyrdom here (around 155 A.D.), and in his youth he ought to have heard this letter read if he did not actually read it himself. In any case, he was the bishop here in 115 when Ignatius of Antioch passed through these tracts on his way to his death in the amphitheater and wrote a letter to Polycarp that was preserved.

The letter to Smyrna is short. We learn the congregation suffers pressure and is poor and that the Jews belong to their sworn enemies. The situation seems to have been the same two generations later when they carried firewood to the bonfire where Polycarp was burned. The congregation learns to expect this. Many of them will be thrown in prison, and really hard times are coming. However, there is a limit set for this—perhaps so that the persecution ceases, perhaps so that it ends with death. Here it is important to remain faithful unto death. It can be hard if a person is tortured. However, the suffering will not be longer than can be endured, and those who endure it are sure to receive "the crown" of life. The Greek word essentially means "wreath," the sort of victory wreath that a person received in athletic events. "The second death" is the eternal, that which follows judgment.

12-17 The Letter to Pergamum

Pergamum was the capital of the province of Asia. The Roman proconsul resided there, and the first temple to the cult of Caesar was built there. It had stood there now for over a hundred years. The god of medicine had a quite famous sanctuary that pilgrims visited in large crowds to be healed. The city was crowned with an altar to Zeus, so richly adorned with sculptures that the remains of them fill a hall of giant dimensions in the Pergamon Museum in Berlin. There was also one of the world's finest libraries (parchment is actually named from this town). The power of both Rome and paganism was concentrated here. To confess Christ must have felt somewhat like evangelizing in Mecca or Moscow.[1]

This is reflected in the letter. "Satan's Throne" can indicate the altar to Caesar, which would be the cause of martyrdom for so many Christians, or it can point to the whole spirit of the city. However, the congregation had shown the courage that was needed even in the severest test, at the time when Antipas was murdered. Who he was we do not know, only that he suffered martyrdom. It was likely not a question of planned persecution. In such a case, he would not have been the only one. Rather, it had been a matter of an uprising when the masses showed their hate for Christians. For this reason, it had to require courage to confess Christ's name. However, the brave congregation receives *one* reproach: Within its midst there are those who hold to "the teachings of the Nicolaitans." We do not know very much about the Nicolaitans. They seem to have been forerunners to the powerful movements that in the following generation became a mortal danger to Christendom with religious thoughts and opinions that were relevant to the era. In the early form that we encounter here, it can be most closely called a hyper-evangelical libertinism, that is, a teaching that drove Christian freedom to a looseness so that everything would finally be permitted for the "enlightened" with the right knowledge.

For those who hold fast to Apostolic Christianity, this was "the teaching of Balaam." Balaam is the Greek form of Bileam, a name that we know from the Old Testament. However, here it is not a matter of Balaam blessing Israel though he was hired to curse them. There is also a story that afterwards he caused the heathen women to entice Israelites to their sacrificial feasts and get them to fornicate (Numbers 31:16, read in light of 25:1f). Here lie the similarities with the Nicolaitans. They apparently held to the Christian's right to participate in heathen sacrificial feasts though such feasts typically ended with sexual abandon, a remnant of old fertility rites. Apparently, some had a poor experience of emancipation. Paul too speaks about this matter (1 Corinthians 10:7f). This time the promise to those who stand fast is to receive a share of "the hidden manna." Here again we have a point of contact with the Gospel of John. There Jesus speaks of the true manna (John 6:31f) that is the bread from heaven—He Himself. What the white stone with the new name indicates is a little uncertain. A white stone was used by jurors when they voted. It meant "not guilty." However, the closest example could be a little tablet in the form of a white stone that was given to the victor in a competition and bore his name. It is uncertain if the new name is God's or that of the recipient. In any case,

---

[1] A reminder that Bo Giertz wrote these commentaries in the mid 80s when Moscow was under Communist control and ruled by atheists.

the meaning is that he who believes possesses something he has received. Salvation is personal; I cannot give my salvation away. It applies to me and no one else.

18-29 The Letter to Thyatira

Thyatira was known as an industrial city. Lydia, one of the first disciples in Philippi, came from there. She dealt in purple dye, one of the fine products from Thyatira's workshops. The city was about sixty miles inland from the coast. It is clear that the order the letters follow, the direction the person who would carry John's message from congregation to congregation would have to follow on the great road.

So, the congregation of Thyatira receives fame for her faithfulness and zeal, which had never been greater than now. However, there is still a serious error here, the same as in Pergamum. She has been too indulgent and tolerant of false teaching. Apparently, this applies to the same direction as in Ephesus and Pergamum, the so-called Nicolaitans. Even here an assumed name from the Old Testament is used. Everyone knew to whom it applied; the woman in question was certainly not named Jezebel, because Jezebel is the same name as Isabel, the name of Ahab's queen, a Phoenician who introduced Baal worship to the kingdom of Israel with everything that went along with it concerning wild orgies and apostasy from the Lord. This Jezebel in Thyatira made open claim to be spiritually gifted. She stepped forth as a prophet. There was nothing wrong about this in and of itself. Women could also be prophets (1 Corinthians 11:5, Acts 21:9). Of course, the prophecy was a message from God that He could give to those He wanted. The risk for the congregation was that someone stepped forward and spoke in God's name without being called by God. And Jezebel was a false prophet. That she "presented herself as a teacher," thus a proclaimer of the gospel before the congregation, was against the apostolic order. Paul had directly forbidden this in a letter to Ephesus (1 Timothy 2:12), which at the time must have been known and read among these congregations. And worst of all: What Jezebel proclaimed led people away from Christ. Once again there was the false freedom. Here it was not only applied but had also been developed as a teaching. We catch a glimpse of it in the talk of "the deep things of Satan." In the later Gnosticism something similar returns. Because the spiritually enlightened were supremely free and inaccessible to Satan, they could allow themselves the greatest freedom, even in the realm of sexuality. By sinking into such "depths," a person showed his contempt for them and his independence.

Now a person should remember that every unfaithfulness to God is counted as spiritual adultery. So, it was already in the Old Testament. God had betrothed Himself to Israel. The people were His bride, and now the church was also. To break with God was adultery. Even here the word "adultery" has this connotation. Yet at the same time, a person must remember that the false freedom—not the least in connection with the sacrificial meals—almost forcibly led a person to immorality. It was then as now: one of the great dissimilarities between a Christian and a non-Christian's way of life lay in the sexual realm. For those who were not Christian, sexuality was—according to, among others, Eusebius, the great Church historian in the 4th century—the highest value. For the Christians, there was a higher value that gave rules even for sexuality. As soon as the true Christianity came into play, it was noticed in the sexual realm. So it was also in Thyratira.

The judgment is strict. For Jezebel herself the time of grace has passed. She will be thrown on a sickbed with some harsh disease. They who sinned with her still have one last opportunity for repentance. What is meant by "children" is uncertain. It often means "children of the same spirit." In such a case, this would point to those who are just as hardened as their spiritual mother.

Then there follows an admonition that says: hold fast what you have. Here there is nothing new needed, only the well-known apostolic order, even in questions about sacrificial meals and fornication (Acts 15:28f). The promise to these hard pressed but faithful Christians is that they come to share their Lord's victory over the heathen. The word is borrowed from Psalm 2:8, which is known as a Messianic psalm. So, the Messiah would do to His opponents. His confessors would share in His victory. A person ought not get too concerned about this word "Morning Star." Again, it is a mysterious name, which will be explained later (Revelation 22:16).

Revelation 3

1-6 The Letter to Sardis

The letter from Patmos is now carried further. First, it has gone north along the coast and reached Pergamum. Then the letter carrier turned inland to Thyatira. Now he follows the great road south down into Hermus Valley and reached Lydia's legendary capital, Sardis, where at one time the wealthy King Croesius had reigned.

The congregation in Sardis is the first in the series that has not received a word of praise. It is dead, though it imagines that it lives. A person can be as living and vital as any and still be dead before God. However, when God's Son lets His voice sound off, then the dead can receive life (John 5:25). It had happened in Sardis, but here death had re-entered, but not through obvious apostasy. Neither is there talk about coarse delusion or immorality as in Thyatira. Worship life seems to have functioned undisturbed. Nothing is mentioned about any persecution. However, the congregation is dead. Perhaps it has died precisely because it is free of enemies. A dead Christendom does not cause offense.

Even here, though, there are some who have "not soiled their garments." The white robes were a picture of all that a person receives through baptism and faith: forgiveness, the new righteousness, the right to be God's child, sanctification. Soiled garments did not require coarse immorality. In Sardis it seems to rather have been a question of tepidity and lack of seriousness.

Again, there is a call to turn back to the point of departure, to that which one "receives," the whole of the apostolic message, the gospel, the Spirit. Christendom is to hold fast to something once given, which in turn works renewal.

The promise to those who hold fast means that they may walk with Christ, thus to life in the disciple's communion with their Lord. They have their names written in the book of life—thus "in heaven" as Jesus also expresses the matter (Luke 10:20)—and Christ shall be known to them on judgment day.

7-13 The Letter to Philadelphia

Sardis and Philadelphia are closer to each other than any of the other seven cities in Revelation, but spiritually the distance was as great as it could be. Sardis did not receive any praise. Philadelphia also did not receive any blame. Just as in Smyrna, the congregation seems to have been a source of joy.

That Christ has the name "David's key" is connected with one of the many foreshadowings in the Old Testament that the Jews had already applied to the Messiah. The prophet Isaiah had spoken about the faithful official in Hezekiah's day who would receive custody of David's palace, symbolized by the key, so that he could open and close all of its rooms and storehouses (Isaiah 22:22). This then became a picture of the Messiah's rule over David's house, and for the Christians, it received a particular meaning through Christ's power over the dead and the kingdom of the dead. Now Christ says here that He gave His faithful Christians an open door, perhaps it is in this meaning that Paul uses the same picture: an opportunity to proclaim the gospel. As a remarkable success, it is mentioned that even some Jews will repent. Two generations earlier it would not have been anything remarkable, but now, towards the end of the first century, the Jews have fortified their unbelief and its consequent rejection of the gospel. They had taken the position that some had taken already during Jesus's earthly life, and which gave Him reason to say to them that the devil was their father (John 8:44). Now they are called Satan's synagogue. Naturally, that some of them shall come to the congregation and "bow down before your feet" does not mean that they shall worship men, but that they shall recognize that "God is really among you," as Paul says that the heathen would do when they came to the divine service and were convinced by the power of God's Word (1 Corinthians 14:24).

The remarkable thing about this congregation was not the sort of power that impresses the world. On the contrary, it speaks about its weakness (literally: "you have but little power"). However, it has kept fast to its Lord's Word, above all the commandment concerning endurance. It has known—what so many contemporary Christians so easily forget—that perseverance is needed because the persecution is a necessary consequence of confessing Christ. If anyone holds fast to Christ's Word, then Christ holds fast to him. Our fathers used to say that he who wants to have something to do with God must first and foremost see to it that they hold fast to God's Word; then he can be certain that God has something to do with him and carries His work further.

So, it does not mean anything new. The command to Philadelphia says: hold fast to what you have. And the promise to them who do this says: you are God's possession; you are a portion of His holy temple; there you are at home, and there you shall stay.

14-22 The Letter to Laodicea

Finally on its long journey, John's message reaches Laodicea, ninety-six miles from Ephesus as the crow flies, within the land of the Lykos valley. Except for Ephesus, this congregation is the only one of the seven that is spoken about in other passages of the New Testament where it is mentioned in the letter to the neighboring city of Colossae. At this time, it seems Colossae is no longer in existence. It was deserted by an earthquake in the 60s, only a few years after Paul had written his letter to them. Even Laodicea was laid to ruins at this time but was rebuilt, while Colossae disappeared from history. This is the likely explanation for why the congregation there is not mentioned in the Book of Revelation.

REVELATION 3:14-22

Like Sardis, Laodicea receives no word of recognition, but only reprobation. It indirectly says that the congregation is dead. It would have protested vehemently against the claim. It seemed that all was well; it lacked nothing. Yet it will hear that it lacked something essential. It lacked profile. It had accepted a smoothness and an inoffensive, colorless existence that did not challenge but neither did it awaken or gain any people. So, it hears that it was better if it took a position against Christ. In any case, then no one could be tricked into believing that this was true Christianity.

The counsel that it receives is to come to Christ and receive—or "buy," in the Biblical sense, for nothing—that which it does not bother to receive. It speaks in pictures that can be interpreted in many ways. However, if a person keeps to similar pictures in the Bible, gold means faith that is refined by suffering, the white clothes are Christ's righteousness, and eye ointment is the work of the Holy Spirit that opens our eyes so that we see our sins.

In the introduction Christ is called the "amen." This approximately means: the reliable, that which is the truth. His faithfulness also shows here. Despite everything, the congregation that He would rather spit out of His mouth, gets to learn that He is now standing at the door and knocking and is prepared to enter. And here it is no longer talk of a congregation, but about the individual man. Receive Jesus: a person can only do this for oneself. And to do it means to participate in His victory and receive His place at God's side. If a person participates in Christ, such a person has a share in all He has won for us.

Christian churches and congregations have often received their names from the Bible. For conceivable reasons, congregations like to choose names like Smyrna and Philadelphia. It would probably be useful if a man occasionally asked himself if the congregation might better fit Sardis or Laodicea, and then act according to the counsel they received.

Revelation 4

1-8 The Heavens Open

There is a line of demarcation here in the Book of Revelation. John has listened and written seven messages that touch on the era that is imminent. Now he *sees* one vision after another, and the visions deal with something that shall come.

It begins with him seeing the heavens open. Forgiveness is withdrawn. The mighty voice that he heard before commands him to come up. He is pulled out. He does not quite know how himself. In the next instant, he is before the throne of God. And here words fail him. He uses idealistic expressions, which indicate that he has nothing but approximate pictures to resort to. He is most restrained when he describes God Himself. He only speaks about "Him who sits on the throne." He gives a vague hint about something that was like a semi-precious stone, jasper or carnelian. In his attempt to describe the heavenly world, John often resorts to gemstones. Unfortunately, we know all too little about what people in antiquity meant by the different names, even if it is the same name that appears today. Yet it is clear that in God's creation, that is "full of his glory," there is nothing that John found better suited to describe the heavenly world than gemstones. We infer that it has to do with the gloss, the depth of the colors, that compares to the luminescence and artistic structure. However, it is still only hints. We stand before something that essentially cannot be described because it has no real correspondence on earth.

Jasper can have many colors, carnelian is usually red. However, what John thought he saw we can only guess at. In any case, it was an interplay of colors because a circle of light (rainbow) shone around the throne, what we might call a mandorla—with the green color of an emerald.

John is more detailed when he describes what happened around the throne. A divine service was celebrated there—if now again we can attempt to point to the nearest correspondence on earth. In nature's kingdom, it was gemstones that best give an idea of heaven. In the life of man, this is the divine service. We come to see this time and again in the text. There is no doubt that John has recognized the divine service as it was celebrated in the early church when he stood before God's throne. At this time, it had begun to receive a form that it would maintain for centuries. It was led by the bishop. We have already seen that the letter assumes that there is a responsible leader for every congregation. At his side, he had the presbyters. At the divine service they were seated in a half circle with the bishop in the middle, so as the older church buildings still show. The word "presbyter" still remains with us in the word "priest." In the very beginning it meant "elder" or "senior." With the Jews, it was the name of the directors for a local congregation. With the Christians, it was taken over as a term for the college that led the congregation and had a hand in the proclamation, the instruction, and congregational direction. From the beginning, it seems that not all presbyters were what we call priests or pastors. However, at about the same time as the bishop became leader, it became this. Here in the Book of Revelation we find ourselves in the midst of this transition, and when John uses the word "presbyter" here, in all likelihood, he means something that a person can best render with the word "priest."

Yet, what are they? Blessed men or heavenly beings? A man cannot answer such questions when John does not do it himself. He does not construct finely thought-out profundities. He describes what he saw. We can also ask why there were twenty-four parts. We can only guess that it has to do with the twelve tribes and the twelve apostles. The number twelve was foundational for both the old Israel and for the new, for God's people in the Old Testament and His church in the new. Perhaps the twenty-four before God's face represent the whole of His purpose, God's Israel in all times.

The flashes of lightening and the rumblings of thunder are a reminder of the Almighty, features of God's being that immediately put everyone else in their place. The glass sea, which like many other features in the picture has its foreshadowing in the prophets, shall perhaps hint that while the heavenly world is completely hidden to us, our world still lies completely open for the One who looks down from heaven. The same can be said of the strange eyes born by the four living creatures. These "living creatures" have counterpoints in Ezekiel and Daniel, but this makes them no less mysterious. We may take them as revelations of a world where everything is different. We can interpret them allegorically—as a person does when he lets them stand for the four evangelists—but we shall not believe that we know what they "mean." Only one thing is certain: They serve and praise God like everything else in the heavenly world. In some way, their many eyes are perhaps also a tool for His all-seeing eye. Nothing on earth is hidden. There is always an eye in heaven that follows us.

9-11 The Heavenly Divine Service

Then follows the description of the never silent song of praise. John has heard it in his ears the whole time. It fills the heavenly world day and night. It testifies to a joy and happiness that breaks forth in constantly refreshed jubilee. The source of this joy is God Himself. It is He who fills the whole of existence with joy.

First the song of praise comes to the threefold Holy, that which Isaiah once heard the seraphim sing. Here John uses the threefold expression "He who was and is and is to come." This is the characteristic expression, linguistically developed contrary to the most fundamental rules of Greek grammar, but clearly used in the divine service as John was accustomed to celebrating. Now John describes how the priests and the four living creatures celebrate the divine service. Their constantly new tributes and thanksgivings apply first and foremost to creation, the amazement that He who was alone sovereign and joyful would create a world that would share His joy and exist like Himself. Yet they have even more to thank Him for.

Revelation 5

1-4 The Scroll with Seven Seals

Then new images are rolled out for the prophet. A seer is not bound by time and space. That which is important shows itself to him. Sometimes he sees and is amazed. Sometimes he receives an immediate, intuitive certainty about the deeper meaning or of the context that otherwise would have been hidden to him.

Now he concentrates his attention on something that rests in the right hand of "him who sat on the throne." It is a scroll, written within and on the back. (The back was normally left blank.) The scroll had been sealed with seven seals. And so, an angel steps forth as a herald—this is what the Greek text means—and looking for someone who can break the seven seals and open the scroll. Yet it shows that no living being can undertake the task. No one can open the scroll, and no one can read what it says. John, who received certainty that the scroll hid something infinitely important is seized by an overwhelming anxiety and worry and begins to cry.

We have now encountered the number 7 numerous times. That there were seven letters may have been a coincidence. However, even here there seems to be a purpose behind the number, because we know that there were many congregations in these tracts. There is no doubt that in antiquity a person thought certain numbers were more holy than others. The Jews put seven in relationship with God. Of course, it is the prescribed number for the days of the week. Nature's own rotation was set up according to the number seven, so that there were two weeks from new moon to full moon. And in the divine service it constantly recurs: seven weeks between Easter and Pentecost, the great candelabras with seven arms, the sacrificial blood that was sprinkled seven times, etc.

In John's Revelation the number seven constantly returns in everything that has to do with God and His work. A person cannot say what this "means," only that it shows that we touch upon holy ground, God's presence, among things and events that He shapes.

5-14 The Lamb who was Slain

Once again, a new picture appears. One of God's priests comforts John. There is *one* who can open the scroll because He won the victory. His name does not need to be mentioned; it has to do with two Old Testament prophecies: the lion of Judah (Genesis 49:9f) and the shoot from David's root (Isaiah 11:1). As soon as He is named, John sees Him. He stands there in the midst of the celebration of divine service. John seems neither amazed nor awed that there is a Lamb, or that the Lamb looks as if it had been slain. So it is in a vision. The peculiar can be obvious, necessary, and convincing. The picture of the Lamb is one we are familiar with. Of course, it is found in the chapter on the Lord's suffering servant (Isaiah 53), and the Baptist uses it. The seven horns appear more peculiar to us. However, for John, the horn was a well-known symbol for strength and power. Most peculiar are the seven eyes that are God's seven spirits. We meet God's seven spirits already in the introduction (1:4), and they come again as seven lamps before God's throne (4:5). Here, they are the Lamb's eyes, and at the same time spirits who are sent out over all the earth, apparently so that Christ sees and knows everything. This means that John does not think of seven different spirits, but of the one Spirit, He whom Jesus sends from the Father as an instrument of His work.

Then the Lamb steps forth and receives the scroll. At the same time, something new happens within the Heavenly Liturgy. All fell before the Lamb with their harps and their bowls of incense. Incense is the classical picture of prayer that rises up before God's throne (Psalm 141:2). Then they sing a new song, a song that could not be sung before.

In this place, it says expressly that they "sang." Even the harps show that it is a question of songs and music. Otherwise, the word "said" is normally used, but it does not mean that it was a question of what we call "speech" or "talking," only that they used the word which then follows. Even in this case it literally says that "they sang a new song and said."

The new song deals with Christ's atoning work. However, this was not the new thing. The new thing was that He, who sacrificed Himself for the world, had come in during a final and decisive phase. And this phase is necessarily connected with the atoning work. Here it is said with a remarkable expression that Christ *purchased* people for God with His blood. It cannot be said any more forcefully that we were lost, and helplessly separated from God who created us and does not want to lose us. Still, we were lost to Him because God and sin cannot be united. For the sinner this means that a catastrophe has entered the presence of the threefold Holy one. No sinner would have been able to live in God's presence if Christ had not come under condemnation and taken the consequences of sin upon Himself. He paid what it cost and purchased man back for God, people of all races and cultures. He made them kings (really a kingdom) and priests before God (sacrificial priests—it is this word that is used here). He reinstates them as sons and daughters to the king and made it possible for them to bring forth pure and holy sacrifices. So, they may share the power and the glory in His kingdom.

However, the kingdom has not yet come. Evil still reigns on earth. God lets the evangelists go out and offer forgiveness and salvation to all. The gospel is to be preached to all people. However, God has set a limit to the possibilities of evil. One day He will audit the account. The curtain will go up for the last act in the great drama. It is this moment that comes when the Lamb takes the scroll and breaks the first seal.

REVELATION 5:5-14

And Jubilee breaks loose. The hosts of heaven and God's people on earth and all of creation have waited for this. It begins among the innumerable angels around the throne, and the entire worshiping congregation in heaven unites with them. Finally, the whole of creation resounds with songs of praise. The four living creatures confirm it with their Amen, and the twenty-four priests fall again and pray.

Revelation 6

1-2 The First Seal is Broken

So the drama has begun. The Lamb breaks the first seal, and a rider rides forth on a white horse. He receives a crown of victory and storms away to conquer.

Who is he? John does not say. Perhaps, he himself wondered. It could have been a champion of the Lord. This would mean that the drama begins with a victory for the gospel. Yet complete scourge then follows, and for this reason most expositors today believe that we have before us a picture of a worldly conqueror, one of them who seems unstoppable—and who God allows to be successful for a time. This success can belong to the misery that comes to inflict the world.

3-4 The Second Seal is Broken

The same scene is repeated four times. One of the four living creatures cries: Come! And a horse and rider come forth. Each time there is something symbolic in the horse's color and the rider's armament. The second time the horse is bright red. The rider receives power to remove peace from the earth and is equipped with a sword. The people slaughter each other. The war gets bloodier than anything before. Perhaps it happens precisely in the trail of the worldly conqueror's successes and as a consequence of the world power's desire to unify the whole world in a single block or under a single ideology.

5-6 The Third Seal is Broken

We have already begun to glimpse the similarities between these scourges and those that Jesus spoke about right before His death (Matthew 24:6f). "People shall rise against people and nation against nation." Then it says: There shall be famine upon famine. This is what the rider on the black horse brings with him. He has a scale in his hand. It is the symbol for the handling of everyday necessities, those which the small people shall live on. A voice is heard—John knows not whose, he only says what he experienced—that gives us the inflation's misery in a nutshell. He mentions a measurement—approximately a liter—that among other things was a soldier's daily ration. A single ration of wheat shall cost a denarius (that is the coin mentioned in the original text). It was the daily wage of a poor laborer. So, he could abstain from wheat and keep to barley bread, the most common ingredient in a poor man's diet. Yet even so, a daily wage would barely suffice for three—and only for one meal. So, it was a matter of a starvation diet. However, wine and oil would still remain for those who had money. We recognize the picture from times of food shortages. Strangely enough, there is still enough to get for those who can pay.

7-8 The Fourth Seal is Broken

The fourth living creature has said his "come," and a horse with the color of a corpse, pale yellow with a greenish hue, appears. The rider has no armament, but he is called death, "the pale death," the death of starvation and plagues, not only of weapons. He has Hades (the kingdom of death) with him—we would like to know in which form, but John does not say. What we may know is that these scourges will take a great toll on human life.

Now all of this is written into God's plans for the world. This is the meaning of the picture of the sealed scroll. This certainly did not deal with something that was God's plan from the beginning because everything He created was good. It is a consequence of the fall into sin, the rebellion, the distortion that in turn triggered all God's work of salvation. All this must happen because the world is such as it is, and God simultaneously carries it to the goal He determined.

Here we also receive a vision of the future that violently collides with what a western man has desired to believe now for over a hundred years. People have believed in progress. They have imagined that everything must get better if not through a natural law, then in any case through wise political measures. However, Jesus clearly tells us—here as in the gospels—that this is not the case. The foundational damage in humanity sits so deep that there is no other final resolution than a totally new creation. Now God carries the world toward this. He offers humanity the invitation to enter into this new world. This is why the gospel is preached. However, God very well knows that most will reject it and that in their blindness and selfishness and the misuse of their reason, they will come to face ever worse miseries. God has held them back for a long time. But now, when the end approaches, the powers of destruction receive a free hand and openly do what they are for.

9-11 The Fifth Seal is Broken

Three seals remain. The four preceding have formed a unity. They have described what the world has to deal with. Jesus's words could be used as a summary (Matthew 24:6): [Such things] "must take place but the end is not yet." This is what the next seal is concerned with.

Now the scene is different. When the seal is broken, John sees—just now?—that there is an altar before God's throne. Under this altar he sees the souls of the martyrs. In Jerusalem's temple the sacrificial blood was poured unto the rock under the altar. Here God has not collected the blood of the martyrs but the martyrs themselves. And now they speak. They come with questions that always burn within people of faith during hard times, particularly when terrible atrocities happen, and it seems God does not intervene. This is the question: How long? How long can You let such things continue, Lord? It is not a matter of revenge. It is a matter of justice, of the victory of good. In order to give this evil world yet another day of grace and yet another opportunity for repentance, God allows the evil to live—and they use their time to do so much evil! How long shall it happen?

The answer is a gift first: a white robe. In some way, this represents God's kingdom and its righteousness. Martyrs are well-protected there. Nothing really evil has happened to them. They learn to leave the rest to God. The time is not yet imminent. God still has something to do on earth. It will cost yet more martyrs suffering and death. However, God knows how many. He keeps His hand on them.

12-17 The Sixth Seal is Broken

Now the end approaches. When the next to last seal is broken, the old creation begins to fall apart. Jesus said the same in His talk about the last things (Matthew 24:29f). Here it is described in similar pictures with a clarity and power that lets us remember how shaken the seer was when he saw what happened. It does not serve anything to try and translate this into normal, scientific prose. It is a matter of the dissolution of the universe, something just as powerful, unfathomable, and overwhelming as the genesis. When men of science try to describe how they believe it happened—with "the big Bang"—we see how it can happen in God's workshop and how unfathomable it is that happens there.

However, one thing is clear. The great day will not be met with the joy of those who do not want to know of God. They will be seized by despair. When all this begins to happen, they try to hide themselves—perhaps literally in their shelters, dug out into mountains—and have only one thought: this is something terrible, something that crushes the whole of our world, all that we believe in and live for. When John spoke about "earth's inhabitants" (as in verse 10), it is always a question of those who do not believe, about those who have earth as their last true home. For them the great day, when all becomes new, only becomes a day of fear, a day of wrath. God's wrath is that aspect of His being that is and remains incapable of uniting with all evil, an unforgiving opposition that can never be softened or smoothed over.

Revelation 7

1-8 The Hundred and Forty-four Thousand

The picture changes again, and after a moment we perceive that we have been carried back in time. This is the way of visions. A person can compare them with a film. Suddenly, all the attention is focused on a little detail or an individual figure that was not seen before. So, it was with the scroll and with the Lamb. Just as suddenly a man can be moved back in time and be able to see a scene that is the background or description of something that has already happened. So, it is here. We find ourselves right in the middle of the final stage of the great drama, when the whole of the old creation is loosening in its joints. Here we learn that God's people had been previously stamped with God's seal on their forehead. We learn this through a particular vision. At earth's "four horns"—we would say: in the four quarters—stand four angels who hold back the winds. Perhaps a person ought rather to translate this "the storms," which was part of the Old Testament's well-known tools for God's punishment. Before they are now let loose, God's people shall be sealed with God's own seal. Later we receive confirmation of what we already think here: it is a protecting sign, something that shall protect them through all scourges.

However, who are these people? Here the opinions are helplessly divided among the commentators—as so often when it comes to the Book of Revelation. Some use entire lines of "proof" that this must be talk of the Jews. Others think that it is obviously talk of the church, the new Israel. With Jesus a New Testament came, and it established a new Israel. The core was formed by the Jews who received their Messiah. With this core then, people of all nations and cultures were united. This new Israel also has twelve tribes (Luke 22:30). For this reason, the apostles were twelve in number. In general, the commentators lean toward the later interpretation. So, there would be talk here of how God sealed His own with a mark before the great tests, which shows that He has not forgotten them and will not allow them to be lost.

But why were only 144,000 sealed? And why exactly 12,000 from every tribe? Here the numbers must have symbolic significance. Unfortunately, we have no certain fact when it comes to that symbolism. A person usually places the number 3 in relationship to God, and 4 with the world. Of course, the number 12 is the product of 3 and 4, so it then stands for completeness: God and the world. If a person then takes 12 times 12 and multiplies it by a thousand, it can then mean the totality of the church, the whole of God's great people in the world. However, such interpretations always have something arbitrary about them. We may remember that John himself seems to have often wondered about what he saw. God's Word directs itself to all eras and all people. There can be details that do not become completely comprehensible before their time comes. The same Word can still have something to say to us. We are right to meditate over it and let it speak to us. In any case, so much is certain, that here there is a promise of God to help His people through the extreme need that may come. Perhaps here there are also other hints that can be worth noticing. 144,000 is a far too small number to compare with the population of the world and with the many of them that are called Christians today. It fits with what Jesus has said to us. Those who believe end up being a tiny minority when the world does not have very long left.

Again, we meditate concerning the 12,000 in every tribe, so perhaps we imagine that there is an inherent harmony and beauty in all of God's plans. Even His plan with God's people constructed something of a well-balanced architecture in the temple that God's people make up, which all shall be revealed when the twelve tribes march in and take possession of the heavenly Canaan. And he who believes that here John speaks about the old Israel, he rejoices to find a confirmation of what Paul has already said: finally, Israel shall also be saved. However, we are reminded the whole time that this concerns things that we today can only imagine. We will see soon enough.

9-17 The Innumerable Host

Then a completely different picture follows. John sees the innumerable host from all the people of the world in white robes who stand before the throne. They have come "out of the great tribulation." We have become accustomed to this translation, and it is not easy to find a better one, though it does not precisely render the original text. It is a question of a word that we encountered before (among others in 1:9 and 2:9, 10 and 22) and which essentially means to be pressed by pressure and hardship. It is used for all that a Christian can suffer under pressure from a hostile environment and especially is used for the persecution that waits for the church when the world becomes old. The "great tribulation" is certainly the last harsh tribulation in the final act of the drama. The tribulation is not the sort of personal worries that hit all people, but real "Christian suffering" of the type that Paul speaks about (Colossians 1:24). However, because such suffering has followed Christendom from the very beginning and belongs to a great context that culminates in the last great persecution, so all earlier witnesses also have their place in the great host. And if a person wants to apply the picture to all of those who have fought the good fight of faith—under very everyday circumstances and without suffering real persecution—it is not incorrect even if Jesus does not quite speak about them here.

They sing about salvation. It belongs to God, is found with God, depends on God. It is God and the Lamb they have to thank that they now stand here. Several of those who sing must have given their lives and shed their blood for God's sake.

However, it is not their blood that has washed away their sins. Their clothes are white because they have washed them in the blood of the Lamb. The blood of martyrs can never atone for any sins. Only the blood of Jesus can do that. Essentially it is a strange picture. Blood that makes clothes white. The picture would have been absurd if Jesus had been only a man, a great martyr who shed his blood. However, He was God's Son, the light of the world, purity itself, and therefore His blood can purify and make all things white.

The whole heavenly host harmonizes in songs of praise. The saved people praise God for their salvation. The angels have other things to thank God for. They thank God because He exists. They list what belongs to Him. It is literally ALL—all that is good, all that brings joy and meaning and makes it a miracle of joy to be alive. It is hard to properly render in English what there is in these words that are heaped upon each other. The word for "glory" is simultaneously the word for God's majesty and glory (*doxa*), that which makes all in His presence be joy and happiness. "Wisdom" (*sofia*) is His unfathomable wisdom, that which already filled the pious of the Old Testament with wonder and adoration and caused Paul and the whole early church to break out in songs of praise. The word for "praise" and "thanksgiving" (*eulogia, eucharistia*) are those which are used for the blessing of God's name and thanks to God, which the Jews brought forth in all shifts of life and which the Christians receive at the climax of the celebration of the Lord's Supper.

Revelation 8

1-5 The Last Seal is Broken

When the sixth seal is broken, John saw how the old world began to come apart just as his Lord said that it would do. Then he heard how the 144,000 were sealed and how the last great persecution had begun.

Now the last seal is broken. The eternal praise song is silenced. The whole of heaven hushes in infinite tension. However, at the beginning nothing happens. Then John receives—as it happens in a vision—a new picture in his field of view: the seven angels that stand before the throne. There are seven particular angels that are well known to all Jews. We usually call them archangels. We meet one of them in the Gospel of Luke: "Gabriel who stands before God" (1:19). Now each of them receives a trumpet.

With this, a new series of visions begins. Once again, it is a matter of seven parts, of which the first four are apparently connected. It is obvious that they all belong with the final act of the world's drama. However, they simultaneously bare the features of such as happened earlier in history and which are constantly repeated anew. This is because the powers that are let loose here have been active ever since the day of the fall. The difference is that God has held them in check up till now. Now they have free rein.

The introduction to this new consequence of terrible events is a scene before the heavenly high alter. An angel steps forward with a censer, receives enough incense to offer the smoke with the prayers of Christians, so that all rise up to God. Then he fills his censer again, but now with fire from the altar—the altar under which the martyrs rest in expectation that God will finally take over and set a limit to evil. The meaning can hardly be anything but: Now God has heard the cry of the suffering on earth—they who cry: Come, Lord Jesus, Your kingdom comes, let Your name be kept holy and Your will be done! Now God shall right the ship. He has tarried long enough before intervening. He has not wished that any should be lost. He has waited for at least a few to yet turn and repent. Now there is nothing more to wait for. The angel fills his censer with fire from the altar and lets it rain down upon the earth. The thunder rumbles, the lightning flashes, the earth quakes. Judgment Day is near. The seven angels stand at the ready with their trumpets.

6-12 The First Four Trumpets

When the first four seals were broken, such miseries as have happened so many times before in history—though on a lesser scale—followed. However, now in the final act the world enters an era when all earlier experiences are shortened. All are on the way to their dissolution, even time and space, and it is meaningless to ask how such things can happen. Such questions assume that we know that even in the future all must happen according to laws that rule now. However, this is precisely what Jesus says will not happen.

Some have discussed if that which is described here with the first four trumpets should be thought of as pictures of something that, in fact, comes to happen within the frame of world history, or if these are events that blow up the frame for all that can happen so long as the old world order remains. Previously, people thought that such things could not happen, and many wanted to regard it simply as symbols and pictures. However, ever since the end of the Second World War we have seen that we men with our abuse of reason and our helpless egotism, in fact, are in place to achieve something that looks awfully close to the pictures that John saw in his vision. We know that it can hail fire from heaven and that the ground, forests, and grass on whole continents can very well burn up. We know that mountains of burning fire can fall over us and that life in the sea can disappear and the water in the rivers can be dangerous to drink. We know that air pollution can cost us. Not even sunlight is certain anymore. It is not impossible that this is the consequence of a third world war, or a natural disaster (or both together), which the pictures here suggest. In any case they say: thereby, the end has not come. Humanity survives. That which happened was rather a final warning.

A person can object that Revelation sees these scourges as something that God sends, while the third world war would obviously be willed by man. However, according to the Bible's way of seeing, there is no contradiction. God and Satan fight for humanity. Satan is the destroyer who wants to destroy and plague. God holds His creation with power so that the gospel shall be preached, and people have the opportunity to find their way home to God. However, when God has done what He could for our salvation, He draws a line and lets the end come. He withdraws His protective hand and lets evil have free course. It is this we see as the narrative unfolds.

13 The Cry of Woe from Heaven

When the first four trumpets sound, an interlude follows. John hears a single eagle scream high up in the heavens. It is a threefold cry of woe that goes out over the earth. The three final trumpets come to introduce up to now unknown miseries for humanity. Up to now God has placed a limit to the evil in order to give humanity time for repentance. Now they have rejected His last warning. They do not want to go His way. Now they may go their own way without Him.

Revelation 9

1-12 The Fifth Trumpet

The fifth trumpet sounds. Again, John's gaze is directed to a figure that he has not noticed before: "a star fallen from heaven to earth." For a Biblically knowledgeable Jew like John, it was clear who he saw. The prophet Isaiah spoke of this star (Isaiah 14:12f). He was once "the shining morning star," created by God. However, he was the one who thought in his heart: "I will ascend to heaven and there I will steal my throne. I will make myself like the almighty." Of course, the prophet was read in Jesus's day—and obviously by Jesus Himself—as a story about Satan's rebellion against God, the great fall that was the cause of all evil in existence. It was this "star" that receives the key to the bottomless pit.

Up until now God had held the worst of the abyss's powers in prison. It is a thought that we also encounter in the other passages of the New Testament (2 Peter 2:4). How and where and when we cannot say other than with the pictures that the Bible uses. However, here the picture is clear enough. Now the powers of the abyss are unleashed. And thereby, the framework for all we can imagine with the help of everyday experience is blown up. We encounter a world that is completely different, a fantastically nightmarish world. It would require a great artist in a surrealistic spirit to paint a picture of the abyss's smoke that billows forth and gives birth to hosts of tormenting spirits, beings that could be taken from the paintings of Hieronymus Bosch. John seeks to describe them with the help of pictures from his environment. He has apparently seen them very concretely and knows how they look. But who can properly describe what none of us has ever before seen?

As so often, the picture is filled with reminiscences from the Old Testament. Of course, there are also foreshadowings, even to that which shall come when God intervenes at the end of time found there. John is deeply familiar with them. Here we see how well he knew the prophet Joel, who gives us a tremoring description of the scourge that swarms of locusts had caused his people. He had seen that the scourges came from God and that the destroyers carried out God's punishment, but simultaneously, it was a warning and a call to repentance. When John sees his vision, he understands that this, which the prophet described—a concrete event that happened many centuries before—was simultaneously a foreshadowing (a "type" as one said in the early church) to that which would come to happen. However, the fulfillment at the end of time is still something different, far more fateful and all-inclusive.

However, there is even here a call to repentance. The tormenting spirits may not kill their victims, and they receive a particular time measured out for their power. The verdict is not yet irrevocable.

It does not serve much to ask how the "angel of the bottomless pit," Apollyon—it means the Destroyer—is identical with Satan, and how, in any case, Satan could release him (if now the meaning is that the destroyer until then had been bound). A vision does not answer such questions. That which is clear is that it is the same spirit, and the same evil will that is active. That Satan has a kingdom and servants that do his will is a concept that was confirmed by Jesus over and over again.

What John says about that which happens when the world falls apart has many times showed itself to be a repeat and a culmination of that which occurred before. Perhaps it is so here too. Time after time people—sometimes naïve and well-meaning—have opened the lock and let the powers loose. People have given pornographic films the go ahead and opened the floodgates that keep criminals in check, and people have encountered demonic powers that they hardly believed to exist.

13-19 The Sixth Trumpet

The sixth trumpet sounds, and John again hears a voice, without really knowing who speaks. It seems to come from the four horns, which rise up from the four corners of the altar, just like the altar that Moses received orders to make. The altar, the temple, the incense, and the songs of praise on earth were, of course, supposed to give a glimpse of heaven. However hard it is then for John to describe how it goes before God's face, it is obvious that of all he has experienced on earth, it is the divine service that comes closest.

That the voice from the altar spoke in God's ways was obvious to John. It was then God who gave the command to release the four angels bound at the Euphrates River. The Euphrates is the river of Babel, and in Israel, Babel became a symbol for Satan's kingdom, and all evil. For men in John's time, the name Euphrates had a sinister sound. It was the eastern border of the empire. On the other side lay the Parthian empire, the only civilization that was experienced as a constant threat and that had time and again crushed the Roman legions with calvary. What John saw was, thus, the old threat from the east but now enlarged to dimensions that surpassed all human measures. Yet even this eruption of destructive powers stood under God's control. It would happen just this way. The year, the day, the hour was already determined.

For the half-secularized Christendom that is so common among us, it is a shocking thought that God would be able let such things happen. For many people, that God is good means that He shall protect us from the consequences of our sins. A person lives according to his own plans and for his own goals without seriously asking for God's will. What a person expects of Him is that He shall see to it that there are no unforeseen charges on the bill. The Bible gives us a different picture. God wants to have communion with His children. So, He calls us to Himself.

When we refuse to come, He can still continue to give us His protection. He gives us more time and opportunities for repentance. In this manner, He also deals in large part with humanity. However, Jesus and the whole New Testament tell us that a limit is set for the time when God continues to call on them who will not come, despite everything. There comes a time when there is no more to gain. Then God withdraws His protection from the unrepentant. Men receive the consequences of their own choices. They become victims for powers that they themselves invoked.

John emphasizes that he can only render the pictures that he himself was able to see. The cavalry that storms forth is innumerable. He may hear that it touches on a dizzying number. The Greek form (essentially "ten thousand twenty thousands") shows that there is no question of exact numbers. And the description of the hosts of evil shows that it deals with pictures, terrifying and fantastic pictures of a reality that is just as hard for us to imagine as the people of antiquity would have to comprehend the description of contemporary tank battles.

20-21 The Last Warning Rejected

The sixth trumpet sounds, and the second series of harsh scourges comes to its end. Till the very end, the door of grace has been kept open. However, it shows that the unrepentant in no way will think of it. They continue precisely as before, first and foremost in the area of religion. They worship their own gods, which they themselves have originated—in modern expression, their culture, their standard of living, their sexuality—themselves. They are gods that cannot help, and behind them stand—now as then—the evil spirits who cause men to put the creation (which in and of itself is good) in place of the Creator. And as it goes with religions, so it is with morals: even there, men continue as before with the same contempt for God and His commandments.

Revelation 10

1-4 That Which May Still Not Be Said

Between the sixth and the last seal there is an interlude in which two other scenes are shoved in. In the same way, an interlude follows the sixth trumpet. Again, John sees a mighty angel descend. At first, a person could believe that it was Christ Himself, because the picture is so close to what John described in the first chapter. However, it is only a messenger, one of Christ's heavenly servants. He sets himself with his one foot on the sea and the second foot on land. It works as if in his vision John sees Patmos in front of him, perhaps precisely the bay where the harbor and capital still lie. If a person stands up on the mountain side and looks out to the sea—as John certainly did many times—the picture of the angel comes alive. The mighty one sets his right foot on the mirror-like sea and lets the left rest on the heights by the beach. Perhaps John saw something symbolic about this: the Lord, on behalf of whom the Lord speaks, rules over land and sea.

And the angel speaks with a mighty voice, and "the seven thunders" answer. For a pious Jew, the seven thunders were a well-known matter—the 29th Psalm, the mighty hymn about God's revelation in thunderstorms. Seven times talk of God's voice in the thunder returns. When the seven voices now sound, John immediately grabs his pen to write down what they said. But then a voice speaks to him from heaven and commands him to forget it as one seals a secret action with his seal. This may not be written down and not carried further.

This little episode gives us an interesting revelation of how John worked. He has not composed his work from previously gathered material from different sources. When he received a revelation, he wrote down—just as St. Birgitta[1] used to do—the content as quickly as he had occasion to do so. Here he could only say that he received a message that was not to be spread further. It can be a useful reminder to us all that would so gladly make Christendom into a complete explanation of the world, where no questions need go unanswered. Christendom is something that has been revealed to us. There are things which God lets us know, and there are other things He has kept from us to let us know at some other time, or not at all.

---

[1] St. Birgitta (1303-1373) was a fourteenth century mystic from Sweden whose memory is still beloved in Sweden. Though she started receiving visions early in life, it was not until after her husband died that she later established monasteries and convents. She was known for charity to single mothers, and agitation for church reform in Rome where she died. She also sent the plans for the famous Blue Church in Vadstena.

5-7 The End of Time

Then the angel speaks again, and this time it is a message that shall be brought forth and which is confirmed with an oath by the Eternal One who created everything. The message says: Now there is no more time. First and foremost, this means that people have no further suspension to expect. Time comes to an end. It can well enough be understood very literally. When God intervenes and creates something new, neither time nor space applies in the same way as in the old creation. Time is not eternal. It came to be with creation. Modern physics has shown that time is bound to material. It is not something absolute but depends on how much material there is in the vicinity and how fast you move.

At the seventh trumpet, the end comes. Then God is finished. He has had a secret plan. His prophets have been able to see it, but no one has correctly been able to understand how God thought to carry His will through. The big breakthrough for this plan was Christ. However, the work will only be completed when Christ comes again and makes all things new. Even Paul has much to say about God's secret plan, for example, in Ephesians chapter 3.

8-11 The Little Scroll

The angel holds a scroll in his hand. It is emphasized that it was little and that it was unrolled, so completely different from the one John had seen previously. Now he receives the command to go meet the angel and receive it. He does this and is told to eat it. Such a command seems almost grotesque to us. In the secularized western lands, a person looks at eating as something completely corporeal, often something crassly material and unspiritual. However, for Jews eating was a miracle of God, a part of God's mystery. So a person would initiate meals with Scripture and prayers, and at ceremonial occasions meals received the character of worship. A person was conscious of the miracle in being able to receive a piece of God's creation and unite oneself in order to turn it into one's own life. So it was completely natural for Jesus to speak about Himself as the bread of life, a bread that must be eaten. To eat a scroll must mean to incorporate that which was written there with his own self and be one with the message that would be carried further. Ezekiel had also once received a similar command (2:8f).

That the scroll should taste like honey was no surprise for a Jew. This was also Ezekiel's experience. Of course, God's word was "sweeter than honey, yes, even the purest honey" (Psalms 19:10). But that this should then be followed by powerful pain was something new. It can point to an experience that Jeremiah had to endure. "Your words were found, and I ate them, and your words became to me a joy, and the delight of my heart" (Jeremiah 15:16). But then came the bitterness. For the words made the prophet "a man of strife and contention to the whole land!" and "a reproach and derision all day long" (Jeremiah 15:10, 20:8). It can be hard to be a prophet. It was to precisely this task that John was called, and he must continue with it.

The experience of this work of the Word is common. Jesus speaks about it in the parable of that which was sown on stony ground. First came pure joy and enthusiasm for the word. Then came opposition and persecution. Our fathers used to speak about the great joy that follows with the call, then all is new and rich and lovely, but it is followed by the awakening's bitter experience when one seriously sees what a sinner he is.

Revelation 11

1-3 The Temple, The Courtyard, and Witnesses

In his vison, John has until now been a passive receiver. Now he is drawn into the events. He is given a measuring rod "that resembled a staff." Here "staff" can mean a shepherd's staff or possibly a scepter. It is really a question of measuring an area that will be put under God's particular protection. Therefore, even those who worship in the temple shall "be measured," while the forecourts are left outside because it is left to God's enemies. The measurement corresponds to the sealing with God's seal, which also preceded the last scourge.

Among Christians the Temple was the well-known symbol for the church. It is she that God takes into His protection. However, mark well "not the forecourts." We also talk about the forecourts of Christendom. In the great national churches, a person often sees "the forecourts of Christendom" as an essential factor to deal with. However, in the great testing it does not come to remain. It is occupied and trampled under by the feet of Christ's enemies. The development in the Third Reich can illustrate what is meant. The religiosity that wanted to be anchored in the people and follow the times, fell short, while a small group of confessionally faithful people offered resistance.

The forty-two months is an apocalyptic number. It reappears in the next sentence as 1260 days (so 42 times 30). It can also be called "time, times and half a time," an expression previously encountered in the Prophet Daniel (Daniel 7:25, 12:7). So, it is also a question of time for a great scourge when it will look as if God's enemies will be victorious. It is hard to say how much is symbolic about these numbers. In any case, it touches upon a limited time, and a time God Himself has established.

The two witnesses are mentioned as if they are well-known, but they are not described until later. The voice that speaks says "I shall…" and speaks about "my witnesses." So, it seems to be Christ Himself who speaks. Even in this great time of apostasy, when the forecourts are occupied by the enemy, Christ comes to let their testimony be heard.

4-6 The Power of the Witnesses

As the narrative continues, it seems to be John himself who speaks. He explains who the witnesses were. When they are first mentioned it seems they were known. It seems that this deals with Moses and Elijah, who were to come back before the great judgment. It fits with the characteristics they have here. Moses had the full authority to slay Egypt with plagues, and Elijah had prophesied drought and annihilates

God's enemies with fire. Yet here the witnesses also identify with two olive trees, that Zechariah had spoken about in connection with a lampstand (Zechariah 4:3, 11f). Here the lampstands are two. It is the same symbolism that we encounter when the seven churches are called lampstands. The two witnesses speak about representatives for the whole church. They personify the apostolic witness that shall also be heard during the last terrible attack against Christendom. For as long as God wants the world to hear the gospel, no one can silence it.

7-10 The Martyrdom of the Witnesses

There comes a day when the last testimony has gone out to the world. Then the particular protection God has given His witnesses will be withdrawn. It looks as if the enemies would triumph. John has apparently seen it in a vision that he now describes for us. From the bottomless pit climbs a wild beast. John does not need to say who it is. His audience knew it already. It was written in Scripture (Daniel 7:7). It would come to bring war against the saints. So now it did, and the two witnesses became martyrs. Their corpses lay in the street of "the great city." In the spiritual context that we have here, it can be called Sodom or Egypt, the city of fornication and oppression. It is a matter of a symbol, an improper name for something that is still a reality. And the reality behind the name can hardly be other than a humanity that is hostile to God, self-adoring and self-assured, the powerful city that worships wealth, subdues its opportunities for happiness, and insists on its freedom to exercise its vices.

Now God's witnesses lie there in the street and are not allowed to be buried—the most extreme shame and disgrace that could befall a person. And the city of the world rejoices. People only experienced the apostolic testimony as a plague. It stood in an irreconcilable opposition to the lifestyle that a person practiced, that which would give life meaning. Here we encounter the end times magnification of the motif that so often lies behind the animosity towards the gospel and the harassment of Christians. A person wants to escape seeing that there is a way of life that shows that he himself has turned in the wrong direction.

When here it speaks of the city where "even their Lord was crucified," it can seem to indicate Jerusalem. However, afterwards it immediately speaks of people from the whole world as its inhabitants. This indicates that it is dealing with the great city of the world, the home of unbelief and apostasy, that has inhabitants in all times and all people, and where Christ really was crucified and is so again even though He is also *their* Lord.

11-14 The Victory of the Witnesses

Once again, we encounter the number three and a half. In the original text it says, "after these three and a half days," as if the number were well-known, though it now touches on days and not on years. Perhaps here there is a hint concerning a connection with Jesus Himself. For three years He testified, after three days He was resurrected. The servants shall follow their Lord in everything, "be like him by dying like him" so then to share in His resurrection.

Now John speaks about something that happened, apparently something he saw in his vision. The dead witnesses come back to life; they are received into heaven in a cloud—as will happen at Christ's return—the great city is shaken to its foundations; many die and people are seized with fear and give "glory to God in heaven." Perhaps for one and another this was a conversion the minute before the stroke of midnight. However, it is more likely that John only means the terror that understands that God exists and therefore tries by any means to get in with Him.

Some believe that that which is described in this vision belongs with the events in connection with Christ's return and the resurrection of the dead. So, the meaning would be that the martyrs receive their restoration, and their persecutors may see that the persecuted still spoke on God's behalf and were in His hand the whole time. Others think that this must be a question of some particular event that plays out before the return of Christ. He who lives will see.

So "the second woe" meets its end. Now comes the last and with that the end.

15-18 The Seventh Trumpet: God takes the Kingdom

The last trumpet sounds. The decisive moment is imminent. Up till now God has tarried with His final intervention, that which shall set a final limit to evil. Up until the end, He has allowed the rebels to live in order to give them the opportunity for salvation. The whole time He has had the power to crush them, but He has not wanted to use it.

Now He takes control. It is that which the voices in heaven cry out as soon as the seventh trumpet has sounded. God takes control to rule for all eternity. No longer shall anyone defy His will.

The twenty-four pastors who step before God's people greet Him and thank Him. They have waited for this and longed for it. No one but God can truly understand why He waited so long and how His eyes have been able to observe so much evil and still have forbearance with this evil. Now His people thank Him because He "made use of his power." Now God may be called "He who is and was" but no longer "he who comes." Now He has come for eternity.

The heathen—or "the people" as a person can also translate: the Jews and the New Testament use the same word for both—have shown their spite, resentment, and anger for God's claim and threat, and so they persecuted his confessors. Now they may see that God really can be angry. God's wrath is His irreconcilable opposition to all evil; they who do evil experience His presence as something unbearable, like a consuming fire. The rebels have destroyed, laid waste to God's good creation, abused His gifts. Now they encounter God Himself and this means destruction for them.

The great day finally entails that the ship is righted. They who must suffer because God was so patient receive their restoration, and all God's servants, small and great, receive their reward. Finally, all mysteries and all "whys" receive their resolution and answer.

19 The Gates Open to the Innermost Mysteries

This verse really belongs to the next chapter. Our chapter separation that came about in the 13th century does not always do the text justice. Here it is a matter of the next great step forward in John's account of his visions. First, he finds himself on Patmos. Then a gate to heaven is opened. He saw a glimpse of God's throne, from which came thunder and lightning. Then follows the vision of the lamb with the scroll and the seven seals. Then come the angels with the seven trumpets and a new series of terrifying events. They too are introduced with thunder and lightning that followed the fire from the altar. Now the gates to God's Temple in heaven are opened. The ark of the covenant is visible. The earthly ark was the sign of God's presence with His people with whom He had made a covenant. It consisted of a box where the tablets of the law were kept. Israel carried it with them through the desert. Gradually it was placed far back in the Holy of Holies in the Temple, hidden from the sight of the people. When the heavenly ark is now seen, it means that God is with His people. The way to Him lies open. Therefore, even God's most ultimate plans and the deepest mysteries of existence are revealed. It is this that is now described. The chief part of that which up till now has been described belongs at home on earth, among people within the frame of history. To some extent, it is such that has already been described. Now it is recapitulated as it appears from the point of view of eternity.

So we have been lifted up a step into that which we in the introduction called the apocalyptic "spiral." We can look down on earth and into heaven from the threshold of God's heavenly sanctuary. And again, the new act in the drama is introduced with thunder and lightning that proclaims God's holiness and majesty.

Revelation 12

1-6 The Woman and the Dragon

John sees a vision in heaven. He knows that it is a "sign," something that must be interpreted, a symbol. It is a heavenly being, a woman who clothes herself with the light of the sun like a coat and stands on the moon and carries twelve stars on her head. Twelve is the number of tribes of Israel, and John perhaps thought that the woman was God's bride, the elect who had called from among all the people of the earth. The woman was pregnant and crying in her birth pangs. Perhaps John thought of Mary for a moment, the Lord's mother. Of course, the baby boy that was born was apparently Jesus, the promised one who would govern all people with an iron scepter. However, when he saw her flee out in the desert and saw how the dragon persecuted all her other children, he must have understood that it was not Mary, but God's bride, she who first is called the daughter of Zion and then became God's church. What he was able to see was the Bride's, the People of God's, the Church's history seen from the perspective of eternity, reduced to a few decisive events. It touches on a fight with life and death between the woman and the great dragon, the strife that was prophesied already in the narrative of the fall, the strife between the serpent and the woman's seed. The opponent in the drama is the old serpent, this monster above all monsters, with seven heads and ten horns and a royal diadem on his head—altogether the sign of power, strength, and prestige—aggressive fire red, with a power to destroy and devour as he exercises sovereignty and pre-eminence, where he goes forward almost in transience. So, he sweeps the stars of heaven with his tail and a third of them tumble to the earth—a ghastly, painted picture for those who knew that he himself was a fallen angel, the fallen Morning Star, and that he took with him a great many of God's angels in the fall.

Now the dragon takes position to devour the woman's child as soon as it comes into the world. The Messiah would be born of the bride, proceed from God's people like a Jew among others, a man who could be tempted and killed. The dragon attempted all this, but he was unsuccessful. John only sees the exit, the final result (he and his audience knew the rest). The Son was taken up to God and received His place by God's side. And then follows the new: the bride, the church is rescued out in the desert—as Israel was saved from Egypt—and protected there for a period of time that is again signified with the apocalyptic number (1260=42=3 ½).

7-9 Michael and the Dragon

Another vision follows. It lets us see how history can appear from heaven's point of view. We find ourselves beyond time and looking back at that which happened on earth. God's Son was born among God's people. Satan took up the fight on earth and lost it. It has decisive consequences for that which happened in heaven. Michael and his angels took the fight with him and his followers. Michael, like Gabriel, is counted as one of the seven archangels who stand before God. In the Old Testament we meet him as the mighty champion and defender of God's people (Daniel 12:1).

That Satan, in fact, had a place in heaven is clearly stated in the Old Testament. He was one of "God's sons," one of the heavenly beings who God created. Only now he definitively lost the place he was created to hold. However, the context only becomes clear through the hymn that now follows.

10-12 The Victory Hymn

John again hears heavenly voices without knowing to whom they belong. It can be angels; it can be the saved people in the great masses. In any case, they speak about the sinful people as "our brothers." And here we now hear what Satan did in heaven. He was "our brother's accuser," restlessly active with his accuser. We encounter one of the deepest uncertainties of the whole drama of salvation. Satan had one point right. We were really culpable before God. We had trespassed all the laws, which may not be trespassed. We had no right to come enter God's heaven. We do not fit there. If we slipped in, Satan himself would follow. It was he who had a right to us.

In this problem there was only one resolution. God could not change the law, which was the expression of His own being, but He could take the consequences of the trespass for His own being. So, Christ was able to take all the world's sins on Himself and suffer and die for them. Through this miracle of atonement, Satan lost his opportunity to act as prosecutor. It was his decisive defeat. Now he is cast out of heaven. It is the same fact that Jesus spoke about already in His lifetime: Now Satan would be cast out (John 12:31: compare with Luke 10:18).

The hymn says how it could happen. He was conquered "by the blood of the Lamb," through Jesus's sacrificial death, and through "the word of their testimony," meaning the gospel of the Savior, Jesus. The witnesses had made the testimony theirs. They had believed it. Only then could they strike the weapon out of the hands of the accuser.

Satan has also been cast to the earth. There he can continue the fight. However, he knows that his time is short. So, he does like Hitler and many other dictators did when their power began to falter. He mobilizes all his resources, scrapes together his reserves, pushes forward more and more ruthlessly, and finally throws off the mask. It is this that comes to characterize history's final stage. And here sounds again from heaven a "woe," the third and final. It sounds over the earth and sea and applies to the whole final act of the drama.

13-18 The Time of the Desert Church

So, the dragon has been cast down. His wrath now goes out over the woman, God's bride, the Church. However, the woman receives "the great eagle's wings." The picture was immediately conceivable for those who know the Old Testament. At Sinai, God had said to His saved people: "You yourselves have seen what I did to the Egyptians, and how I bore you on eagles' wings and brought you to myself" (Exodus 19:4). In some way, God comes to carry His bride on eagles' wings to the protection that only He knows. No one today can know how it will happen. However, so much we can understand—that in the last days of the world there will be a persecuted catacomb church that goes underground. Yet this comes to remain. This does not mean that all those who remain Christians escape death and martyrdom. Death threatens each and every one of us "who keep the commandments of God and hold to the testimony of Jesus," just as it was during the persecution in the Roman empire.

Again, we encounter the mysterious number that well may be counted to the words that will not be understood before their time is imminent. Neither is it possible to translate the river of death from the dragon's mouth into common newspaper English. We get the idea that the persecution comes to means something of a flood of sin that seems determined to wash away all traces of Christendom from the earth, but that God, in some way, allows it to disappear in the sand.

That the dragon set himself on the beach is only a threatening hint that his resources are not exhausted. He waits for something that shall come.

Revelation 13

1-4 The Beast

Now there follows the first of seven visions, which are all introduced with an "and I saw." It is possible that John himself conceived of it as a new cycle of seven events that complete and shed new light over the previous two. We see the world's drama from above, as a man only can see it when a person is lifted up above history and notices what really happened in the jumble that the world events seem to constitute. We are suddenly moved back to a point in time that we seemed to have passed by. We heard about the two witnesses that were murdered by the beast. Now we are carried back to the moment when the beast climbed up out of the sea (in actual fact from the bottomless pit—abyss—as it is said in 11:7). It is a monster that is reminiscent of the great dragon. It bares all the symbols and insignia of power: ten horns with the royal crown and seven heads. However, it is a question of a power hostile to God—the heads bare blasphemous names that show that here comes a possessor of power that has put itself in God's place. John does not need to ask what power it has. The beast looked like the summary of the four beasts in Daniel. It is most reminiscent of the fourth and the worst, but it also had features of the others. This beast represents a powerful state. And here, it was a question of the state in its absolute perfect power, a state that is demonic and hostile to God. The beast has the great power of the dragon, of Satan himself. Every Christian otherwise knew that all earthly powers received their authority from God. Jesus, Paul, and Peter had all emphasized this. God wants there to be a just order on earth. The state is placed to protect and maintain. The state can do this without being Christian. However, then it has to have respect for justice, for the law, which God has written even on the hearts of the heathen. It has something above it that it may not violate. If it sets itself over all else and takes power to determine what is just and unjust, then it is no longer a servant of God, but of Satan. Then it no longer has its authority from God but has put itself above God. And the vision John saw says with terrible clarity: It has received its power from the dragon, from the destroyer that defies God.

Naturally, John and his fellow Christians thought of the Roman state when they heard this. It was supposed to serve justice. Paul had still seen it in this way. However, from the day Nero unleashed his persecution, the situation was different. Perhaps John saw a direct hint of Rome and the Caesars in the number of heads, but it is uncertain because the same number is already found with the great beast in Daniel. Some have even tried to interpret the mortal wound that one of the heads received and still survived as one of the Caesars, namely Nero. There was a rumor that he would come back, perhaps from the realm of the dead or perhaps from lands where some thought he had successfully fled. However, all this is uncertain.

The only clear thing is that here we encounter a demonic attempt to set up a competitor to Christ, an anti-savior, who shall also have died and received life again. And at the same time, it is a picture of the life force in the ideologies that give birth to totalitarian states that are hostile to God. They can fail and be exposed for their demonic character. A person can believe that they made themselves impossible for all time. They still come back and live again.

Now the whole world submits to this beast. People worship it as a savior. We receive an eerie but not unrealistic perspective of the future. Of course, the worse the conditions get the more prone people become to praise the totalitarian state, the saving dictator, and the great leader.

5-10 The Demonic Totalitarian State

The beast had received its power from the dragon. Gradually it receives more power. It is also clear that this means with God's consent. Again, we encounter the mysterious number which sets a limit for the power of evil. It may go so far, but no further. This time would be hard enough. The state uses all its power to root out the Christian faith. Of course, it has declared itself sovereign. It is from itself and not from anything else that all power should proceed. Therefore, God and His will become something unbearable that cannot be allowed to exist. It can seem as if the state really has the advantage. It becomes the sole power, a superpower that crushes all opposition and rules over the whole earth. It regulates everything. A person must be registered to be able to show the right stamp, not only on paper but in his soul, so that he has the right views, uses the right phrases, makes himself approving or protesting, according to what the state does. Otherwise, a person is shut out and may neither buy nor sell. And then it is not easy to stand fast in their faith. However, there are some who do it. Christ has their names written in the book of life. This does not mean that some are predetermined to salvation and others to damnation. However, God, who has overseen the whole of the course of the world, knows who comes to preserve His love. He loves the others also and is serious about His call, but He knows who will come to answer yes and stand fast. They are the children of His joy, and their names are written in a book that will not be opened before it is all over.

In this extreme distress, it does not do to make any external opposition to the demonic state. If a person is imprisoned and dragged away, then you have to take the martyrdom. A person shall not take up arms. He who does this will perish. Here comes the great test for the Christian faith: to remain steadfast and suffer for their faith, certain that finally Christ will be victorious.

The text for the last verse is uncertain. The translation we have goes back to a textual variant that is late and incorrect. And perhaps the next to last sentence ought to read: If anyone is slain with the sword, so shall he let himself be killed.

11-17 The False Prophet

Then vision number two comes. Yet another monster rises up, this time from the earth. It only has two horns, and they are similar to the Lamb's. However, John immediately hears that the beast speaks a different language than Christ. And soon it is clear what it is a matter of. The beast has received a servant who is clothed with extraordinary power and becomes a sort of grand vizier or vice president, or perhaps rather a propaganda minister and an ideologue of the state.

John becomes so eager that he begins to speak in the present tense concerning all that the new monster does. Here the totalitarian state receives its master of ceremonies and culture leader, such as people want to have. He does great signs and miracles. People want to have a miracle. They are drawn to the sensational. They want to be impressed. So, the new monster creates a false faith and a false cult around the picture that convinces people to glorify the beast. The new monster has imposed upon him the task that the Spirit has in Christ's kingdom: to create faith. We glimpse a satanic mirror image of the holy Trinity. The Dragon, who is Satan, sends the beast, the anti-Christ, and this carries out his work through its representative, he who will later be called the false prophet.

For John and his contemporaries this had a horrible actuality. Everywhere in the empire there were erected pictures of Caesar to which a person was supposed to sacrifice. It was a sign that a person was a loyal citizen. He who declined was killed. It only required offering a little incense to the idol's altar. If a person did this, he was free. However, this bit of incense means that a person received the mark of the beast. What John could not imagine was that he had seen a vision that would take on new realities in constantly new situations, where Christ's followers would be placed before the state's and the public's opinions, and the apostate church's demand to accept what all the others had accepted.

Already in the Roman Empire it happened that people were denied the opportunity to make a living for themselves if a person did not join in. In our days, the totalitarian states have far greater opportunities to rob a recalcitrant Christian of his fundamental rights. Imagine what the future can bare in its womb.

18 The Number of the Beast

The sentence with the number 666 has not been successfully interpreted in a convincing way. John apparently knows that this had something to say to those he wrote to. Yet already with the church father Irenaeus—barely a hundred years later—we see that no one was clear about the meaning. The "number" likely means that a person counted the sum of the numbers corresponding to the letters. The letters were namely used by both Jews and Greeks the way we use numbers. A person can get both Nero and Domintianus and a series of other names to give the sum 666 if a person uses more or less meaningful operations. "Caesar Nero" is the proposal that has been most popular in our era, but the counting comes together only if one uses Hebrew letters—which John's audience did not know—and, in addition, spelled in a less than common way. Moreover, it is not certain that it was meant to account for the numerical worth of the numbers. The numerology of antiquity knew other complicated ways to find hidden messages in a number. And there were some who thought that John did not at all wish to admonish his audience to go home and count. Perhaps here he only asks a question of them: which number fits you? And so, he himself gives the answer: 666. Because 7 was God's number, 6 was a step lower, however much a person repeats it. And it is precisely this that characterizes the beast. With all his fearful power, he still comes a step under God and draws the shortest straw.

However, a Christian must say again: The day we need to know it, then we will also understand it. It does not serve to speculate before then.

Revelation 14

1-5 The 144,000 on Mount Zion

The 14th chapter of Revelation contains a series of unresolved mysteries, and a commentator feels admonished to be more careful than ever. It starts already in the first scene, the fourth of the visions that John now describes in sequence. What is it he sees? Where is Mount Zion? In the heavens or on earth? The commentators are deeply divided. Perhaps we stand before the deep mystery that the Church exists simultaneously in heaven and on earth. God's people are found on both sides of the border of time and, although separated, they celebrate the divine service together.

Which is this new song? John does not say. We probably do best to cease questioning. It is enough to know that the heavens are full of praise, mighty like the thunder of great waters, full of the beauty that our earthly music can sometimes resemble. It is a new song, which can never empty its possibility to beauty and joy. This can also be learned by men, but only if they have received God's seal. There are those who remain deaf without the ability to perceive the hymn that still belongs to the innermost essence of existence.

Who are the 144,000? Must it not be the same as we had heard about before who had been sealed with God's seal? But how can it then be described as John does here? Is it only men who were sealed? Have they all lived a celibate life? It literally reads that they have not "defiled themselves with women." Does this mean that a sexual life is something impure of itself? Such thoughts can be found in the early church already at the time when John wrote, but they are rejected by the New Testament. Does John merely mean that there is no living in fornication? It literally says that they are *"Jungfrur."*[1] This word jungfru could also be used for males. Does it here mean to live in celibacy or does it have another transferred meaning? Even in the Old Testament it was known that God's people were His bride that should belong to Him alone. Paul speaks about the church as a bride, betrothed to Christ to be set before Him as a pure virgin (2 Corinthians 11:2). According to the good rule that "Scripture shall interpret Scripture," it is perhaps best to understand this word in that spirit.

"Firstfruits" were the first of the new harvest that was dedicated to God. In the same way, the 144,000 are the first part of the unfathomable harvest. What was sacrificed was flawless. The thought lying behind the words "no lie in their mouths,"

---

[1] This is a bit hard to translate in English. The word jungfru/Jungfrau could be translated maiden, but literally means a virgin girl, composed of two words that mean young and woman, not just a virgin, and maiden does not really mean that in English.

and "blameless" does not mean that they had been free of sin. Like all the others, they had to "wash their clothes and make them white in the blood of the Lamb."

6-13 The Last Rebellion

The next vision—the fifth—carries us to the last moment before the eternal irrevocable decision. There comes a threefold commandment from heaven. The first is the last call to come along before it is definitively too late. Here too the questions pile up. Why is this called a gospel? It is, of course, a question of a simple obedience to God. The gospel may well be thought to lay in the fact that this invitation comes even in the last minute of the world. But why is it then called an "eternal" gospel?

The second message is the shaking news that Babylon has fallen. Here for the first time in Revelation we encounter "Babylon" as the name of the "great city," the world city, the self-glorifying culture that is hostile to God, the human kingdom that wanted to be self-sufficient. We do not hear when it has fallen. That comes later. We touch upon the border between time and eternity, where the moment flows together with the past and future.

The third message directs itself to those who believe. We must read it just as a word to the Christians in the seven congregations that now stand before the threat about a hard persecution. Everyone can count on being denounced, incarcerated, commanded to deny Christ and to sacrifice to Caesar, perhaps under torture, to then be tormented and shamefully executed, perhaps in an arena amidst the jubilation of thousands of spectators who revel in seeing the Christians torn apart by wild animals. The temptation to apostatize must be unfathomable. It is to such people the message is directed. It wants to clarify how foolish and fateful it will still be to try save their lives. He who receives the mark of the beast certainly escapes the arena, but there comes a day when he shall stand before Christ and all His angels. He who denied Him comes to receive His judgment "before the holy angels and before the Lamb." What the judgment means is described with fearful words. It is a question of pictures. Fire and sulfur had destroyed Sodom and Gomora. However, the actual fact is in all its seriousness already in the words of Jesus concerning the great judgment. There are those who "shall go away to eternal punishment."

So, a person remembers that this word is not intended for those who believe. God calls through the gospel. No one can be scared into heaven. It is directed to those who stand before the persecution and can expect the worst that can happen to him on earth. Then he can be helped by hearing them.

Finally, a particular message comes to those who still come to die "in the Lord," so in faith in Jesus before they have been able to see Him come as the victor. They may hear that they are saved. Again, we encounter questions. Were they not blessed before they died in the Lord? Why are just these blessed? Perhaps because they escape the last great tribulation? What does it mean that they can rest? Is there no work in heaven? And how can their deeds follow them? Is it for the sake of works that they should be blessed?

All such questions are rooted in an incorrect manner of reading. What we have here is not a timeless teaching but a word of comfort to people in extreme distress. When the persecution breaks loose everyone shall know that death carries him straight into the rest before Jesus. For "the pain," a word is used that means wear, tear, and torment. This will be over forever. However, the deeds follow along, those which a person did from love for his Lord Christ. These are no basis for salvation. That foundation is far better; it is found at Golgotha. However, to have been able to serve is, and remains, something to be thankful for. Perhaps this shall show itself that it bears more fruit than one himself knew or was able to see. The deeds may in some way continue. The pain is over, but not the service that is a constant new joy.

In this passage the wine of wrath is spoken about twice. The picture is from the Old Testament (Isaiah 51:17, Jeremiah 25:15). Babylon let the people drink the wine of fornication, its wine of lechery and godlessness, and they drank it willingly. But then they also drank the wine of God's wrath at the same time. They would notice it when the moment was imminent, the moment that the three angels now made known.

14-20 The Harvest is Fully Ripe

A new vision follows with new mysteries. Who is it "that looks like a son of man"? The picture is taken from Daniel (7:13), and immediately we think of Christ. But how then could the other angels speak to him as he did? And why does it say that "another angel" stepped forth? A person could translate it, "another, an angel" (so that one translates Luke 23:32 "two others, who were criminals" where it literally says "two other criminals"). However, the same expression will later appear two more times, and there it must mean "another angel."

We can drop the question because the answer does not matter. What the vision says is that the harvest is now finally ripe. God has no more to wait for. Now the harvest can begin. ("Scythe" is a misleading translation. There were no scythes at that time, and a scythe in a vineyard is silly.) Harvest time had come, that which Jesus speaks about in the parable about the wheat and the tares. Now the Master sends His servants out (Matthew 13:39f). Even the picture of the vineyard was well known to all, both as a picture of Israel and of the church. Meanwhile, here it speaks of "the vineyard of the world." This means the whole of humanity. And the ripeness is not a ripeness for God's kingdom, but for judgment. God has waited long enough; now the clusters are cut down and thrown into the wrath of God's great wine press. Here again comes a picture that is hard to interpret. What does it mean that the wine press is found outside the city? What do the 1,600 stadia mean? This corresponds to 180 miles. It can be seen to correspond to Palestine's northernmost point to its southern border, and some have speculated over what sort of role the Holy Land can play in this last event. But it is likely as symbolic as the 144,000. Four used to be considered the world's number. Ten stood for the whole. If now a person squares both the numbers and multiplies the numbers a man gets from this with each other, the result is 1,600. So, it could mean the whole of the old world. However, all such speculations are uncertain. The actual picture is vivid and clear: from the wine press streams the red blood of the grapes. There is a flood that overflows; it climbs a meter high and spreads out over the ground as far as the eye can see. But what does it indicate? A fearful shedding of blood when the grapes of wrath are ripe, and God lets people harvest the fruit of their endless selfishness, their abuse of reason, their spite for the laws that the Creator has written in their heart? We think this but cannot be sure.

Revelation 15

1-4 The Bowls of Wrath and the Great Song of Praise

The sixth and seventh visions—if now John really attached some importance to the number seven here—constitute a transition to the seven bowls of wrath that shall follow. First the seven angels step forward. The vision is not described; John only notes that with their seven plagues God's wrathful judgment is fulfilled.

Then the scene grows, and we again stand before the throne, just as in the first series of visions. Again, the sea of glass spreads out before us, but now it is "mingled with fire," perhaps lighted from within, perhaps permeated by streaks of light, perhaps reflecting the flames from the apocalyptic fire burning the world. Standing at its edge are the victors who conquered Satan's forces on earth, which now passes away. They sing a song—likely meaning one and the same—that is called the song of Moses and the Lamb. It does not say why, but Moses stands for the Old Testament and the Lamb for the New, and the meaning is that all God's work in the light of eternity appears as one great unity, a divine harmony that immediately causes the song of praise to break out. Great and wonderful is God's work—and righteousness. Here in the hour of judgment, God's people rejoice in His righteousness. All God's ways are just. Perhaps here we have the answer to the question: how shall anyone be able to rejoice in heaven when some others are lost? The answer is that God alone is holy. When a person finally sees God, such as He really is the true good, the only truth, and see how completely incompatible His being is with all selfishness and impurity, then a person understands why God did as He did—and is amazed that He will pay such a high price to save us. Finally, the greater question is not how God can condemn anyone, but how has He waited so long with His judgment?

15:5-16:1 The Bowls of Wrath are Poured Out

The temple is opened again. While the scenes develop, the view in heaven opens and now John sees the Temple again, which in some way is a prototype for the tabernacle in the desert, "the tent of witnesses." There the seven angels step out, clothed as priests in white linen with golden sashes just like Christ Himself (1:13). They receive the seven golden bowls that are filled with God's wrath. Then the temple is filled with smoke, just like Isaiah saw it in his vision (Isaiah 6:4). John understands that it is God's glory that descends, and that God dwells in the cloud, just as He did in the pillar of cloud in the desert or in the cloud on the mount of transfiguration. So, no one could enter the temple. The wrath of judgment must first have its course.

Revelation 16

2-7 The First Three Bowls of Wrath

For a third time, a series of visions begins, which John clearly marks with the number seven. We have climbed yet another step up in the "spiral." That which happens has a certain likeness with that which already has happened. The similarity with the seven trumpets is somewhat striking. And there are similarities in the history of the world, even back to the plagues that struck Egypt during the time of Moses. However, at the same time, it is a matter of something completely new. When the trumpets sound, a third of the world is struck. In the catastrophe, there is a warning, a call to repentance, an opportunity for salvation. Now all is struck. The world has chosen the beast. God no longer waits but settles the account with evil. The seven bowls of wrath are part of His judgment.

We find ourselves in a world that passes away. That which happens cannot be described with the help of such as happens today. It does not do to translate these visions into common prose. No German in the 1930s could have imagined how his country would look fifteen years later in the last days of the Third Reich. And that was merely a matter of an historic catastrophe—certainly one that more than any earlier catastrophe can help us understand how it will be during the last days of the world, when the kingdom of the beast perishes.

So here are questions about catastrophes that most deeply meant that the Creator stops holding His creation together. He withholds the protection He had given the spiteful and unthankful. They may experience what it is like to be without God. This applies to bodily tissues as well as the water of the sea and the springs in the ground. All is destroyed, persistent and sore, toxic and disgusting. And from the point of view where we now stand, it shows itself to be something consistent and inevitable, something that the truth and justice demand.

What is meant by the "angel in charge of the waters" we cannot know. Earlier we heard about angels who have authority over the winds (7:1) and over fire (14:18), and we can at least imagine that God's servants in the heavenly world also have their tasks in our world and in that which daily happens around us. That the altar spoke perhaps means no more than what John said earlier: He heard a voice that came from the four horns of the altar (9:13).

8-21 Hardening and Perishing

With the fourth bowl of wrath the total hardening comes to daylight. The sun scorches the people with an insufferable heat. Then they begin to curse God. They blaspheme; they revile and mock Him—all this is contained in the Greek word that

John uses—despite everything they know that exists. They do like so many modern men: they say that He does not exist; they live as if He did not exist, but when they are struck by misfortune, they reprimand God for being so cruel.

When then the fifth bowl is emptied upon the beast's throne—this is already evidence of God's sovereign power—catastrophe falls upon the whole world, the whole of the existence that man has made for himself with the help of God's gifts, and in spite of God Himself. The light goes out. The whole system is deadlocked. The totalitarian state no longer functions, despite terror and force. Life becomes unbearable. It is in the night's long dark hours that we feel the pain the worst. So now the kingdom of the beast sits in the dark, and the people bite their tongues in pain. But no one repents. They blame God for everything.

The sixth bowl takes away the last protections from chaos. We have already seen that the great Euphrates river was the border to the east. Here it stands as a symbol for the last protection against war and destruction. Now it is gone. The way is open for all the powers of violence. The beast, that thinks that his days are numbered, acts like Hitler and gathers up all he can gather and throws it into the fight, taking it with him into destruction. John sees it in a picture that is not easily forgotten. Frogs come out of the triumvirate of evil's mouth: the dragon (Satan), the beast (his earthly representative), and the false prophet (the beast's propogandist). The frogs go out into the world until all of them have power and gather them up to the last battle. This is an eerie picture of propaganda, long before the time of mass media.

Armageddon means Mount Megiddo. Meigddo lies in a hillock at the foot of Carmel where the great plain begins. There were ancient battlefields here, where hosts have drawn up over the millennia and clashed with each other. Perhaps the names shall be mentioned again when the world experiences the last, totally destructive outbreak of war's insanity. Perhaps it is only mentioned as a symbol for blood drenched ground.

The little outcry that breaks up the description (in verse 15) is typical for an early Christian prophet. We can imagine that the divine services, both the sermon and the prophecy, as well as the prayers, in this way could be broken by a prophetic interjection. Because they come from the Lord, they would have free course in the congregation, independent from the order that a person otherwise followed (that this could have certain problems associated with it and a certain order needed to be created, even for the free prophets, we see from the instructions Paul gives in 1 Corinthians 14:29f.).

The last bowl of wrath means the end. A voice—that must be God's own—says: it is done. On the cross, Christ could say, "It is finished." God had done what could be done to open the opportunity of salvation to everyone. Now God has done what remained to do: He has offered salvation to all. He waited as long as there was something to wait for. Now He has drawn the line and settled the account with evil. Here is the final point of the drama that began when God said His "Let there be!" The time has come for a new creation.

The old creation is all together destroyed. The great city, the great Babylon, the proud creation of man, the godless culture, now stands in ruins. Hundred-pound hail stones rain upon it from heaven. John could not have known what rain of destruction people would pour out over its great cities with the help of their abused reason. We sometimes understand his visions better than he himself. And still, we can do no more than imagine what it is about.

This belongs to the picture that man himself may be there to carry out God's destruction. The beast gathers up the powers of the earth for the last destructive war. And it is precisely their selfishness that becomes the tool for God's justice. Perhaps they come to take part in another way too when the last plague falls upon the beast's kingdom.

Revelation 17

1-6 The Prostitute and the Beast

One of the seven angels who emptied the bowls of wrath takes John with him to let his see the judgment that falls upon "the great whore." John can see what the angel means. It is the question of a new incarnation of the world powers hostile to God, something we would call the secularized society of abundance with its status symbols and gadgets, its luxury and worship of sex.

John is carried out into the desert. It was in the desert that Israel received its law and entered into the covenant with God. They had lived in the presence of God there, directly from God's hand. Then temptations came in the rich land that flowed with milk and honey, the land with vineyards and Baal idols. The desert was the right place to see the great whore with undisturbed eyes. In the stillness before God, she seems frightened and disgusting, where she comes riding on the seven headed beast that John easily recognized. He had already seen it climb up from the bottomless pit in order to take control over men and establish the demonic state, that which would usurp the place of God and demand total submission under its absolute power. It is this that now carries the great whore. She sits there in her bright colors, covered in jewelry, and drunk. And on her forehead, she—as the whores of Rome used to do—bore her name. She is The Great Babylon.

What was Babylon? It had once been a world city and a mighty power, which had crushed the kingdom of Judah and carried her people into captivity. Now it was laid waste, but for those who read the Bible, the name Babylon had for a long time become a synonym for the kingdom of Satan and all its manifestations, including the political. At this time, there were many who saw Rome as the place where it most clearly stepped forth in the day.

The whore held the symbol of her power in her hand: the golden cup from which the people drank to their intoxication. This wine had two ingredients: fornication and idolatry. Abominations (or scandals) were what the Jews called the idolatry they had to fight with so hard, the Canaanite fertility rites and their idols of Baal and Asherah with their wild feasts and debauchery. Now they encountered the same spirit in the Hellenistic culture with their worship of sexuality. Idolatry and fornication belonged together. Apostasy from the Lord was spiritual adultery. God's people were His bride and were not to belong to anyone else. However, in practice, this spiritual fornication included the bodily, such as life once was in antiquity.

The prostitute rode on the beast. She had it good in the kingdom of the antichrist. There was a common interest between them. He who lives to get the most of enjoyment from life must experience the gospel as a threat, something that a person wants to escape seeing and hearing. The hatred of Christ is always a temptation in the kingdom that is simply of this world, and it can as often as not break out into bloody persecutions. There is a need to silence the gospel. It seems beautiful when it can finally be declared dead. The woman was drunk with the blood of the martyrs.

The Greek word that is here translated with "witness"[1] is precisely "martyr." From its basic meaning of "witness," it was already on the way to become synonymous with blood witness, martyr.

7-18 The Mystery of the Beast and the Prostitute

Now something follows that is unusual in the Book of Revelation: an oral commentary on the vision that John is allowed to see. He learns "the mystery" of it. The Greek word is "*mysterium*." It is not a question of a riddle that can be solved with the help of a sharp mind and experience, but of a mystery of the same sort as "the mystery of Christ," something that God reveals to His own, something they themselves could never comprehend on their own. Now we hear what the mystery with visions like this is; it does not mean that we may know what it "essentially means." So a person often thinks concerning the matter: a person has been able to see a picture that essentially represents something else, and now they may know what it "really" represents. However, this is not how it is with God's mysteries. Certainly, they can be matters of "symbols." However, the symbols accommodate a reality. This reality can certainly also be expressed with other words or pictures, but these can never replace the symbols. What we receive as an "explanation" is never exhausted. It says the same thing as the picture, the vision, the symbol, though in a different way. Perhaps it gives us a counterpart to the reality that the symbol speaks about. Or it sheds light on it from a new side. So, the prostitute's mystery is not that there will, at some time, exist a person, or city, or state that she represents. Rather that it is a question of "the mystery of her being" (as the word is rendered in verse 5). The mystery is that she, just as she shows herself, reveals a reality that a person can then recognize in both history and in their environment.

Therefore, it is said that "understanding and also wisdom" are needed to understand this mystery (or "understanding that is wisdom" as it is literally written). The understanding is our natural reason with its ability to observe and logic. It is not sufficient. It needs "wisdom," by which the Bible means a gift from God that makes it possible for a person to understand what He means when He reveals His mysteries.

Concerning the beast, we now know that its seven heads are (not mean!) seven mountains and seven kings. The seven mountains are immediately thought to be Rome's seven hills, and this is certainly the meaning. This says that the prostitute,

---

[1] Here Bo Giertz is commenting on how he translated this text in his translation that accompanied this commentary.

the great Babylon, is enthroned upon the seven mountains. Worse is it with the seven kings. Some have tried to show that they touch upon Roman Caesars, but the counting does not work. This shall namely be written during Caesar Domitianus, who was the 8th, 9th, or 11th of the Caesars, depending on how a person counts. Here it clearly says that John lives during the 6th. This would be Caesar Galba (68-69) or possibly Vespasian (69-79), again depending on how a person counts. The difficulty is so obvious that people during the glory days of liberal theology did not see any other thing to do than assume that Revelation was collated from different sources of which one came in the year 69; this was so unskillfully done that incompatible sources came to stand right next to each other. It is a highly arbitrary way to come to terms with a text that a person finds hard to understand. The difficulty is usually because a person reads the text with modern lenses that do not fit it.

We stand before a mystery, which we cannot resolve. We can comfort ourselves knowing that neither could the expositors of the early church. We may note that the text itself says that it touches upon something that will happen in the future. And we have good reason to try understanding it from the symbolic language that the Old Testament uses, and which immediately tells us that this text—even if it also has something to say about concrete figures and places—first and foremost wants to say something about the beast and his kingdom.

The head and the mountains and kings altogether are namely symbols for power. If the heads stand for will and authority, then the mountains are symbols of the power's lasting foundation. The number seven is the divine, essential, perfection. The beast's seven heads, like the dragon's, then mean the claim to divine power. Here comes the authority, the foundation, the king.

Some have tried to apply this mysterious speech about "he who was, who is not, but who shall come but go to destruction" to Caesar Nero, who some believed would return. It is possible that John has figured that the anti-Christ would manifest himself in this way. However, the essential thing, the beast's true being, is something different. It is to appear as a counter-savior, a demonic and false copy of Christ, who is believed to be dead but shall come again. John uses the same verb that is included in the word for Christ's return, his Parousia, when he speaks about how the beast "comes again." The imitation extends that far. The beast shall say, like Christ (1:17), I was dead, but see, I live. However, then comes the addition, the decisive—he goes to meet his death. Yet Christ could say: I live forever and ever.

So, the beast has already appeared. Now he hides himself, but it will appear again. We at least imagine how it expresses itself in world history. The beast with its kingdom can appear—at least ideologically—in concrete figures and particular events. Then it seems to disappear again. Yet it returns, perhaps more visible than ever. And finally, it comes in earnest to establish his totalitarian superstate. For the moment, it can be hidden and even declared dead. It belongs to the great irony in the 20th century, the cruelest and most bloodstained in history, that within Christian circles it was possible to say, the devil is a myth.

The ten horns that are ten kings apparently belong to the future. They can well enough be understood as an indication that the anti-Christ in his kingdom receives a total affiliation from the powerbrokers on earth and that this becomes a total alignment. It is this total world power that begins the last great persecution, and which will finally suffer defeat when Christ comes. However, before this there comes a strange interlude: the beast and its vassals turn against the great prostitute. She believed that she sat securely under the beast's protection. Now instead, she is plundered. The wealth, welfare, and the life that received its purpose through enjoyment is finished.

And in all this lies God's judgment. All the evil powers have finally done His errands and carried out His judgment that must come when one obeys them.

The ten vassals come to the power "in the same hour as the beast." A person could also translate it: They receive their power together with the beast for a single hour. In such a case, it must be "for a short time."

A person ought to note that the beast can, at the same time, be said to be one of the heads that it bears. It is not a lack of logic, but an expression for how the beast is a spiritual power with worldwide dimensions that can take form in different people and events in different times. Therefore, a person can encounter it in changing forms, which are still children of the same spirit. When we get a step higher in "the spiral," we can think that we encounter the beast seriously for the first time. At the same time, we can look back on the kingdoms and dictators where it manifested itself in the past. The beast has many heads. This is part of its mystery.

Revelation 18

1-3 The Fall of Great Babylon!

A messenger comes from heaven. His power is apparent. The whole earth is lit up. John has heard his message before (14:8): Fallen, fallen is Babylon the great! Only now does it fall so that John can see it. And even now it somewhat sounds like a prophecy. We touch upon the border between time and eternity. What for us is a series of events in time is, from the eternity of God, a single reality. What God has now determined is already a fact. Babylon had fallen. Already when it fell in sin and apostatized from God, "the great city" had fallen and bore within it the final catastrophe, that which is now revealed for all. The reason is indicated with the same words as before: her wine of wrath and fornication. Fornication was both spiritual and bodily, both her unfaithfulness to God and her worship of sex. And the wine of fornication was, at the same time, a wine of wrath.

The visions from the great Babylon's defeat are full of allusions to the Scriptures. The prophets had prophesied how Babel and Tyre would be punished for their arrogance. Long before Jesus, the Jews had understood that this applied to all the powers of the world and the authorities that blasphemed God. As a pious Jew, John knew his Bible. In his vision he saw how the Scriptures were fulfilled. When he describes what he saw, it constantly happens in Scripture. He does not cite and never refers to the prophets. Yet a person understands that he has seen the connection with all these new things that he sees and that which God once revealed to the fathers. About one fifth of this chapter can be found in small fragments of the Old Testament (Isaiah 13 and 47, Jeremiah 50-51, Ezekiel 26-27). Some scholars who like to imagine that John worked somewhat like an academic think that a chapter like this is hobbled together from different written sources. This is to totally misunderstand both the prophets and vision's essence.

4-8 The Day of Retribution

John still hears a voice from heaven. Now it is revealed what it means that God judges. He withdraws. He is finished with His protection and His good gifts. The great city had defeated them, enjoyed them, made themselves sure and hard in their conviction to be able to hold them. Now God commands His people to withdraw. Even before, the command had applied in questions of the world's godless manner of living. Paul was able to say it with great emphasis (2 Corinthians 6:14). Now the final exodus happens, like Lot's from Sodom. God withdraws His hand. All of His servants, even the heavenly, follow. The evil powers are given free rein to play. They occupy the great city—and then the judgment comes. The great city was the self-glorified civilization, he who was himself nearest and believed that he ruled over the wealth of the earth, which the insane exploited to create a hitherto never before seen abundance. They had worshiped power and declared that there is no other right that the state found to impose good. Now they receive all that they have done to others.

Who did the voice speak to? John does not say and perhaps only knew that finally it was God who spoke. Perhaps He spoke to the angels of judgment. Or perhaps to the men and the powers on earth, which suffered from the world's evil and themselves were just as evil, and who now received the freedom to settle the score—and become the vessels of judgment, both for their enemies and for themselves.

9-19 The World's Danger concerning the Defeat of the World Powers

Thus, the catastrophe had come—suddenly and surprisingly for all of those who believed in the powers of this world and meant that reason and their own well understood interests were the supportive forces in their culture. They did not think that it was the Creator who in His goodness held everything together with power. Now when the catastrophe comes, everything is destroyed. Perhaps it is not so hard for us to think that—we who experience how the whole of our daily life become more and more dependent on a complicated and vulnerable machinery that provides us with what we need daily.

In his vision, John sees how the catastrophe hits three categories of people. First are the governing, the top of the world kingdom, they who had foremost opportunity to see to the good and who had whole heartedly accepted faith in this kingdom that is only of this world. Then it is the merchants, those who gathered all that the abundant society needed and were themselves right through humanity's never measured desire for ever higher standards. And finally, it was they who were responsible for communication and transportation. All are signs with concrete pictures from the Roman Empire's glory days, but it is not hard to see how these pictures would be able to be applied today.

Now the disturbing thing is that all those who complain about the catastrophe have no sympathy for the great city. They only think of themselves. No one extends a helping hand. All stand a long way off and look on. What terrifies them is that the whole could go so fast. They had invested in the great prostitute and her manner of life. They had never dreamed that such an abundant society could be completely destroyed so fast. And they had not thought of what fateful consequences it would have for all that they themselves invested in, that which would give meaning to their lives. Even in their complaint, they call the city "the mighty." It is the same word that the angel used for the Lord God, He who judged her. He alone was mighty.

The listing of all the wares that were freighted to the great city gives us a good picture of the status of the time and the gadgets. Some of these words are so special that today we do not rightly know what it is about. "All sorts of scented woods" literally says "all sorts of thuja wood." Even with us, a person can sometimes come across woodwork of the wood that we call thuja, but we are not sure what the Greeks meant by the same word. When the translation talks about "rare spices," the original text says "*amomon*," so far as one knows an Indian spice that among other things was used to perfume cosmetic hair products. And when finally, it says—literally—"bodies and human souls," it touches on slaves. For antiquity, it was only a matter of "bodies." John adds, with a tone of accusation, the biblical expression "human souls." For the Jews, it meant people with body and soul, wares that God created in His image.

When John describes the complaint of the sailors, he transitions to tell how it *was*. It is clear that he describes what he saw before his eyes. There stand all the sailors in the whole world. It is not a question of a single city that burns, it is the world power, the whole of the secularized culture, that which finally turned its back to God. All must see what happened. For a long way off a person sees the smoke rise from the burning city—that too is a picture with eerie actuality for us people in the twentieth century.

20 Rejoice over God's Justice

Now is an admonition to rejoice for God's judgment follows for all of heaven and all God's servants. Some consider this admonition highly inappropriate: Can a person rejoice over God's judgment? They usually forget that they, at the same time, complain that God does not judge. They cannot understand that God allows so much evil on earth. It is not seldom that they say they cannot believe in a good and righteous God precisely because so much injustice happens. Even the Bible is full of such questions: How can God permit? We may remember that John speaks to all men, who without exception lived under the threat of torture, abuse, and murder—perhaps while providing amusement for the great audience in the amphitheater. They really knew the seriousness in the question: how can God allow? We may also remember that the Book of Revelation applies to the end of time, when humanity says its final no to God and finally chooses to go its own evil way. Then God finally intervenes. It is this "Finally!" that releases the jubilee in heaven.

21-24 The Content of God's Judgment

Now John may see how one of the angels performed an action with prophetic meaning—as the prophets also did. He slung a huge stone into the sea, where it disappears. The end comes just as violently and quickly when God has waited long enough. And then it is really over. God was the giver of all good gifts. When God finally withdraws because they have been abused, then everything stops. Nothing functions without God. Above all these goods that even the godless enjoy—music, art, job satisfaction, life's amenities, and joys—a person can now write, "never more."

The great city had ruled with the help of its wealth, and its finances were the result of its power. It had deceived all the people with its "sorcery," its ability to attract with false reflections and the appearance of glory and imaginary benefits. Now it is all over. All that which was of real value, it came from God. Yet everyone wants to keep Him completely shut out, so completely that people killed those who confessed Him.

All the blood that was shed by the martyrs has been shed in the great city, it finally says. Here we receive one last reminder that the great city has no particular place on a map. It is a question of the world city, the kingdom of Satan, the society hostile to God, where people believe they rule alone, but, in reality, serve the beast.

Revelation 19

1-5 The Joy of Victory in Heaven

Silence has spread over the fall of Babylon. However, John hears a peculiar noise. He cannot really describe it. However, he comprehends the words. It is a mighty *Halleluja*, the most concentrated expression of the Psalms for the joy before God's face. That it is used in the early church's divine service is certain, but strangely enough, we do not encounter it anywhere in the New Testament except for in this chapter from John. John does not know who is actually singing. However, he sees how the heavenly liturgy before God's throne confirms its song of praise with its Halleluja and his Amen. And the song of praise again moves around this, that now God—finally—rights the ship and shows His power. People wonder how God can allow so much evil. They hit upon the strangest theories to defend Him, even that He, in actual fact, is not almighty. The heavenly hosts know better. However, even they seem to have wondered how He could tarry so long with setting a limit to the evil. Of course, He had sovereign power to crush all evil. However, the evil people were so dear to Him that He tarried to the very last with His judgment, so long that even His servants stood in wonder. Now the smoke from the great city rises, the smoke that on earth awoke fear and complaint for lost money. In heaven, a person sees that this proved that God is both almighty and just.

6-8 The Marriage of the Lamb

Again, the song of praise from the unknown crowds sounds. Now it is mighty like the roar of surf and thunder. Once again it is a jubilant Halleluja because God has taken control. Yet it is something more: the jubilee that the time is ready for the Lamb's wedding. The bride makes herself ready. Already in the Old Testament the bride is God's people who have the Lord as its true bridegroom. Jesus called Himself the bridegroom, and Paul says that His bride is the church. She has looked forward to this moment in hope. Faithfulness has cost her persecution and shame. Now the wedding shall happen.

So, it is the church that is Christ's bride. The individual Christian is a guest at the wedding invited to Lamb's wedding.

The bride is contrasted with the great prostitute. The contrast is striking: the prostitute is flamboyant and glitters with jewels; the bride is clothed in pure white. "It was granted her" to clothe herself, is how it literally reads. People have debated whether "righteous deeds" really is the right translation of the words that John uses to declare what the white dress means. Usually the word means a command, a legal provision. In Romans (5:16) Paul uses it for God's justifying judgment, but that is an exception. There is nothing unreasonable in that here John means the righteous deeds of the Christians. He has said before that it is a gift of God, a grace, that the bride may wear the dress. The great crowd before the throne has washed their clothes in the blood of the Lamb. However, he who has done this will also preserve their dress pure and, through forgiveness, this is possible. Christ wants to present the church as His bride "splendor...holy without blemish." (Ephesians 5:27)

9-10 The Word from God Himself

Ever since the beginning of chapter 17, John has been able to listen and receive spoken words rather than visions. There are those who think that here we again have the number seven, seven messages about Babylon and the prostitute, their perishing and their contrast, the bride. Now there is a summary. Someone—the same angel who spoke from the beginning (17:1)?—commands John to write down what he now hears: A beatification of guests at the Lamb's wedding. Then a statement follows about "these words," most probably all the words John was able to hear ever since he was carried out into the desert and was able to see the prostitute on the beast. It is God who speaks now. John is deeply shaken and falls down to worship. He is reprimanded. They who present the Word from God are only servants. John is himself one such servant, just like all those who have "the testimony of Jesus." Literally it says the "Jesus witness." In Greek, it can mean both the testimony *from* Jesus, that which He presents, and the testimony *about* Jesus, that which speaks about Him. Here we can figure both meanings. It is this that is the Spirit of prophecy. Prophecy is inspired by the Spirit, and the Spirit witnesses about Jesus (John 15:26). The prophet's deepest mystery is that he makes Jesus alive and that Jesus Himself speaks through His Spirit.

11-16 Christ is Drawn out to Fight

John sees the heavens open again—a sure sign that something great is about to happen and that we can expect a new series of visions. We are carried into a new cycle, into yet a new plan where we may see what we have already seen, but in a new light that exposes more of the event's real contents, as simultaneously new things are revealed to us.

John sees a white horse with a rider. Immediately, he remarks that it is something other than the rider he saw when the first seal was broken (6:2). Then it was the Lamb who broke the seal. Now it is the Lamb, Christ, who rides out. He is still that Lamb who was slain, and His mantel is soaked in blood—even His own blood, though some will see it as the enemy's and invoke a prophecy by Isaiah (63:1f). Now He comes as the King of Kings, in His divine power. We sometimes forget that Christ who died for everyone, is also He to whom all judgment has been transferred

(John 5:22). He is placed for the fall or rectification. The world that did not want to receive Him as a savior, now receives Him as the knight on the white horse.

Four times he mentions his name in this vision. First, he is called "Faithful and True." He does as he promised, and it is as he said. Next, he speaks about the name that none of us knows. The Son's deepest being is a mystery that no one but the Father knows. However, in the letter to Philadelphia (3:12), we heard the promise that he who wins the victory will bear the Lord's new name. The third name is "God's word." It is used here in the same meaning as in John's prologue. Christ is the Word. And the fourth name says that will now be revealed: that the crucified, whom the world rejected, really was the Lord of all lords.

"The armies of heaven" brings to mind angels. However, we heard before (17:14) that He who is the Lord of lords and King of kings comes to conquer the beast and its vasal kings, and that the victory shall be shared by "those called and chosen and faithful who follows him." It is possible that it is they who have now become "the armies in heaven."

17-21 The Enemy is Lost

An angel standing in the sun is again one such picture that a person can only see in a vision. We can perhaps ask ourselves how the blinding light of the sun—high up in heaven down there in the south!—forms itself into the shape of a heavenly herald. So, his cry sounds, unreal and scary, directed to the vultures that circle above. There are foreshadowings of this in the prophets. Birds of prey and vultures about a battlefield were a scene many saw with their own eyes. In the prophets, it was a picture of destruction and defeat that would strike God's enemies. Here the angel now calls upon the visible companions of death and destruction. And he does it before the battle began. The production is given. When now the beast with all his vassals consolidates his armies, they are already consecrated to destruction. No real battle is necessary. "The Heavenly Armies" never engage. The enemy falls before the sword that John already saw at the first encounter with the Resurrected One, that which proceeded from His lips. Just as the Creator in the beginning "By the word of the LORD the heavens were made," (Psalm 33:6), so now the Almighty's word drops all who opposed it to the ground, however, only when the leaders are captured, the beast and the false prophet, which is apparently the name of the other beast, he who became the "propaganda minister" (13:11f). And here for the first time is mentioned—apparently as something largely well-known so it did not need further explanation—"the lake of fire that burns with sulfur." We may hear more about the matter later.

Revelation 20

1-6 The Thousand Year Kingdom

The six verses that now follow have given rise to endless discussions. In general, Lutherans have been restrained in their exposition. There is only one interpretation that is expressly named and rejected by the Lutheran confessions, and it is the conception that before Christ comes, the pious shall conquer the worldly powers and root out all the godless. The Reformation era had seen fearful examples of the consequences this false teaching could have. These adherents are normally called "Chiliasts" (from the Greek *chilioi*, which means thousand). But "chiliasm" can also be used for other forms of belief in the thousand-year kingdom, though a person more often speaks of "millennialism" (from the Latin word for thousand: *mille*). In the course of time, many forms of millennialism have come about. During the Middle Ages, it was common that a person thought that Satan had been bound and Christ came to power when Christendom was victorious over the Roman empire. Augustine had already taught this, and the reformers commonly held with him. During the 19th century, the conception received new strength when it once looked as if the Christian people would rule the world and—as some hoped—spread the gospel and the Christian culture to all people. Then it became very clear that Satan was certainly not bound, and it has been all the more common to see the thousand-year kingdom as something still to come. However, if we ask how it will take shape, then the answers are as varied as they are contradictory.

The reasons are obvious. This place is the only place in the Bible where it directly speaks about a thousand-year kingdom. And John is seer. It is not always certain that a seer always understands the visions he sees. Here John only suggests what he has glimpsed. How did he see the thousand years? How did he know that Satan would be released again? Who spoke to him about the first resurrection and the second death? Or did he see them? Do the thousand years come before or after Christ's return? Who are they who rule with Christ? All faithful Christians or just the martyrs and the confessors who experienced the last hard persecution? Who do they rule? In heaven or on earth? John does not clearly say, and the commentators have given the shiftiest answers. Whatever answer a person gives, it hardly affects the Christian life of faith that we live today. Concerning all this, we can draw the conclusion that here there is no unambiguous answer to retrieve and that it is not meaning that we shall look for answers to such questions.

REVELATION 20:7-10

What is it that John has to say to us who live today?

Only that Satan shall be definitively defeated. Jesus tells us the same. Satan fell from heaven and will be cast out (Luke 10:17, John 12:31). The Stronger Man has come, and He shall bind the strong man (Mark 3:27). The battle is already underway; the decisive victory was won at Golgotha. Satan defends himself by mobilizing all his resources, but he finally loses the battle—even if he comes to do one last desperate rebellion. And those who do not falter in the battle, they come to share in Christ's victory and "reign" with him. Some are allowed "to sit on the throne who judges over Israel's twelve tribes" (Luke 22:30). He has made all "a kingdom, priests to his God and Father" (Revelation 1:6). To be at the same time a king and priest means to simultaneously govern and serve. This means to share in Christ's victory, His power and His glory, and at the same time to be His devoted servants, "a holy priesthood, to offer spiritual sacrifices." (1 Peter 2:5) Here, "priests" means, as usual, sacrificial priests, who all have entered the Holy of Holies and all have their joy in presenting constantly new sacrifices of prayer, and hymns and ministry. If now whether this ministry may take place in a happy kingdom on earth or before His throne in heaven, is essentially a completely meaningless question. Just as the question of whether the thousand years shall be counted according to our accounting of time or—as so much else in the Book of Revelation—is a symbolic number. Those who live shall see.

Here John speaks about "the first resurrection" and places it in contrast to "the second death." Apparently, he means that there is a second resurrection, that which applies to all of humanity, while it is only a small number of martyrs and confessors who share in the first resurrection. Even with Paul, we find the thought that the dead shall be made alive in a particular order: First Christ, then at His return those who belong to Him, and only then shall the end come (1 Corinthians 15:23). Jesus too speaks about how it is when He comes: then one is taken up, the other left. However, here, as elsewhere, it is impossible for us to establish an action calendar for the end of days. God has kept the matter to Himself. When Jesus speaks about these things, He always has the same admonition to us: Keep ready. You know not the day when it will happen.

7-10 The Last Battle

Gog and Magog are names that are taken from the prophet Ezekiel (chapters 38-39). There Gog is a prince and Magog a land. Neither has been able to be identified with any people or any kingdom that was found at the time. Here with John, it is apparent that we have been presented a prophecy that touches on an unknown future. Gog and Magog have become names of earthly powers-states, government leaders, ideologies—that are Satan's last resources in the fight against God. In the same way, Israel and Jerusalem have become symbols for God's kingdom on earth.

"The beloved city," the Lord's city, has become God's church. And the church is still God's people who are on a pilgrimage to Canaan, a person has yet to get there. So, it talks of the "camp" of the saints, just as during the desert sojourn. Now it is a matter of the last camp, immediately before the goal.

This is the last battle. Some have thought that it is only a new aspect of the great final showdown, that which before was called the battle of Armageddon (16:16, compare 19:19f), but it hardly looks as if John thought of the matter that way. In any case, Satan is finally defeated. Apparently, he cannot die since he once received a share of God's life, that which is eternal. However, he is cast into the sea of fire, the place where evil is eternally isolated. He is no longer the Prince of Darkness, not the lord of evil, but its victim.

11-15 The Great Judgment

Then comes the final scene. The drama of world history has come to the end. John sees "a great white throne and he who sat on it." Before, these words have always meant God's own throne, but here John means that he sees it as Jesus spoke about it in the description of the Son of Man's great judgment of the people, when He shall "sit on his throne of glory." That we all shall "step before Christ's judgment seat" (2 Corinthians 5:10), all Christians knew. Yet even Paul could sometimes say that we all shall "step before God's throne" (Romans 14:10). It is God's judgment that comes. And it is God's overwhelming power that is revealed here before John's eyes. Who can remain before God's sight? Heaven and earth flee away. They fold away and disappear like a fog, dissolved forever. In this world, which now comes, there is no place for them. They have been called forth from nothing and return to it.

What remains is the people, the earthly beings who have "eternity put in their heart" (Ecclesiastes 3:11). They seemed to be gone, drowned by the sea, decaying in the earth, engulfed by death and the kingdom of death. However, now they stand there and shall answer for what they made of the life God gave them. John sees how the books are referenced—or perhaps rather rolled up because he probably speaks of scrolls. The books are the sign of God's immeasurable, exact, indelibly preserved knowledge, His omniscience, even of every single human life, for every second that it existed. So, the judgment is already clear. There is no talk of any hearing, just as little here as in Jesus's description of the Son of Man's great judgment. Everyone is judged according to his deeds, which—according to all that the New Testament tells us—means how we reacted when God sought us, and we received the invitation of His salvation. And now it shows that there was "another book," conducted in a different way. It is "the Book of Life," that can also be called the book "of the lamb who was slain." (13:8)

There is written the names of all those who receive what God wants to give to all, but so many pushed away: the perfect forgiveness through participation in

Christ's great atoning sacrifice. It is this that is finally decisive. "There is therefore now no condemnation for those who are in Christ Jesus." (Romans 8:1)

Death and Hades now are shown to belong to God's enemies. In some manner, they are connected with Satan's rebellion. They are tormentors who come under the same judgment as Satan himself. It is the same thought as we find with Paul: the last of Christ's enemies to be destroyed is death. (1 Corinthians 15:26)

Revelation 21

1-8 A New World

So it is done. God is finished with this tremendous work that the Bible describes that began when God created heaven and earth. Now we are presented with the end. God is finished with His work in the old creation, where the rebellion happened and where God now did what could be done to save what could be saved. Now the hour has come for a new beginning, and now God creates a new world. The old is no more.

What now happens in this passage, John sees and hears in a series of revelations. Once again, it is a question of seven parts. He first gives them in seven short, content-saturated sentences. Then he turns back—as usual—and allows us to see the same vision anew and hear about the same thing in the same order, but in a new manner. First, he may see the new Jerusalem, the church in her perfection. Then he may hear that which is the new and great with this new world: God Himself lives among His people. All the old is past, all mourning, no crying, no pain. All has become new. The fourth is a confirmation of the word's truth, the fifth is a confirmation that the work is now finished. And finally, the proclamation of God's final salvation and His final judgment. To these seven points we may now turn back to them in order.

9-21 The New Jerusalem

It is again an angel who takes John with him. It could have been the same who in spirit carried him out into the desert to show him the great prostitute and her punishment. Now he is carried instead up to a high mountain to see the counterpart to the prostitute, the Lamb's bride, in all the beauty she received from her bridegroom.

That which in one moment is called a bride, is in the next moment presented as a city. Both are symbols for a reality that we cannot describe without using just these pictures. In the Bible they lie closer to each other than in our everyday world. Jerusalem was, of course, "Zion's Daughter," she who God chose as His Bride, the faithful city that still became a prostitute (Isaiah 1:21). Both pictures complete each other. On the one hand, the Church is Christ's bride whom He loves and watches over (Ephesians 5:27). At the same time, she is His Temple, with walls that envelope and protect the beloved. It is this that John now describes.

The picture of God's city is full of details that are also in the Old Testament prophets. But—here as otherwise—it does not need to mean that John "retrieved them" from there. Rather, he recognized them. He has understood that what he is now seeing is what the prophets had already seen. However, he has something new to add.

The new Jerusalem comes down from heaven. It belongs to a different world. So, it cannot be described in a manner that is vivid for us who have only seen the old world. Already "its radiance" is a mystery. John uses a word that essentially means a light source or a celestial body. However, he later says that the city had neither sun nor moon. It was illuminated by God's own glory. And it is something that he indicates here. John looks for a word that describes the peculiar and captivating light. Here it is hard for us to understand what he means. Some "jasper," clear as crystal, is nowhere to be found on earth—as long as "jasper" means the same thing then as it does today.

John sees a mighty ring of walls before him. With his visionary intuition, he perceives that it has twelve gates, which face the four directions. They are guarded by twelve angels and bear the names of the twelve tribes. Even the new Israel consists of twelve tribes. Even in the new world they witness to what God did to save the world that is now past.

The city's construction is full of symbols. It opens itself to every direction. "People shall come in from east and west, from north and south" and be guests at the wedding feast of the Lamb. The gates stay open. There is salvation for all. However, they are guarded by angels who know what is required of the wedding guests: to have made their clothes white in the blood of the lamb. The walls have twelve foundations. "Foundation stones" is not really the best translation. These foundations are completely visible, somewhat like the reinforced plinths and buttresses that at this time could be used to hold up and support a city wall. They have the names of the apostles. The church is built on the foundation of the apostles. Paul says this (Ephesians 2:20). The foundation that was laid at the time of the apostles is laid for all time and can never be changed. It also remains in the new Jerusalem.

That John speaks about apostles in this manner is usually cited as evidence that he himself could not have been an apostle. This would mean self-exultation, is the thought. However, this is not quite so certain. The apostles knew that they were not chosen because they were more worthy than others. They were Christ's witnesses and representatives, obligated to disseminate what they had learned from Him. So, they would lay a foundation that could not be erased. It was their duty to make clear how unchangeable it was.

With his golden measuring rod, the angel now measures up the city. It is—as when John measured the Temple (11:1)—a symbolic event. This is God's city, established by Him, measured for His people. Every inch-wide mark is God's, overshadowed by His hand. The actual measurement seems to happen in a moment though it touches upon huge dimensions. So, it is when God measures, He "Who has measured the waters in the hollow of His hand and marked off the heavens with a span," (Isaiah 40:12). The actual measurement is baffling. We cannot imagine such a city. It is described as a cube, just as large in all three dimensions (approximately

1,380 miles, almost as far as from Stockholm to Vienna [San Diego to Austin]). We perceive that our common dimensions have ceased to apply. We can try to see with different eyes, eyes that have been trained by the foreshadowing of the Old Testament. In the Temple, the Holy of Holies, the Most Holy Place, was such a cube, (1 Kings 6:20). It was God's presence on Earth. Here in this new Jerusalem everyone is able to enter the Holy of Holies in an unbroken communion with God and each other. It is perhaps the first thing we should think of when we are placed before this strange picture. And next, we shall hear the ring in the holy number of 12. It appears again in the 12 stadia and the 144 cubits. We have encountered it before in the 144,000 that were sealed with God's seal, 12,000 for each and every one of Israel's 12 tribes. We encounter it in the creation of the 12 months, and in the salvation history of the 12 patriarchs, and the 12 tribes and the 12 apostles. God's architecture has its own harmony. It has a pattern that emerges in his work on earth as well as in the new Jerusalem. However, if we attempt to turn these numbers over in a construction drawing on paper, we are helpless. What was it that was measured on the walls? Height or thickness? Whichever we choose, we cannot get the 144 cubits (approximately 66 meters) to fit together with the city's dimensions. We would like to have asked John what he really meant. Perhaps he would answer with something just as hard to conceive. None of us will be able to comprehend such things before we—like John—have it before us and can see everything "in the spirit," with new eyes.

John attempts to describe the city's beauty. Even the foundations upon which it rests sparkle with gemstones. Again, we hear that each of these foundations bear the name of an apostle. And as different as the apostles were, so different are the gemstones in color and structure. God has an inexhaustible wealth in His creative joy, but all are united in the new Jerusalem. Even on earth these twelve gemstones are united into a work of art. It was the "Breastpiece of Judgment" (Exodus 28:17) that the high priest bore on his chest, an artistic piece with twelve inset stones, the same as in the new Jerusalem's walls (with two deviations that may be caused by the difficulty of translating Hebrew to Greek). The stone bears the name of one of the 12 tribes, and the high priest bore them in his heart when he entered "the Most Holy Place to constantly bring them into remembrance before the Lord's face." So, he bears "constantly the judgment of Israel's children on his heart before the Lord's face." Do we not comprehend the symbolism? The tribes were different, the apostles were different, we are all different, but the great high priest bears us all in his heart when he carries our judgment, and in the new Jerusalem, there is a place for all. While every foundation opens a gate, the gates are similar. There is no particular entrance reserved. Every gate is made of a single immense pearl. Whether John also sees a sign in this is uncertain. Perhaps he has only seen a beauty, completely like in the wider streets of a transparent gold that does not appear on earth.

When John looks for counterparts to all this beauty on earth, his thoughts grab onto the most beautiful in God's creation. It is the same sort of treasure that the great Babylon and the great prostitute had stolen for themselves and flaunted. In and of themselves, these valuables were not evil. They were something that witnessed to God's glory—for He who could see it and take it from His hand.

22-27 God Dwells with Men

The mighty voice from the throne had said: Behold, the dwelling place of God is with man. Now John learns what that means. In the new Jerusalem, no temple is needed. God Himself is there. He has again united Himself with the children of man. He is all in all. Everything is permeated by His light. What the prophets promised the old Israel is now fulfilled in the new Jerusalem. "The kings of the earth will bring their glory into it. They will bring into it the glory and honor of the nations." The earth that passes away was still full of God's glory that shined with the splendor of a sunset, in the colors of flowers and in a butterfly's wings. It sounded in the child's joyful laugh, in the songs of birds on a Sunday morning, in the music that let the heart perceive that there was something beyond the realities of everyday life. This comes to be carried into the new world and encounters us completely differently and still remarkably well-known: melodies and rhythms, colors and smells, shapes and lines of play, the ring in a poem and warmth in a voice. Only the impure and lying shall be excluded forever, thus that which was loveless, foul and false in that which people found.

Revelation 22

1-5 The New Creation

He who had sat on the throne said: Behold I make all things new. In the beginning He had created heaven and earth. Now He creates again, and John is able to see the new, even if only a glimpse. Again, this was something already glimpsed by the prophets. They had spoken about the wonderful river that would at one time be allowed to well forth. Every Jew had many times sung the psalm concerning "a river whose streams make glad the city of God," the city of which it could be said "God is in the midst of her" (Psalm 46:5f). And now John gets to see the river, where it floated through God's city, glittering clear, surrounded by trees. And the tree (or woods, both translations are possible) was the same wonderful tree of life that once stood in the middle of Eden's garden that which no one had seen or was able to eat from since the fall into sin. Now life and healing are here again. So, there shall never be heard any complaint anymore. No longer shall God need to speak judgment over His children. They shall see His face, bear His name on their foreheads, celebrate and worship His glory and serve Him. And they shall experience this ministry as a perfect freedom, a happy ability to do what they want unhindered. So to "serve" [minister] can also be called to "rule."

6-10 The Firm Word

Write! These words are trustworthy and true.

So had He said, who sat on the throne, now the angel speaking to John repeats them. First that these words are trustworthy and true, and then why they should be written and distributed. The message comes from God. It is He who speaks through the prophets. He is "the God of the Spirit of the prophets" as it literally says. It is He who inspires them. And now He has spoken in the same way to John. We may hear the same, which is already said in the introduction in the first chapter. He has sent His angel to show His servants what will soon happen.

Then a sudden change follows so that it is no longer an angel that speaks, but Christ Himself. It cannot very well be anyone but Him who says: Behold, I come soon! The change was completely natural to John. Of course, the angel came from Christ. He spoke Christ's words. Christ spoke through him the whole time. The angel was only the tool. John wanted—as once before—to pray to the tool but was once again corrected. In this context, God says something very important: John and all the other prophets and everyone who carries this message is an instrument of the same sort. These words are trustworthy and true, whoever speaks them. It is the matter of a word that was written down to be preserved and distributed. So,

John has the command: Write! And so, he now receives the command to not forget what he wrote. Daniel had once had the command to forget the vision he had seen because it pointed to a distant future (Daniel 8:26). But this which John has been able to see and hear, it was a message to contemporaries, just as to anyone who might read this book.

11-13 The Beginning and the End

It is done. I am Alpha and Omega.

This was the fifth point in that which was said from the throne. This theme is now taken up again, though the interpretation is a bit unclear. Part is very clear—the words about Alpha and Omega, the beginning and the end, as it literally reads. The addition "the first and the last," in fact, says the same thing. Here it is Christ who speaks. He is the one who encompasses time and eternity. He is "born of the Father before all time" as it says in the confessions. Here is the King of eternity, the final goal of all that is created. "All things were created through him and for him" (Colossians 1:16). It is this work that is now finished, and which the words "it is done" indicate. Both creation and salvation have reached their goal. On the cross, Jesus could say, "it is finished." The first mile marker was reached. Now we stand at the last. This means that nothing more can be done when it comes to salvation. All have landed where they belong at home. It is possible that it is this that is referred to with the words saying let everyone continue what he was doing: evil or good. It belongs to the act of the new creation that everyone receives the form that is given to him. The actual verb form (aorist imperative) is the same as in the story of creation in Genesis. That which has been translated here "yet a little while" can also be rendered "still" for all the future.

However, in these words can also lie another meaning. The scene will change again. John has stood on the border of a new world, and was able to see the era, that which comes after the new creation. But now his gaze is directed back again to the world where we live. John is reminded that he shall turn back. He carries a message with him. It begins already with the command to not seal the words of the prophets because the time is near. So, time continues, but it is short! And everyone shall know this—both those who live in debauchery, and those who sanctify themselves. The word can all be understood so as they have been translated here.

14 The Promise Stands Fast

All the letters ended with a promise to those who believed and remained faithful. The same promise is repeated by Him who sat on the throne (21:7). Here it returns once again, as a confirmation of the most essential. What it means is to wash your clothes in the blood of the Lamb. It is about salvation through faith in Him who died for us. This is the only condition for entering the city. However, this condition is inflexible. It is also said in the "little Bible" (John 3:16). God gave His Son so that everyone who believes in Him shall not perish but have eternal life. This is precisely what John says here: He shall receive the right to eat of the tree of life—the right that was lost in the fall, when man was driven away from the tree of life and the gates shut. (Genesis 3:22)

15 Judgment Also Stands Fast

The seventh and last thing that is said by Him who sat on the throne contained the inevitable judgment over those who chose evil. He repeats the condemnation. The first time it began with "the cowardly and unfaithful." So cowardice is mentioned first among the sins that draw people to destruction. What that follows presents what many Christians consider to be worse. But John lived in the midst of a time of sifting. When it cost something to stand fast to Christ's Word then it shows what a deadly sin cowardice can be.

In place of the cowards, unfaithful and nefarious, it speaks here about "dogs." The Jews could use this word about the gentiles, and even Jesus does it in the conversation with the Canaanite woman (Matthew 15:26). Paul uses it concerning the Jews who distorted the gospel (Philippians 3:2). Perhaps here it has the same meaning as "the unfaithful."

Among the excluded are mentioned in both cases, the liars. Lying in the Bible is not just an untrue statement, something that does not fit the facts. The truth is something more than the facts. It is a share of God's being. It is His good purpose, His intention with creation. So, a person can "do truth." A person can "be of the truth." The lie, therefore, is the evil power that perverts and distorts God's good intention with everything. The devil is the father of lies. In the original text, it speaks about he who "does lies," which is here translated with "who loves and practices falsehood," though the expression does not mean as much as the original text.

16-17 The Final Word

So John has interpreted the last sentence in this symphony that built up around the holy number of seven. Now the final word is said. It carries him from the dawn of the new world down into the old world's evening twilight, where persecution is still a reality and lives are at stake. Now Christ speaks directly to the people who shall be reached by His message through John. It shall be read "before you—in the congregations." However, it is Christ's testimony that He sent through His angel. It comes from Him who is "the root," the promised one (Isaiah 11:1) and the bright morning star, which announces a new day.

So, we are back in the seven congregations. This shall be read before them. It shall be heard by them who still stand in the hard fight. And the answer from the bride, the church, can be nothing but that which she has learned from the Spirit. It is a longing cry from a burning heart: Come! Everyone who listens, shall join in the cry; Come, Lord Jesus! This applies to all those who hear it, in every people, and in all coming days, so long as the old world with its fight and agony remains. Yet we live in an era of grace. The water of life is still acquired for nothing. So long as the bride still waits for her bridegroom, the doors stay open to the wedding feast. So long as the Church can say "come Lord Jesus," so long can she also say "Come you who thirst." Here is the water of life. The same water that flows clear as crystal in the wide river through the new Jerusalem, that a person many also drink even now, here on earth. There is a deep well in the cup of blessing and in the Word, that is like rain that falls from heaven and makes the earth fruitful and fertile.

18-19 Let the Word Stand!

The message is now finished. It shall be sent out into the world. It shall be read before the congregations and reach addresses that John could never have imagined. Now it brings a greeting with it on the path, a warning to all those who will disseminate it. Nothing may be added to it, and nothing may be taken from it. This is God's word and testimony from Jesus Christ, as it already says from the beginning (1:2). The message from God may not be handled as the word of man. Man's word is time bound. Later times can change, strengthen, and add to it with the help of their reason and their increased knowledge. However, Christ's Word cannot be changed. It shall remain even when heaven and earth pass away.

So, these words are prophetic. That which characterizes prophecy is that it has not come through the will of any man but because men were driven by the Holy Spirit and spoke what they were given from God (2 Peter 1:21). But—as it says in the same place—no prophecy can be uttered by a man's own power either. Even for this matter, the Spirit is needed. The prophetic word cannot be used like a telephone book or a reference book about the birds of Sweden. Respect for the word, just as it stands, also means respect for its secrets and mysteries. Neither may a man take them away. And a person may not add his own answer to it when the Word does not answer all our questions.

The punishment for he who adds to it or takes away—as with all other punishment—applies to him who does it in spite and unbelief. Fortunately, for our mistakes and faulty understanding, there is always forgiveness, if in the midst of the misconception there is a heart that believes in Jesus. However, the mistake in questions of the Word can be more fateful than others, because they so easily pervert our faith.

When John sends this message from his exile, he could not imagine his writing would end up being the last book in Holy Scripture. There it is now, and we believe that it has happened through God's direction. The admonition to let the Word stand as it stands—that which John received from his Lord Jesus—has come to conclude our Bible and stands there as a warning for all times and to all who receive a Bible in their hand.

20-21 Final Greeting

So the message has gone out. It reaches those who should hear it—perhaps a congregation on the coast of Asia Minor, perhaps a lone Bible reader in our day. Now there are only three short words to add.

The first comes from the Lord Christ: Behold, I come soon.

The second is the congregation's answer. We can almost hear them join in, the persecuted in Ephesus, Smyrna, and Philadelphia, with a resounding "Amen!" as they were accustomed to doing in the divine service. An amen that is then followed by their prayer: Come, Lord Jesus! It was this prayer that ever since the beginning had followed the gospel, from the very first Pentecost, through all persecutions, out along the paths where the apostles wandered. Even among the Greeks in Corinth, it always sounded in the form received from the Jesus in the very oldest congregation: Maranatha! You our Lord, come! (1 Corinthians 16:22).

With that the message is presented. John, who was able to send it, reminds us that it was, in fact, sent as a letter. So, he concludes it with a greeting that normally concluded a letter when a Christian wrote to other Christians. He wishes them that the grace of the Lord Jesus would be with them. The visions he was able to see also witness to this grace. No desire and no words could better conclude the content in this book when they today stand as the very last.

APPENDIX

The Bible's View of Itself and Other Views of the Bible

Visby 1970 con Gothenburg's Pastor's Conference 1970
Bo Giertz
Translated by Bror Erickson

Can a person say that the Bible has its own view of what we call a "view of the Bible"?

The answer is yes.

The New Testament has a peculiar way of looking at what it calls "Scripture" or the "the Scriptures"—what we call the Old Testament. Therefore, we are in a position to say how the New Testament looks at Israel's Holy Scripture, and it is very important and meaningful that we know this. Most importantly, we have the view of Jesus Himself concerning "Scripture"—no one can say that this is peripheral and irrelevant, but it only applies to the Old Testament. Neither can we say that the appraisal of the Biblical Word we encounter here should be applied to the words of Jesus Himself, let alone the rest of the Bible.

What is the Bible's View of Itself if We listen to Jesus?

"O foolish ones, and slow of heart to believe all that the prophets have spoken!" (Luke 24:25 [ESV])

We are reminded of the Word Jesus spoke to the two disciples on the road to Emmaus. Venting their heartfelt disappointment, they could not fathom what had happened in Jerusalem. In answer, Jesus tells them the tragedy they had witnessed was what God had already said would happen. It was determined that the Messiah

APPENDIX

must suffer all this to enter His glory. What God had determined in His council, He had also told His people in advance. He had given them the promise and let the Scriptures witness to his plan and intentions. As the three men continued on the road, Jesus went through Moses and all the prophets explaining what was said about Him in all the Scripture.

The Scriptures witness concerning Christ. The whole history of which they tell points forward to Him. They are filled everywhere with types and allusions, promises and prophecies. Therefore, the Old Testament's Scriptures are something that need to be "fulfilled"—this is the chief thought in all the New Testament from the Gospel of Matthew to Revelation: the Scriptures must be fulfilled—in full. And this fulfillment happens through Jesus Christ. Therefore no one can understand the Old Testament other than in light of Christ. It was a part of the work of Jesus to then expound on the Scriptures. He did not just do this on the way to Emmaus. Luke says at the end of his gospel that after the resurrection, Jesus instructed His disciples precisely about this, "that everything written about me in the Law of Moses and the Prophets and the Psalms must be fulfilled" (Luke 24:44). After that, it says He opened their minds so that they could understand the Scriptures.

We come across the same thought again in Paul. When the Old Testament Scripture is read, a veil hangs over the hearts of those who listen to how Moses is read. Only in Christ does the veil disappear. When a person converts to the Lord, it is taken away, and then they can understand the Scripture's true meaning.

Hebrews says the same, the law contains a shadow of the good to come, but it does not produce the thing in its real shape [its true gestalt]. Yet Christ has come as the chief priest for the good we now possess and shows us the true meaning, for example, of the sacrificial service, the great day of atonement, and the story of Melchizedek.

So, Jesus can say that the Old Testament Scripture's witness to Him. "But these are they that speak of me." (John 5:39)

Therefore, even the New Testament Scriptures are permeated by the conviction that all this that was written so long ago was written for our sake. It all pointed to the future. It had content that the people of the time could never completely understand. Only now that we live in the times of fulfillment can we apprehend the scope of which God has recorded in Scripture.

Perhaps these short hints already suffice to explain what a gulf there is between the Bible's view of Scripture and the most popular view concerning Scripture that in our day is called "The Historical View of the Bible."

THE BIBLE'S VIEW OF ITSELF AND OTHER VIEWS OF THE BIBLE

A Person can mean many things by "The Historical View of the Bible"[1]

In everyday language, people most often mean by "The Historical View of the Bible" that the Bible came about in the same way as all other books. Its authors were children of their time; they wrote and spoke as men did in their time. For unbelief and atheism, this view is obvious. There is no accounting for God in this view. He does not exist, nor can He intervene in history. So, they conclude that the Bible cannot be God's Word.

Even people who say they believe in God and, in a certain manner, are Christians often mean the same thing when they say they have a historical view. They actually do believe God exists and that people can have religious experiences. However, everyone has his own way of experiencing God, and when we attempt to speak about Him, it is only weak human attempts to express what is essentially inexpressible. So then, the biblical authors made human attempts to describe their encounters with God in their own way. A person can listen to them in the same manner that a person listens to the thoughts of good friends. Jesus is in a class of His own, but it is impossible to know what He has said because His Word was mediated to us through simple men that shared the delusions of their times. Therefore, to have a historical view of the Bible means to view it with the help of better knowledge, which one assumes we modern men possess, to criticize and sift out that we do not believe to be true.

"The Historical View of the Bible" in Swedish Theology

However, the concept of "The Historical View of the Bible" often has a different meaning in Swedish theology. Here it means that God's revelation happens in history, primarily through events in which God has intervened in the world; God elected Israel, liberated them from Egypt, gave them their law, sent them their prophets, and, in the fullness of time, His Son. A word of interpretation also belongs to these acts of salvation. The prophets and Jesus have spoken to men. These words are a part of the revelation, one of the ways in which God has intervened in the world.

This Swedish use is not primarily a view of the Bible but a view of God. God is the living God, He who intervenes and operates in history. So far, it is all good.

The critical point now is the view of the Bible. What meaning does one allot oneself for the Biblical Word? Here there is a whole range of conceptions in our

---

[1] Here Bo Giertz will start attacking what is known in English Academic Circles anyway as "Higher Criticism." But not just in its academic manifestations, but in all the manifestations in which this view of the Bible has permeated culture down to the least educated men. The view he attacks is the one employed in virtually every PBS documentary that even remotely touches on the Bible and has thus also permeated our culture.

time. On the one hand, some only see God's action in the events of history and the Word as something once spoken. Now the interventions of God are finished. The process through which these events have been distinguished and this Word has been entrusted to us is purely human. So, the Bible is full of mistakes, and our knowledge of these deeds and works is very poor in many parts.

In other nuances of the same basic view, one allots the written documents greater value. In large part, it is believed that they give us a correct picture of these deeds of God in history, but the basic view itself remains. The standpoint is summarized so: In our meaning, "The Historical View of the Bible takes into account that God speaks in concrete events of history through his ambassadors. But this message has been mediated to us through a complicated handing down, editing, and process of interpretation that is available for historical criticism."

The Gulf Between the Modern "Historical View" and the Bible's View of Itself

If we compare the Historical View of the Bible to the classical Lutheran teaching of inspiration, we see the Historical View cannot account for any inspiration when they wrote it down. It is possible that the words came from God when they were spoken, but the mediation of them is a human process. So, there are numerous sources of error here that we can examine with normal empirical and worldly means.

It is here that the gulf between the modern "Historical View of the Bible" and the Bible's own view widens. For Jesus, the apostles, and the whole of the early church, it was an outstanding feature that the wording of Scripture had meaning beyond that of other books. All their manner of reading and citing shows that they are convinced that God has allowed these words to be written in just this manner so that they could be a proclamation of Christ. Their meaning had long been hidden, and the contemporaries of the authors could not see it, at least not clearly. Yet in the light of Jesus Christ, these places find their right interpretation and are understandable. This means God Himself has shaped the process through which the Scriptures received their shape and speak to us. The process itself belongs to God's work in history.

It seems obvious that classical Lutheran doctrine of inspiration, which recognizes the Holy Spirit gave the authors of the Bible what they would write, gives better expression to the New Testament's view of Scripture than the Historical View of the Bible.

How the Holy Spirit influenced the Biblical authors is something that the Christian church has never defined. In the time of orthodoxy, certain theologians thought that the process was approximately a dictation. We might rather express the manner so: that God has linked the whole long history through which this Scripture has come to be: the oral narration, authorship, editing, selection, and canon formation. So then, the Bible has received the shape that it should have so that in its completeness, it would carry God's message to all people in all times if read in the right manner.

We are also conscious that the Bible has its own history of origin, where men have contributed at every stage. This history of origin can naturally be investigated in the same manner as other histories. Naturally, a researcher has the right to approach the books of the Bible with the same questions that a researcher asks in such circumstances: questions of authorship, dating, source writings, linguistic peculiarities, historical veracity, and many other things. We must always find it valuable to know what the times were like when these Scriptures were written, what the different concepts and thought processes meant for the people of the time, and more. But such analyses of the text can never give us the final answer to the question of their message; the message comes from God. If the New Testament is correct, one cannot understand the message simply by letting the texts be illustrated from contemporary events and notions.

On the contrary, they must be illustrated from the person of Jesus Christ. Only in Him have we found the completion that reveals the Scriptures' deepest meaning. The exegetes can endlessly discuss who the Lord's Suffering Servant is in the 53rd chapter of Isaiah. They can come up with diverse theories concerning Melchizedek. They can make it probable that some of the Psalter's most known Christocentric Psalms originally concern an Israelite king. Nevertheless, the New Testament sees in all this one of the God-given types of Christ and a part of the Christian proclamation that God intentionally shaped in this manner to help us understand who Jesus is and what happened to Him. It is this New Testament's view of the Bible that we confess in our church on a true holy day such as Annunciation Day, Good Friday, Epiphany, Midsummer, when we read Old Testament texts that would hardly have any connection with the day topic if one understood them the way modern scholarship maintains is likely they were understood when they were written. If, therefore, one has the New Testament's view that these texts must be read and understood in light of Jesus Christ, then they have their given and well-motivated place in these holy days.

So here, it is believed that already in their origin, God had placed in them a meaning that would be revealed only in the fullness of time. The Holy Spirit was operative when these texts were conceived as we now have them.

If in contemporary speech we attempt to express the New Testament's view of Scripture, then I find no better formulation than this: "The Scriptures are such as God has willed that they should be." If I am not mistaken, this formulation was coined on the West Coast[2] 50 years ago, when the fight over Biblical authority was

---

[2] The West Coast of Sweden, Gothenburg and its environs where Bo Giertz was bishop, has long had a history of strong Christian belief and a particular piety fostered by the students of Henric Schartau who led a revival in Sweden during 18th and

hot. The first author where I found this saying—I.D. Wallerius—adds that he would like to place a period there and not need some closer definition. He means: This is Biblical and clear, and it is accurate. The Scriptures are such as God has willed them to be. It is tacitly understood as obvious what God's intention was: to speak to all people at all times about their salvation.

The Scriptures also have a particular purpose. They may speak through historical narratives, poems, philosophical essays, letters, or prophecies. This purpose is to witness to salvation through Jesus Christ, testify to the way to God through him, and of the life that one lives in his communion. So, the Scriptures have a center from which all must be understood. Our fathers knew this well. Christ is the Scriptures kernel and star. The promise and preparation separate themselves from the fulfillment. This is not the matter of a development where we men so gradually develop our spiritual capabilities and make ourselves right representatives of God. It is instead God who develops His plan and His meaning step by step. He is the same in the Old Testament as in the New, but in the time of the Old Testament, the most important is still partially withheld. He is there as the promise, the insinuation, and the types.

The Bible has been given with a particular purpose and must be read in a particular manner

That the Bible has been given to us with a particular purpose also means that it must be read in a particular manner if we are to make any use of it. Because the Word deals with God's salvation, it is, in essence, law and gospel. It speaks about God's demands and God's gifts. There lies a pearl of endless wisdom in the simple word that we on the West Coast so enjoyably use: The Bible shall be read with the intention of salvation. If a person wants to hear God speak in the Bible, he must ask about Him and His salvation. If a person approaches Scripture and reads it with completely different questions, he cannot demand that God shall speak. The unconverted curiosity has no value for God's Word. It has been so in all times, also in the epochs of church history, when it was obvious for all that Scripture was God's Word. It has always been a *theologia irrigenitorum*, on the unconverted theology. To this also belongs the misuse of Scripture that occurred in the old days when it was read as a profane encyclopedia without asking after God Himself. The unconverted man can be curious and inquisitive of the Bible but wary of letting it burn with the fire of the Lord that condemns and forgives. Instead, they will search for cool, neutral, and safe facts about events and relationships that have freed themselves from any connection with salvation. In this way, one avoids searching Scripture for real theology that always deals with God and our relationship to him.

19th centuries which emphasized the liturgical life of the church and the means of grace in the life of the Christian.

THE BIBLE'S VIEW OF ITSELF AND OTHER VIEWS OF THE BIBLE

Rather they search for geology, cosmology, archeology, zoology, and many other kinds of human knowledge. But the Bible was not sent out into the world for that.

Such misuse always carries its own punishment. One of the dangerous consequences was an unfruitful fight with science on points where Christianity had no reason to fight. When science began to question the accuracy of some points concerning human knowledge that one had made for himself by using the Bible as it should not be used, one felt forced to take up a fight that had little to do with faith in Christ.

When the Bible is read with the intention of salvation and used for that which it should be used, then it functions completely as we see Scripture functioning in the New Testament. It becomes, as Paul says, "profitable for teaching [namely about Christ], for reproof, for correction, and for training in righteousness" (2 Timothy 3:16). Everything falls in place. God may say what He wants to say in His Word. And when a man receives the word as God's Word in this way, then it also becomes as Paul says, "The word of God, which is at work within you believers" (1 Thessalonians 2:13). This also belongs to the essence of Scripture's inspiration. Because the Word is "thoroughly inspired" by God, it can be a living, operable Word that is a tool of the Holy Spirit. It is a means of grace. Just as the Scribes in the New Testament, despite all their knowledge of the Bible and their firm faith in the Word, could not understand it because they would not receive Scripture's real message about justification by faith from God, neither can a man in our day understand that which is written in God's Word if he does not have this personal, living contact with the Spirit in the Word. And the Spirit is—we do well to note—not our own spirit that gives us inspiration or wisdom that perhaps exceeds the Word, or actually gives us inspiration to criticize the Scripture but the Spirit that lives in the Word. It is the Spirit who makes the Word alive. It is just this that Jesus says is the Spirit's only task: to witness about Him and remind people of what He said.

For us Lutherans, it has always been a matter of the heart to emphasize Scripture's task in the world: to witness about Christ. If a person understands this, then everything in Scripture functions correctly. This is where we Lutherans distinguish ourselves from the reformed. They read the Scripture like a law book, in a different manner than we, without seeing everything in the light of Christ. That is why they preserve the Old Testament's forbidding of images as the second commandment in the Decalogue. That is why they have always attempted to apply the law as God gave it to Israel to our own society in an extension that is foreign to us. The difference has very deep and penetrating consequences for both divine service and everyday life. It is for this reason that it can be so hard for a Lutheran to feel at home in a reformed church.

Even among confessional Lutherans, there can be profound nuances in conception. But they do not depend on the essentials. That which is essential and common is the conviction that the Bible is such as God has willed that it should be, and we receive it as a message from God. However, when one listens to a message and reads Scripture, one must always keep the Word's value clear. A person must know what form the author has chosen for his message. A person listens in one way to a protocol and in a different way to a poem. A story can have something infinitely important to say without thereby reporting a factual event. When we listen to the parable of the Merciful Samaritan,[3] we do not ask for a name or year. A historical distinction can be consciously vague, concentrated upon the essential. There are always different ideas about how a person should understand certain parts of God's Word, if they are conceived as parables, as poems, or as history, and to what extent this history, in any case, might be stylized, vague, or concentrated on the essential, and drawn in a shortened perspective.

Yet wherever God speaks in one manner or another, the message is the same. And it can be understood by whoever will receive it in its intention of salvation.

The crucial distinction between different ways of seeing the Bible consists in the answer to this question: Do we believe that there is a God who speaks to us here and that He has something to say to us through these words, or do we not believe it? Are we prepared to receive this message and correct ourselves according to it or not?

Here the paths diverge. If we separate the New Testament view of Scripture, which has been confessed by the universal Christian Church in all times, we are convinced that we have found something here that men cannot change but is given for all times. To this conception stands the contrary, out of which a historical outlook relativizes the Biblical message. A person can concede that Jesus or the apostles actually mean or say one thing, but then dismiss it as time-bound and obsolete. This can apply to the historical perspective of the world, this world's course, and the return of Christ. It can apply to marriage and the sexual life. It can apply to the division of tasks between man and woman that the New Testament says shall apply in God's congregation. There are new questions constantly arising that are asked of us Christians before choosing between the Bible's way of seeing and another that lies more in line with the way of thought in a secular world. How we choose in the end depends on our attitude toward the Word. It exposes whether we share the Bible's view or have some other view.

For we who want to hold fast to God's Word, it is always a conscious question. Do we also share the Bible's view when it comes to our own life? Do we share

---

[3] In English this is the story of The Good Samaritan. However, in Swedish they use the term merciful. And it makes a bit more sense because the whole parable is one about showing mercy. This is I think an example of some of the theological heritage that is inevitably lost in the transition to English. Something as simple as the title of a parable, subtly changing the way we think about it, even if our theology is Lutheran. If for no other reason it is small things like this that should propel younger theologians to not only study Greek and Hebrew, Latin and German, but also other languages in which Lutheran Culture has flourished, and then languages in which we want Lutheranism to flourish, Spanish, Arabic, etc.

THE BIBLE'S VIEW OF ITSELF AND OTHER VIEWS OF THE BIBLE

the biblical view when the New Testament speaks of suffering and persecution as a normal thing and not something about which to be surprised or embittered? Do we do this when it means taking up our cross and not living for ourselves comfortably, without giving in to the everyday tests of patience and small annoyances? Is this what we do when it comes to not passing by the man who has been beaten and wounded by life's hard knocks?

The Bible's own view shall apply. Not only its view of the Word but also its view of the cross, discipleship, love, and service. God help us all.

Printed in the USA
CPSIA information can be obtained
at www.ICGtesting.com
LVHW091036300923
759548LV00002B/2